THE NECROMANTICS

THE NECROMANTICS

REANIMATION, THE HISTORICAL IMAGINATION, AND VICTORIAN BRITISH AND IRISH LITERATURE

Renée Fox

THE OHIO STATE UNIVERSITY PRESS
COLUMBUS

Copyright © 2023 by The Ohio State University.
All rights reserved.

Library of Congress Cataloging-in-Publication Data
Names: Fox, Renée Allyson, 1977– author.
Title: The necromantics : reanimation, the historical imagination, and Victorian British and Irish literature / Renée Fox.
Description: Columbus : The Ohio State University Press, [2023] | Includes bibliographical references and index. | Summary: "Critiques the boundary between Victorian studies and Irish studies and interrogates how Mary Shelley, Robert Browning, Charles Dickens, W. B. Yeats, and Bram Stoker leveraged reanimated bodies in their work to reimagine the past"—Provided by publisher.
Identifiers: LCCN 2022059674 | ISBN 9780814215494 (cloth) | ISBN 0814215491 (cloth) | ISBN 9780814282922 (ebook) | ISBN 081428292X (ebook)
Subjects: LCSH: Shelley, Mary Wollstonecraft, 1797–1851—Criticism and interpretation. | Browning, Robert, 1812–1889—Criticism and interpretation. | Dickens, Charles, 1812–1870—Criticism and interpretation. | Yeats, W. B. (William Butler), 1865–1939—Criticism and interpretation. | Stoker, Bram, 1847–1912—Criticism and interpretation. | English literature—19th century—History and criticism. | English literature—Irish authors—19th century—History and criticism. | Reincarnation in literature. | Zombies in literature. | Mummies in literature.
Classification: LCC PR461 .F69 2023 | DDC 823/.809353—dc23/eng/20230216
LC record available at https://lccn.loc.gov/2022059674
Other identifiers: ISBN 9780814258736 (paper) | ISBN 0814258735 (paper)

Cover design by Sarah Flood-Baumann
Text design by Stuart Rodriguez
Type set in Minion Pro

CONTENTS

Acknowledgments		vii
INTRODUCTION	Necromantic Victorians	1
CHAPTER 1	How *Frankenstein* Got History	38
CHAPTER 2	Dickensian Zombies in *Great Expectations* and *Our Mutual Friend*	79
CHAPTER 3	Robert Browning's Necropoetics	112
CHAPTER 4	W. B. Yeats and the Necromantic Museum	138
CHAPTER 5	Bram Stoker's Irish Mummy Gothic	177
EPILOGUE	The Undead Reader, or the Perils of Resuscitative Reading	215
Notes		225
Works Cited		241
Index		261

ACKNOWLEDGMENTS

This book has emerged into the world because many organizations and people have helped me breathe sparks of life into what sometimes felt like cold bones. Thank you to Becca Bostock, Elizabeth Zaleski, and Kristen Ebert-Wagner for humanely guiding this project through its publication process, and to the anonymous readers for The Ohio State University Press for their labor and deep, gracious engagement with my work. My writing and archival research has been supported by the Josephine de Kármán Foundation, the Mrs. Giles M. Whiting Foundation, the UCLA William Andrews Clark Memorial Library (including the Kanner Fellowship in British Studies and the Ahmanson-Getty Fellowship), the William B. Neenan, S.J. Visiting Fellowship at Boston College Ireland, the Hellman Fellows Program, the University of Miami Provost's Research Awards, the University of California Humanities Research Institute, the UCSC EVC Writing Fellows Program, the UCSC Committee on Research, the Humanities Institute and the Humanities Division at UCSC, and the UCSC Literature Department.

The organizations and institutions that provided this support also introduced me to many friends and colleagues whose help and brilliance have been indispensable. At the Clark Library, Scott Jacobs and Nina Schneider offered constant assistance in the archives (and excellent snacks outside of them), and I am indebted to Joseph Bristow, Neil Hultgren, Elisha Cohn, Dustin Friedman, and Patrick Keilty for all their intense thinking with me about the late

viii • ACKNOWLEDGMENTS

nineteenth century. At Boston College Ireland, Mike Cronin introduced me to exciting new work in Irish studies and became a collaborator who fundamentally changed the way I experience my relationship to the field—I am grateful to him in so many ways. Gabriele Schwab, organizer of a UCHRI Residential Research Group on "Artificial Humanity" meant to begin in March 2020, did a masterful job helping us feel connected to one another even in those first strange weeks of virtual pandemic isolation. I'm especially thankful for the conversations with Long Bui and Annie McClanahan that emerged from the work of this RRG. I also thank Sylvanna Falcón for her enthusiastic guidance during my year as an EVC Writing Fellow, which made the project of book-writing feel actually manageable.

This book has benefited from years of generous readers and interlocutors. I'm deeply grateful to Joss Marsh for mentoring me into the world of Victorian studies and introducing me to the joys of mummy fiction, as well as to Bill Solomon and Suvir Kaul for their early reading and guidance. Deborah Nord and Diana Fuss read many drafts of its chapters, shaping my thinking with their incisive feedback, intellectual rigor, and endless encouragement—this book wouldn't exist without them. Simon Gikandi's astute critiques helped me situate my Irish studies work in a wider postcolonial context. April Alliston, Michael Cadden, and Paul Muldoon all provided opportunities to test out my necromantic arguments with new gothic and Irish texts, offering unflagging support and thoughtful advice about my readings. Joseph Valente has been a steadfast mentor, friend, and reader, a "dualitist" across many years and countless conversations about Stoker, Yeats, and the merits of sablefish. Thank you as well to Aviva Briefel, both for enthusiastically reading chapters and for thinking with me about mummies and spirits. Luke Gibbons, Seamus Deane, and Kevin Whelan provided essential introductions to the field of Irish studies over several summers at the Notre Dame Irish Seminar. Wendy Lee, Rebecca Rainof, Alyson Shaw, and Jacky Shin were an invaluable nineteenth-century working group at the beginnings of this project, and I thank Abby Bender, Greg Londe, Ellen Scheible, Julieann Ulin, and Siân White for being my first Irish studies compatriots. I am profoundly grateful to Sara Maurer and Mary Mullen for creating a space in Irish studies for those of us also working in Victorian studies, and they, along with Gordon Bigelow, Amy Martin, and Patrick O'Malley, have been crucial friends and colleagues as I've navigated the complexities of working at the intersection of these two fields. Eric Falci provided extraordinary feedback on the chapters he read, and he, Michael Rubenstein, and Seán Kennedy deserve extra gratitude for always convincing me to keep writing. J. K. Barret, Jason Baskin, Hannah Crawforth, Erin Forbes, and Casey Walker have been listening to me talk about reanimated corpses for a very, very long time, and these amazing friends have been especially present and encouraging from afar and across Zoom screens during the pandemic.

My Dickens chapter started its life as a lecture at the Dickens Universe, where Kathleen Frederickson, Claire Jarvis, and Elisha Cohn all patiently helped me untangle my argument with mere hours to spare (and have continued to help me untangle things over the intervening years). Since that Universe, the Dickens Project has become a central part of my professional life, giving me an intellectual home in Victorian studies that's full of field-changing colleagues and dear friends. John Jordan has been a mentor for longer than he even knows, and is one of the smartest, kindest, and most dedicated humans I could ever conspire with. Courtney Mahaney's remarkable ability to keep the Project thriving even in times of crisis has meant that I had time to finish this book, and I am incredibly grateful for all her work. Dickens Project people have been among my primary support networks throughout this project, reading, encouraging, and inspiring me: Rae Greiner, Jason Rudy, and Ryan Fong have been tireless, and I also owe thanks to Tanya Agathocleous, Ian Duncan, Jonathan Grossman, Nancy Henry, Tricia Lootens, Teresa Mangum, Elizabeth Meadows, Helena Michie, Andrew Miller, Cornelia Pearsall, Catherine Robson, and Carolyn Williams.

Huge thanks to Pam Hammons, Romy Lerner, Brenna Munro, Manohar Narayanamurthi, Jason Pearl, Gema Pérez-Sánchez, Kurt Voss-Hoynes, Tim Watson, and especially John Funchion (my gothic partner-in-crime): during and since my time at the University of Miami they have supported my work, read chapter drafts, watched *Buffy* with me from across cities and countries, and talked me through sticky moments. At UCSC, I have an extraordinary family of colleagues and friends who have sustained me as I brought this book to life. Jody Greene is an unfailing source of strength, love, and advice, and Vilashini Cooppan has nourished body, soul, and brain throughout my writing process. Casey Coneway, Kate Jones, Greg O'Malley, and Elaine Sullivan were (always will be) my amazing pandemic pod-mates—their friendship and cheerleading have been especially meaningful throughout this difficult time. I owe special thanks to Susan Gillman, who has provided wonderfully thoughtful feedback on drafts and talked me through many iterations of my arguments. I am also deeply grateful to Jasmine Alinder, Lindsay Baker, Anna Maria Barry-Jester, Dorian Bell, Michael Chemers, Carla Freccero, Muriam Haleh Davis, Jennifer Derr, Kirsten Silva Gruesz, Alma Heckman, Sean Keilen, Kim Lau, Marsh Leicester, Mark Massoud, Marc Matera, Samantha Matherne, Adam Millard-Ball, Maya Peterson, Thomas Serres, Amanda Smith, and Zac Zimmer.

I wouldn't be who I am and this book wouldn't be what it is without the unconditional love, support, and confidence of my family, Lynda and Lee Fox and Ian Segal—thank you for everything.

A portion of chapter 3 was first published in *Victorian Poetry* (vol. 49, no. 4, Winter 2011, pp. 463–83) under the title "Robert Browning's Necropoetics," and an earlier version of chapter 4 appeared in *Yeats and Afterwords* (edited by Joseph Valente and Marjorie Howes, U of Notre Dame P, 2014, pp. 15–41) under the title "The Revivalist Museum: Yeats and the Reanimation of History."

INTRODUCTION

Necromantic Victorians

REANIMATING BODIES

In the second edition of her *Poems* (1871), Lady Jane Wilde—mother of Oscar Wilde and publishing under the Irish nationalist name "Speranza"—added a prefatory dedication poem to an impassioned collection calling for the Irish nation to rise in fiery revolution against its "proud oppressors, for . . . centuries of wrong."[1] The dedication poem, called "To Ireland," describes both the potential and the limitations of poetry's power to resurrect a dead, enslaved nation into liberatory modernity, imagining Ireland as a murdered body that might be miraculously brought to life with a few jolts of outside energy:

> MY COUNTRY, wounded to the heart,
>   Could I but flash along thy soul
> Electric power to rive apart
>   The thunder-clouds that round thee roll,
> And, by my burning words, uplift
> Thy life from out Death's icy drift,
> Till the full splendours of our age
> Shone round thee for thy heritage—
> As Miriam's, by the Red Sea strand
> Clashing proud cymbals, so my hand

2 · INTRODUCTION

> Would strike thy harp,
> Loved Ireland! (Wilde iii)

Wilde's fantasy of restorative electricity has a dramatic gothic tinge to it, channeling both the dark and stormy nights of gothic fiction and the galvanic power that *Frankenstein*'s 1818 publication made nearly synonymous with the dangerous animation of dead matter. Yet these opening lines also embed the poem's resuscitative desires in a strange longing for historical revision. Unlike Wilde's better known poem "The Famine Year," in which a "ghastly, spectral army" of the Irish dead "rise as witnesses" at the Second Coming to wreak their vengeance on the cruel British, "To Ireland's" vision of reanimation turns from the earlier poem's zombie revenge fantasy to a meditation on the revivifying powers of both poetry and the present.[2] Wilde's wish for poetry to have electricity's life-giving force, for her "burning words" to raise Ireland "from out Death's icy drift," is also a wish for the wakened national corpse to be newly illuminated by the contemporary moment, or even to be transformed by it. The grammatical ambiguity of lines 7–8 above suggests that the present moment, the "splendours of our age," might at once brighten the heritage contained in the electrified body of Wilde's dead nation and *become* its heritage, replacing the tradition with the shining glow of modernity. Reanimating the dead in this poem isn't just a nationalist dream of electrifying a cold Irish corpse. It's also an uncertain question about the relationship that reanimation produces between heritage and current events, between the past and what the past inevitably becomes when it's made to live again in the present.

Wilde's poem captures the primary argument of this book as well as several secondary threads that weave through it. Ireland in this poem isn't a ghost that haunts the present, demanding retribution for past wrongs: the dead nation won't, or can't, return of its own free will or act in its own interest. Instead, it lingers in the grave as a historical body that must be acted upon—revived and transformed—by literary, political, and scientific forces outside of it. *The Necromantics* contends that English and Irish writers across the nineteenth century use such images of reanimated corpses to scrutinize how the Victorian historical imagination makes the past legible and useful in the present moment. These revived bodies allow writers to examine how much the historical imagination relies on art, literary genre, and sentiment; to dissect the value and vulnerabilities of its presentist impulses; and especially in the case of Irish writers, to anatomize its underlying imperialist assumptions that give some bodies the power to resurrect the past and render other bodies dead objects to be willfully resurrected into new histories. Even as the book builds its argument out of English corpses—recombined creatures, ancient scholars, murdered brides, and zombified narrators—the dead body of the Irish nation lies buried at its center. This body emerges in multiple reanimated guises in my final chapters as I explore the fragments and scathing critiques of Victorian resuscitative history that underlie the late nineteenth-century Irish Literary Revival movement. While the Irish writers in these chapters postdate the English writers in earlier chapters, the book's turn to Ireland does more than just recontextualize the Literary Revival as a uniquely Victorian cultural phenomenon.[3] As Wilde's poem makes manifestly clear, the clarity of these Irish writers' political agendas, the literalness with which they imagine reanimating the dead, and the stark connections they make between reviving bodies and "creat[ing] a vibrant future . . . by resuscitating the past" all illuminate how profoundly earlier Victorian writers used reanimated bodies to agonize over the aesthetic and political forces that make the past alive to the present (Howes and Valente 1).

Like Wilde, many of these writers turn to electricity either as a metaphor or as a quite literal force for reanimating the dead, tapping into its intertwined nineteenth-century associations with grotesque science, bodily and aesthetic vitality, quackery, the subjugation of nature, and destructive force to measure both the viability of their resuscitative ambitions and the dangerous ramifications of their rare successes.[4] Wilde's poem clings to its image of Ireland as a corpse, a wounded body with heart, eyes, and soul, that must be resurrected into a new life of freedom. Yet unlike other writers of the Irish Literary Revival that emerged at the end of the 1880s who believed, as W. B. Yeats wrote, that power over the "body and soul" of Ireland lay in its poems and stories, Wilde offers a more circumspect reflection on what literature can and can't do for dead bodies, especially at a moment when "Electricity is Life" screamed from the pages of newspaper advertisements and spectacular displays of medical electricity were stunning London audiences (Yeats, "Introduction" 25).[5] In the 1864 first edition of her *Poems,* Wilde borrows Percy Shelley's idea of poetry as "electric life which burns within . . . words" to describe poetic language as flashes of "electric light, strong, swift, and sudden."[6] By the 1871 second edition, she has added both the dedication poem and a new closing poem to the collection in which a comparison between poetry and electric life only reveals the breaking point of a poet's capabilities.[7] Like Charles Dickens's 1865 *Our Mutual Friend* and Robert Browning's 1868–69 *The Ring and the Book,* Wilde's new 1871 poems simultaneously bestow the writer with resuscitative powers and lament the incapacity of these powers to fully restore the dead to life. As both Dickens's and Browning's texts do, along with texts by Mary Shelley, Standish O'Grady, and Bram Stoker, Wilde's poems turn to the contemporary language of electricity to imagine a corpse nearly but not quite alive again.

4 • INTRODUCTION

Dead bodies serve as such writers' experimental objects, jolted to not-quite-life by electrical energies representing both the aspirations and the incapacities of what the historian Jules Michelet described in 1874 as history's desire to "exhume [the past] for a second life" (Barthes 101).

I call this body of nineteenth-century literature preoccupied with the possibilities and perils of bringing the dead to life "necromantic" literature. Necromantic literature distinguishes itself from ghost stories by its disinterest both in spectrality—"how the past lives indirectly in the present, inchoately suffusing and shaping rather than determining it," as Wendy Brown describes it—and in traumatic recurrence: "The specter begins by coming back, by repeating itself, by recurring" (145, 149–50). Necromantic literature instead focuses on how material corpses, even metaphorical ones, are exhumed, reanimated, and manipulated by the powers of the present into lively, readable historical bodies. In some texts, like *The Ring and the Book,* waking a corpse into modern readability is a nearly literal poetic act: when Robert Browning asks in the poem's introductory book, "How title I the dead alive once more?" he grammatically collapses reanimated corpse and new poem into a single entity (44). Others, like *Our Mutual Friend* and Bram Stoker's 1903 *The Jewel of Seven Stars,* make the desire to resuscitate a dead body into readable life into a monstrous mandate, whether that resuscitation happens at the level of form, as in Dickens's novel, or in a dark cellar crammed with electrical equipment and Egyptian curios, as in Stoker's.

Bodies and stories are often interchangeable in necromantic literature, revival and rewriting presented as analogous in kind, if not always in degree. The first stanza of Wilde's poem offers a stark example of this as it jumps from its fantasy of reanimating Ireland to revising the biblical Exodus story to better suit Wilde's needs as a woman poet. However, the parallel structure of this stanza doesn't present revival and rewriting as metaphors for one another the way Browning's poem does. Instead, it presents two different but intertwined versions of the work of the poet, one resuscitative and one revisionary, each demonstrating that reimagining the past into present-day lives requires both active aesthetic work and a recognition that such work will leave an inescapable imprint on whatever new lives it produces. In the case of Wilde's first stanza, we can see the imprint in two ways: nearly literally in the image of the present age lending its glow to the newly revived body of Ireland, and effectively in her transformation of Exodus from a story of liberation to one of revival. Whether reanimating dead Ireland or reimagining Miriam as a necromancer in her own right, this stanza encapsulates the impulse of necromantic literature more largely to revive its dead bodies in order to reconstruct the past into new literary and political stories. As I argue throughout this book, texts that bring bodies back to life simultaneously reimagine the past to suit present-day needs and self-consciously reflect on the mechanisms, ambitions, and dangers that inhere in such daring acts of reanimation. Yet necromantic literature isn't simply historical revival literature in a different guise, self-conscious of its inauthenticity though such revival literature may be.[8] Necromantic literature is *about* the ways poems, stories, and histories try to revive the past. It literalizes the aesthetics and politics of such revivals to examine them, question them, undermine them, and sometimes even celebrate them.

Wilde's poem demonstrates this in its opening stanza, which focuses not precisely on bringing Ireland back to life but on wondering and doubting what kind of work a poet's "burning words" can do to revive something that has long been dead. It's a poem about the resuscitative imagination, in all its glory *and* all its failure: "Could I but flash along thy soul," the poem's second line asks, pouring both longing and lamentation into that one small "but." The metaphoric connection between poetic words and resuscitative electric power dreamed in this first stanza recedes as the poem unfolds into an acknowledgment that poetry alone can't provide sufficient "new energies" to "make [Ireland's] strong life-currents flow" (Wilde iv). The poem instead calls for "a hero heart to lead" Ireland into a life of awakened liberty, insisting that the woman poet can't really "make the slumb'ring Soul arise"—she can only "lift the funeral pall" and ready the nation for its heroic revival. And yet, Wilde can't quite abandon the idea that a woman's poetic voice might have just enough life force to stir Ireland's "mighty heart . . . even with one pulse-throb," that poetry will always have some small bit of resuscitative efficacy that wakens the dead to the stronger forces that can fully raise them.

Although Wilde's deference to a male hero's big strong powers of revival here feels delightfully perfunctory—she does, after all, choose Miriam rather than Moses as the true hero of Exodus—throughout the nineteenth century the question of who gets to reanimate the dead is often as gendered as it is fraught with colonial power dynamics. While Mary Shelley's *Frankenstein* and its early adaptations mark the starting point of *The Necromantics,* most of the texts I examine are by male writers whose aesthetic audacity remains tempered, in Browning's words, by their limited ability to "create . . . , no, but resuscitate . . . , perhaps" (42). As Shelley's own originary investment in dysfunctional creativity increasingly became the stuff of male writers' reflections on how artists repurpose old material into new forms, the story of nineteenth-century necromantic literature became rooted in a masculine aesthetic that both chafes against and explores the nuances of its creative incapacities. A few writers, like Browning and Stoker, explicitly engage with the challenges an alive-again female corpse presents to masculine aesthetic and political dominance, either by relying on a dead woman to speak against the fiction of objective historical truth or by having her kill everyone rather than cede her historical knowledge to them. Yet despite the primacy of the reanimated female corpse in the work of critics like Carol Christ, Elisabeth Bronfen, and Brian Norman, many of the necromantic writers I examine show little interest either in dead women's ability to catalyze and flummox masculine representational mastery[9] or in the power of a posthumous female voice to intervene in crises of injustice.[10]

The gendering of the resuscitative imagination inheres less in who the corpse is and what the corpse does than in how and why the corpse is (or isn't) reanimated, and to what extent the ability to reanimate resides in what Mike Goode calls the "manliness . . . of historical authority" (20). From the late eighteenth century, in which "historical thinkers' competence to know the past depended on the manliness and sociality of their bodies' constitutional power to feel," through the early twentieth century when debates about the validity of different historiographical methods and historical revival movements shaped themselves around shifting discourses of what constituted manliness, stories of reanimating the dead regularly traced the rise and fall of ideas about masculine prowess (23).[11] While issues of gender aren't central to this book as a whole, the resuscitative impulses in many of its texts expose and unsettle assumptions about forms of masculine power, even when texts glide over such assumptions with little fanfare. For instance: "are'nt I the hero of the piece?" one stage version of Frankenstein from 1849 asks insistently at the beginning of his play, shamelessly declaring his authority vested in being a "made m[a]n" of industry, only to end up ceding his heroic power to a strapping educational reformer who manages to tame the creature that all the industrial force in the world can't control (Brough and Brough 230, 233). As Wilde's arch submission to (and clever undercutting of) the supposedly superior resuscitative power of a male hero in her poem suggests, the erotic and implicitly masculine act of "enter[ing], spark-like" (Robert Browning's words) to bring a dead thing back to life might not always be the most productive way to coax a cold heart back to beating. And even when it does work—when brides speak and mummies rise, when funerary monuments pulse with spirit and voluptuous vampires glow with feeding—successfully reanimating the dead can be far deadlier to the present than failure ever could have been.

RESUSCITATIVE READING

This book traces the promise—both generative and destructive—of the resuscitative imagination from the sentimental historiography of the late eighteenth / early nineteenth century to its most absurd extreme in the zombies and mummies that early twenty-first-century mash-ups set loose in classic nineteenth-century novels—they're your reward if you read all the way to the epilogue. Each chapter explores a very different facet of necromancy as the book moves from explicit historicism in its first chapter, through novelistic and poetic form in chapters 2 and 3, to the political pressures of the Irish Literary Revival in the final two chapters. By focusing on texts both within and without the conventional nineteenth-century gothic canon, I aim to show how pervasively the necromantic imagination both saturates and reanimates nineteenth-century British and Irish literature, even (or especially) when writers aren't operating in an explicitly gothic mode. For instance, I begin with *Frankenstein* not because this gothic novel itself is a necromantic exemplar but because the relationship between Shelley's novel, her reflections on the historical imagination, and the later proliferation of *Frankenstein*s into a cultural myth of reanimation provides a paradigmatic *ars necromantica* for the book as a whole. Rife with necromancy though the gothic canon is, my aim isn't to reiterate arguments about a genre in which "repetition and revivification rule," and so I haven't focused on texts like Charles Maturin's *Melmoth the Wanderer* (1820); the vampires of Lord Byron, John Polidori, J. R. Planché, James Malcolm Rymer, Dion Boucicault, J. Sheridan Le Fanu, and Stoker; or mummy-ish stories by H. Rider Haggard and Arthur Conan Doyle (Lutz, "Gothic Fictions" 76). Instead, I turn to Browning, Dickens, and Yeats, in part because all three of these writers engage with the reanimation myths of both Shelleys that I discuss in my first chapter, but also because all three bring the gothic impulse of necromancy to bear on distinctly different formal projects, which themselves have their own necromantic afterlives. These projects—the dramatic monologue, the realist novel, and Irish Literary Revival literature—return to life in countless ways across the last three centuries: in the Irish Famine zombies that borrow from the dramatic monologues of Shelley, Browning, and Tennyson,[12] in James Joyce's modernist resurrections and recombinations, in the *Jane Slayres* and *Grave Expectations* that the twenty-first century delights in producing, in J. M. Synge's returning fathers and Yeats's rag and bone shop of the heart, in the mummy novel by Stoker that I address in my final chapter, and in the endless iterations of Stoker's vampires and mummies that have become pervasive in contemporary culture. Although *The Necromantics* doesn't address all of these afterlives, its extensive and genre-crossing exploration of reanimation demonstrates the inescapability of necromancy both as a nineteenth-century literary strategy and as a contemporary critical methodology for theorizing nineteenth-century literary forms and politics.

The Necromantics is about the literal afterlives of history that literature produces: about the bodies, forms, and words that allow us to give the past new life in the present, and about the ease with which such resuscitative desires can set loose old monsters to rampage through the contemporary world. Taking seriously Sir Walter Scott's 1819 image of the historian "walk[ing] over the recent field of battle, and [selecting] for the subject of resuscitation by his sorceries, a body whose limbs had recently quivered with existence," this book explores the reanimated corpses—monstrous, metaphorical, and occasionally merely electrified—that populate nineteenth-century British and Irish literature ("Dedicatory Epistle" 22). It argues that these alive-again bodies represent serious engagements with political and aesthetic debates across the late eighteenth and nineteenth centuries about how to make history ethical, useful, and affecting to a present-day audience. The past does not haunt anyone in this necromantic literature so much as provide an apparently dormant form through which writers and their characters—poets, scientists, archaeologists, playwrights, and bone collectors—try to channel their own ideologically and aesthetically relevant versions of history. As Caroline Levine and others have shown us, however, forms are never actually dormant, and the claim underlying this book as a whole is that even while necromantic literature dreams that the past can be usefully resuscitated in and for the present, it dreads the repercussions of this inevitably appropriative and delusive act of historical reinvention.[13] For every imaginary blushing lady that necromantic literature offers us, it also gives us a blood-sucking vampiric bride. For every ecstatic hope that the past can live vibrantly again in the nerves and tissues of present-day bodies, a galvanized corpse grimaces horrifically from its slab to remind us that not every past can, or should, be brought to life again.

Reanimated bodies, though imbued with history, are not spectral bodies. They do not bear with them intractable pasts that demand resolution, and necromantic tales are not ghost stories. They have none of what Vernon Lee in 1889 mockingly called "specters that can be caught in definite places and made to dictate judicial evidence" (40). My book follows the work of Brian Norman's *Dead Women Talking* in assembling a cache of the literary undead that often falls between the cracks of works that focus on ghosts, haunting, and "history's horrors" on one side, and aestheticized corpses imagined into modern representation on the other (Goddu 3). Victorian studies has devoted copious attention to both of these: to theories of spectrality, histories of spiritualism, and analyses of the mediums who channel ghosts;[14] and to the representational possibilities of dead bodies themselves, which sometimes serve as "the beginning of stories rather than their end" and sometimes simply produce "poems oozing aqueous putrefaction" (Lutz, *Relics* 8; Franklin and Franklin 73).[15] The dead-but-living literary character who is neither ghost nor corpse is what Norman calls a "bewildering figure," both in credulous and in critical terms (5). As Lee sardonically wrote, "murdered people, I am told, usually stay quiet, as a scientific fact," but when the dead do get lively again, literary criticism's inclination is either to return them to their graves or to make them into ghosts (38).

The dead generally either stay dead or are still present. They may be objects, as Elisabeth Bronfen argues, that "elude . . . the effort at recuperation which representation seeks to afford," but more often they are lingering subjects, as Carla Freccero puts it, with "a demand to which we must somehow respond" (Bronfen xii, Freccero 70). As Lee's derision suggests, this demand needn't always be juridical, but if the dead past makes an active guest appearance in the nineteenth-century present, its ghostliness is hard to avoid.[16] Even Lee's nonjudicial "genuine ghost," which she describes issuing from the mind rather than more literally from the grave, can't help but be an ethereal trace of the past, come to linger in and truck with the present. It "spr[ings] from the strange confused heaps, half-rubbish, half-treasure, which lie in our fancy, heaps of half-faded recollections, of fragmentary vivid impressions"; it emerges from "the Past, the more or less remote Past" of our imaginations, where "a legion of ghosts, very vague and changeful, are perpetually to and fro, fetching and carrying for us between [the Past] and the present" (39). Such ghosts, whether old-fangled or new-fangled, move through the nineteenth-century present of their own accord, delivering justice for past wrongs or giving memory a sensory form, but the irrepressibly agential pasts they hazily embody aren't the stuff of necromantic literature.

The willfully unghostly bodies of *The Necromantics*—mummies, galvanized corpses, and old men riding horses out of the land of the dead, among them—represent a concern with how the present recreates and uses the past rather than with the lingering past itself: with the political and aesthetic agendas that inhere in the aspiration to bring the past to life in modern forms. Tales of reanimation resist the critical truism, in the words of Julian Wolfreys, "that all forms of narrative are, in one way or another, haunted" and that "all stories are, more or less, ghost stories" (3). Unlike ghost stories, necromantic stories are invested in how language can actively excavate and rewrite history, not in history's own disruptive malingering. They demand that we understand modernity's relationship to the past in terms of resuscitation, revival, and reanimation, not in the paranoid terms of haunting, spectrality, and ghostliness. These texts teeter precariously on the boundary between miracle and monstrosity as they imagine what the art of the present can do to history, and their fantasies about the world-bending possibility of reanimating the dead are often creative and destructive in equal measure.

Necromantic literature is a deliberately unhaunted gothic. It mucks around in the grave, it obsesses over the potentially monstrous relationship between past and present, and it worries incessantly about literature's capacity to produce its own worst nightmares, but it does so without ghosts, buried secrets, or repressed anxieties. In this respect my focus on the necromantic instead of the ghostly builds on recent work in gothic studies that seeks to untangle gothic literature from critical frameworks that read the gothic as "ineluctably haunted" by "the inescapability of the past," full of guilty secrets that criticism needs to excavate (Moynahan 116, Lloyd-Smith 41).[17] Like Jack Halberstam and Joseph Valente, who argue that the gothic makes monsters out of the demonizing tendencies intrinsic to cultural prejudices instead of by repressing/expressing those prejudices themselves, I read necromantic literature as an active interlocutor in the production of history. Abandoning what Siân Silyn Roberts calls *"the guilt thesis"* undergirding the confrontational assumption that it is criticism's job to expose gothic texts' repressed sins, my aim in this book is to emphasize the generative over the reactive work of monster-making (21). As Silyn Roberts points out, if we take seriously the gothic's original aesthetic practice of deliberately manufacturing terrifying situations in order to maintain what Horace Walpole called "a constant vicissitude of interesting passions" in its readers, we will see how often "the gothic *defines* rather than *reflects* the object of fear" that critics have purported to unearth from it (Walpole 6, Silyn Roberts 21). In other words, plumbing gothic novels for their buried historical or cultural terrors misses the extent to which they explicitly render history and culture terrifying. Assuming that such novels are participants in—not ciphers for—their myriad contextual networks allows the novels themselves—not their penetrating critics—to stand as powerful engines of cultural analysis.

This reorientation away from the symptomatic reading practices that have long attended the gothic invites us to read the same gothic texts differently, as these critics do, but it also creates a new gothic space particularly suited to the literature of reanimation and its attention to the possibilities, precarities, and dangers of literature's generative capacities. If the work of paranoid reading, in Eve Kosofsky Sedgwick's terms, is to expose the "unfleshed skeleton of . . . culture," then necromantic literature's ceaseless efforts to reflesh, revoice, and reanimate the dead have far more in common with the "additive and accretive" impulses of reparative reading that Sedgwick proposes as an alternative (149). If Sedgwick can't quite explain what a reparative reading actually looks like beyond its affective attunements with camp, neither can most necromantic writers quite imagine a happy ending to Mary Shelley's fundamentally camp fantasy of a philosophical novel in which the dead return to life, "their souls endued with the same sensibilities and capacities as before, [but] turned naked of knowledge into this world, again to dress their skeleton powers in such habiliments as situation, education, and experience will furnish" ("Dodsworth" 48–49). In fact, Bram Stoker's unhappy ending to *The Jewel of Seven Stars* quite literally sends a reanimated corpse running off naked into the world, murderous, guided by outraged queenly sensibilities, and rife with the capacity for colonial domination. It's hardly shocking that foundational necromantic texts like *Frankenstein* and *Dracula* have long and rich queer/camp afterlives—I like to think that Mary Shelley reanimated in her own philosophical novel would have enjoyed the undying cultural vitality of her tragically dismembered Bride. Like reparative reading, necromantic writing is laden with the revolutionary possibility of new transhistorical attachments ("the irrepressible fascination with ventriloquistic experimentation; the disorienting juxtapositions of present with past"), new faith in the power of the aesthetic, and a profound wish to believe that there's more to be gained from giving life to a corpse than from defleshing it (Sedgwick 150). It just often ends disastrously.

My reading strategies follow the lead of necromantic writers' revolutionary desires, if not their often-destructive finales, seeking ways to read stories of reanimation as culturally transformative and always enraptured with what the literary imagination has the capacity to do, make, and remake in the world. Instead of understanding reanimation as an act of antagonistic exhumation, I approach necromantic literature seeking ways to discover a more generative—or, better, a more resuscitative—logic at work in its exhumations of the dead. Inspired by the desires, if not always the methods, of what Rita Felski has called "postcritical" or "reflective" reading, I take seriously the often metaphorical language of resuscitation that Felski uses (or borrows) to describe postcritical reading as a dynamic interaction between reader and text. Such reading "galvanize[s]" words, empowers us to "speak with the dead," renders texts "living . . . voices that speak back to our own axioms and convictions," and allows a text to "spring . . . to life via a mundane yet mysterious process in which words are animated by readers and reanimate readers in their turn" (*Hooked* 32; *Limits* 156, 159, 175).

My epilogue looks briefly at writers who take this zombie-making potential of postcritical reading to its most absurd extreme. But taking seriously—not literally—the idea of reading as a process of creative remaking liberates nineteenth-century texts from the bonds of history that have had such a hold on them. Felski insists that "the literary text is not a museum piece"—a point that I argue playfully against in my third chapter, given the opportunities that museum pieces offer to a necromantic imagination—but it would be more accurate to say that the literary text is not a ghost, tied irrevocably to an ever more pressing past (*Limits* 182). The ghost is a figure of historical persistence, while the reanimated body is a figure of historical recuperation. Tales of

12 • INTRODUCTION

reanimation foreground the processes by which contemporary literary forms remake the rags and bones of the past, whereas stories of haunting dwell on the disruptive presence of the past itself. I thus propose a model of resuscitative reading that takes its cues from necromantic texts themselves. It is our job as readers and critics to give the old bones we excavate new life, always aware of how our subjective energies fundamentally act upon materials with which we interact, and knowing that acts of critical resurrection run the risk of producing monsters instead of miracles. As Robert Browning wrote in *The Ring and the Book,* describing how poetic practice, in his words, "starts the dead alive," the work of the poet is to "put old powers to play, / Push out lines to the limit" (43). This, to me, is an apt directive for resuscitative reading: to give texts an experimental jolt, to push them to their limits by creatively remembering rather than dismembering their relationship to the world at large.

THE NECROMANTIC IMAGINATION: RESUSCITATIVE, HISTORICIST, PRESENTIST

I borrow the "historical imagination" in my title from Hayden White, whose foundational *Metahistory: The Historical Imagination in Nineteenth-Century Europe* reconceived what he called the "golden age" of history as an ongoing reflection on the aesthetic patterns through which history tells its stories (xii). By characterizing the nineteenth-century historian's work as "an essentially *poetic* act" and nineteenth-century historical works themselves as "formal verbal structures" constituted by recognizable plots, tropes, styles, and ideologies, White made it possible to recognize historical writing as a representational and linguistic mode fundamentally determined by present-day consciousness (x, 4). As he writes, "the very claim to have distinguished a past from a present world of social thought and praxis, and to have determined the total coherence of that past world, implies a conception of the form that knowledge of the present world also must take, insofar as it is continuous with that past world" (22). The past, like the raw material of any story, gains its meaning through the mediations and affordances of aesthetic form, which in turn emerge from the social and political forces shaping the present moment.[18] In this sense, history will always have a distinctly presentist sensibility, even when it appears to be the driest recitation of provable facts from the past. The most unfeeling nineteenth-century histories still refract and resist an inheritance of a "feeling-based Romantic historicism," and the most "technical scientific" histories, as J. R. Seeley wrote in 1879, reflect "the leading wants of the time" just as clearly as those whose "literary magic" can "fill the ears of men with a glorious tale" (M. Goode 150; 295, 299, 294, 293).

White's point is that historical works—even those that dismiss "presentist concerns" to focus on difference rather than continuity—are still presentist because they can't escape their own metahistorical reflections, their attentiveness to the mediating capacities of their own forms (4). More recently, in an explicit call for scholars of the nineteenth century to embrace presentism as a "robust interpretive mode," V21 Collective founders Anna Kornbluh and Benjamin Morgan reiterated White by insisting that historical-mindedness isn't antithetical to presentism because "pastness must always be theorized" (n. pag.). V21 aimed to push current nineteenth-century studies scholarship away from thinking of presentism as "the deformation of our objects of study in our own image" and toward an interpretive mode that embraced the complex interleavings of past and present (n. pag.).[19] Yet while this redefinition of presentism invited a field-wide conversation about how contemporary scholarship contextualizes its nineteenth-century archives, it also reiterated a debate about the nature of historicism that had been ongoing since the late eighteenth century.[20] Is the purpose of studying the past to embalm long-dead corpses—to "exhaustively describe, preserve, and display the past"—or to "write a history of the present" that brings those corpses back to life (*Manifesto* n. pag.; Foucault 31)?

As I demonstrate throughout this book, the Victorian corpses that V21 hoped to reanimate had their own ideas about history's resuscitative potential. Work by Porscha Fermanis, Jonathan Crimmins, Devin Griffiths, Ian Duncan, and others has demonstrated that neither the complicated theoretical and scientific landscape of nineteenth-century historicism nor the strategies by which—to borrow Duncan's words—such scholarship "give[s] history back a human form" bear any resemblance to the "bland antiquarianism" that V21 both invented and rejected (*Human Forms* 61; *Manifesto* n. pag.).[21] However, the field's debate about the relative values and methods of historicist and presentist reading practices, both of which in their own ways risk "the deformation of our objects of study," reiterates precisely the uncertainty, the desire to experiment, and the speculative productions of nineteenth-century writers who imagined their own aesthetic projects as acts of resuscitation. The question of whether presentism deforms or makes new shapes; whether historicism deadens or revives; whether the two are distinct from one another or whether presentism simply represents a creative attentiveness to historicism's capacity to intertwine past and present—all of these questions equally animate Mary Shelley's insistence in her 1831 introduction to *Frankenstein* that every "beginning must be linked to something that came before," Bram Stoker's fantasy in 1903 that resurrecting a mummy "can link together the Old and the New, Earth and Heaven," and countless dreams and nightmares of reanimating the dead in between (Shelley, "Introduction" 349; Stoker, *Jewel* 155). While these writers certainly aren't historians, they borrow the idea that history can be a form of necromancy—Seeley's "literary magic," producing statesmen "before us . . . posing and declaiming with dramatic gesture" (294)—from its persistence in the work of historians, historical fiction, and criticism of historiographic method across the nineteenth century.

From Thomas Rowlandson's 1816 engraving "Death and the Antiquaries," in which a very lively skeleton watches with interest as antiquarians crowd around the exhumed body of a king, and Scott's melodramatic 1819 image of the historical novelist as a "Scottish magician" picking his way through still-quivering corpses while the poor English author must work with "dry, sapless, mouldering, and disjoined bones," to Charles Kingsley's 1860 argument that history should "ma[ke] a friend of the dead, and br[ing] him to life again" and Michelet's impassioned claim that the fundamental "duty of the Historian" is to give life to "the too-forgotten dead," necromantic language and imagery suffused nineteenth-century theorizing about history's relationship to the past (Scott, "Dedicatory Epistle" 22; Kingsley 5; Barthes 101). Necromancy doesn't serve the same specific function across these different registers any more than it does across the work of Shelley and Stoker, but in each case recourse to necromancy signals a much closer attention to historicist methodology than to whatever actually constitutes the dead past.[22] Necromantic metaphors focus on what history *does* instead of on what the past *is,* and the writers I treat in this book explore the aesthetic and political possibilities of this active historicism when they transform history's figurative necromancy into literature's literal reanimated corpses: Shelley's creature in its countless iterations, Dickens's zombie characters, Browning's dead but speaking bride, Yeats's reborn Celtic heroes, and Stoker's *very* angry mummy.

PROMETHEAN HISTORY, IRISH REVIVAL

Before I turn to this literary phenomenon, however, I want to look more closely at the work of two of the nineteenth-century historians—Jules Michelet, briefly, and the Irish historian Standish O'Grady, at greater length—whose particular versions of resuscitative historiography animate my approach to reading literary reanimation as an engagement with nineteenth-century historical-mindedness. Michelet, whose preface to his *History of the Nineteenth Century* includes the language I quote above about the duty of historians, presents resuscitative history as an ethical imperative. The whole of the passage emphasizes what Roland Barthes describes as the "magical action" of the historian, "a magus" who gives the dead "a place in History's universal memory" (Barthes 82). Michelet's dream of resurrection focuses on the inability of meaning to inhere in the past: one can't look to it for understanding, and the historian should not imagine himself backward into it—in the Smithian sense—but instead must resurrect the dead in the present moment so that the historical present can render meaning from lost lives:

> Never in my career have I lost sight of that duty of the Historian. I have given many of the too-forgotten dead the assistance which I myself shall require.
>
> I have exhumed them for a second life. Some were not born at a moment suitable to them. Others were born on the eve of new and striking circumstances which have come to erase them, so to speak, stifling their memory.
>
> . . .
>
> History greets and renews these disinherited glories; it gives life to these dead men, resuscitates them. Its justice thus associates those who have not lived at the same time, offers reparation to some who appeared so briefly only to vanish. Now they live with us, and we feel we are their relatives, their friends. Thus is constituted a family, a city shared by the living and the dead (101–2).

History exhumes, renews, resuscitates, repairs; it disintegrates distinctions between past and present; it brings back the dead as people—relatives, friends, and family—not as emblems; and most importantly, by giving the dead a second life in the present, history acts as an agent of justice, not by setting the wrongs of the past to rights but by making the past matter *now*. Several decades before, in an earlier exploration of what constitutes historical justice, Michelet describes the historian as a "Prometheus" who gives the dead fire so that "they might begin to speak[:] . . . words must be heard which were never spoken" (102). Prometheus, as any reader of either Shelley knows, first created man and then gave him fire before being punished for his transgressions against the other gods. Michelet here fuses both creator and fire-bringer in his image of Prometheus by investing the historian with the power not only to illuminate the words of the dead but also to create new words for them. Although this earlier passage moves away from the resuscitative image of making the dead speak to end with them lulled back to sleep by the historian's gentle ministrations of justice, Michelet imagines the historian in Promethean terms to make history's relationship with the dead past agential, transgressive, and part of a larger early nineteenth-century fascination with Prometheus as an emblem of social and political resistance.[23]

White characterized Michelet's historical sensibility as both Romantic and "Anarchist," and his mode of historical emplotment as an attempt to safeguard

16 • INTRODUCTION

"the memory of the race, against any tyranny which might have offended that memory by systematic suppression of the truth" (162, 158). In this, and with the Promethean historian in mind, we can hear echoes of Percy Shelley's preface to his poem "Prometheus Unbound," inspired also by the events of the French Revolution, in which he writes that his aim is to "produce a systematical history of what appear to [him] to be the genuine elements of human society," embodied in Prometheus's "highest perfection of moral and intellectual nature impelled by the purest and the truest motives to the best and noblest ends"— the story of "a Champion" who refuses to be reconciled with "the Oppressor of mankind" (*Poetical Works* 267, 264, 263).[24] Channeling Michelet's own poetic impulses, White describes Michelet's histories in similar terms as dramas of the "liberation of a spiritual power fighting to free itself from the forces of darkness," and it is this sense of history's power to liberate the oppressed dead from the "the disfigured and perverted past" that Michelet not only describes as "the aim of history" but explicitly names as a resuscitative practice: "Let it be my part in the future to have not attained, but marked, the aim of history, to have called it by a name that nobody had given it. . . . I have named it *resurrection,* and this name will remain" (qtd. in White 152; original italics). To choose "resurrection" over other formal labels—Michelet mentions and rejects "narration" and "analysis"—makes clear that he wants the work of the historian to do more than plot, reflect, or even set its aspirations somewhere reachable. He instead wants history to strive toward the miraculous, to wish to do the impossible in the name of creating a more ethical and more truthful world. He longs for history to resuscitate the dead not because it truly can, but because imagining that history could bring the dead to life invests history with the power, or at least the potential, to remake the past into an ideal future. This idealistic dream of reanimation as a second life for the past—a new life, an aesthetic life, a useful life, a real life—undergirds the work of many of the writers in this book, whether they believe in the dream like W. B. Yeats does or whether, like Bram Stoker, they quote from "Prometheus Unbound" only to foreshadow how dangerous this dream can become.[25]

The Irish historian Standish O'Grady, the "father" of the Irish Literary Revival movement, believed wholeheartedly in the power of history to bring the past back to useful life, and his Romantic approach to writing ancient Celtic history in the 1870s and '80s stands at several key crossroads of this book: chronological, national, conceptual, and methodological (Boyd, "Introduction" 7). In his bizarre multivolume *History of Ireland* (1878–81), O'Grady unabashedly borrows ideas, tropes, and even quotations from the same late eighteenth- and early nineteenth-century thinkers that I argue in my first three chapters underlie the resuscitative work of Mary Shelley, Robert Browning, and Charles Dickens, but he does so explicitly to create an Irish national mythos that ultimately gives rise to the work of W. B. Yeats and Bram Stoker that I explore in my final two chapters. By embedding a resuscitative British literary tradition in a resuscitative Irish historiographical project, O'Grady's *History* serves as the connective tissue both between the English and Irish necromantic imaginations, and between necromantic literature as a whole and nineteenth-century historiography. In the *History's* own eccentric muddling of British and Irish literary and historical sources and its direct influence on the resuscitative aesthetics of late nineteenth- and early twentieth-century Irish literature, O'Grady's work embodies both the complicated bidirectionality of Irish and English necromantic writing throughout the nineteenth century and the importance of these necromantic literatures as active interlocutors in nineteenth-century historiographic theory.

In looking both backward to early nineteenth-century British Romantic poets and historians and forward to the quite literal Celtic revivals that Yeats and Stoker envision at the turn of the twentieth century, O'Grady's *History of Ireland* reveals an ambiguous colonial politics writ small as literary form.[26] O'Grady's "Fenian Unionis[m]," as one contemporary described it, which later in his life became what can only be described as queer socialist unionism, glorifies Irish history and culture while also firmly endorsing the British imperial project (qtd. in Castle, "Wild" 3).[27] His work in the nineteenth century became an origin point for late nineteenth- / early twentieth-century Irish cultural nationalism, and yet his own early twentieth-century writing glaringly omits internationally acclaimed Irish writers like Yeats from his lists of "great modern poets" (Byron, Shelley, Wordsworth, Walt Whitman[28]) and ham-fistedly includes the ostentatiously Scottish Sir Walter Scott in his list of "our great Nature poets, the English poets" ("Nature" 38). Unlike the Irish writers who follow in his footsteps and whose work is at least equally indebted to earlier English writers, O'Grady celebrates his English inheritances rather than distinguishing his work from them and doesn't see this celebration undermining the Irishness of the cultural masterpiece he believes he's creating. He makes no effort to enmesh himself in anything like an Irish national tradition because Irish history and the English literary tradition aren't antithetical to O'Grady. He unapologetically conceives the form of his Irish *History* in explicit relation to the nineteenth-century English literature he admires, not to the nineteenth-century Irish literature that he barely acknowledges, and he finds in this English Romantic tradition aesthetic and political models for a revival of Irish identity.

While O'Grady relies on the translation work of mid-nineteenth-century Irish-language scholars to furnish him with the raw bardic materials from

18 · INTRODUCTION

which he draws his *History*, he disregards any connections between his work and other nineteenth-century Irish historians also writing Celtic histories in favor of an intense approbation for Thomas Carlyle, whose notion that "the Bible of any nation should be its history" O'Grady lists among his primary influences (qtd. in Higgins, *Heroic* 13). As others have suggested, the Scottish Carlyle's avowedly anti-Irish sentiments, which went so far as to call for Irish extermination in the immediate aftermath of the Famine, make him a dubious father figure for the Father of the Irish Literary Revival.[29] Yet O'Grady's own revivalist sensibilities followed Carlyle in their privileging of heroes over peasants and leaders over masses.[30] Instead of seeking an Irish uprising against the oppression of British colonialism or planting the seeds for an independent Irish nation, O'Grady conceived the *History* as a glorification of Celtic feudalism, a story of aristocratic heroes waking a sluggish people with their dominance and splendor. Praising Carlyle's "blazing" words for their power "almost to wake the dead," O'Grady imagined his own words wakening the Irish spirit not to a call for modern self-determination but to a recognition that their glorious heroic past offered a model for an Irish future limned by an equally heroic Anglo-Irish aristocracy.[31]

Like Michelet, O'Grady represents history in both resuscitative and Romantic Promethean terms, using lines from Shelley's "Prometheus Unbound" as epigraphs to chapters of his *History of Ireland* and explicitly borrowing Shelley's language and imagery in his descriptions of Cuculain, the Celtic hero that he wants readers to recognize as kith and kin with Shelley's Prometheus. Fusing Irish heroic literature with this canonical Romantic literary tradition had a profound effect on the young Yeats, who would later ecstatically reiterate in an essay on Shelley's poetry that it "seek[s] to awaken in all things that are, a community with what we experience within ourselves" ("Shelley" 55). As I discuss further in chapter 4, this translation of Irish legend through Romantic poetry offered Yeats a model for how his own poetry could create symbols that "transcend particular time and place . . . and bec[ome] living souls" ("Shelley" 62). But O'Grady's turn to Prometheus, specifically, embeds his project both in the Promethean mythos of creativity and in a literary history most famously associated in the nineteenth century with both Percy and Mary Shelley. In invoking Prometheus, O'Grady's interest lies less in the revolutionary possibilities of historical resuscitation that Michelet found so compelling and more in Prometheus as a vehicle for and an emblem of literary inheritance and revival. As much as the myth of Prometheus itself offered a blueprint for tales of heroic (or antiheroic) creativity and resistance to authority, the myth's literary trajectory across the early nineteenth century also took on its own symbolic resuscitative weight as writers acknowledged not only the usefulness of

Prometheus as a character model but also the value of reimagining an ancient story to best suit a modern imagination. For instance, Percy Shelley describes his work in the preface to "Prometheus Unbound" not only as producing a morally ideal history but also as finding "new life" in ideas that were already present in man and nature (*Poetical Works* 264). He doesn't simply rewrite Aeschylus's ancient drama of Prometheus in different language. Instead, he aims to create a new, modern, moral vision out of the skeleton of Aeschylus's plot—to resuscitate ancient mythology with the "uncommunicated lightning of [his] own mind" into a modern form rooted in "the moral and intellectual condition" of contemporary England (265). For O'Grady, Shelley's Prometheus represents both the transformation of a mythical hero into a modern archetype and the strategic regeneration of old source material into new and relevant literary forms.

The *other* Shelley's Promethean venture isn't quoted anywhere in O'Grady's *History of Ireland*, but *Frankenstein: The Modern Prometheus* is as important an intertext for O'Grady's historicist imagination as "Prometheus Unbound" is. Between the end of the 1840s and the beginning of the 1880s, no fewer than three iconic political cartoons titled "The Irish Frankenstein" appeared in British newspapers, in each case depicting an independent or resistant Ireland as a monster turning either on whatever political architect was attempting its liberation or on Britain itself. These cartoons resonate with O'Grady's own unionist politics, and when he himself scathingly describes what an independent Irish nation would look like, his language is indebted to the popular idea of a Frankenstein's monster as an amalgamation of unsynthesized and violently animated parts: the monstrous nation would be "an accumulation of great numbers of different kinds of people with a multitude of separate selfish and conflicting interests, all held violently together by armed force."[32] This proliferation of Frankenstein imagery across the nineteenth century bespeaks the widespread cultural capital that Mary Shelley's novel acquired in the decades after its 1818 publication, when the bare bones of its plot (and occasionally its Promethean subtitle) propagated in theatrical adaptations whose huge popularity gave the novel itself new life and a new, revised edition in the 1830s (which I discuss in detail in chapter 1).[33]

While Mary Shelley's subtitle creates its own revisionary relationship to Aeschylus, insisting that we recognize both the novel's inherited mythos and its explicitly modern reimagining of the ancient story about gods creating humans, the plays that follow Shelley's novel rely far more explicitly than their source text on their status as new incarnations of texts that came before. While Shelley offers us Prometheus as one of several literary models for understanding Frankenstein's creative power and his moral failing as a creator, she doesn't

20 • INTRODUCTION

write Frankenstein's creature itself as a symbol for literary revision. The theatrical adaptations that follow her novel, however, transform Frankenstein from a character who creates life into a character who reanimates the dead and focus our attention directly on the recycling of old parts into new monsters. They do this literally, of course, in the many creatures that stage-Frankensteins stitch together out of dead bodies—these Frankensteins "breathe the breath of life into a mass of putrefying mortality" rather than create a new species of life, as Shelley's Frankenstein does (Milner 192)—but the plays do so equally in their self-conscious attentiveness to their own resuscitative relationships with both the original text of Shelley's novel and the other theatrical adaptations of *Frankenstein* that precede them. "You must excuse a trifling deviation / from Mrs. Shelley's marvellous narration," says a character in one of the plays, while a character in another worries that "a Drama of th[is] title has already been many nights before the Town" (Brough and Brough 229; Peake, *Another* 162).

While such dramas may seem far afield from O'Grady's *History of Ireland,* their constellation of inheritances and resurrections helped keep both Shelleys' Promethean efforts alive enough in nineteenth-century culture to be tapped as recognizable resuscitative models for historians like O'Grady and Michelet. It's difficult to imagine that these plays' enduring transformation of Mary Shelley's modern Prometheus into a reanimator wasn't somewhere in the back of Mary's own mind when she describes Percy's Prometheus as "the regenerator" in her 1839 edition of his poetical works, reimagining him as a redemptive version of her own creator-god whose self-renewing heart resuscitates human virtue rather than decaying body parts ("Note" 371). O'Grady's own Promethean quotations acknowledge not only the relationship he wants to create between British Romantic sensibilities and his own historiographic project, but also the degree to which his history relies on the mechanisms of literary revival for reimagining the past in ways that can do useful work in modern world.[34] If O'Grady imagines his foremost Celtic hero Cuculain as Promethean in Percy Shelley's heroic sense, he presents his historicist method as Promethean in Mary Shelley's regenerational sense, "superadd[ing] a realisation more intense" to old stories in order to produce a passionate new life for them that he thinks nineteenth-century Ireland sorely lacks (1:xii).[35] Like Frankenstein's many creatures whose new lives rely on creative superadditions to the archive of creatures that precede them, O'Grady's history comes to life only when he infuses the archives of the Irish past with a "profound and vital humanity," the imaginative and aesthetic lightning that transforms calcified bits of information into moving stories (*History: Critical and Philosophical* 203).

Unlike Michelet, O'Grady imagined his work resuscitating both historical bodies and modern bodies. For him, the point of historical revival was to produce an immersive, experiential history that enlivened contemporary readers by infusing them with its vitality. Again, nineteenth-century *Frankensteins* offer a monstrous model for this utopian historical project: while these *Frankensteins* push the idea of history living in the body to its gothic limit in the form of an animated monster composed of dead body parts, O'Grady uses similar philosophical sources to imagine Irish history ecstatically coming to life in the bodies of his contemporary Irish readers.[36] His *History* borrows heavily from debates about the relative veracities of romance and history that both William Godwin and Mary Shelley reflected on when, for instance, Godwin argued in "Of History and Romance" that romance is not only "one of the species of history" but also a "nobler composition" than "what ordinarily bears the denomination of history" (465).[37] The "novelist and the romancer," as O'Grady writes in the introduction to the first volume of his *History*, have become the bastions of "pure historical composition," because "nearly every work . . . affecting to treat the past in a rigid and conscientious spirit, is merely archaeological" (1:iii). The distinction Godwin makes between romance and history, reconceived by O'Grady as the difference between "pure history" and the "merely archaeological," is precisely the difference between a dead history of "sorry remnants" and a history that can bring the dead to life (1:iv). "Out of the sad leavings of the past," O'Grady asks, "how can even the most cunning mechanical arrangement evolve a living, adequate, affective representation of the life of our ancestors?" (1:iv).

In the spirits both of Adam Smith and of Edmund Burke, O'Grady insists that in history "there must be sympathy, imagination, and creation," for only then will a "vivid picture" of the past "impress itself upon [the] mind" (1:iv.).[38] He also offers what might well be a deliberate invocation of Scott's argument in *Ivanhoe*'s "Dedicatory Epistle to the Rev. Doctor Dryasdust" that translating antiquated language and manners will both save readers being "trammelled by the repulsive dryness of mere antiquity" and demonstrate that "the passions. . . . are generally the same in all ranks and conditions, in all countries and ages" (26, 28). O'Grady borrows Scott's point when he argues that he takes his own artistic license and "disregard[s] . . . the literal statement of the bard" because "the same human heart beat in their breasts as beats amongst us today. All the great permanent relations of life are the same" (1:xi, xii). O'Grady trades historical accuracy for continuity and familiarity because his aim isn't to provide modern Ireland with information about its Celtic past. He aims instead to make modern Irish readers *feel* their Celtic history as an integral part of their embodied experience of Irishness, as a new source of national vitality, even as erotic excitement. The student of his version Irish history will have their senses "touch[ed] and stir[red]" to life by their ability to immerse

22 • INTRODUCTION

themselves in the stories of humanity he offers them (*History: Critical and Philosophical* 204).

O'Grady's deeply aesthetic and poetic historical sensibility is clearly enmeshed in of-the-moment debates in the 1860s and 1870s about the proper disciplinary form of history that Seeley outlines in the article I discuss above—about whether history should be an art or a science, whether the past should be "adulterated, corrupted, falsified" by the "black magic" of poetry, or whether the historian should "restore the prosaic truth in all its tiresome dryness and intricacy where poetry had reigned before" (Seeley 293).[39] But the frames through which O'Grady defends and elucidates his methodology, as well as his repeated insistences throughout the *History* that readers should experience history with their enlivened senses, not apprehend it with their "frozen" minds, have far more in common with the early nineteenth century than they do with the moment of his writing (2:18). He has been described by Gregory Castle as a "presentist historicist" precisely because he recognizes both this recent British past and the ancient Celtic past as fully applicable to late nineteenth-century Ireland, but Castle's further elucidation of this presentism as an awareness of the past's "ability to haunt and thereby alter the way we think about our contemporary moment, which in turn alters how we think about the future," misses the fundamental principle underlying O'Grady's presentist creation of Irish history (Castle, "Wild" 26). The past doesn't haunt the *History of Ireland*. The past in and of itself has no purchase on O'Grady's contemporary moment or on his dreams for Ireland's future. Instead, O'Grady's presentist historicism is rooted in his aesthetics of revival, which explicitly remake the past into contemporary forms that frame his desires for Ireland's present and future. This presentist aesthetics determines O'Grady's relationship to early nineteenth-century inheritances as much as his relationship to the centuries-old bardic past. He both embeds British Romanticism in the foundations of the Irish Literary Revival and reimagines British Romanticism as an Irish literary form, reshaped by his deeply self-conscious reflections on how, why, and to what aesthetic and political ends the Irish past could be made both to live and to matter in an Ireland struggling to write itself into a national identity. His *History* always looks simultaneously backward and forward, anchored by the power of present-day history to reconstruct the past into a model for an ideal Irish future.

I linger on O'Grady here because his historicist methodology offers me a model for reading the nineteenth-century resuscitative imagination both developmentally and recursively. His *History of Ireland* reveals the English literary inheritances of late-century Irish Literary Revival writing while simultaneously enabling the politics and aesthetics of the Irish Revival to reframe the resuscitative experiments of earlier-century English writers. My own book borrows his practice of looking forward from England to Ireland and backward from Ireland to England, arguing that the Irish Literary Revival is both the apotheosis of nineteenth-century necromantic literature and the critical origin point for recognizing the historical, political, and formal investments that shaped necromantic literature across the century as a whole. As this book unfolds, I show writers across both national traditions engaging the same hopes for language's resuscitative power, the same uncertainties about the past's accessibility, the same skepticisms about technological modernity, and the same turns to monstrosity to theorize the extremities of a sentimental historical imagination. Yet the *History of Ireland,* which equally embodies these hopes, uncertainties, skepticisms, and turns, also reveals how inextricable they are from the ideologies and cultural appropriations of the British imperial project. And while the imprints of imperialism clearly shape the Irish Literary Revival writing that follows O'Grady, the *History*'s strange attuning of English and Irish necromancies equally illuminates these ideologies and appropriations straining the resuscitative aesthetics of the English writers who precede him.

I make no counterfactual claims here for early and mid-nineteenth-century English writers as inheritors of late-century Irish Revival politics, but as critics like Mary Mullen and Elaine Freedgood have shown, discovering new ways to read relationships between texts—ways of reading that resist what Mullen describes as "the institutionalized practices of literary study" (13)—will produce new understandings of how texts operate beyond the expectations of form we've been trained to seek. While I show the evolution of the British resuscitative imagination from Mary Shelley to Bram Stoker, O'Grady's *History* serves as a critical inflection point, allowing me to argue that reading literature of the Irish Literary Revival as explicitly necromantic breathes new and different life into the English necromantic literature that came before it. By clearly laying bare the political instrumentalism and aesthetic idealism that together can transform the past into an undead historical monster, Irish literature wakes us to the same mechanisms less obviously at work in the English literature that precedes it. Along with critics like Mullen, Amy Martin, and Patrick O'Malley, my approach resists both the denigrating and the celebratory critical narratives that situate nineteenth-century Irish literature on the colonial periphery of British literary production.[40] I argue instead that the second lives, revived heroes, and reanimated monsters of late-century Irish writing illuminate a systemic necromantic impulse threading its way from British Romanticism to Victorian realism. In other words, I read Irish necromantic literature as a resuscitative rather than as a derivative tradition, both

24 • INTRODUCTION

resurrecting and allowing me to resurrect the strategies, desires, and dangers of the British necromantic imagination as a whole.

GALVANIC HISTORY

As my introductory reading of Lady Wilde's poem demonstrates, this nec-romantic imagination relies heavily on the language of nineteenth-century electricity to express both its resuscitative longings and its ideal modes of historical apprehension. Even O'Grady electrifies his past, describing the "dazzling" light of heroes in a lively history and the "lightnings" of the giant Fomorians, "raised by sorcerers from their tombs" (*History: Critical and Philo-sophical* 200, 2:191). The galvanic story underlying the resuscitative fantasies of almost all the writers this book discusses begins in 1802, when Giovanni Aldini, nephew of Luigi Galvani and professor of experimental philosophy at the University of Bologna, began a European tour in which he set out to prove the existence of what his uncle had called "animal electricity." Debates raged at the end of the eighteenth century about the nature of the electrical force that Galvani, in his famous experiments on frogs' legs, claimed originated in ani-mal tissue itself, and Aldini turned to the anatomical theaters of Paris, Oxford, and London to show that, with the right kinds of experiments, he could reveal "the power of Galvanism to excite the vital forces" (Aldini 2).[41]

Aldini's public experiments on oxen and human corpses worked to shrink the not-trivial distance between stimulating muscle movement and actually restoring life. In one of these, for instance, Aldini connected a wire from the spinal column of a recently beheaded ox to the ox's sphincter, and, as he tells us, performed the miraculous task of "obtain[ing] a very strong action on the rectum, which even produced an expulsion of faeces" (57). In trying to make the ox defecate, Aldini may have been recollecting one of the eighteenth century's most famous automatons, Jacques Vaucanson's "Digesting Duck," which stunned spectators in the 1730s with its apparent ability to swallow corn and other grains and expel them a few moments later in a form that closely resembled duck feces.[42] Like Vaucanson's digesting duck, Aldini's defecating ox troubled the boundary between life and nonlife by putting the most unerr-ingly organic of bodily functions at the center of a disquisition on the role of artifice in producing, or replacing, natural vital forces. But whereas the duck's simulated body confronted people with the possibility that life might be far nearer to nonlife than we want to imagine, the ox's very real shit pushed in the opposite direction by intimating that nonlife might always be just on the cusp of becoming real life, if the right sorts of artificial stimulation could stir material vitality into action. While several of his earlier experiments produced movements that Aldini compared to lifelike phenomena—sheep eyeballs roll and ox tongues protrude—the defecating ox seemed to cross an important biological line between lifelike and life itself by performing a function that was essential to life rather than simply mimicking the motions and appearances of living creatures. Even if the dead, headless ox couldn't actually be resuscitated (and the spectators, "very much alarmed" by all of the violent movements this ox was suddenly making, were undoubtedly grateful for that [57]), it could be galvanized into some definition of living, with enough of its vital force replenished to recommence its mundane organic operations. The sudden feces appeared to reveal that circulatory processes of life could be set in motion even after they had ceased to move of their own accord. It may have been messy, but for Aldini it was a triumph, nonetheless.

In experiments like these, Aldini set out to prove that the same galvanic power supplying the world with postmortem ox feces also filled the human body, and could be the source of even greater miracles of reanimation:

> From the experiments already described, one might by analogy conjecture what effect the action of Galvanism would produce on that noble being man, the sole object of my researches. . . . It was therefore necessary to obtain the human body while it still retained, after death, the vital powers in the highest degree of preservation. (67)

It was possible, he suggested, that he would discover important instances in which "interment ought to be retarded" because a corpse could, indeed, be resuscitated (89). And so, to "promot[e] the welfare of the human race," he commenced experiments on hanged criminals, frightening unsuspecting spectators by producing "horrid grimaces" on the faces of their severed heads and making their bodies move so much "as almost to give an appearance of re-animation" (91, 71, 193). He insisted that his object in these experiments wasn't actually to bring these dead, beheaded criminals back to life but to discover the extent to which galvanism could function as a rejuvenating force, particularly on slightly less dead people. And yet he also described one of these experiments "surpass[ing] our most sanguine expectations," and wrote ecstatically that "vitality might, perhaps, have been restored, if many circumstances had not rendered it impossible" (194). By "circumstances," in this case, Aldini undoubtedly refers to the pesky separation of heads from bodies that also rendered his oxen far too dead to be genuinely restored to life, but as with the defecating ox, these human experiments imagine both life and death as spectrums rather than as singular states.

Galvanic scientists that followed in his footsteps, like Wilson Phillips and Andrew Ure in the 1810s, made much of galvanism's power to transform life and death into interpretive phenomena rather than definitive conditions. The former again turned to the digestive system (this time of dead rabbits) to prove that the "nervous influence" and galvanic electricity were interchangeable if both could help a bunny digest its parsley, and the latter scandalously induced the corpse of the hanged murderer Matthew Clydesdale to expressions of "rage, horror, despair, and ghastly smiles" such that some of the experiment's spectators believed "he had come to life" (Ure 287, 290, 291). Ure, especially, borrowed Aldini's sensationalized habits of description to translate the stimulated muscle contractions of his corpse into the language of human affect, underscoring his audience's shock at the corpse's apparent reanimation with his own representation of its convulsive movements as lively feelings. In the hands of Aldini and his successors, resuscitation from "apparent death" might be possible even if reanimation of the *really* dead isn't. Actual vitality might be just on the heels of muscle spasms, grimaces, ghastly smiles, and ox feces, even if headless corpses weren't leaping off the tables to polka (Aldini 91). The appearance of death wasn't always quite death, and the appearance of life wasn't usually quite life, but galvanism seemed to have the remarkable potential to cloud the distinctions both between death and life, and between appearance and reality.

Setting aside the irony of using literal bullshit as evidence of animal electricity, and overlooking the questionable ethics of Aldini's and Ure's glee at snatching bloody bodies straight from the gallows (not to mention the mass rabbit killing), the notion in the early nineteenth century that "life" might be little more than stored electricity was both seductive and radical, to scientists and philosophers alike.[43] If the physical matter of which bodies are composed contains electricity, and that electricity is what makes all bodies live—be they oxen or human, by analogy or by experiment—then there's no such thing as a divine spark or a human soul. Was electricity truly life's vital force, or might it just serve as a useful metaphor for the mystery of vital force? Was electricity a pale, specious imitation of whatever divine spark truly made piles of organic matter into living, feeling human beings, or, as Coleridge thought, did the presence of electricity in all matter mean that the divine spark was everywhere? As I discuss in chapter 1, *Frankenstein* and its 1820s theatrical adaptations offer clear examples of how early nineteenth-century literature probed the complexities of the relationship between the "vital warmth" that sparks a creature's ragtag parts into animation, and what it means to actually *be* or to *become* a human being.[44] Real galvanic experiments like Aldini's and

Ure's didn't have the same power that literature or theatre did to produce a human soul out of bits of flesh and flashes of lightning, but they nonetheless dangled the tantalizing possibility that human vitality—or something very near to it—could be renewed, or even manufactured, without any need for divine intervention.

Throughout the next several decades of the nineteenth century, the association between electricity and vitality hovered somewhere between scientific miracle and quack-magnet. While the field of medical electricity itself still had purchase in the scientific community, the old idea of animal electricity fell entirely out of fashion. As an 1843 article in *John Bull* puts it, describing a Belfast doctor's recent claims that the lungs "act as a galvanic battery in generating 'electro-nervous influence,' and not, as commonly believed . . . in evolving carbon from the blood," making such claims that the physical phenomena of the body are akin to "mysterious agents" like electricity and galvanism "is only explaining an *ignotum* by an *ignotius*" ("Lungs" 685). In tandem with the waning validity of animal electricity, belief in galvanism's actual reanimating potential faded almost completely as it became clear that galvanized criminals weren't anywhere near as close to returning to life as their enthusiastic scientists wished them to be,[45] and the idea of a body galvanized to actual life became the stuff of parodic fiction rather than anatomical inquiry.[46] Satirical journals from the mid-nineteenth century into the early twentieth would even reprint articles about galvanic experiments on executed corpses from early nineteenth-century scientific journals, recontextualizing the now passé attempts to prove that there was "a probability that life might have been restored" as patent absurdities or "famous crimes."[47] Andrew Ure's original article from the *Quarterly Journal*, which in 1818 and 1819 had been reprinted by several respectable British and American newspapers, was particularly useful fodder for satirical magazines, given his melodramatic language and his insistence that the expressions on his corpse's face "surpass[ed] far the wildest representations of a Fuseli or a Kean" (Ure 290). In the 1840s sections of the article were reproduced in the *Penny Satirist* alongside other useful gems like "The Science of Astrology," "How to Flatter Successfully," and "How to Make the Donkey Go."[48] Galvanism's connection to vitality more broadly conceived also came under fire, as an increasing number of readily available medical devices utilizing the "Mysterious Power of Galvanism" to increase bodily strength, cure illness, or stimulate the nerves—devices like the electric corset, the electric hairbrush, galvanic rings, belts, bracelets, and amulets—began popping up in the marketplace.[49] As one satirical article suggests, galvanic rings, especially, could have all sorts of enticing vitalizing effects:

However inelegant it would seem, we are sure there are hundreds of thousands of virgins now "wasting in despair," who would hail with pleasure our recommendation that unmarried swains should wear [the rings] through their *lips*. The impulsive action which galvanism would give causing a basial reciprocity—... a magnetic tendency to attract the lip, would bring about the "consummation devoutly to be wished" far more rapidly than at present. We have [also] received from some male correspondents queries as to what would be the effect of a galvanic ring of sufficient size worn round the "upper leg."[50]

Not everybody thought electrical and galvanic cures were quack medicine, however, and the association between electrical energies and vitality persisted into the later nineteenth century. In 1837, for instance, an 1803 150-page mock epic poem called "Terrible Tractoration" (about the curative powers of an American doctor's late eighteenth-century galvanic "metallic tractors") went into its fourth edition, including a new preface in which its author, "Christopher Caustic, M.D.," explains that the tractors "were said to cure diseases . . . by conducting from the diseased part the surplus of electric fluid which in such cases, causes or accompanies the morbid affection" (Fessenden iii).[51] Although by the 1830s the effectiveness of the tractors had been thoroughly debunked, "Caustic" isn't quite willing to abandon his endorsement, writing defensively that "the author would have never written a syllable intended to give Metallic Tractors favorable notoriety, had he not believed in their efficacy," and never saying that his belief has diminished (iv).[52] The poem is exaggeratedly satirical (it clearly doesn't think the galvanic tractors can really "reanimat[e] daily, / Rogues that were hung *once*, at Old Bailey" [85]), yet its critique remains directed at the medical community that dismisses the tractors rather than at the curative galvanic potential of the devices themselves. Even more, its elaborately long and comic footnotes about the marvels of early nineteenth-century galvanic experiments also remain untouched. Again, while these admit to embellishing the stories and poke fun at credulous observers who believed in the miracle of galvanic reanimation, it is precisely these absurd exaggerations of galvanism's power—at the expense of the real therapeutic potential it might have—that the poem denounces.

The market in electrical medical implements proliferated from the 1850s forward, despite atrophied belief in the revitalizing power of galvanism and its tractorian offshoots. As an article about an electrical device called Pulvermacher's Chain (which Dickens himself ordered in 1870)[53] in the *Lady's Newspaper* claimed in the late 1850s, "the numerous cures everywhere obtained in a variety of maladies" by the application of electrical remedies "has led to the electric fluid being ranked among the most powerful and astonishing of therapeutic agents. In a comparatively brief space proofs of this have multiplied to infinity," and, the article concludes, therapeutic electrical apparatuses like Pulvermacher's are thus indispensable in "elucidat[ing] the yet obscure question relative to the mechanism of life" (Jamin 108). Pulvermacher's advertisements claimed to open "a new Era in the History of Electricity," which it calls a "Wonderful Agent of Nature"[54]; some of its advertisements even promised "Health Without Medicine," insisting that "ELECTRICITY WILL CURE when all other Remedies fail." While undergirded by avowals of scientific advancement, advertisements like these nonetheless elevate the "extraordinary" powers of electricity above the prosaic workings of mere medicine by suggesting that electricity is more akin to a transformative mystical force than to a doctors' tool.[55] Words like "powerful," "astonishing," and "wondrous" echo the earlier Romantic belief that electricity was a gnostic source both of life and of sublime sensory experience, even as we supposedly enter a whole "new Era" of electrical innovation.[56] By the 1860s Pulvermacher's advertisements were headlined "Electricity is Life," and this was the vitalist tagline that other, even more quackish purveyors of medical electricity borrowed for their own advertisements.[57]

For every instance of potentially effective therapeutic electricity, there were half a dozen advertisements for other devices, like "Boyd's Galvanic Battery" (1878), that pushed belief to the breaking point. Boyd's batteries, which used the highly original "The Blood is the Life" rather than "Electricity is Life" as their slogan, were wearable batteries made of decoratively arranged flat metal discs of alternating metals, promised to cure "nearly all diseases" by constantly electrifying the blood of the wearer: "It is true that the blood is the life," the ad says hyperbolically, "and it is also true that corrupt, poisoned, diseased, impoverished, and vitiated blood means DEATH." Dr. Boyd claims to be able to cure anything from impotency to loss of confidence, although the fine print of the ad includes a disclaimer saying that the battery can't help with whooping cough, cholera, worms, or a number of other actually diagnosable diseases. What underlies the widely inclusive curative claims of this battery, however, as it does most similar devices between the 1850s and 1870s, is the restoration of sexual vitality waning with age. As the image of a naked, battery-wearing Zeus-like man with a remarkably full and jutting beard that accompanies Boyd's advertising copy suggests, electric wearables had particular appeal for men looking for a "magic" return of the "vital power" that the advertisement suggests may have been lost to a passionate overabundance of youthful "self-abuse." Dickens, of course, only turned to such devices to cure chronic leg pain. And, given that he had his fatal stroke the day he received his Pulvermacher's chain, its efficacy even to raise neuralgic legs remains uncertain.[58]

As an 1860 article from *All the Year Round* called "Infallible Physic" suggests, the British public was notoriously susceptible to such medical "arch-quackery," and galvanic medical devices were among the worst offenders (448). The article uses these devices to begin its long list of hoax cures because they most clearly demonstrate the propensity for quack medicine to capitalize on gnostic forces and forms of knowledge, twisting the inscrutabilities of nature into ineffectual shams. Beginning with a description of the same early nineteenth-century tractors satirized in "Terrible Tractoration," the article suggests that what all quack-artists have in common is their pretense of possessing "some secret hitherto undiscovered, which is an infallible remedy for some single accident or disease, or which, properly applied, cures all the ills that flesh is heir to" (448). And, the writer goes on to say, "Electricity and magnetism . . . those mysterious forces, the physical laws concerning which are little understood by the majority of persons, are made scapegoats" (452). The article carefully brackets off quack doctors and quack devices from the force of electricity itself. Rejuvenating tractors and "stimulating" rings and baldness-curing hairbrushes might not be the miraculous curatives they purport to be, but the energies behind them—electricity and magnetism, the scapegoats—remain mysterious, secret, unknown and universal forces animating the world, just as they were in the early nineteenth century. People were particularly susceptible to the lure of galvanic medical devices *because* electricity itself clearly had such impressive power. If a lightning strike could kill hundreds of people in an instant and its power could be harnessed by the telegraph to send messages thousands of miles in mere seconds,[59] then why couldn't a device supposedly full of the same vast power cure baldness and impotence?[60]

By the 1850s and '60s, descriptions of electricity and galvanism needed to make a distinction between electricity as an instrument and electricity as an energy: a distinction between electricity harnessed, reduced, and made mundanely material in the service of domestic life, and electricity as an all-pervasive natural miracle, described in one magazine article as the "subtlest, most Protean of all forces of nature . . . invest[ing] every atom of earth, air, and ocean, and of all they contain, but giv[ing] no outward sign of its existence" ("Indestructibility" 338). Electrical devices that seemed to bypass or imitate nature were often suspect. An 1857 article about an electric cooktop in *Punch,* for instance, asks skeptically whether "the old *batterie de cuisine* will soon be replaced by a galvanic battery" ("Cooking" 198). But electricity out and about in the world, invisible and working its natural miracles, was a source of wonder. One writer in *Macmillan's Magazine* goes so far as to suggest that the ubiquitous presence of electricity gave rise to belief in the supernatural world, insisting that "the peopling of the air with spirits, the existence of the idea of Djin, Kobold, and Fairy, all point to the prevalence of the idea that unseen agencies are for ever about us. Ten thousand motions sweep by, bathing us in their current, and we cannot recognize them" (Rodwell 343).

In this supernatural form, electricity could be an apt metaphor for the miraculous workings of certain human systems, like the nervous system, while the inverse metaphor—using the body to explain this "mysterious form of force"—was a valuable rhetorical tool for making vast electrical phenomena like the telegraph network comprehensible without also domesticating them ("Wonders" 224).[61] By contrast, electricity "enslaved" by humans, especially in their homes—and many periodical press writers throughout the middle and late decades of the nineteenth century relied on the language of enslavement, servitude, torment, and subjugation to describe the ways in which new technologies transformed electrical power into useful domestic tools[62]—and made to *stand in* for nature, whether that nature was bodily vitality, household tasks, or natural sunlight (as in the case of electric lighting), often invited uncertainty and critique.[63]

This distinction between electricity as a miraculous natural force and electricity as an ersatz manmade tool appears in modified form in Thomas Carlyle's 1843 *Past and Present*, which wields similar language to distinguish between true social resurrection and the sham animation of the contemporary economy. Carlyle uses galvanism in its debauched early nineteenth-century sense as a metaphor to characterize the inauthentic life of a society driven by money, industrialism, and dilettantism, while a society guided by what he calls "hero worship" has the potential to genuinely bring the dead spirit of England to life: only a civilization led by an "aristocracy of talent," rather than one led by a laissez-faire economy, will allow "the awakening of the Nation's soul from its asphyxia, and the return of blessed life to us,—Heaven's blessed life, not Mammon's *galvanic* accursed one" (Carlyle, *Past* 32, 34; my emphasis). Without always specifically referring to electricity, Carlyle's language in the opening chapters of *Past and Present* underscores his choice of explicitly galvanic metaphors to consider England's social life force. His use of the word *quack* a number of times to describe lawmakers who place profit above human wellbeing, as well as his repeated lamentations for the dread fate of the "Asphyxied" if they are not somehow resuscitated, borrow from the fraught debates about electricity's life-giving efficacy that were ongoing in the first half of the nineteenth century (34).[64] Against the possibility of society's truly "resuscitated soul," with all the "travail-throes" that such a fully changed state will

32 • INTRODUCTION

require, Carlyle persistently pits his metaphor for artificial life (35): the "Life of a Society" that worships Mammon is "galvanic and devil-ridden, too truly possessed by a devil"; "ghastly, dead or galvanised Dilettantism" cannot begin to compare to true religiosity; and dilettantes and industrial workers go "about as if by galvanism, with meaningless glaring eyes, and hav[ing] no soul" (65, 113, 180). Carlyle's galvanic workers are pale imitations of living people, animated by industrialism to repeat and produce without soul or individuality. The nineteenth-century shopping arcades in England and Paris might not yet have reached the capitalist heights of twentieth-century suburban shopping malls, but Carlyle was still the George Romero of the 1840s, imagining industrialism and the mindless accumulation of wealth to be responsible for the zombification of society.[65]

Carlyle's galvanized zombies are more than just nineteenth-century industrial drones, however. They're also a reflection on the same practices of scientific, progressivist, "Dryasdust" historiography that Sir Walter Scott and Mary Shelley so vehemently write against in the earlier part of the century. For Carlyle, borrowing Scott's "Dryasdust" offers a handy shorthand for antiquarian history composed of superficial and inert collections of facts, dates, and scraps of evidence: "Dryasdust, looking merely at the surface, is greatly in error," he writes toward the end of *Past and Present,* having regularly made "Dryasdust" his scapegoat for useless bits of historical information (234). Against this version of history that sees the world, as Walter Benjamin puts it, as "an endless series of facts congealed in the form of things," Carlyle pits his own imaginative practice of mining the past for sublime and redemptive models of the future (14). He seeks a "human soul"—the same soul he sees missing in zombie industrialism—in the "Paper-Masses" of history that lay before him, imagining the relationship of past, present, and future not as a scientific progression from savagery to civilization but as a "an ever-living, ever-working Chaos of Being" or an Yggdrasil, "in all times and in all places . . . one and the same Life-tree" (*Past* 37; "On History" 7; *Past* 37). Finding and animating old bones isn't the same thing as discovering actual life buried amid the skeletons of the past: "what mountains of dead ashes, wreck and burnt bones, does assiduous Pedantry dig up from the Past Time, and name it History," he asks, "till, as we say, the human soul sinks wearied and bewildered; till the Past Time seems all one infinite incredible grey void[?]" (*Past* 46). Over this bone-filled ash heap of a "Historical Library," Carlyle suggests a sign that reads "DRY RUBBISH SHOT HERE!," identifying the dead fragments of this version of the past as little more than a collection of trash (46).

In contrast to this dead rubbish of dryasdust history, imaginative history—Romantic history, Scott's history, Shelley's history, O'Grady's history,

Carlyle's history—less concerned with distinctions between fact and fiction than with the power of the sympathetic mind to find sparks of life in heaps of old bones, might be able to accomplish something far greater than gathering a heap of inert and ossified fragments: "fancy a deep-buried mastodon were to begin to *speak* from amid its rock-swathings, never so indistinctly!" (*Past* 42). Notwithstanding the inability of mastodons to speak even before time buried them, Carlyle's point is that we need to wade through the dust heaps of History, where along with the dinosaurs the "most extinct fossil species of Men or Monks" also linger, ready to perform this same "miracle" and speak (42). Our work isn't to collect their bones but to find lost and asphyxiated souls waiting in these fossils to be resuscitated: souls, as he says over and over when he talks both of current historiographical practice *and* of accursed galvanic life, that are "somewhat wanted at present" (47). Present-day industrialism AND present-day historiography have let souls go missing. Like the galvanized zombies of the present, the "broken blackened shin-bone[s] of the old dead Ages" recovered by historians who concern themselves with historical facts rather than transhistorical souls can be nothing but "dry rubbish," gray "fantasm" (47).

Galvanized dilettantism, as Carlyle calls it, strips the "Heaven-blessed life" from present and past alike, and thus, inevitably, from any possible future. "O dilettante friend," he pleads, gesturing dramatically to what he calls the "old osseus fragment[s]" of the past, "let us know always that it was a world, and not a void infinite of grey haze . . . a once gigantic Life lies buried there! It . . . was alive once, and spake" (47). Galvanism, in Carlyle's case, thus isn't just a metaphor for bad industrialism. It's also a metaphor for bad history, history that falls short of its true resuscitative purpose, history that strives only for "lifelikeness." True history restores true life, as J. A. Froude says of Carlyle's, "bring[s] dead things and dead people actually back to life," while other, "scientific" history only *looks* like true life (qtd. in H. Fraser 16). True history will produce neither galvanized zombies nor phantasms, but real, living, speaking people (and mastodons). This is the dream of nineteenth-century resuscitative historiography, the dream of Michelet and O'Grady, the dream I trace from Mary Shelley's necromantic imagination in chapter 1 all the way to its monstrous mummy incarnation in chapter 5.

ARTICULATING THE BODY

My own necromantic imagination has stitched these bits of history—Promethean, galvanic, maybe full of eloquent mastodons—together with an unlikely collection of nineteenth-century British and Irish texts, forging an awkwardly articulated body, reanimating its assemblage of poems, novels, dramas, essays, and histories into a singular story about literature's dreams and nightmares of resuscitating the past. The body may stagger sometimes as it learns its new shape; its parts will sometimes grind frustratingly against one another, but it moves, and it breathes, and it hasn't yet left me for dead in a dank basement (n.b.: there are no basements in California). My hope is that in the end it will speak for itself.

I begin *The Necromantics* with Mary Shelley's novel *Frankenstein*—Western culture's most famous reanimated body—only to argue that *Frankenstein* isn't where the story of nineteenth-century reanimation begins. This chapter starts by reading *Frankenstein* as a novel about human animation—how a thing becomes a person—rather than about reanimation—how dead things are brought to life—and then turns to the decades after *Frankenstein*'s initial publication to look at how theatrical adaptations of the novel, as well as Shelley's later essays and fictions, recreate the novel's creature as a cultural myth about embodied history. Exploring connections between Romantic sentimental historiography, early nineteenth-century ideas about vitality and embodiment, and characters ranging from Valerius the Reanimated Roman and Roger Dodsworth the Reanimated Englishman to Frankinstitch the Tailor and What Is It, the Automaton, this chapter lays a foundation for the chapters that follow by arguing that coming to life and being brought back from the dead have distinctly different historiographical and affective resonances. The contrast between *Frankenstein,* its Shelleyan successors, and its later adaptations offers a model for the emergence of necromantic literature from other gothic forms and allows me to theorize the ways in which popular literature (and drama) can reimagine debates about historiographical method as stories about the ethics and capacities of the resuscitative artistic imagination.

My second chapter turns from the monsters of resuscitative historiography to the realist zombies that interrupt narrative history and telos in Charles Dickens's fiction. This chapter intervenes in debates about Dickens's success or failure as a realist novelist by arguing that *Great Expectations* (1861) and *Our Mutual Friend* (1865) both mount ferocious critiques of the hollow "lifelikeness" of realism's characters, narrative modes, and teleological plots. Through a preoccupation with epitaphs in the earlier novel and galvanism in the later one, both novels experiment with, and so lay bare, the very unreal fictional devices and forms at the heart of realism. In *Great Expectations,* I use the term *epitaphic realism* to identify a zombie problem at the center of the text's narrative structure: the more Pip attempts to animate a history of himself—his life—out of language, the more he produces lifelessness, just as the epitaph's gesture of conjuring life from language always inevitably conjures the absence of life, instead. *Our Mutual Friend,* by contrast, makes no attempt to create a coherent narrative life out of language, instead using its plentiful episodes of and references to reanimation to expose the artifice of realist telos. I argue that the history of nineteenth-century galvanism and quack medical electricity that I outline above hisses on the edges of Dickens's final completed novel, and that the galvanic metaphors, references, images, and allusions that pepper the text bring mid-century electrical quackery and artificial vitality to bear on realism's canny substitution of lifelikeness for life. Although Dickens both figuratively and literally reanimates characters throughout this novel, he never allows reanimation to be an escape from social legibility, instrumentalism, or telos. Galvanic reanimation instead becomes a metaphor for these aesthetic expectations, and social expectations, of realism, expectations that the novel as a whole resists.

While Dickens's novels use the language of reanimation to rail against the circumscribed artificiality of novelistic life, Robert Browning finds in the artifice of reanimation an ideal model for poetry's relationship to history. In my third chapter I focus on Browning's book-length poem, *The Ring and the Book* (1869), in which he not only fleshes out an ars poetica with reanimation as its central tenet but also takes as his central character the gothic figure of a cruelly murdered wife telling the story of her suffering. This twelve-book "murder poem" begins by insisting that the poet's work is to "resuscitate" rather than to "create," to "start the dead alive" but not to "make" out of nothing as God can make. Browning explicitly conceives poetry's relationship to the past as an effort of galvanic reanimation, and unlike Dickens's dismay at the artifice of such aesthetically produced life, Browning identifies this artifice as precisely the liberation poetry needs from historical objectivity. The notion that poetry can do only as much as reanimate the dead becomes a way for Browning to propose a kind of literary innovation that remembers, but refuses to be bound by, the past. Browning genders this poetics in the figure of Pompilia, who both straddles the line between life and death and, as a female corpse through which Browning speaks, blurs the line between subject and aesthetic object. This reanimated female speaker embodies Browning's resuscitative theory of poetic innovation: her testimony offers a memorial poetics that interrogates the very mechanisms by which we remember, and that sees the process of remembrance as one inextricable both from revision and from invention. For Browning, the reanimated body epitomizes not only the potentially transcendent relationship between art and the "scraps" of the past but also this relationship's sometimes crushing limitations.

My fourth chapter also considers reanimation as a form of productive aesthetic constraint as I turn to W. B. Yeats, Irish nationalism, and the Victorian museum, exploring the intersections between the politics of poetry and what Theodor Adorno calls the "second life" of objects trapped in national museum collections (182). I frame this chapter by looking at British Museum poetry by Dante Gabriel Rossetti, Thomas Hardy, and others, whose work dwells with guilty distress on the way museums culturally decontextualize the objects within them. I argue that Yeats, by contrast, saw the museum as a model for the culturally revivifying power of poetry, and I trace O'Grady's legacy in Yeats's certainty that fragments of the past can be positively resuscitated by the modern aesthetic imagination. This chapter focuses primarily on Yeats's folklore collections and long poem "The Wanderings of Oisin," written in the 1880s just as Dublin was trying to figure out what its own Irish National Museum might look like. These early works, as well as Yeats's autobiographical reflections on the 1880s, reimagine the alienating Victorian act of collecting as a process of Irish national revitalization, but with an important caveat: the modern artist who resurrects the dead past might also be endangered by absorption in it. In "The Wanderings of Oisin," Yeats allegorizes the act of folklore-collecting as an immersion in the land of the dead and the process of shaping that folklore into poetry as a return to life, but the poet-bard who returns does not truly get to live again. I argue in this chapter that although Yeats's efforts of literary collecting demonstrate an idealistic captivation with the artistic and political potential of reanimating the dead, they always also reveal a deep anxiety about the price the poet pays for Irish cultural revival.

Yeats's poets may suffer to bring the Celtic past back from the dead, but in Bram Stoker's fiction the Irish Literary Revival becomes a truly monstrous phenomenon. My final chapter, on Stoker's mummy novel *The Jewel of Seven Stars* (1903), reconsiders this classic tale of gothic reanimation gone awry as an engagement with the aesthetic and political strategies of late nineteenth- and early twentieth-century Irish cultural nationalism. The novel operates at the historical intersection between Irish and Egyptian nationalist movements at the turn of the twentieth century, and Stoker's strange synthesis of ancient Egyptian and ancient Celtic references makes this overtly colonial story of British characters resurrecting a stolen Egyptian mummy into a story that is equally about Ireland's own appropriations and misappropriations of Celtic history. What if a history isn't really yours to bring back from the dead? At what point does the desire to recuperate the past through art—the desire to "save the thing," as Browning would have it—become a violence perpetrated upon it rather than a revitalization of it? This mummy novel, I argue, toys with the political fallacies of the nationalist historical imagination, repurposing a conventional nineteenth-century plot of colonial appropriation as a cautionary tale about the instability and danger of reanimating an imaginary national past.

And yet, dangerous though Stoker's mummy may be, the idealistic Egyptologists in his novel *do* bring her fully to life. She may go off on a killing spree as soon as she vacates her sarcophagus and they may all end up dead, but Stoker's characters still manage to accomplish their impossible task of reanimating her. Although the texts I address in *The Necromantics* range from the cautiously optimistic to the truly terrifying—as I show in my epilogue on the zombies, mummies, and vampires that contemporary writers have imagined into canonical nineteenth-century novels—they share a unifying belief that literature has the unique power to bring the dead back to life. What returns from the dead may not be friendly, nor will it ever be the same as what was once alive, but even the monsters are their own form of literary miracle.

CHAPTER 1

How *Frankenstein* Got History

We all remember the scene from Mel Brooks's 1974 movie *Young Frankenstein* when Igor, sent by Dr. Frederick Frankenstein to steal the brain of the brilliant "scientist and saint" Hans Delbruck to use in the creature he's making, accidentally drops the historian's brain and steals another brain, not telling Frankenstein that it's a different brain from the one he asked for. When the creature comes to life without the dazzling eloquence and intelligence Frankenstein was expecting, he questions Igor. "Would you mind telling me whose brain I did put in?" he asks. "Abby . . . someone," Igor replies. "Abby someone? Abby who?" "Abby Normal." "Abby Normal?" Frankenstein repeats, and Igor replies, "I'm almost sure that was the name." And then Frankenstein explodes: "Are you saying. . . . that I put an abnormal brain . . . into a seven-and-a-half-foot-long . . . fifty-four-inch-wide . . . ***GORILLA***?!?!?! *IS **THAT** WHAT YOU'RE TELLING ME!?!?*" Spoofing 150 years of *Frankenstein* adaptations that focus on the specific parts that go into the making of the monster, *Young Frankenstein* draws particular attention to the investment these adaptations have in the historicity of the monster's body. The real Hans Delbruck was a German historian, not a scientist, whose military histories were especially interested in the methodological value of re-examining original antique sources, and Frederick himself spends the whole movie trying to deny, and finally ultimately capitulating to, his inheritance of the Frankenstein family "curse." At the center of the movie's self-conscious parody of all the *Franken-stein* movies (and plays) that have preceded it lies a preoccupation with the mechanisms of adaptation: with the back-and-forth movement between original texts and new contexts and with the dialogic process by which old parts and new forms mutually impact and change each other. History matters to *Young Frankenstein*, but what matters even more is what we can *do* with history. As the "monster" learns how to love music, sing, and dance (even before a dose of Frankenstein juice turns him into an eloquent gentleman), the movie reminds us that a body, like a film, can pay homage to its origins while still adapting new ideas in order to become something novel. *Young Frankenstein* values the constituent parts that it recombines and reanimates by refusing to be contingent upon them, imagining that even the most abby-normal original has the potential to be reanimated into something brilliantly new if it's just given the right kind of treatment.

Adaptations of *Frankenstein* like *Young Frankenstein* and its nineteenth- and early twentieth-century predecessors dwell at length on the old parts out of which their new creatures are composed. But tropes like the problem of the wrong brain that have been such a persistent part of dramatizations of the *Frankenstein* story draw attention to the very absence of such moments in Shelley's novel—they spotlight Shelley's *lack* of interest in the lingering effects of old parts on her creature's new consciousness.[1] Although the monster has come to be our most popular cultural image of a reanimated corpse, only in *Frankenstein*'s later adaptations does a preoccupation with *re*animation become central to the monster's development. In Shelley's hands, who or what the monster once was—how and why old parts have been reshaped—means almost nothing in comparison to how a new creature *becomes* a living, feeling human. In other words, a principle of animation, rather than an interest in reanimation, underlies the novel's allegory of creativity. Memory and history remain extrinsic rather than constitutive aspects of artistic production.

How, then, did the idea of *Frankenstein* shift from a novel about human animation (how a thing becomes a person) into a story about reanimation (what happens when dead things come to life)? In the decades after *Franken-stein*'s initial publication in 1818, several theatrical adaptations of the novel as well as Shelley's own essays and fictions resurrect the novel's creature as a cultural myth about embodied history. These texts, whether philosophical or popular, engage debates about Romantic historiographical methods to produce stories about the ethics and revolutionary capacities of the resuscitative artistic imagination. Two of Shelley's stories, in particular—"Valerius, the Reanimated Roman" (1819) and "Roger Dodsworth, the Reanimated English-

40 • CHAPTER 1

man" (1826)—dwell at length on how we might rethink the present moment if we were forced to experience it through the eyes and body of someone long dead who has been brought back to life. These stories are snippets of revivalist historical fiction taken to its most literal extreme.[2] The term *reanimated* in their titles bears little relationship to Victor's creature or to the gothic, grave-stitched bodies we remember from *Frankenstein* films, but instead signifies a preoccupation with contemporary modes of historical apprehension and the onus we lay on the past to produce our understanding of the present. They bear out necromantic literature's desire to resist the deadening confines of historicism by resurrecting the past into valuable forms of life in the present, even as such literature also exposes the dangers of presentist thinking by showing us how easily the desire to bring the dead to life in our own image and to fulfill our own needs can morph into stories of horror and ruin.

In "Valerius" and "Dodsworth," reanimated bodies walk a fine line between miracle and immiseration as they encapsulate the presentism of the historical imagination that has brought them to life. Rather than offering a window into the past, these bodies serve as tools to articulate the problems and demands of present-day politics, art, technology, and national identity, even as they also resist the instrumentalized role they inevitably come to occupy. Shelley's stories wonder what has been lost to time and what might be found again. They trouble the conceptual gaps between the past and accepted history, and they idealize the value and effects of bringing historical knowledge to bear on the present moment. In other words, they create explicit necromantic fantasies about the presentist nature of the historical imagination, engaging with and troubling contemporary models of historiographical thinking by offering literal resurrections of the past in a way that *Frankenstein* makes no attempt to do. And yet these necromantic stories, written in the decade after *Frankenstein* when theatrical adaptations of the novel were beginning to attach historical significance beyond Shelley's to the creature's recycled parts, create important intellectual conduits between the 1818 novel about becoming human and its afterlife as a parable about the monstrosity of indiscreetly mucking around in the grave to make something "new." Moving between Shelley's *Franken-stein*, her "reanimated" stories and her 1831 introduction to the novel, and stage and screen versions of *Frankenstein* between 1823 and 1994, this chapter argues that while the novel itself always remains a Romantic meditation on the principle of life, the ongoing centuries-long *Frankenstein* story is a necromantic tale of its own: a story of the dead reanimated over and over again for present-day use as the modern historical imagination progresses from late eighteenth-century sympathetic historiography to the resuscitative aesthetics of nineteenth- and twentieth-century adaptation.

ANIMATING THE MONSTER

Emerging into the English literary world on the heels of a half-century of gothic specters that trained readers, as Jane Austen writes in *Northanger Abbey*, to understand that every old building "is undoubtedly haunted" and every family is tormented by "past scenes of horror being acted" out repeatedly by the ghosts of wronged ancestors, *Frankenstein*'s creature, disturbingly solid and without a historical ancestor to be found, proved a baffling and resistant body to interpret (Austen 150, 153). "No one can love a good ghost story more than we do," one scathing review of the novel begins, and then continues: "Our prejudices in favour of legitimacy, of course, are proportionably shocked by the pretensions of any pseudo-diabolism; and all our best feelings of ghostly loyalty are excited by the usurpation of an unauthorized hobgoblin, or a non-descript fee-fa-fum" (*British Critic* 432). Neither an apparition of the sort Horace Walpole or Ann Radcliffe had taught us to pleasurably expect nor a shockingly supernatural demon in the Matthew Lewis vein, the creature in Shelley's novel was simply, as this reviewer puts it, "grotesque and *bizarre*" (438; original italics). Critics from the nineteenth century forward have worked to find an interpretive framework that makes sense of this gothic body that is neither spirit nor devil, neither supernatural nor natural, neither haunting nor, somehow, free from the problem of the past it nonetheless does not possess. "If Frankenstein could have endowed his creature with the vital principle of a hundred or a thousand human beings," another reviewer writes, "it would no more have been able *to walk* without having previously acquired *the habit* of doing so, than it would be to talk, or to reason, or to judge" (*Literary Panorama* 414; original italics). That is, how can the creature develop humanity unless he already has a history of being human that his mind and muscles can remember? Bodies should have histories, this reviewer suggests (lest they exhibit "a strong tendency toward *materialism*") and gothic bodies especially so, overflowing as they usually are with disruptive history (412; original italics). But *Frankenstein*'s newly living creature defies these mandates.

Fast-forward nearly two hundred years and critics are still trying to account for the creature's body within a lineage of the haunting and haunted gothic, looking for ways to breathe historical life into a body that so vociferously resists it. Elizabeth Freeman, for instance, uses *Frankenstein* to trace the sentimental genealogy of her idea of "erotohistoriography," a queer mode of encountering the past "in the present," using the body "as a tool to effect, figure, or perform that encounter" (95). Yet the bodily pleasures of history, as she explains, have been "the loser in bygone battles over what the discipline of history itself should become," with cognitive understanding and objectivity

42 • CHAPTER 1

overtaking sensory feelings as the primary and proper mode of writing and apprehending the past (95). She presents *Frankenstein* as a "counterhistory" to the primacy of cognitive history, finding in the relationship between Victor and his creature several competing versions of historical consciousness that both map onto and undermine the disciplinary transition between late eighteenth-century sentimental understandings of history as an affective, sensory experience and the Victorian turn to an objective, scientific approach to history. To make this argument, however, Freeman claims that Frankenstein's creature "contains a history of bodies" and is thus akin to a ghost, an embodied form of historical encounter that tests the limits of rational, cognitive understanding (103): although the creature "is not a ghost, precisely, his striated and heterogeneous anatomy can certainly be read similarly, as a figure for both the social conflicts of which history consists and the genre in which history announced itself in other terms" (98). In this formulation the creature is history embodied, quite literally, a composite of mismatched and dead artifacts, whose literally historical constitution enables him to experience history sympathetically but also dangerously.[3] As Freeman writes, "Frankenstein's monster is monstrous because he lets history too far in, going so far as to embody it instead of merely feeling it" (104).

While I return in later sections of this chapter to Shelley's strong investment in the eighteenth-century historiographical debates that Freeman outlines (debates, I argue, that have much more purchase in pieces of Shelley's later writing than in *Frankenstein*), here I want to focus on the problem of Freeman's assertion that Victor's creature can be read as something akin to a ghost—that the literal historicity of his body's dead raw materials make his constructed body inherently historical, and that the phenomenon at the center of the novel is thus an embodied pastness whose materiality makes that past even more profoundly present than a gossamer specter would. The creature is not just not "precisely" a ghost, as she describes him. He is explicitly and *definitively* not a ghost, especially in the terms by which Shelley defines ghosts in an essay of 1824:[4] shapes "that rise all pale and ghastly from the churchyard and haunt their ancient abodes; who, spoken to, reply; and whose cold unearthly touch makes the hair stand stark upon the head; the true old-fashioned, foretelling, flitting, gliding ghost,—who has seen such a one?" ("On Ghosts" 337). For Shelley, a ghost is at worst a silly superstition and at best a psychological phenomenon of soul and memory and guilt and longing, a return of something that has been lost and is "beyond our soul's ken" (336). That the creature in *Frankenstein* is no such phenomenon—no spirit lingering after death to try the soul and the imagination, no ethereal remains of some history preceding the moment of his wakening to life—is not an incidental technicality in a novel that hinges on a crisis of creativity for both its plot and its philosophical and aesthetic reflection. What "produce[s] a painful and bewildered state of mind" in readers and reviewers accustomed to the gothic ghost stories of the eighteenth century is the novel's express fixation on something they'd never seen in a novel before, "the creation . . . of a living and intelligent being," and the relationship (aesthetic, ethical, and technological) between creator and created that plagues its aftermath (Scott, "Remarks" 615). The whole point of Shelley's creature is that he is a new, originless person, even if Victor feels "haunted by a curse" because the creature exists (*Frankenstein* 165). The creature may read *Plutarch's Lives* like a Burkean, but the novel goes to great lengths to de-emphasize, even to forget, his piecemeal origins in the graveyard as it shapes him into a living, feeling human.

Despite the fact that our cultural impression of the creature, dating back to even the earliest adaptations of the novel (more on this soon), fixate on the reverberations of the specific parts out of which he is composed, the novel itself explicitly does not. To the extent that the parts of the creature are addressed at all, they are addressed specifically for their aesthetic function, not for their historicity: for what they look like now, not for what they used to be.[5] Even as Victor contemplates his "capacity of bestowing animation" on a human frame, he considers not the means by which he'll acquire the frame but instead the "intricacies of fibres, muscles, and veins" that make up a human body (*Frankenstein* 79, 80). Even as bones from charnel houses and materials from "the dissecting room and the slaughter house" (which, incidentally, do not explicitly furnish *human* parts[6]) come together to form the body of the creature, Victor's immediate horror at the result of his labors is an aesthetic horror at his own artistic failure—his inability to see how human features might best harmonize with one another—not an uncanny horror at the composite dead made live again (81). "His limbs were in proportion, and I had selected his features as beautiful. Beautiful! Great God! His yellow skin scarcely covered the work of muscles and arteries beneath; his hair was of a lustrous black, and flowing; his teeth of a pearly whiteness; but these luxuriances only formed a more horrid contrast with his watery eyes, that seemed almost of the same colour as the dun-white sockets in which they were set, his shrivelled complexion and straight black lips" (83). This is not to diminish the fact that the creature is bound to the border between life and death that Victor has been so eager to transgress, as his fever dreams about the decaying corpses of Elizabeth and his mother that immediately succeed the creature's waking demonstrate. Rather, it is to suggest that the creature in his initial

44 • CHAPTER 1

moments of transgressing this boundary poses an aesthetic crisis rather than a historiographical one: a crisis about creative vitality, not a crisis about historical apprehension.

Throughout *Frankenstein,* the word *animate* (used close to a dozen times in the first fifty pages of the novel, only to vanish almost entirely from the remainder) is nearly always synonymous with the idea of a vital spirit or eager liveliness. "From this time a new spirit of life animated the decaying frame of the stranger," Walton says of Victor in one of his opening letters, describing Victor's reaction to Walton's sighting of the monster on a distant sledge (*Frankenstein* 315).[7] An "active spirit of tenderness animated" Victor's parents, he tells us (315); Elizabeth Lavenza is "ever there to bless and animate" his family, Henry Clerval has an "animated glance," and Victor himself is "animated by an almost supernatural enthusiasm" for his laborious scientific task (321, 324, 78). Although this task, as we know, is one of "bestowing animation on lifeless matter," until the moment at which Victor actually achieves his goal the novel imbues the notion of animation and what animates with an intense and unwavering optimism (79). Filtered through Victor's blemished retrospective view, the spirit of animation is a generative, uplifting, vital force right up until he discovers it as a literal force. From that moment on, the generative form of animation drops out of Victor's vocabulary. While the creature, in telling his own story, still uses it to tenderly describe the Arabian Safie, for Victor the idea of animation has become inextricably tied to the monstrosity both of his act and of his creature. "A mummy endued with animation could not be so hideous as that wretch," he says upon seeing his creation's newly living face, and as the creature later curses him with the destruction of his heart and life, Victor sees only the "fiendish rage [that] animated him as he said this," a twisted and horrifying translation of the tenderness and spirit that he once described animating his loved ones (84, 156). The artificial creation of life has destroyed the innate life force Victor was trying so desperately to emulate. Just as his discovery of life demanded that his studies "must first have recourse to death," so too does the power of animation fundamentally de-animate—literally as well as rhetorically—the natural vitality of humans that the word "animate" so often emphasizes in the first quarter of the novel (78).

As Shelley's circle of acquaintance, reading habits, and 1831 introduction to *Frankenstein* make clear, she conceived *Frankenstein* while immersed in the Romantic poets' fascination with "the nature of the principle of life" (350). For poets like Coleridge, Shelley, Byron, and Keats, as Denise Gigante has argued, "the unpredictable vitality of the living form, its very liveliness—protean, procreative, for some terrifying—served as a model for 'genuine' art. . . . Yet too much power, or power potentially unhinged or gone awry, lay forever on the horizon of Romantic vitalism" (4–5). In *Frankenstein* Shelley nightmarishly captures not only the obsessive Romantic seeking after the "living principle" that marked the difference between inert form and authentic art but also the near-invisibility of the boundary between this kind of vitality and monstrosity. To the extent that the creature can be seen as a metaphor for aesthetic production, as Shelley suggests in her introduction when she bids her "hideous progeny go forth and prosper," the horror of Victor's literal act of animation refutes the viability of an aesthetic theory that bases artistic authenticity on its "vitality" (351). The novel envisions to desire to make art live as the most monstrous and destructive desire imaginable.

Gigante demonstrates that late eighteenth-century scientific probing into the "principle of life" provides a useful point of critical entry into a canon of Romantic poetry that seems obsessed with the symbolic and aesthetic relationship between organicism, vitality, and the imagination. "As the concept of vital power sparked a pre-occupation with self-generating and self-maintaining form, it quickened the category of the aesthetic," she writes, working to "recover this era of vitalism, roughly 1780–1830, as a context for making sense of the life contained in the poetry of the time, at the level not only of content but also of form" (6, 45). In claiming that the Romantic obsession with organicism offered poets both formal structures and metaphors that analogically attempt to access the animating spirit of poetry, however, Gigante also offers an implicit claim about what the Romantics were *less* interested in: words without any kind of animating spirit, or forms upon which some false animating spirit was imposed from without. Coleridge wrote in his *Biographia Literaria* that the imagination was the "living Power and prime Agent of all human Perception . . . It is essentially *vital,* even as all objects (*as* objects) are essentially fixed and dead" (*BL* 304). He insisted that, "could a rule be given from without, poetry would cease to be poetry, and sink into a mechanical art. It would be [a fashioning], not [a creation]" (83–84). Or as he wrote in an earlier essay on Shakespeare, "The form is mechanic, when on any given material we impress a pre-determined form . . . as when to a mass of wet clay we give whatever shape we wish it retain when hardened. The organic form, on the other hand, is innate. It shapes, as it developes itself, from within . . . Such as the life is, such is the form" ("Shakespeare" 46–47). The line between natural vitality and the discoveries of "artificial life" by Erasmus Darwin and Luigi Galvani (so compelling to Byron and the Shelleys, especially) was a fine one, but a line nonetheless, and although Percy Shelley, for instance, imagined that the words of an ideal poet might be "covered in the ashes of their birth" and in need of a "conductor," he still believed wholeheartedly that the words had in them an innate spark, without which they would be nothing ("Defence" 693).

46 • CHAPTER 1

The principle of life might be discoverable through science, but this discovery interested the poets primarily for the insight it could offer them into the origin point of life *within* human beings, and thus symbolically within literary forms. Vital art wasn't an artificial simulacrum of organic life; it was another incarnation of it. James A. W. Heffernan has suggested that Victor Frankenstein's ultimate aesthetic problem is his application "to corpses a [neoclassical] formula calculated to produce ideal beauty in painting and sculpture" (144)—that is, he tries to make beautiful art out of the wrong materials—but this oversimplifies the aesthetic crisis of the novel by locating it only in what Victor *uses* for his experiment, rather than in the relationship between his materials and his practice. His project isn't the Romantic discovery of a lively force in these materials that he will "conduct" to life. Instead, he wants to use his new knowledge of the principle of life to animate the inanimate, to produce artificial life where no life exists on its own. It is this desire to "impress a pre-determined form" on materials with no organic spark of their own—a fundamental violation of Romantic aesthetic principle—not the problem of the scraps themselves (whatever their inanimate nature might be), that generates a monster instead of a work of art.[8]

In Victor Frankenstein's deliberately mysterious discovery of galvanism, in the sensory, emotional, and aesthetic means by which his creature acquires a literate and conscious soul, and in the mythic fashion by which Victor's creation comes to stand in for the ideals of Romantic poetry, *Frankenstein* reiterates the question that Gigante claims "is asked a thousand times in a thousand ways by all the major British Romantic poets writing in the period from 1760 through 1830" (2)—in Percy Shelley's words, "Then, what is Life?" ("Triumph" 621). Although centuries of adaptations have transformed *Frankenstein* into the urtext for thinking about reanimation in nineteenth-century British literature, this is explicitly not a text about bringing anything *back* to life. "I thought, that if I could bestow animation upon lifeless matter," Victor says, "I might in process of time (although I now found it impossible) renew life where death had apparently devoted the body to corruption" (*Frankenstein* 81). *Re*animation is secondary to the principle of animation itself.[9] As chapter 3 discusses at length, Robert Browning, half a century later, would revise Percy Shelley's sense of the ideal poet whose words are "a spark . . . pregnant with a lightning which has yet found no conductor" into a theory of resuscitative poetry ("Defence" 693), a liberating imitation of godlike creativity. In contrast, Mary Shelley offers up an allegory of an artist trying to *be* God: "A new species would bless me as its creator and source," Victor imagines, embarking on no less an exploration of "the principle of life" than "the creation of a human being" (*Frankenstein* 80, 78, 80). He may form this creation out of scraps, but he remains willfully uninterested in their origin or in the notion of his process as a recycling of old parts. His passion, his guilt, and his disgust all stem from the act of creation, not the act of reanimation. It is only *after* the creature has woken and shown himself to be anything but the "beautiful" form Victor thought he was making that he labels his creation a "demoniacal corpse to which I had so miserably given life," more "hideous" than a "mummy endued with animation" (84).[10] Only when the creature seems monstrous does Victor transform him from a simple "inanimate body" into a living corpse (83). And yet still, this is a nightmarish description of ugly art, not a true recollection of the monster's origins. The creature remains throughout the novel the first member of a hideous new race, not an animate mosaic of dead parts.

By her 1831 introduction to the third edition of the novel, though, Shelley has begun to refocus her theory of aesthetic creativity on the need for "something that went before," more than on the animating spark itself: "Invention, it must be humbly admitted, does not consist in creating out of void, but out of chaos," she writes (350). It is in this introduction, not in the novel itself, that the creature's body gains a history, as Shelley reimagines her own creative process as a historically contingent phenomenon shaped by and shaping past experience into something new. The introduction retroactively makes history central to the novel, offering as its purpose "some account of the origin of the story" in order to answer the perennial question of how "a young girl, came to think of, and to dilate upon, so very hideous an idea?" (347).[11] Shelley reiterates this insistence on the inextricability of art and origins a few years later in her preface to *The Poetical Works of Percy Shelley* (1839) when she writes that her desire for the volume is both to put the products of "sublime genius" before the world *and* to detail "the history of those productions, as they sprung, living and warm, from [Shelley's] heart and brain" (vii). Percy Shelley's genius may itself have been a form of Olympian vitality, but to make this genius legible and lively now that he's gone, Mary Shelley needs it to have history. Even more, this recourse to "the history of those productions" serves as Shelley's way to make her dead husband himself feel living and warm again, as she uses the language of vitality throughout the preface (vii)—"These characteristics breathe throughout his poetry," "No poet was ever warmed by a more genuine and unforced inspiration," "His extreme sensibility . . . rendered his mind keenly alive to every perception" (ix, x, x–xi)—to remind us that as long as we can reach our minds back into the past, the poet will be alive again in his work.

In her introduction to *Frankenstein,* Shelley describes her foray into personal history as "an appendage" attached to the novel, forging a link between the monster's body and the remnants of history that is often overshadowed

48 · CHAPTER 1

by the more explicit link she creates at the end of the introduction between the monster's body and the novel itself ("I bid my hideous progeny go forth and prosper") (347, 352). The novel's origin story begins with Shelley's "distinguished" parents and her childhood penchant for "forging castles in the air," then continues to trace her personal history through to the now famous summer in Switzerland in which Lord Byron dared everyone to write ghost stories (347). Here, Shelley moves from a personal origin story to a creative origin story for the novel, laying out an aesthetic theory in which historical origins are themselves an incontrovertible necessity. "Every thing must have a beginning . . . and that beginning must be linked to something that went before," she writes, after describing the paralyzing "blank incapability of invention which is the greatest misery of authorship, when dull Nothing replies to our anxious invocations" (349). The vital spark of creative life must come from *somewhere*—not only can it not come from nothing, but it also *must* be part of a historical process, a link in a chain where only something old can become something new. In order to create, "the materials must, in the first place, be afforded; [invention] can give form to dark, shapeless substances, but cannot bring into being the substance itself" (350). These familiar lines explicitly borrow their imagery from Victor's construction of the creature from dead parts and often serve as evidence for reading the novel as an allegory of artistic creativity—this is well-trodden ground for any introductory literature class. But they also resignify Victor's creative process as a historical process, one that builds on what came before rather than generating something entirely new.

The materials themselves become significant, not simply as raw substances but as "link[s] to something that went before," as the physical incarnations of an origin story ("Introduction" 349). To argue that "invention consists in the capacity of seizing on the capabilities of a subject" is to argue that the capabilities of a subject pre-exist invention—that the materials themselves have meaning, and that creativity is a process of transformation or translation, giving new shape to old substance (350). The "materials" to which Shelley attributes *Frankenstein*'s origins reinforce this point. Conversations between Lord Byron and Percy Shelley on the "nature of the principle of life" had suggested to her the possibility that "a corpse would be re-animated; galvanism had given token of such things: perhaps the component parts of a creature might be manufactured, brought together, and endued with vital warmth" (350). These philosophical "materials" emphasize not Victor's ambition to create a "new species" or even to "create a human being" (although the idea of parts being "manufactured" gestures industrially in that direction) but rather the re- intrinsic to artistic production. Bodies might be reanimated, component parts might be recycled, and when the young student of unhallowed arts sees "the thing he had put together," all he wishes is for it to return to "the dead matter" from which it is composed (351). If we take as a given the idea that this introduction prompts us to read *Frankenstein* as a novel about the ethics of creativity, it equally prompts us to read *Frankenstein* as a novel about the historically contingent nature of creativity and about the blood-curdling possibilities of historical materials reanimated in new lives. But this reading of creativity as historical contingent is belated. Only after thirteen years of the novel living in the world, only after more than a decade of toying with the idea of "reanimation" to explore historiography's reliance on sympathy and affect to produce meaningful understandings of the past, does Shelley reimagine her creature and her novel as meditations on the historical imagination as much as on the nature of creative vitality.

VALERIUS: THE REANIMATION OF HISTORICAL FEELING

Two of Mary Shelley's other pieces of fiction, "Valerius, the Reanimated Roman" and "Roger Dodsworth, the Reanimated Englishman," demonstrate that Shelley clearly did not consider animation and reanimation to be synonymous phenomena, despite a number of critics who group these texts with *Frankenstein* to argue for Shelley's large-scale interest in reanimation.[12] In each of these stories, a man from a different historical moment comes back to life in the present, inexplicably in "Valerius" and after being discovered in and thawed from a frozen mountain in "Roger Dodsworth." But these stories' philosophical interest in the problem of the past spontaneously resuscitated and necessarily misplaced bears no clear relationship to the gothic transgressions of *Frankenstein*. "Valerius," in particular, takes at unperturbed face value the idea that an ancient man has been brought back to life. Rather than worrying over the mechanics, ethics, or dangers of this unprecedented reanimated body out of time, the story instead revolves around the ancient Roman's desolation at the state of contemporary Rome and his inability to be moved—animated—by the remnants of history around him. By contrast, Dodsworth's spontaneous defrosting and return to life, although equally ungothic, provides Shelley an opportunity to reflect more broadly on how the present might change if there were mechanisms that allowed historical personages to come to life more regularly. Reanimated bodies in both texts primarily spur philosophical meditations on the utility, the seductiveness, and the speciousness of sympathetic ties between past and present, even as the bodies themselves stand as impossibly literal testaments to the power of Shelley's own historical imagination.

In "Valerius," Shelley uses the title character's reanimated body as a tool to explore how the past might move inspirationally in the present world, but she

50 • CHAPTER 1

never lets her readers forget that while *we* might be inspired by such historical resuscitations, Valerius himself remains a walking dead man, never more
lively than an instrumental fiction. Valerius does not inhabit a liminal space
between life and death, but instead seems to be a living ruin, "a statue of one
of the Romans animated with life" ("Valerius" 332). When Isabell Harley, Valerius's Scottish interlocutor, tells us that "his semblance was that of life, yet he
belonged to the dead," she quickly adds that she "did not feel fear or terror"
at this state of being (343). The lamentable problem she identifies as Valerius's
death-with-the-appearance-of-life is neither a gothic nor a ghostly problem, as
her lack of terror suggests, but rather a problem of Valerius's failed sentiment
that Isabell tries to balance with her own sentimental excess. Early nineteenth-
century Romantic historicism was an epistemology of sentiment, not a concat-
enation of objective information, and, as Mike Goode explains, "a man needed
to feel the idea of history in order to think it" (8). Feeling mattered precisely
because proper sentiment (in Adam Smith's terms) was the connective moral
tissue between past and present, the conduit for a sympathetic identification
with the plights of others that made history relevant, educative, and construc-
tive to present-day society. But despite *being* the living past, Valerius has no
capacity to experience the past in this way. Not even the "sight of the exquisite
statues and paintings in Rome" can prompt feelings of joy in him, a condition
that seems like aesthetic insufficiency but actually reflects Valerius's incapacity
for sympathetic sociality (343).

The historical remnants of classical Rome should, according to Shelley's
Isabell, inspire "worship . . . of those noble heroes . . . who have enlightened
the whole world by their miraculous virtue" ("Valerius" 340). That is, one's
apprehension of classical history should transcend attention to whatever facts
of oppression and violence undergird the presence of the ruins and should
instead rely on a felt, spiritual relationship to the heroic historical virtues that
have produced the contemporary enlightened world. Isabell articulates and
tries to talk Valerius into a sentimental theory of history in which he can be
socially acculturated to the present by learning to properly—morally, virtu-
ously—feel the value of the past. To "recognize history's social relevance," one
had to be suitably sentimental: all moral judgments emerged from the ability
to feel, but *proper* moral judgments were specifically predicated on the ideal
social acculturation of these feeling constitutions (Goode 11). Isabell's desire
to bring Valerius into the fold of the contemporary society he "shunned"
assumes the inverse relationship between historical relevance and acculturated
feelings to be true, as well. Her "task to interest his feelings and to endeavour
by what ever means to draw him from the apathy under which he was sunk"
relies on the supposition that guiding the apathetic Valerius to a sentimental

understanding of history's value to the present will precipitate the emergence of his properly feeling constitution, which will in turn allow him to integrate himself into the contemporary society from which he currently feels alienated ("Valerius" 339). As she explains, "I wished to interest the feelings of Valerius and not so much to shew him all the remains of his country as to awaken in him by their sight a sentiment that he was still in some degree linked to the world," an effort that emphasizes the relationship between the sentiment inspired by historical ruins and one's ability to be fully present in the current moment (342).

Valerius seems "not a being of this earth" because he does not feel history as moral pleasure (343). When Isabell looks from the top of the Forum across the Tiber River, the ruins she sees have "an interest and feeling that sinks deep into [her] heart," but when Valerius looks at same view, he tells her that he "behold[s] nothing but destruction" and it "all appears void" (341). In the sense that this story ties life—or at least lifelikeness—to the ability to feel pleasurable sensation, we can find connections to *Frankenstein* and the creature's description of his coming to consciousness as the development of his ability to feel delight in the beauties of the world around him. But Valerius, in contrast to the creature, describes his "first sensations upon awakening to life" as a series of disenchantments and detachments, "agony," "despair," an increasing recognition that he has returned to a "mean and debased reality" and that this world is little more than "a spectacle in which he had no concern" (337, 339–40). As Isabell says, "the links that had bound him to [the world] had been snapped many ages before," and what remains is a figure who cannot feel history because he *is* history: history not as a tissue of affective connections between past and present but as something closer to Walter Benjamin's Angelus Novus, staring at the pile of historical wreckage that he cannot prevent as he moves helplessly through a future to which he does not belong (340).[13]

Isabell's desire to awaken Valerius's sentiments—to reconstitute his historical sensibility as positive emotion rather than as backwards-looking despair—does not aim to strengthen his attachment to the past but instead to help him develop feelings that attach him to the present. This story about a "reanimated Roman" explicitly figures these two modes of attachment as the difference between living death and actual life. The story sympathizes with Isabell's desire to bring the reanimated Valerius fully to life through historical sentiment but does not ultimately endorse these life-giving efforts as a real possibility. Although the fragmented tale clearly articulates a theory of sentimental historicism in line with late eighteenth- and early nineteenth-century Burkean ideas of historical embodiment, it also doubles down on the idea that embodied history can be a deadening rather than enlivening phenomenon.[14]

Valerius may be awake and walking around—he is indisputably an incarnation of revived history—but as the story draws to a close and Isabell finds her efforts to bring Valerius to present-day life frustrated by his inability to feel history in the way he should, her fascination with him begins to bear an uncanny resemblance to necrophilia. The less Valerius feels, the more Isabell "love[s] and revere[s] him" (343). The less connected he is to the living world of the present, the more she feels a "repulsive" wonder at him, "a sentiment for which [she] can find no name," an "uneasiness" at his touch that she nonetheless admits "encreased [her] affection" for him instead of interfering with it (344). If, as Goode contends, the late eighteenth-century understanding of sentimental historicism vacillated between, on one side, a Burkean insistence that the relevance of history could only be apprehended through an embodied attachment to the past, and on the other side, a countering certainty that the inherent eroticism of an attachment to "the once-living bodies of the past" gave off a perverse "whiff of deathliness and necrophilia," then Isabell's uneasy and slightly disgusting love for all that is dead in Valerius demonstrates how easily the distinction between these two poles can dissolve (Goode 49).

Yet Shelley's story uses its two main characters to engage and critique both positions simultaneously. As Ian Duncan has argued about the contemporaneous historical romances of James Hogg and Walter Scott, "revival" treads a fine line between commemorating the deadness of the past and refusing to lay it to rest, often resurrecting not a lively homage to lost tradition but a "bereft and traumatized . . . animated corpse," a "resurrection that perpetuates the 'agony' it was supposed to cure" (*Scott's* 212, 214). These not-quite-living bodies "parody . . . the moral philosophers' account of sympathetic exchange," animated not by the enlivening transhistorical spirit of fellow-feeling that characterizes Adam Smith's sense of sympathetic historical inhabitance but instead as an uncanny reminder that death never really dies, especially when it seems to be alive again (208).[15] In Shelley's story, Valerius, like Hogg's corpses, literalizes the Burkean dream of the past revived by embodiment in the present as well as the sympathetic connection that such embodiment creates with long-dead actors, but embodied historicity does not automatically produce a lively historical consciousness. Even as Valerius's historical body reinforces the deadness of the past and its fundamental detachment from the present, Isabell's attempts to produce enlivening sentiments in him only precipitate her own increasingly morbid attachment to a past that refuses to come fully to life. If necrophilia is one of the risks of trying to make history live again through sentiment, then swapping in actual eros for Freeman's erotohistoriography might be all that can hold its dangers at bay.

"Valerius" does not dismantle the Burkean relationship between sentimental history and revivification so much as suggest that this mode of historical apprehension—this felt connection between past and present—is itself an impossible fiction. The story stops short of denying that if Isabell had succeeded in her efforts to raise the right feelings in Valerius—aesthetically appreciative, ennobling, hopeful feelings—she would have been able to bring him fully to life, and the past could live again in the present such that the valuable complexities of Roman history could emerge in nuanced and productive ways in the contemporary imagination. Valerius is, after all, technically alive again, walking and talking and being grouchy. He represents both the fantasy of embodied history and the breakdown of this fantasy's viability in the face of the realities of time's movements. Valerius's ongoing despair at the "grand" remnants of the Roman Empire serves as a cipher for Shelley's own disconcerting sense (as she expresses it in a later essay) that "the confused mixture of monuments of all ages [in Rome] disturbs the imagination," and Valerius's criticism of the most revered Roman monuments voices Shelley's own dismay at the "austere self-denying" and "degraded" aesthetics of Catholicism that both she and Valerius so despise ("Modern Italy" 359, 361). Valerius's agonistic relationship with the monuments to which Isabell believes he should feel connected estranges contemporary aesthetic and political reverence for a monolithic notion of ancient Rome, reminding us that "ancient Rome" is itself a historical process rather than a singular entity, and one that is as rife with violence as it is with enlightenment and beauty.[16]

In other words, part of the problem with Valerius is that he represents only one small moment in an ongoing and complicated historical trajectory and cannot finally embody more than the single moment of his own life. Isabell's hope that she can help Valerius feel history's connective tissues across the vast breach of time between his circumscribed experience of the past and the present moment is a hope that, while idealistic, nonetheless collapses the specificities that distinguish historical moments from one another. It is a presentist hope, perhaps even an anachronistic one, and one that ultimately stands at odds with Shelley's presentation of the classical past as a series of distinct, conflicting moments. That Shelley offers Rome through two individual points of view—Valerius's and Isabell's—each of which sees the ruins as a completely different historical referent, only serves to emphasize the heterogeneity of the past, even if Isabell willfully idealizes the republican inheritances of later periods of Roman history. Elena Anastasaki has described this "fragmentariness" in the story's narrative form—it is both composed of several embedded narratives and unfinished as a whole—as an analog for the fragmentary nature of the reanimated character, whose inability to integrate into the contemporary world reveals the fragmented, discontinuous nature of the individual (30). Yet more than expressing a Romantic notion of the "fragmentation of the self," these multiple narrative perspectives work against an understanding of classical history as a unified, anachronistic, fully comprehensible phenomenon (36). Isabell wants Valerius to feel history as continuity, but he is no ghost and he does not incarnate history as persistence. His reanimated body can only feel history as a breach, as a disunity, as the painful death of the discrete past by a series of violent presents.

And yet this story presents neither Valerius nor Isabell as fundamentally wrong in their relationships to the past, nor does it suggest that there should be only one singular way of apprehending it. What it does insist is that reanimating the past is not equivalent to making it live again, and that bringing history fully to life in the present is a fundamentally aesthetic act, if also a fundamentally impossible one. Valerius himself is a profoundly fictional figure, one who exists only as a literary creation. The ancient Roman is resurrected in the present without any gesture of scientific, philosophical, or religious justification. He is neither monstrous nor miraculous, neither an invitation to suspend disbelief nor an invitation to relish the affective sensations he produces in us. Instead he is an embodied impossibility and a literary tool whose very presence in the story resists the hope for necromantic historicism even more than his active resistances to Isabell's desires do. The living Isabell, not the reanimated Valerius, is the character with the potential to fully embody and thus to enliven history in this text, for although Valerius himself is an aesthetic figure, it is Isabell who has a sympathetic connection to "the spirit of beauty" in architecture, nature, and literature and who uses this "penetrat[ing]" connection to discover the liveliness of the past ("Valerius" 342). While her narrative makes clear that her primary aim is to make sublime historical views wake Valerius's higher feelings and thus his spirit as a whole, she herself is the character whose feelings, both spiritual and erotic, are awakened by the magnificence of the historical remnants around her and who thus experiences the past as a sensory phenomenon.

Valerius may be back from the dead, but it is Isabell's capacity for "feeling inspired by the excess of beauty . . . which may inspire virtue and love" that comes closest to what Charles Kingsley a few decades later described as the ideal necromantic hope of sentimental historiography: the enlivening power of historians who "see with their eyes, feel with their hearts" and discover beauty in "sympathiz[ing] with all noble, generous, earnest thought and desire" ("Valerius" 342; Kingsley 4, 3). And yet, although Isabell's aesthetic sensibility allows her to be receptive to this sensory experience of the past— she is an ideal *reader* of Kingsley's historiography—when she fails to similarly inspire Valerius she also fails as a sentimental historian, whose ultimate revivifying task would be to connect with the dead through what Rae Greiner calls "a sympathetic form of imagining" that recreates the feelings and perspectives of the past in order to make "history a vibrant and perpetual project"

(56). As Kingsley explains, "When you have thus made a friend of the dead, and brought him to life again, and let him teach you to see with his eyes, and feel with his heart, you will begin to understand more of his generation and his circumstances, than all the mere history books of the period would teach you" (5–6).[17] Isabell certainly befriends Valerius, but her narrative makes clear that she cannot ultimately see Rome through his eyes or feel the pain that his heart feels when he looks out over the ruins. She instead seeks his conversion to her own sympathetic connection with a Roman past alternative to the one he lived, and she imagines that exciting his feelings in this way will finally succeed in bringing him back to life. Facing a vast swathe of Roman ruins, Isabell's imagination can discover the virtuous feelings that inspired them and "know the human heart" behind them in precisely the way Kingsley insists a historian must if she is truly to understand the past (Kingsley 4). But faced with a dead man literally reanimated, Isabell's historiographic necromancy fails utterly, even if her necrophilia gains a beloved object. She cannot sympathize Valerius back to life, cannot—to borrow Sir Walter Scott's words—put her "potent magic" to use "embodying and reviving" the historical moment Valerius represents, cannot—in the historian R. G. Collingswood's words— "decompose and recompose" Valerius into a living, feeling being in the present ("Dedicatory Epistle" 22, qtd. in Greiner 57).

That Shelley does not ultimately fulfill the fantasy of necromantic history with the story's actual necromantic body suggests a deep skepticism about the efficacy of Romantic historiography. Her portrayal of Isabell endorses the value and pleasure of sentimental historicism, but Valerius himself, the dead man walking, belies the illusion that such historicism is equivalent to a realistic understanding of the past. If Valerius at the story's beginning seems to represent the dream of sentimental history's resuscitative power, by the fragment's end he is little more than zombie historiography, a dead body reanimated but cursed to inhabit the present without connecting to it, bound by an unbreakable "earthly barrier" of unshared sympathies that keeps the reanimated past from living a full, real life in the present (344). Historiographic method goes awry in this story somewhere between Kingsley's invocations to "ma[k]e a friend of the dead" and to "br[ing] him to life again." Instead of assuming these two processes are synonymous, the story identifies a flaw in the historicist logic that equates a sentimental attachment to the past with what Scott describes in his "Dedicatory Epistle" to *Ivanhoe* as the "resuscitation" of the past's "dry, sapless, mouldering, and disjointed bones" by a historian's "sorceries" (22). Unlike *Frankenstein*, in which Shelley suggests that sympathy with the creature's out-of-time body might be *all* he needs to live fully in the social world from which he has been so alienated, "Valerius" insists that while sympathy might serve as connective tissue between individuals, it has little efficacy as an actual life force. A body built anew can flourish in a sympathetic present, but a body brought back from the dead has no such chance. In Valerius's view, his reanimated body can find purchase in the present only as a mouthpiece for contemporary judgment, for as he says at the end of his narrative, all he can usefully do in this time is "examine the boasted improvements of modern times and . . . judge if, after the great fluctuation in human affairs, man is nearer perfection than in [his] days" (339).

To the extent that this story is less interested in accessing the Roman republican past than it is in criticizing Romantic British history—criticizing Romantic classicism specifically as well as criticizing sentimental historiographical methodology more generally—it positions Valerius not as a key to rediscovering the past but as a mouthpiece for the problems of how the present understands the past. Shelley makes no pretense that we will learn things about Rome from Valerius that we could not know without him, and neither his nor Isabell's narrative demonstrates any real interest in Valerius's own history. Instead, both narratives focus on his alienation from and assessments of the contemporary moment, emphasizing the essentially presentist nature of his reanimated historical body. Both the characters within the story and the story itself are guilty of forcing Valerius into a utilitarian role, demanding that he embody a relationship between past and present in which the past is subject to the imagination of the present. The tale may critique Isabell for trying to talk Valerius into seeing Rome through her eyes, but Shelley, too, uses him as a fictional conceit to reflect on nineteenth-century Britain's ways of understanding, valuing, and politicizing the past. That Valerius constantly frustrates the attempts of his interlocutors to make him see and feel the present as they do exposes—even as it refuses—what Goode calls the "artificiality and anachronism" of sentimental historicism (84). But reanimating a recalcitrant Valerius still remains a way for Shelley herself to use a historical body to produce her own reading of the present. The fiction that Valerius's impossible presence most clearly represents in this text is the fiction that reanimating the past is anything but a way for the present to fulfill its own needs and desires.

ROGER DODSWORTH:
HOAX, ROMANCE, REANIMATION

Written seven years after "Valerius, the Reanimated Roman" and clearly alluding to this previous story with its title, "Roger Dodsworth, the Reanimated Englishman" revisits the value and politics of a sympathetic historical imagination in a more optimistic, if also a more sardonic, way. This piece capitalizes on a hoax story making the rounds in French and British newspapers throughout 1826, which claimed that a man frozen in ice since 1660 had recently been found, thawed, and resuscitated in Switzerland by an English doctor returning home from Italy.[18] Shelley's "Roger Dodsworth" takes a more philosophical approach to Dodsworth's newly defrosted life than other Dodsworth pieces, which focus less on what Dodsworth's reanimation might mean to our understanding of history and more on how much the three-hundred-year-old Roger reminds them of dusty nineteenth-century Tories. In conversation with her own and William Godwin's reflections on the value of romance and imagination in producing true, living history, Shelley's "Dodsworth" is a rumination on the capacity of resuscitative history to enable political change in the present moment. While Valerius's reanimated body both offers and withholds the possibility of feeling with the past, Dodsworth's body—imaginary as it is, irreverently though Shelley engages with it—encompasses the revolutionary potential of transhistorical sympathy.

The Roger Dodsworth "discovery" story was first published in France in June of 1826 and then translated into English for the London *New Times* a week later. After the initial news broke, several other newspapers and journals published the story, many appending humorous or satirical reflections on Roger Dodsworth's politics, stiff joints, or general preposterousness to the basic "facts" of the case. Writers like Thomas Moore wrote satirical Dodsworth poems in which the centuries-old Roger embodies the antiquated and conservative views of the Tories, while anonymous letters purportedly from Dodsworth himself contemplate historical consciousness, history-writing, and the porous relationship between past and present. No one in the periodical press seems mired in any gothic anxiety about Dodsworth's sudden aliveness or worried about his likeness to a revenant. Instead, Dodsworth shares more imaginative space with the historicity of Shelley's reanimated Valerius than with the monstrosity of her animated creature, and inspires similar thinking about the narrative mechanisms through which the early nineteenth century produces historical understanding.

Shelley's own article on Dodsworth, submitted to the *New Monthly Magazine* in the fall of 1826 but not ultimately published there, begins by attending to this question of Dodsworth's usefulness to contemporary England and makes it clear that his value to the nineteenth century lies in the degree to which his embodied historicity can be instrumentalized by historians, writers, and the public at large. Her first paragraph dwells on the resuscitated man's accountability to the modern era in which he has returned to life, objectifying and atomizing him according to the various uses to which the present would like to put him. That he has not yet appeared in England has begun to interfere with these uses. The antiquarian society has been frustrated in its plots to acquire his clothes and "treasures in the way of pamphlet, old song, or autographic letter [that] his pockets might contain," countless poets have had to leave their Dodsworth encomiums unfinished, Shelley's own father, William Godwin, has suspended his work on his history of the Commonwealth as he awaits "such authentic information" as Dodsworth can provide, and the nation and world as a whole have been generally deprived of a "new subject of romantic wonder and scientific interest" that they hoped would be immediately forthcoming ("Dodsworth" 43). Like almost all the Dodsworth periodical pieces, Shelley's article has a snarky tone, but she directs her wit explicitly at the popular impulse to exploit the miracle of Dodsworth's supposed emergence from the ice, not at the similarity between his own inescapable historical backwardness and the current political climate of Britain. While the article goes on to mount its own historicist critique, it approaches this aim by openly acknowledging that the Dodsworth story is an imaginative catalyst and that Dodsworth's impossibly reanimated body is a narrative tool. Unlike many of the other substantive Dodsworth publications that followed the initial burst of reporting, Shelley's article neither claims to be in Dodsworth's own voice nor directly addresses him. Instead, she embraces the fictionality of this "youthful antique" and the possibilities for storytelling that inhere in it, spinning out a series of speculations about the scientific and religious bases for his resuscitation before finally ventriloquizing the voice that she freely admits she must invent (44). "Since facts are denied to us," she writes, we must "be permitted to indulge in conjecture" about Dodsworth's first waking moments and reactions to his new era of existence (44). As she describes her suspicions about Dodsworth's seventeenth-century political leanings, his concerns about his inheritance, and the questions he might have asked when powers of speech returned to him, she repeats the phrase "we may imagine" like a mantra, reminding readers even as she records a "dialogue" between Dodsworth and the doctor who found him that his voice is entirely her invention (45).

The Dodsworth she invents is a "moderate, peaceful, unenthusiastic" thinker whose lack of political doggedness suits him as equally to one time as to another (48). Stripping Dodsworth of any particular political leaning and emphasizing his middling sensibility allows Shelley to imagine his capacity to adapt to the modern moment, even if his initial reaction to his resuscitation is to lament that everything familiar to him "are now antiquities" (47). She presents Dodsworth's seemingly effortless acclimation to modernity to argue for the consistency of character, of politics, and of power relations across vast swathes of time and circumstance (even if Dodsworth is only consistent in his easy acquiescence to new ideas). Education, manners, technologies, and styles may vary across centuries, but the fundamental nature of human relations just repeats itself over and over again, much to everyone's detriment. Dodsworth's value, for Shelley, is not his embodied pastness but the transhistoricity of character that his reanimation exposes. He is a literal incarnation of the past given new life in the present, and even if he himself is fairly useless there, his existence (fictional though it may be) offers Shelley an occasion to fantasize about the value of more dazzling pasts making themselves known in the contemporary world.

Shelley makes her point about Dodsworth's uninspiring transhistorical moderation in order to fantasize about a world in which other, more exhilarating characters could be "reborn in these times" and use the knowledge of their past selves to positively influence the modern political condition ("Dodsworth" 48). Although she begins this meditation by alluding to Virgil's theory that "every thousand years the dead return to life, and their souls endued with the same sensibilities and capacities as before, are turned naked of knowledge into this world, again to dress their skeleton powers in such habiliments as situation, education, and experience will furnish," her philosophical investment quickly moves from this hopeless vision of historical repetition to the possibility that sympathetic attachment to a seemingly disconnected, even contradictory past can create revolutionary change in the present (48–49). Lisa Kasmer has argued that "Roger Dodsworth" offers a "dystopic vision" of history doomed to repeated cycles of mediocrity, with Virgil's "macabre vision of the dead returning to life" underscoring Shelley's fatalistic belief in the "failure of historical progress" (Kasmer 124). Yet Dodsworth's mediocrity and Virgil's vision are Shelley's starting points, not her endpoints, and she transforms their lackluster models of resurrection into an invitation to imagine how socially valuable remembering the past to life can be. As Kasmer also argues—although she explicitly excludes "Dodsworth" from this argument—Shelley's historical long-form fictions during the decade in which she wrote "Dodsworth," including her 1823 novel *Valperga, or the Life and Adventures of Castruccio, Prince of Lucca* and her 1830 novel *The Fortunes of Perkin Warbeck,* demonstrate Shelley's clear interest in the narrative and political efficacy of historicist sympathy. Stories of the past matter not because they offer us an "old Chronicle" of facts but because "of the romance" they contain, Shelley writes in her preface to *Perkin Warbeck,* riffing on the same distinction between history and romance that William Godwin dwells on at length in a 1797 essay called "Of History and Romance" (*Perkin Warbeck* iii).

Godwin's essay explicitly embeds his reflections on historical truth in a distinction between dead and lively bodies. As Godwin argues, the most technically truthful history, "the mere chronicle of facts, places and dates" is "in reality no history," is "the mere skeleton of history": "The muscles, the articulations, everything in which the life emphatically resides, is absent" (462). Real

60 • CHAPTER 1

historical understanding, the kind that inspires virtue and elevates the mind, can only be produced by intimate contact, the exchange of "real sentiments," "the friction and heat" of knowing the past in all of its voluptuous fervor (458). Dry, lifeless skeletons of historical fact—themselves as rife with "falsehood and impossibility" as any other kind of narrative, despite their appeals to objectivity (465)—offer none of the fleshy joinings that Godwin believes make the past rousing and fruitful. As he explains it, the best histories are a form of queerly carnal pleasure, allowing us to "follow [the man of "great genius"] into his closet" rather than holding him aloof and distant on the "public stage" (458). If the past is truly to stir men to aspirations of virtue, it "must be made, as it were, to slide into" everything we are and wish to be, and these deep, personal connections with the masculine bodies of the past will make greatness possible.

But if the historical imagination is to reach this apotheosis of queer necrophiliac fulfillment, the past must be more than a collection of calcified fragments. Nothing slides easily into a jagged, dusty pile of bones, and the historian who relies on disarticulated skeletal facts can never give flesh to the warm, muscled body that Godwin wants to "enter into . . . feelings with" in the closet, making virtuous history (460). The more time that has elapsed between the past being narrated and the present moment, the closer history approaches to something like fable, "pregnant with the most generous motives and the most fascinating examples" (Godwin is nothing if not nonbinary in his erotics) (460). By contrast, recent and geographically proximate pasts bind historians to the "unsatisfying" demands of the "evidence of facts" and "broken fragments," blocking them from the "genuine praxis on the nature of man" that more ancient history can offer (461, 2). To properly give life to a more modern past, Godwin proposes "romance" as an embodied alternative to skeletal historical chronicle, calling romance writers the "real" historians in contrast to "he who was formerly called the historian . . . a romance writer without the ardour, the enthusiasm, and the sublime license of imagination, that belong to that species of composition" (466). Neither history nor romance can objectively represent an unmediated past, but romance achieves a tantalizing authenticity unavailable to history because it has the imaginative liberty and the erotic energy to know the innermost lives of the characters it represents.

Shelley's historical novels in the 1820s and 1830s channel Godwin's insistence that "nobler" history, or romance, will always "interest our passions," while the "dry and repulsive nature" of objective national history will leave our souls in a state of "torpid tranquility" (Godwin 464, 454). Shelley makes this distinction explicit in her preface to *The Fortunes of Perkin Warbeck,* explaining to readers that no narrative "confined to the incorporation of facts" could ever do "justice" to the complicated human emotion and desires that structure the pretender's story and make him a "true man" and a "hero to ennoble the pages of a humble tale" (iii, iv). In Shelley's justification of moving beyond historical chronicle into a narrative that dwells on feelings and relationships instead of on names and dates, she maintains that sympathetic personal history offers a clearer window into the complexities of Warbeck's political position than any political history possibly could. The purpose of learning about history, she argues, is not to evaluate or judge the accuracy of three-hundred-year-old information but to understand how and why people thought or acted the way they did in their historical moment. The writer of romance, unlike the writer of historical chronicle, has license to imagine human relationships and motivations into their stories, and can thus present a more complete and morally sound portrait of a historical moment than a historian limited to known facts. Readers of romance in turn can develop an intimate acquaintance with the past that will excite sympathy and virtuous feeling.

Shelley's preface to *Perkin Warbeck* makes a clear case for a historical epistemology that mobilizes sentiment to create continuities between past and present, a case she makes equally but more obliquely in "Roger Dodsworth." As she writes explicitly in *Perkin Warbeck,* sympathy should be the foundation for historical understanding because "human nature in its leading features is the same in all ages" (iv). A narrative of history that enables one to imagine oneself into another's experiences of the past will also illuminate and enable empathy for present-day human experiences because human nature does not change. She makes the same point about the consistency of human nature across time and space in "Roger Dodsworth," even though this earlier piece has none of her historical novels' investments in the methodological differences between history and romance. In "Dodsworth" she instead borrows the material figure for sentimental historiography—the reanimated corpse—to reflect on the ethical and political value of bearing the experiences of multiple historical moments in a single mind. It would be "an instructive school for kings and statesmen, and in fact for all human beings," she writes, to recognize that their existence in the present moment is inextricably entwined with their existences in other historical moments ("Dodsworth" 49). Acknowledging one's connections to the past will enable more virtuous action in the present. Shelley imagines that everyone now living had many past lives that we—unlike Dodsworth—cannot remember, and that could we all be "tremblingly alive to the historic records of [our] honour or shame," we would inevitably inhabit the present differently, being less hypocritical in our judgments and refusing to reproduce policies that once led us into crisis (49). "If at the present moment the witch, memory, were in a freak, to cause all the present generation to recollect that some ten centuries back they had been somebody else," she writes, "nothing but benevolent actions and real goodness would come pure out of the ordeal" (49). She offers tongue-in-cheek fancies about who certain current statesmen might have been in past lives, but she's not actually interested in philosophies of reincarnation. Instead, she thinks that an "excellent" philosophical novel (were such things "in vogue") might be written "on the development of the same mind in various stations, in different periods of the world's history" (49). By this she means, first, to reiterate her earlier insistence that people's core selves remain fundamentally the same no matter what historical moment they live through, and second, to reinforce her point that an ethical mind in the present moment is a compendium of self-aware past minds.

Without providing overt critiques of philosophical materialism or dry historiography, Shelley's "Dodsworth" nonetheless insists that a sympathetic historical imagination is essential to an ethical and revolutionary politics. Less than a century later, George Santayana would drop his endlessly misquotable warning that "those who cannot remember the past are condemned to repeat it," reminding us that progress is a function of "retentiveness" rather than "absolute" change (284). "Dodsworth" anticipates Santayana's attention to the importance of historical memory, but Shelley makes this point more aggressively by suggesting, through Dodsworth's literally reanimated body and her meditation on various versions of reincarnation, that we must do more than simply remember the facts of the past. We must inhabit past minds, experience past lives, use our imaginations to feel beyond the confines of our singular lives because only through this kind of affective immersion in lives that are not our own will we be able to enact political and cultural change. In other words, "the witch, memory" that Shelley invokes in this essay is not simply a call to recollect the past ("Dodsworth" 49). It is something closer to Scott's witch in his "Dedicatory Epistle," who selects corpses for "resuscitation by his sorceries" in order to bring the past and present into living, breathing contact with one another (22). Only through such an imaginatively embodied historical experience can the past offer the present new "political possibilities," possibilities that Kasmer argues Shelley has already foreclosed on by the time she writes "Roger Dodsworth" but that the piece itself still clearly makes space for.[19]

Shelley's final petition to Dodsworth at the essay's end is to "make himself known personally to us," to bring his knowledge and experience and habits not only fully into the modern world but also into the author's personal world so that she can interact with him on a purely human level ("Dodsworth" 49). She acknowledges that this might not be possible, that the alive-again man (like Valerius) might have found "no affinity between himself and the present state of things" and returned to death, but the essay as a whole builds toward its climactic supplication for real human contact between past and present, for an opportunity to speak, feel, and think with a past that that might not really be dead and gone (50). Like Valerius, Dodsworth ultimately becomes a utilitarian instrument for Shelley to consider the ethical impact of imagining the past to life. But while Valerius (the character if not the story) resists the inevitably utilitarian nature of the sentimental historiography his reanimated body represents, Shelley writes Dodsworth as a figure for the redemptive and even revolutionary potential of a sympathetic historical imagination, even if Dodsworth himself is middling and conventional. The contrast between Dodsworth's own mundane politics and the political promise intrinsic to his reanimated body bespeaks Shelley's point that the sympathetic imagination itself, rather than an attachment to particular heroic acts peppering the past, will be the wellspring of ethical action and political reform.

REANIMATING *FRANKENSTEIN*: OLD PARTS, NEW BODIES

These two short stories, steeped as they are in late eighteenth- and early nineteenth-century historiographical thinking and debate, offer us a filter through which to understand why, by 1831, Shelley has begun to assert the historicity of *Frankenstein*'s origins and underlying aesthetic theory. By 1830 Shelley had fixated on history in its various scales, writing to her publisher that she would like to write a book on the "History of the Earth—in its earlier state—that is an account both of the anti diluvian remains—of the changes on the surface of the Earth, and of the relics of States and Kingdoms before the period of regular history." Or, if this topic wouldn't interest the public, she might instead try "a history of Woman—her position in society & her influence upon it—historically considered, and a History of Chivalry" (Shelley, "Letter" 409). Her "Reanimated" stories embody a roused excitement about the creative energies of history, which comes to more traditional fruition in the historical novels she wrote in the 1820s but which these short necromantic stories retrospectively and more weirdly tether to *Frankenstein*'s gothic animated body. They function as the connective tissue between *Frankenstein* and Shelley's fascination with the historical imagination, for even though they are in no way revisions of *Frankenstein*, they reveal the extent to which Shelley's writing and thinking after 1818 was preoccupied with the ethics and politics of reanimating the past into real, tangible life.

Her forays into historical resuscitation in the "Reanimated" stories are literal in ways that Scott's are not, but they bear more resemblance to his investments in the sympathetic historical imagination than they do to the spectral bodies of most gothic fiction, or the experimental body of her own famous fiction. Although the reanimated Valerius is quite literally a living embodiment of antiquity, his alive-again body acts as a sanitized cipher for Shelley's reflections on modern Europe's historiographical modes of apprehending the past, not as a threatening disruption of the present. Similarly, the satirical reflection in "Roger Dodsworth" on a mild mid-seventeenth-century royalist participating in nineteenth-century England offers up a contrast between Dodsworth's dryasdust concerns that his only value to the present is as an antiquary and Shelley's own primary point that his reanimation emblematizes the vibrant political potential of resuscitative history. If antiquarian history devitalizes lived experience and renders it obsolete, "Roger Dodsworth" fantasizes about an alternative historiography in which the lived experience of the past emerges usefully and personally into the present.

Reanimated bodies in both of these stories have little to do with death and the grave and much to do with the strategies contemporary history might use to make past and present legible to one another. The stories spend significantly less time on their characters' own centuries-old lives than they do revealing how different the current moment looks when the past is alive and well within it. Their point, which Shelley troubles as much as she endorses, is that an intimate connection with the past (made literal by reanimation) has the capacity to produce an alternative present, but not a wholly new one. Her reanimated bodies, unlike her animated creature, represent a revolutionary philosophy of creative remembering that is absent from *Frankenstein*'s primary investment in the nature of the human. Yet these necromantic stories lead Shelley forward to her 1831 introduction to the novel and thus also backward into it, forming a network of connections between being human and the value of origins and historical pathways. As Shelley's thinking about uncanny embodiment shifts increasingly toward a preoccupation with the imaginative historiographical implications of returning to life, she begins to reconsider where to locate the aesthetic theories that inhere in a new body composed of old parts: to move from an investment in its newness to a meditation on its oldness, from a parable of invention to a legend about the value of origins.

But, again, *Frankenstein* came late to the historiographical game. It is telling that Sir Walter Scott's 1818 review of *Frankenstein* in *Blackwood's* draws no parallels between Shelley's novel and his own project of historical fiction, despite his recourse to the reanimated corpse as a metaphor for the writing of history less than a year later. Instead, Scott aligns *Frankenstein* with the generic conventions of the gothic that Horace Walpole lays out in his prefaces to *The Castle of Otranto*, describing Shelley's novel in Walpole's familiar terms of expanding the mind, fidelity to probable human behavior, and the truth of character that the pressures of supernatural circumstances will reveal. "The author's principal object" in creating fantastic scenarios, Scott writes, "is less to produce an effect by means of the marvels of the narrations, than to open new trains and channels of thought, by placing men in supposed situations of an extraordinary and preternatural character, and then describing the mode of feeling and conduct which they are most likely to adopt" ("Remarks" 614). For Scott, *Frankenstein*'s creature is a circumstance of supernatural impossibility, not a metaphor for historical form, and he emphasizes the novel's investment in the dangers of Victor's "art," which he describes as "the creation (if we dare to call it so) or formation of a living and sentient being" (615). Faithful to the novel's own insistence on Victor's "produc[tion] of a new species" (even as he attributes the novel to Percy Bysshe Shelley and disparages the creature's eloquence and ability to acquire a humanistic education), Scott's interest lies in the power of such an improbable incident to "excite . . . new reflections and untried sources of emotion" by convincing readers to suspend their disbelief and immerse themselves in the extreme reverberations of Victor's unlikely creation (615, 620). He also pokes fun at readers' willingness to engage in such an immersive experience, pointing out not only the implausibility of the creature reading Plutarch but also the practical likelihood of "so curious a specimen of natural history" getting swept up by an unscrupulous museum proprietor and displayed for the world to gawp at (619).

Both his praise and his criticism of *Frankenstein*'s supernatural excesses depend on his assertion that the creature at its center is something wholly new, formed as much from Victor torturing the living as from his mucking around in graves. At the review's end, the deliciously horrific newness of the creature resonates metaphorically in Scott's repetition of the words "original" and "new" to describe the novel itself and its power to "enlarge the sphere of that fascinating enjoyment" produced by fictional novelty ("Remarks" 620). Despite being the early nineteenth-century novelist most credited with a resuscitative imagination[20]—"all the dead bones that *he* touches come to life," Andrew Lang wrote of Scott's 1816 novel *The Antiquary* (xii)—Scott recognizes nothing of this impulse or aesthetic in the novel now most culturally synonymous with a feat of reanimating dead flesh. If Scott himself produces resuscitative historical fiction that enables readers to sympathetically experience the lives of people who are dead and gone, he characterizes Shelley's gothic fiction as doing the complete opposite, animating a creature rather than reanimating the dead in order to create entirely new affective experiences for readers.

Scott's review, written immediately after the novel's publication, reinforces the curious belatedness of *Frankenstein*'s historicity. Even if some twenty-first-century critics see *Frankenstein* marking the death of the gothic genre that "was given life in 1764" with the publication of *Otranto*, in the novel's 1818 moment Scott sees it firmly entrenched in, or even an exemplary version of, Walpole's experimental project of "creat[ing] a new species of romance" that could liberate the imagination from a fictional "adherence to common life" and allow it "to expatiate through the boundless realms of invention" (Wolfreys 8; Walpole 12, 7). Walpole may trace his new gothic romance back to Shakespeare and with false modesty write that he would "be more proud of having imitated" the great playwright than he would "enjoy the entire merit of invention," but he makes this claim to provide his experiment with a foundation of legitimacy, not to diminish its originality (12). Scott's association of Shelley's novel with Walpole's insistence on the emotional heights that can be produced by the creation of something new reproduces Victor's own insistence on the "unremitting ardour" and "the variety of feelings that bore [him] onwards" when he imagines that at the end of his experiment "a new species would bless [him] as its creator" (*Frankenstein* 81, 80). Apparently both fiction and scientific experiment need new [or novel] forms to generate sustained emotional intensity. It may seem counterintuitive to suggest that by identifying *Frankenstein* with the then fifty-year-old Walpolean gothic Scott explicitly dehistoricizes the dead matter out of which Victor creates his monster, but Scott takes his cues from Victor and locates the affective force of gothic creativity in the "new trains and channels of thought" it produces, at the expense of any mouldering historical bones that might undergird it ("Remarks" 614). For Scott, bringing the dead to life is a project for historical fiction, not for the gothic (or the galvanists), and the text of *Frankenstein* resides firmly in the latter category's self-reflective preoccupation with experiment and innovation.

However, as the idea of *Frankenstein*, if not the novel proper, is itself reanimated across the nineteenth century, in Shelley's own 1831 introduction and beyond, the historicity of the creature's body becomes central rather than secondary to the process of creation, and that body comes to represent—to return to Freeman's terminology—an erotohistoriographic theory of creative production. If Shelley's novel itself pays little attention to the creature as a historical body, the collective tradition of *Frankenstein* adaptations writes its engagement with literary history on the body of the creature, using this body as a corporeal "tool to effect, figure, or perform [its] encounter[s]" with its literary past (Freeman 95). Between Shelley's novel and the century of *Frankenstein* adaptations that follow (including in that mix Shelley's own new introductory apparatus in 1831), we can excavate a shift in aesthetic theory from Shelley's Romantic vitalism to what will later become Browning's resuscitative poetics (see chapter 3): from a theory of creativity as the discovery of innate vitality to an understanding of creativity as the reanimation of old bones. *Frankenstein* adaptations offer us both a revisionary process and a material metaphor—the historicized body of the creature—for theorizing art as a self-conscious form of necromancy, equally attentive to the skeletons in the grave as to the energy it takes to give them new life.

One key transitional moment in the transformation of the creature from something new to something old happens in 1823, the year of the first major theatrical adaptation of *Frankenstein*. In practical terms, this play inaugurated a decade of popular *Frankenstein* plays in France and England, renewing public interest in the novel and leading quite literally to the 1831 third printing of *Frankenstein* that Shelley's introduction accompanied.[21] Richard Brinsley Peake's *Presumption; or, The Fate of Frankenstein* borrows prodigiously from Shelley's language in the novel, although it relies more on current melodramatic conventions than on the novel for its love stories and plot. As Shelley wrote when she and Godwin went to see the play together, "the story is not well managed but Cooke plays ——'s [the unnamed creature's] part extremely well . . . I was much amused, & it appeared to excite a breathless eagerness in the audience" ("Letter to LH" 404). New Romantic allegiances aside, the play's most significant deviation from the novel is the muteness of the creature, who must communicate by gesture both his desire for acceptance and his rage at the cruel treatment the world visits upon him. Without the eloquence Shelley gives her creature, Peake's creature lingers in a liminal, prehuman state, following no developmental path nor inspiring the same degree of sympathy the creature does in the novel.

The play's language emphasizes the creature's nonhuman status (although images of T. P. Cooke playing the role look distinctly unmonstrous), parroting chapter 3 of Shelley's novel when Frankenstein crows that he has discovered "The vital principle! The cause of life!" and has "daringly attempted the formation—the animation of a Being" but diverging drastically from the novel as he begins the animation process itself (Peake 139). "The object of my experiment lies there," he says as a storm blows outside his laboratory, "a huge automaton in human form" who rises only after a mysterious blue flame—"the Devil's own flame," a panicked servant calls it—produces some form of combustion and brings the form to life (143). As Michael Chemers has pointed out, the storm in this scene, which connects the play to a history of Prometheus plays where storms "signify the presence of a wrathful Zeus hurling a thunderbolt at the imprisoned Titan," is an origin point for the connection between electricity and the creature's animation that is now so prevalent in *Frankenstein* adaptations (*Monster* 56). Even more than the storm, however, the "Devil's" blue light and the reference to the creature as an "automaton" gesture toward a distinctly inorganic vision of the creature, mechanized and powered by electricity rather than a flesh-and-blood body infused with vital spirit. Belatedly horrified by what he has done, Peake's Frankenstein, like Shelley's Victor, later reimagines the "automaton" as "the horrid corpse to which I have given life," but this fleshy language remains overlaid with a more mechanistic sensibility even when Frankenstein dismisses the infanticidal possibility of extinguishing the spark he has generated. "Yet that were murder—murder in its worst and most horrid form—for he is mine—my own formation" (Peake 144). This slippage between investing the creature with the humanity of a child and maintaining the creature as a built "formation," something constructed instead of something born or brought back, is famously reiterated in James Whale's 1931 film when Frankenstein says of his creature that "that body is not dead; it has never lived. I created it. I made it with my own hands" (qtd. in Friedman and Kavey 92). Whale's film wavers between insisting that Frankenstein is a creator and imagining him as a reanimator, as Frankenstein earlier says that "the brain of a dead man is waiting to live again in a body I made with my own hands," but the film at least partially shares Shelley's and Peake's interest in locating the aesthetic and moral quandary of "personhood status" in the inhuman, constructed form of the creature rather than in a transgression of the boundary between life and death (qtd. 111–12, 94).

When Peake labels his creature an "automaton" and hints at electricity as its animating force, he taps into more than two decades of scientific and political debate about the relationship between electricity and the human spirit that sought to establish or disprove the vitalist idea that "life was something superadded to matter" (Morus, "Radicals" 266). Radical materialist philosophers and scientists claimed that life and matter were one and the same, with the body itself producing the necessary biological conduit between "the divine immortal essence, and the dull inertion of created matter" (qtd. 266). The only possible substance that could have the "ethereal" power to stimulate matter into human life, the late eighteenth-century radical John Thelwall said in 1790, was "electrical fluid," the very substance that the conservative Edmund Burke associated with the French revolutionaries that he called "the true conductors of [radical] contagion to every country" (qtd. 264). Electricity for conservatives like Burke was itself "a dangerous revolutionary spirit" that interfered with the divine political order, and by the first few decades of the nineteenth century what Iwan Rhys Morus calls "the heresy of electrical life" was distinctly unrespectable ("Radicals" 264; *Shocking* 67).[22]

Peake's Frankenstein dabbles in this radical materialist idea that humanity might be a product of the vital electric fluid running through the tissues of the body rather than a divine spark bestowed by God, but just as nineteenth-century physical chemists worked to distance their electrical experiments from this materialist association of electricity with humanity, Frankenstein too dissociates electric vitality from human life. He may dabble in materialist experiments, he may even prove radical philosophers like Thelwall right by using electricity to create a being who elicits human sympathy, but he ultimately distances himself from this transgressive materialist project by declaring his creation an electrical automaton, not a person, and by proclaiming that the creation is impossibly and disgustingly inhuman. Even if Peake and the play don't overtly endorse any kind of political agenda, the nineteenth-century association of electrical vitality with political radicalism make the creature's electric body a menacing cultural proposition rather than a viable biological phenomenon from the outset.[23] The play's initial emphasis on the body's mechanistic and inorganic qualities reminds us that Peake's Frankenstein (at least initially) believes wholeheartedly in himself as a revolutionary creator above everything else.

Presumption was not Peake's last word about *Frankenstein,* however. The play's wild success in 1823 inspired him to write another, more farcical *Frankenstein* play mere months later. *Another Piece of Presumption,* also written in 1823, marks a decided turn in the myth of Frankenstein, comically pointing out the vagueness of Victor's grotesque grave-robbing in both novel and first play and providing a nascent model for the accidentally used criminal brain that we see in so many twentieth-century *Frankenstein* adaptations. The hero of the farce, Frankinstitch the tailor (an artist instead of a scientist), decides he wants to "manufacture a gentleman itself" rather than just manufacture clothes for them, but realizes that such a project has important material needs (Peake 166):

> Oh give me the Limbs and you'll see
> A Being so quick stitch'd up by me.
>> Give me material
>> He won't appear ill
>> Legs for his walking
>> Tongue for his talking. (166)

70 • CHAPTER 1

Frankinstitch has to make his "gentleman" out of something, and each of these pieces has a purpose. Where to get these pieces poses a problem—tailors don't necessarily make good grave-robbers—but Frankinstitch solves it by killing off nine of his fellow tailors and reassembling them into his own form of a gentleman: "There's Jemmy Wilson's hair—Billy Borough's [*sic*] head—Bobby Blumenthal's arms—Old Nicholas's neck—Christopher Cabbage's back—Ben Baste's one leg, and Patrick Longmeasure's tother—Dreadful incorporation of nine Tailors—but my man *is* made!" (167). From its beginning, the play jokes about the dual meaning of "parts" in a theatre, with an Underprompter character complaining that the "Ladies and Gentlemen are not pleased with their parts" before the play moves on to focus on the important parts of the tailors who will end up composing Frankinstitch's gentleman (161). "Christopher Cabbage is my name / I'm known by my one Eye. / I'm Patrick Longmeasure the lame . . . Nine as civil *bodies* as I ever met with and good *hands* too" (165; emphasis mine). The slippage between theatrical parts and body parts not only creates a parallel between the intrinsic artifice of both artistic projects at hand in the play (the play itself and the making of a man) but also foregrounds the intense suspension of disbelief required to imagine a bunch of disparate parts fusing together to form a composite whole (again, in both the theatrical sense and the Frankensteinian sense). The play continuously breaks the fourth wall as behind-the-scenes characters comment on the on-stage action, ensuring that the audience can't lose itself in the drama of either the play or Frankinstitch's project. It schools us to remember that the parts are always just parts, no matter how they are assembled into something that appears to be greater.

Peake's emphasis on the tailors' parts sets the stage for later *Frankensteins* (both serious and parodic) in which the origins of stolen parts have a material impact on the character of the creature who receives them. In this farcical version, the specificity of the parts accounts for the "hobgoblin's" near-instantaneous eloquence: "I beg pardon for interrupting," says one of the characters, "but the Demon or Hobgoblin appears to speak English very well for a newly made man!" "Why, he has got Billy Burrow's head on," replies another. "That's the reason" (168). It also lays the groundwork for a final scene in which the ghosts of the dead tailors return to reclaim their parts—"Give us all these and make us men, / Hold and divide us into nine again!" (176)—and the body of the hobgoblin "disappears" through a trapdoor in the stage "*a la Vampire*" (176). The length at which Peake dwells on the materials Frankinstitch uses to sew together his hobgoblin, their influence on the character and capabilities of the new-made man, and the ease with which they can be sundered and that "man," vanished, parody most particularly the way in which Shelley's novel (and Peake's own first adaptation) explicitly conceives the "principle of life" apart from historical determinism or any concern with origins or originality. Peake's farce reminds us that in Shelley's hands, who or what the monster's parts used to be have no bearing on the monster's development into a person.[24] Art is a vital force in the novel, not a resuscitative one, and the materials that compose its creature have no—have never had, for the text's purposes—lives of their own that can be remembered or repurposed. Victor Frankenstein may produce a failed work of art because he tries to imitate and even better the operations of nature in the body he creates, but he produces a successful person because his creature develops his own singular consciousness rather than relying on inherited and incoherent fragments of pre-owned consciousnesses.

By contrast, Peake provides his creature an explicitly historical, artificially recombined body, one whose past lives refuse to be suppressed when they are reanimated into a newly "made man" that can never be as novel as Frankinstitch wants him to be. Bouriana Zakharieva has argued about Shelley's original creature that "the composite Monster problematize[s] the idea of the natural man as integral being and questions the limits and nature of the organic as axiomatic given," but it is Peake's farce, rather than Shelley's novel, in which the creature's composite body rises to the level of inorganicism (741). Again, Victor may build his creation of disparate parts, but once the creature wakes to human life he becomes an integrated whole, the novel abandoning any reference to him as an admixture of scraps no matter how unpleasant he may be to look at.[25] Frankinstitch's creature, however, never rises to the level of "integral being" because he remains a collection of unsynthesized history for the duration of the play, with the threat of disaggregation and reclamation always implicit in his actions. The farce emphasizes his resolutely unnatural state. He is an artist's creation, made entirely out of bits of other artists, and this artifice serves as material figure for the play's own pastiche of stories and conventions that have come before it. "I am come out as a *play* thing," the creature sings, soon before the theatre manager character exasperatedly complains to the playwright that his "Drama has not an atom of nature in it"; the writer replies, "What has nature to do with the Drama of the present day?" (173, 174). The farce's word games with "play" and "parts" to describe both the drama and the creature, as well as its reflections on the artifice of both, render the creature's aggregate body, composed of bits of other bodies that refuse to settle into their new form, an apt metaphor for the relationship between a new work of drama and the plays (or novels) that have come before it. Writing this in the same year as his first *Frankenstein* play, Peake uses the farce and its creature to suggest that the line between adaptation and grave-robbing is a thin one, and that creation might just be shorthand for stitching together

72 • CHAPTER 1

useful bits of art that have come before to see whether the results can be made to sing and dance. Comical though *Another Piece of Presumption* may be, it makes no bones about the violently appropriative and contrived nature of art that uses old parts to make new bodies. In doing so, it inaugurates a tradition of *Frankensteins* that self-consciously reflect on the resuscitative aesthetics of adaptation.

Mid-century stage adaptations emphasize the innate absence of a historical consciousness in Shelley's creature by reimagining him not as a collection of organic relics but as a mechanical automaton, a foil and a testament to the optimistic Victorian belief that industry and a scientific knowledge of history could remake the world better than ever. In Richard and Barnabas Brough's *Frankenstein; or, the Model Man,* which opened in 1849, Frankenstein creates "a mechanical man with skill supreme. / Each joint as strong as an iron beam / And the springs are a compound of clock-work & steam" (231): a fully industrial creature who, as Audrey A. Fisch has argued, is "designed as a more efficient Victorian labourer" even as the play uses the mystical trope of a magical elixir, not a scientific discovery, to actually animate him (112). Set insistently and often absurdly at the mid-century moment of its production, this play is nearly hysterical about its own modernity. *Model Man* marks its explicit difference from the archaic European atemporality of 1820s *Frankenstein* melodramas by allowing of-the-moment Victorian popular culture to furnish the materials and conditions for Frankenstein's project. It begins with a newspaper account of Frankenstein's new work, intersperses its sentences with "stop" and laments the telegraph's "blow to poor old Gretna Green," alludes to industrial exhibitions and waxworks, laments current working-class labor conditions, and even makes sure that the primary life-giving ingredient of the magical elixir is the much-advertised quack curative Parr's Life Pill (Brough and Brough 229, 233).[26] If earlier plays—even *Another Piece of Presumption*— dwell on the dangers of Frankenstein's godlike (or not godly enough) creative hubris, *Model Man* imagines his creation of a man as social zeitgeist, a logical product of the new ascendancy of English industrial and scientific middle classes. "I'm engaged upon a great invention," Frankenstein excitedly tells the audience, the word *invention* moving his efforts firmly out of the realm of divine experimentation and into the world of industry (230).

Invention here refers specifically to the mechanical man Frankenstein then goes on to describe. However, his glee at the fame this feat of engineering will bring him, as well as his clear sense that such inventions are necessary to streamline the operations of workers who make themselves ill barely getting through "half the thing they're wanted to get through," reveals that he's also simultaneously engaged in projects of self-invention and industrial reinvention (Brough and Brough 230). "My workmanship and I are both made men," Frankenstein crows, just in case audiences need hitting over the head with the idea that his "superior manufactured article" ("rather large, you'll say," "a gent ready made") is a metaphor both for the nineteenth-century myth of the self-made giant of industry and for Frankenstein's own social and financial elevation (233, 238, 239):[27]

> Already my imagination views
> My portrait in the *Illustrated News.*
> Madame Tussaud the glowing picture backs
> And seals my fame with her approving wax. (233)

In a "Ready-made Age," as James Russell Lowell put it in 1853, the idea that anyone or anything needs to be accountable to history, origins, component parts, or narratives of development would seem as archaic as a melodramatic, mute, blue-painted creature roaming the fake Italian countryside (Lowell 39). Instead, ingenuity and some sleight of hand are all it takes to make a whole new class of English monsters, threatening not because they are assemblages of history but because they are the exact opposite, newly manufactured and "ready-made" for immediate use in, by, and of the world around them.

Model Man emphasizes the idea that anything—even history—can be manufactured in this ready-made world by listing the monster as "What Is It?" in the dramatis personae, a noticeable update to the corpus of *Frankenstein* plays that simply list the creature as "****" (or some other typographical blank).[28] In 1849 "What Is It?" was recognizable as the title of an infamous P. T. Barnum exhibition at the Egyptian Hall in 1846. "WHAT IS IT?" Is it an Animal? Is it Human? Is it an extraordinary FREAK of NATURE?" the advertising poster for the exhibition read, featuring an image of a dark-skinned, bearded man with the body of what looks like a bear, supposedly "caught in the wilds of CALIFORNIA" where "it ha[d] been with a tribe of Indians." "The Exhibitors of this Indescribable Person or Animal, do not pretend to assert what it is," the poster goes on to say: "they have named it THE WILD MAN OF THE PRAIRIES; or, 'WHAT IS IT,' because this is the universal exclamation of all who have seen it" (British Library). The exhibition was briefly a phenomenon in anticipatory advertising (so much so that Barnum resurrected it in the 1860s with a different performer) but the *Times* quickly exposed it as a hoax in a letter to the editor from "OPEN-EYE," who writes of his "surprise when, at the first glance, I found 'what is it' to be an old acquaintance—Hervio Nano, alias Hervey Leech, himself!" (Open-Eye 6). Harvey Leach[29] was an American actor whose legs, described in his obituary looking like "the thigh-bones and muscles had disappeared, and the knee joints raised to the hips," made him a sought-after performer on the freak-show stage ("Hervio Nano" 5). By the end of the 1830s newspapers were calling him "the celebrated Hervio Nano, otherwise the Gnome Fly, otherwise the Dwarf, otherwise the Demon, and really Harvey Leach," and when he died in 1847 obituaries remembered him as "the well-known Gnome Fly and Man Monkey" (unsurprisingly omitting the embarrassing "What Is It?" role from his list of theatrical triumphs).[30]

At first glance, an invented mechanical man and Harvey Leach's "missing link" character have little in common, but labeling Frankenstein's monster "What Is It?" brings the weight of this strangely specific cultural referent to bear on *Model Man*. In the 1840s "What Is It?" wasn't a vague equivalent of ****, especially given the number of (perhaps self-referential) times throughout the play that exhibition and performance are imagined as avenues to fame, success, and social status. But the Brough brothers had endless remarkably bodied performers they could have chosen if they simply wanted to suggest a correspondence between the creature and the myriad "freaks" being displayed across London for the pleasure and profit of ruthless managers. "What Is It?" differed from other missing-link exhibitions not in kind but in story. Leach had only been performing for a half hour before an acquaintance recognized him and walked into his cage to say hello, giving very public lie to the explicit story Barnum was telling about the origins and history of "What Is It?" "The thing was blown up in a minute," one of Leach's fellow showmen supposedly reported to Henry Mayhew: "The place was in an uproar. It killed Harvey [*sic*] Leach, for he took it to heart and died" (qtd. in Cook 143). No one had any interest in seeing a hoax with no exotic history attached to it, and visitors were outraged that they had been duped into believing that the wilds of California had yielded a savage but politely tea-drinking throwback to a primitive stage of development. "What Is It?" burst onto the London stage as a racial and anthropological wonder and slunk away from it as an artificially manufactured product of Barnum's freak factory.[31] This transformation from miracle to industrial merchandise took less than an hour and exposed the ease with which identity, social status, and history could be made and unmade by manipulating public curiosity and approbation. *Model Man* calls its monster "What Is It?" to remind us that however singular and extraordinary Frankenstein might imagine the creation of his "gent" to be, his project is representative rather than unique, enmeshed in a social world that allows identity to be produced out of nothing and transfigured into reality through desire and a good publicity blitz.

It makes perfect sense, then, that when Frankenstein sees his manufactured hybrid of technology and quack mysticism wake, his immediate reaction is neither horror nor paternal pride but instead an impulse to exhibit him (at the same venue that housed "What Is It?") as a wondrous specimen, maybe freak and maybe industrial marvel:

> I'll get out bills at once, a cab I'll call
> To hire a room at the Egyptian Hall.
> Or p'raps he'd make more powerful sensations
> At the art exposition of all nations. (Brough and Brough 238)

Frankenstein imagines that he has produced the perfect industrial laborer of the future, marked as nonwhite by its association with "What Is It?" and itself a product of industrial entrepreneurialism, but the monster resists Frankenstein's assumption that the "thing" he has produced will be a vacant, easily controlled, laboring automaton.[32] The monster has higher aspirations than to be a testament to Frankenstein's genius, even if he has "no connexions" and "no advantages of education" (239). As soon as he wakes, the play transfers its satirical attention from Frankenstein's industrial pride to the monster's social standing, doubling down on its send-up of the "made man" transcending his upbringing (or lack thereof) to find a triumphant place in Victorian society. "I dare say it's a common thing, / For folks from nothing all at once to spring," the monster muses, comically transforming his quite literal industrial originlessness into a parody of Victorian class mobility (239). He is by turns a "gent ready made" who understands "propriety" better than his creator and a marauding representative of working-class riots (and slave revolts) "who breaks the peace" and gets "completely out of control" (248, 246). Frankenstein makes sure we understand the monster's socially revolutionary capacity when he whines that he's "not the only man who's set a-going / A horrid monster that he could'nt [sic] stop. / For precedents across the Channel pop" (248). In the modern fairy tale of *Model Man,* however, all it takes is a little bit of musical "Education" (supplied by a sprite named Undine in the form of a magical flute whose "notes will bring to calm subordination" because it "plays a simple tune called Education") to rein in the riots and remind the monster that the real social revolution will be his ability to rise from nothing into something (246). Education, we learn, in the play's one potentially sincere (if also entirely abstract) call for reform, is a

> weapon small,
> Whose unobtrusive power would conquer all
> The ills that o'er the earth hold domination
> If people understood its application,

and the monster's blank developmental canvas proves easily receptive to all the improvements a magical Education flute can provide (249). In this case, Education-by-magic-flute has racist rather than intellectual connotations, "sooth[ing] the savage" monster into following a set of dance steps that will allow him to fit into society (249). It's a far cry from the ethical, historical, and literary education that Frankenstein's creature gets in Shelley's novel, and instead blends Victorian ideas of social reform (colonialist, racist, and classist though they may be) with the melodramatic convention in other *Frankenstein* plays of taming the creature with music. This so-called monster, who ultimately ends up in "a situation" rather than dead, succeeds precisely *because* he has no history and no preconceived sense of his place in the social world (249). He can thus learn how to become whatever he needs to be, to dance whatever dances he needs to. For all that the play might seem ultimately conservative in the fun it makes of how easily manipulatable Victorian industrial, racial, and class hierarchies are, its satire also imagines a social structure without the dead weight of history holding it back, in which a "made man" really can triumph in the end.

Of course, in order to truly envision such a world, the play requires a water fairy, an aging devil, an elixir of life, a magic flute, a mad industrialist, and a mechanical man who loves to polka. In its desire to transform an organic monster into an industrial machine and an allegory of the Romantic artistic ego into an overthrowing of Victorian class structure, *Model Man* palpably demonstrates the ways in which Shelley's *Frankenstein isn't* a Victorian story. "You must excuse a trifling deviation / From Mrs. Shelley's marvelous narration," one of the characters says in an aside to the audience, just before the play spins off into its mad burlesque of modern industrialism, race, and social class (Brough and Brough 229). While both play and novel imagine what a "made man" might (or might not) become in a society to which he has no hereditary claim, the play, written two decades after new incarnations of *Frankenstein* began rendering the creature an inevitably historical body, openly acknowledges that its parody of nineteenth-century industrial England must jettison any investment in history and legacy in order to make space for new social relationships. That the novel manifests no similar accountability to a consideration of its creature's lacking historical consciousness shows, as much as other adaptations with their stitched-together bodies do, the ways in which *Frankenstein's* relationship to embodied history shifted across the first half of the nineteenth century. Although *Frankenstein* is in many ways a novel about history—about the specter of revolution, about the inescapability of the past, and about the subjectivity of recollection—it is primarily interested in what can be discovered, acquired, and imagined rather than in what can be remembered. It's a novel about creating a person, not a novel about reanimating a corpse. Julian Wolfreys, in *Victorian Hauntings*, cites *Frankenstein* as the death knell of the gothic novel as a "vital literary genre," suggesting that as the nineteenth century progressed beyond 1820, the gothic became "spectral" (7–8, 10). By using *Frankenstein* as the end of "the gothic novel proper," Wolfreys locates the novel at a critical juncture of modernity: not, perhaps, between vitality and spectrality, as he suggests, but between vitality and revitalization, in its most literal sense (3). *Frankenstein* may imagine that creativity can be severed from a consciousness of origins, but its horror at the result paves the way for a nineteenth-century gothic that reconceives creativity as an always complicated engagement with the "materials" that came before.

By the time we reach the 1990s and Kenneth Branagh's film *Mary Shelley's Frankenstein*, Shelley's text itself has become fully enmeshed in the crisis of historical embodiment that plays, movies, and critics have been feeding into her myth for two hundred years. The film, which Branagh insists aims "to use as much of Mary Shelley as had not been seen on film before," introduces a meditation on the problem of materials that won't shed their pasts into the central confrontation between Victor and his creature that otherwise explicitly emerges from Shelley's novel (9).

CREATURE

Who were these people of which I am comprised? Good people? Bad people?

VICTOR

Materials. Nothing more.

CREATURE

You're wrong. (*picks up the recorder*) Do you know I knew how to play this?

[He puts down the recorder.]

CREATURE (CONTINUED)

In which part of me did this knowledge reside? In these hands? in this mind? In this heart? (*beat*) And reading and speaking. Not things learned . . . so much as things remembered.

VICTOR

Trace memories in the brain, perhaps.

CREATURE

Stolen memories. Stolen and hazy. They taunt me in my dreams. . . . Who am I? (Lady and Darabont 115)[33]

Victor's unwillingness to acknowledge that the histories he has stitched into his creature matter marks his refusal to recognize the creature's humanity, or to recognize humanity in any of the parts that eventually became him. When the creature follows his questions about the memories inhabiting the fibers of his being with his final question about himself—"Who am I?"—he insists that human identity is inextricably bound to a historical consciousness, and that self-knowledge emerges from an empathetic understanding of the many pasts that have contributed to his current existence. Neither one of Duncan's uncanny historical zombies nor Freeman's monster of embodied history, Branagh's creature is *least* monstrous—most human—in his recognition that he is composed of countless pasts to which he gives new and valued life in the present. Rather than being mired in history, his body resuscitates history into humanity. If Shelley's novel locates the human in the development of an aesthetic, moral, and intellectual consciousness, Branagh's film relocates it to the ability to *remember* such a consciousness. In this scene, Victor has forgotten all the lives that his creature experiences as muscle memory, and in this gap between Victor forgetting and the creature remembering, the film makes its case for a resuscitative rather than a creative *Frankenstein*. "Perhaps I believe in evil after all," the creature says when Victor admits he paid no mind to who and what his "materials" had been in life (Lady and Darabont, 2nd revised draft 92). He suggests—as Shelley does in her 1831 introduction, as many necromantic writers that succeed her in the nineteenth century would— that "creativity" might be little more than bringing the dead to life, that artistic responsibility is indistinguishable from historical responsibility, and that shapeless substances are simply shapes we must remember how to see.

CHAPTER 2

Dickensian Zombies in *Great Expectations* and *Our Mutual Friend*

But what if the shapes we remember, the shapes of past lives conjured into materiality by the artistic imagination, aren't the right shapes? What if they are recognizably unreal resuscitations of the dead? In the third paragraph of Charles Dickens's 1861 novel *Great Expectations,* our first-person narrator Pip confronts just this question when he declares that he gains his "first most vivid and broad impression of the identity of things" one cold afternoon in a graveyard:

> I found out for certain that this bleak place overgrown with nettles was the churchyard; and that Philip Pirrip, late of this parish, and also Georgiana wife of the above, were dead and buried; and that Alexander, Bartholomew, Abraham, Tobias, and Roger, infant children of the aforesaid, were also dead and buried; and that the dark flat wilderness beyond the churchyard, inter-sected with dikes and mounds and gates, with scattered cattle feeding on it, was the marshes; and that the low leaden line beyond was the river; and that the distant savage lair from which the wind was rushing was the sea; and that the small bundle of shivers growing afraid of it all and beginning to cry, was Pip. (*GE* 3)

He has told us in the paragraph above that his entire sense of his family name and lineage comes from "the authority" of tombstones and the words graven

80 • CHAPTER 2

into them (*GE* 3). Having never seen his parents, his "first fancies regarding what they were like were unreasonably derived from their tombstones," the forms of the inscriptions allowing Pip to imagine to life the physical and personal characteristics of people long moldering in the ground: "The shape of the letters on my father's, gave me an odd idea that he was a square, stout, dark man, with curly black hair. From the character and turn of the inscription, '*Also Georgiana Wife of the Above*,' I drew a childish conclusion that my mother was freckled and sickly" (*GE* 3).

Pip's older, retrospective narrating self recognizes that these imaginative flights have no basis in reason. As Elaine Freedgood argues, he "reads unreasonably" because he is "trying to interpret a set of desperately unreaderly texts," but his younger self, coming to consciousness of his own identity constituted by the tombs and the churchyard around him, sees little difference between using the tombs to unreasonably read his family into being and perhaps equally unreasonably writing himself into being as an intrinsic part of these tombstones (*Ideas,* 18, 17). He conjures both his idea of his family and his idea of himself through fundamentally nonsensical associations between what he sees and what he imagines to be true. In the case of his parents, this association is an aesthetic one, the mistaking of artistic forms for real things: the shapes of the carved letters must transparently reflect the bodies they represent.[1] In the case of himself, the association is a grammatical one, an act of serial naming that makes no distinction between what he sees, what he feels, and who he is. Pip's "broad impression of the identity of things" moves freely between naming material things (the churchyard, the marshes, the river, the sea) and describing states of being ("dead and buried," "growing afraid of it all"), before finally enacting a transformation of an object ("the small bundle of shivers") into a self ("was Pip"). By the time Pip gets around to naming himself, the distinction between things and descriptive states, between objective material realities and feelings, has collapsed. Just as for his young self the letters on his family's tombstones unequivocally and "unreasonably" represent the shapes of the people below them, so too for his older narrating self "the identity of things" ultimately and unreasonably becomes indistinguishable from the identity of Pip.

These opening paragraphs of Dickens's second-to-last completed novel use tombstones and a churchyard to reflect, cynically, on what George Levine in *The Realistic Imagination* calls realism's moral "quest for the world beyond words," or its desire for "the validation of imagination in the visible world" (12, 18). As Levine suggests in his foundational book, one of the bedrocks of the realist novel is its faith in the idea that there is a meaningful world beyond language that can nonetheless be represented by language, a world that the novel hopes is not "merely monstrous and mechanical, beyond the control of human meaning" (22). But what happens to the form of the novel if there isn't such a world? Or, more precisely, as the beginning of *Great Expectations* asks, what if the problem isn't that there's no such world but that the only tools novels have to represent this world—words, graven in stone or organized into sentences—*make* it monstrous and mechanical? Although Pip's churchyard isn't quite populated with zombies—not every novel can be *Pride and Prejudice*—the people that Pip tries to recall to life by reading words on tombstones and finding names for abstract ideas bear no relationship to a world that might actually exist beyond these words. Pip's parents, siblings, and even his own younger self are the stuff of words, representations that shiver without their own warmth, figments of realism's [re]incarnating imagination.

This chapter faces head-on the possibility that monstrosity and mechanization are essential conditions of the realist novel, rather than the defects hovering just beyond its horizon, and argues—perhaps counterintuitively—that Dickens's novels are their most realist selves precisely where critics for the last century and a half have identified Dickens's "shortcomings and exaggerations" as a realist writer (Lewes 142). In his final two completed novels, *Great Expectations* and *Our Mutual Friend* (1865), where Dickens dabbles gleefully in the grotesque, in the evisceration of narrative temporalities, and in the eerie gothic liminalities between life and death, he also mounts his most scathing critiques of realism's attenuated production of lifelike characters and worlds. Both *Great Expectations* and *Our Mutual Friend* imagine literary realism as a form with a zombie problem. These novels suggest that the more painstakingly fiction tries to bring characters to life, the more monstrous are both the creatures that come to populate its worlds and those worlds themselves. If such characters seem to "come alive," as Elaine Auyoung puts it, and "endure in a reader's mind long after a story has faded," it's not that far a stretch to suggest that Dickens resists the ways these brain-eating realist zombies remake the messy, maddening, inchoate world into a coherent, organized, industrialized, and socially stabilizing artifice that lingers in our minds long after the fiction of it comes to an end (2).

Each of these novels experiments with, and lays bare, the very unreal fictional devices and forms at the heart of realism, although they do so in different methodological ways and on different scales. In *Great Expectations*, Dickens offers us what I call "epitaphic realism" as Pip's narrative crashes again and again into the illusion of language as an incarnating and representative phenomenon. Pip's story is not a failure of realism so much as it is a story *about* the failure of realism, writ large across the narrative form of the novel as a whole. As Pip's narrator-self demonstrates by beginning the story of his past with the problem of epitaphic language, the already-attained narrative revelation at the heart of the novel's desire to produce a fully fleshed character is that there's only zombie life to be found there: the more Pip tries to recall his past to life through language, the more doomed he is to produce a lifeless version of the very life he's trying to animate. The entire retrospective narrative structure of *Great Expectations* becomes a failed act of reanimation as narrator Pip's attempt to craft his life history deadens not only his own character but the characters of all the other potentially lively Pips the novel offers up to him.

Our Mutual Friend, in contrast, abandons the belief in an authentic representation of character before it even begins, making no attempt to think in large structural terms about how realist narrative tries and fails to bring characters to life. Instead, the novel peppers its action with sly references to (and open mockeries of) synthetic and imitative life, even opening its plot of endless animations and reanimations with a startling image of an animated corpse that the characters know better than to confuse for real life. Against a backdrop of subtle allusions to early nineteenth-century galvanism (the history of which I detail in my introduction), *Our Mutual Friend* moves its characters between the banalities of marriage-bound lifelikeness and the domestic liberty of being dead, artfully tying the former to the quackery and simulations of mid-century medical electricity while painting the latter as an unfettered opposition to all such forces of artifice, electrical *or* literary. In this interplay between nearly alive and safely dead that often takes place in the margins of the novel's main plots, *Our Mutual Friend* mounts a resistance to the aesthetic expectations of realism and toys with alternatives to the legibility, instrumentalism, and telos that realism so often demands. Dickens's preoccupations with epitaphs in the narrative form of *Great Expectations* and with galvanism on the edges of *Our Mutual Friend* reimagine the signifying power of language as a ghastly act of animation. But while *Great Expectations* ultimately finds no way to escape its zombie form, *Our Mutual Friend* offers the condition of "being dead" as a lyrical respite from realism's compulsive striving toward lifelikeness.

DICKENS'S GROTESQUE, EPITAPHIC TRUTH

Dickens's own relationship to the aims and representational strategies of realism has never been entirely clear (if such a thing could ever be entirely clear, for any writer). His waffling in the preface to *Bleak House* between assertions that all the technicalities of the novel are "substantially true, and within the truth" and his aesthetic choice to "purposely dwel[l] upon the romantic side of familiar things" limn the long-standing critical gymnastics that situate Dickens among the realists even as critics debate how his version of realism twists representation, truth, artifice, romance, and the everyday into a comprehensive "vision of contemporary life" (qtd. in Reed 3).[2] Victorian realism in general tends to be definitionally elusive, often demarcated in oppositional relationship to other generic forms ("realism vs. romance, realism vs. epic, realism vs. melodrama"), and yet as Fredric Jameson and others have argued, also "inextricably combin[ing]" these very narrative impulses that would appear to undermine its specificity (*The Antimomies* 2, 6).[3] While realism at its most foundational level "seeks to represent everyday life through thick description, references to the real world and a focus on the ordinary rather than the extraordinary," figuring out what, precisely, constitutes "everyday life" or "the real world" and what the best representational strategies are to render these evasive ideas in language remains formidably mutable (Mullen 4). And even this foundational premise has become increasingly shaky, as critics like Elaine Freedgood and Mary Mullen have explored the twentieth-century institutional and theoretical conditions that invented "a smoother, more formally impressive 'realism'" to shore up the "greatness" of a Victorian novel tradition that might not be especially real at all (Freedgood, *Worlds* 21).

And yet, for all of its internal contradictions, indefinable definitions, and dubious coherence, realism still holds a monolithic status in our narratives of nineteenth-century fiction, retaining what David Lloyd calls a "gravitational force . . . as the generic centre of canonical judgments about the novel as form" (230). Realism has long been as much a value judgment as a set of generic expectations, and whether critics pull nineteenth-century texts and writers into its ever-expanding orbit to contest the Anglocentric exclusions of canon formation or to challenge the terms and limitations through which "the real" is constituted, the importance of realism itself as a category only increases.[4] As Freedgood argues, "literary form is assigned, not discovered," and realism's investiture by twentieth-century Anglo-European literary criticism as the gold standard of novel-writing means that even as critics explore nineteenth-century scientific, ethical, philosophical, and technological shifts that put pressure on singular notions of truth or reality,[5] they do so within a framework of realism's limitless malleability and an ever-receding idea of the real (*Worlds* 138).[6]

A writer like Dickens, whose "romantic side of familiar things" inevitably flummoxes conventional notions of realism, enables critics to develop new historical and aesthetic formulations by which to prove that the "real" exists, even if it's something completely different from what we thought it was. For instance, Daniel Novak's reading of Dickens's relationship to Victorian pho-

84 · CHAPTER 2

tography enables him to argue that, like photographic realism, Dickensian realism "itself exaggerates, sliding insensibly into its presumed opposite—distortion and the grotesque" (34). Andrew Mangham, who analyzes Dickens's attachments to Victorian developments in forensic science, goes even further, arguing that the novels' attempts to "show that it is difficult, if not impossible, to throw the light of truth on anything with any confidence" align with a new forensic understanding of "truth" as a matter of interpretation, not as an empirical fact (loc. 203). Mangham contends that the forms Dickens found to represent conflicted interpretive processes at work are every bit as realistically referential as realisms that do the interpretive work for their readers, and that Dickens's self-conscious attention to the subjectivity of representation and interpretation "enables us to reconsider what interpretive strategies we have come to associate with realism and to recast Dickens as central to this discussion" (loc. 446). In this formulation, Dickens becomes central to discussions of realism only when realism is reconstituted as a forensic examination of "the real" rather than left as an attempt to represent it in any direct sense. Realism and the real both fundamentally shift to accommodate Mangham's reading of Dickens's often grotesque and sentimental representations of the world, which we can newly understand to represent the reality that truth is a teetering and subjective interpretation.

Dickens was very clear that the grotesque and the sentimental need not be at odds with truthful representation, but unlike contemporary critics who remake realism to accommodate his grotesque truths, Dickens himself simply insists that realist representational strategies have nothing to do with real life. As he writes in the preface to *Oliver Twist*, "It appeared to me that to draw a knot of such associates in crime as really do exist; to paint them in all their deformity, in all their wretchedness, in all the squalid poverty of their lives: to show them *as they really are* . . . it appeared to me that to do this was greatly needed. . . . And therefore I did it the best I could" (xxvi; emphasis mine). The more monstrous, the more counter to reality as we know it these criminals seem, the more real they are, and the more necessary such representations are to illuminate the self-perpetuating and subjective nature of the reality that readers assume to be true. A few pages later in the preface, Dickens reiterates the value of what appears to be artificial embellishment in pushing representation closer to reality. Not only does the appearance of artifice not diminish the truth of what is being represented, what seems like melodramatic aggrandizement might, in fact, be necessary to fully represent the real: "It is useless to discuss whether the conduct and character of [Nancy] *seems* natural or unnatural, probable or improbable, right or wrong. IT IS TRUE. Every man who has watched these melancholy shades of life knows it to be so . . . there is not one word exaggerated or overwrought" (xxviii; emphasis mine).

In this early novel, Dickens invokes readers to shift the terms by which we recognize the truth of character, moving away from the evaluative language of nature and probability that eighteenth-century novelists like Henry Fielding and Horace Walpole made central to their realistic aspirations: "every good author will confine himself within the Bounds of Probability," Fielding writes in *Tom Jones*, and although this does not mean "his characters, or his incidents, should be trite, common, or vulgar," it does mean that for a character "to act in direct contradiction to the dictates of his nature, is, if not impossible, as improbable and as miraculous as anything which can well be conceived" (421, 419). Instead, Dickens asks readers to replace probability with what J. Hillis Miller skeptically calls a slightly "too emphatic" affirmation of "historical verisimilitude," a version of the real that asserts its truth without being confined by the rules of representation ("Fiction" 141). For Miller, such claims of mimesis in *Oliver Twist* stand at odds with the novel's explicitly theatrical gestures of imitation: its role-playing, its melodramatic inheritances, and its false identities, among them. As Miller argues, the tension Dickens creates in the novel between the apparently mimetic and the clearly imitative calls into question the presumption that there is any "real" real at all to be represented or imitated. And yet, even more than Miller's point that Dickensian realism thus makes no claims to any sort of reality outside of the conventions of language—that he instead "expose[s] . . . life's thoroughly conventional quality," as Rae Greiner puts it (90)—Dickens's insistence on the unreal appearance of historical verisimilitude, on the idea that what's true might not look at all like what we imagine "real" to look like, produces less a particularly "Dickensian realism" than an insistence on realism's insufficiency as a truly mimetic form.[7] Rather than "Dickensian theatricality reveal[ing] the 'counterfeit quality' of realist mimesis," as Greiner describes Miller's point, it is more precisely that Dickensian verisimilitude looks more theatrical than mimetic, more grotesque than realist (90). Dickens's emphasis is less on the exposure of realism's— and life's—intrinsic fictionality than on the desire to imagine mimetic forms beyond realism that can more fully represent the real and the true.

This is much the point he makes in the opening paragraphs of *Great Expectations* when Pip's "unreasonable"—also "childish" and "odd"—readings of the words on tombstones produce ideas about real people that have no relationship to the reality of who they were. What makes Pip's readings childish is his presumption that language transparently represents material reality—that letters on tombstones transparently trace the shapes of the bodies lying beneath him. What makes his readings unreasonable, however, is his attendant presumption that there is no reality of his family's bodies beyond the language that memorializes them. These are two sides of one epitaphic coin, of course, where memorial language simultaneously conjures the pres-

86 · CHAPTER 2

ence of the dead and reinforces its absence, but they are also two sides of the realist fallacy:[8] that language transparently represents reality, on the one side, and that there is no reality outside of the mediating capacities of language, on the other.[9] We might think of these opening lines as an experiment in epitaphic realism, although one that we are supposed to recognize will always be a failure. The epitaph animates the dead by giving it a voice from the grave, yet it can only do so at the expense of an actual life. As Jolene Zigarovich has argued, "all epitaphs embody a contradiction as they often ventriloquize for the dead . . . [they] simulate a life as they mark a death" (154). When Pip uses the language of his family's tombstones to incarnate their bodies, he participates in the paradoxical project of the epitaph itself, performing a linguistic act that substitutes the simulation of a life for a life that no longer is.[10]

The dead bodies in the grave make this a more complex effort than the simple substitution of language for reality. Where there are tombstones, there can be no ignoring the fact that (in Pip's universe, at least) there are real bodies moldering in the ground beneath them, wholly distinct from his flights of fancy that produce them as living bodies. The incantatory power of the epitaph, which for little Pip functions almost literally as a magical incantation, brings his parents back to some semblance of material life. The older, retrospectively narrating Pip, however, recognizes that this imagined epitaphic act of reanimation is "unreasonable" and "childish": little Pip can incarnate nothing more than a simulation of real lives, real bodies, real parents. If this is what realism can accomplish, narrating Pip is having nothing of it. As he moves from the reanimation of his parents to the incarnation of his own young self in the graveyard—"the small bundle of shivers growing afraid of it all and beginning to cry, was Pip"—a similarly epitaphic logic seems to be at work, in which the linguistic coming into being of the child ("the identity of things") indicates not the absence of any real child but the difficulty of actually representing the real child through the magical, detail-laden language of realist description. A grown-up, narrating Pip makes it clear to us that there was, once, a child Pip (again, within the fictional universe of this novel), but the "Pip" who comes into being against a backdrop of tombstones can never be anything but an epitaphic paradox, a simulation of a life that indicates simultaneously the existence of a real life and its absence in the language that incarnates it.

Narrator Pip both exposes this paradox and relies on it. Unlike *Our Mutual Friend,* whose opening corpse expands into a novel fully preoccupied with the rhetorical, social, and economic complexities of death and corpses, the graveyard opening of *Great Expectations* doesn't lead explicitly into a novel about death and burial, even if Miss Havisham's "haunted house," as Hilary

Schor calls it, with its living "waxwork and skeleton" inhabitant, reminds us that corpses that remain undead and unburied can do far more damage to the living than the bodies lying quietly in their graves (94). Yet this opening relies on the complex epitaphic space of the churchyard to expose the deficiencies of realist representation, to put six feet of earth between language and the bodies it is meant to bring to life, and to reveal that the identity of things we unreasonably perceive to be real in novels might be little more than zombies of our imagination.[11]

Critics have long argued that Dickens's fiction has an animist sensibility, one that ranges from his inclination to vitalize inanimate objects to his resuscitation of the dead, and one that always carries with it an equal and opposing impulse to mechanize or automatize what should be living.[12] If this chapter were focused on Miss Havisham, I might suggest that *Great Expectations* begins by testing out epitaphic realism in order to pave the way for the zombie formpocalypse that Miss Havisham so nearly brings to full fruition as she sits, "corpse-like . . . the frillings and trimmings on her bridal dress, looking like earthly paper" (64). But instead I'll simply say that by the 1860s Dickensian animism had taken on a darker, more pessimistic cast than it had in the 1830s, when, as Miller argues about *Sketches by Boz,* imagining the dead to life out of their inanimate traces functions primarily as a metonymic gesture to forge a coherent narrative of London life out of the broken and disjointed trifles that have long since lost their meaning and use-value.

Miller imagines the early Dickens as an archaeologist, "resurrect[ing]" entire cultures "from the bric-a-brac of a dead civilization," and he argues that this literary strategy for *Sketches* can be seen in perfect miniature precisely at the moments in the text where Boz conjures the living dead out of the forlorn inanimate objects that once mattered to their lives (127). Miller points particularly to a passage from "Meditations on Monmouth-Street" in which Boz's wandering through this "burial-place of the fashions" inspires a necromantic fantasy of the bodies that once wore all the clothes he sees in the shops, "the extensive groves of the illustrious dead" (*SB* 98). There is a metonymic slippage between dead clothes and dead people in this passage about a street that Boz has just labeled a fashion graveyard rather than a human one, a slippage that enables an equally tricky diffusion of animist energy across both things and people:

> We love to walk among these extensive groves of the illustrious dead, and to indulge in the speculations to which they give rise; now fitting a deceased coat, then a dead pair of trousers, and anon the mortal remains of a gaudy waistcoat, upon some being of our own conjuring up, and endeavouring,

88 • CHAPTER 2

> from the shape and fashion of the garment itself, to bring its former owner
> before our mind's eye. We have gone on speculating in this way, until whole
> rows of coats have started from their pegs, and buttoned up, of their own
> accord, round the waists of imaginary wearers; lines of trousers have jumped
> down to meet them; waistcoats have almost burst with anxiety to put them-
> selves on; and half an acre of shoes have suddenly found feet to fit them, and
> gone stumping down the street with a noise which has fairly awakened us
> from our pleasant reverie. (*SB* 98)

As Miller describes it, this passage demonstrates how Boz's (what I would call
necromantic) imagination works. "Confronted with the clothes of the dead,
Boz's speculations bring to life in an instant the personages who wore these
clothes," he writes, although quite quickly in his analysis Boz's authorial animism shifts from personages back to clothes: "they leap up with an unnatural
vitality to put themselves on the ghostly owners conjured up by Boz's speculative imagination" (128). For Miller, this is evidence of Dickens's metonymic
imagination bursting at the seams as the clothes that stand in for the bodies
that once wore them erupt from their figuratively spectral purpose to become
more fleshed and more vital than those bodies they inspire Boz to summon
in the first place.

Yet the clothes in this "burial-place," like the tombstones at the beginning
of *Great Expectations,* also function epitaphically: the deceased coat, the dead
trousers, the mortal remains of a waistcoat—all, we assume, in perfectly fine
condition themselves, despite their pesky mortality—represent the bodies of
the dead who once wore them, even as their denuded forms intimating the
shape of bodies also remind us insistently that these bodies are now absent.
Boz does with these clothes precisely what Pip does with his family's tombstones, relying on the arbitrary form of inanimate objects to produce fictional
versions of the people these objects stand in for. We endeavor, he says, "from
the shape and fashion of the garment itself, to bring its former owner before
our mind's eye" (*SB* 98). Unlike Pip's, however, Boz's conjuring project doesn't
end with the "childish" incarnation of bodies. Instead, using the clothes to
revive the bodies in turn revivifies the clothes, which then seem to garner
their own power to revive more bodies ("half an acre of shoes have suddenly
found feet to fit them"), and by the time we reach the end of this passage, fashion's burial ground has become nothing less than a staging ground for a tony
army of the dead, already "stumping" its rampant way all across the streets of
London (98).

Boz retreats momentarily from this reverie but doubles down on it in the
paragraph that follows, and in terms that make the trajectory from the meton-

Victor rather than with the "misshapen creature" when he describes being pursued by Magwitch; and he quickly pivots to condemn his maker as "the creature" when he admits his repulsion at being part of this relationship in the first place. There is a deliberate shiftiness in how Pip brings the weight of *Frankenstein* to bear on his character's artifice, one that avoids aligning monstrosity with discovering himself to be a gent ready-made in favor of adopting something much closer to Victor's narcissistic sense of victimization. Self-pity notwithstanding, however, this allusion explicitly positions Pip within an ongoing necromantic narrative. As soon as he describes his character and relationship to his benefactor in Frankensteinian terms, Pip can't help but become yet another creature resuscitated by language into a story that has never really belonged to him.

Throughout the novel, protagonist Pip is plagued by anxiety that the story of his life isn't of his making, that his character and his narrative have slipped out of his control and into the hands of other writers and readers, a "perilous" lack of mastery that Deborah Lutz argues "leads to a measure of self-haunting" (*Relics* 80). His discovery that he is Magwitch's creation—even if he refuses to call himself a creature—is only the most dramatic instance of the lost narrative control that Pip experiences at other moments in the text. For instance, upon returning home after Joe visits him in London and already shaken by hearing a convict in the coach discussing him without recognizing that the older Pip is the boy he's describing, Pip sits in the Blue Boar and reads a newspaper story recounting Mr. Pumblechook's instrumental role as the "founder of [Pip's] fortunes" (*GE* 231): "Our readers will learn, not altogether without interest, in reference to the recent romantic rise in fortune of a young artificer in iron of this neighborhood . . . that the youth's earliest patron, companion, and friend, was a highly respected individual not entirely unconnected with the corn and seed trade" (230). This, of course, is a complete rewriting of history, and narrator Pip makes light of it by telling us (in the present tense) that he "entertain[s] a conviction" that even if he were now to go to the North Pole he would find somebody there who would tell him that "Pumblechook was my earliest patron and the founder of my fortunes" (231). Yet this newspaper story, reproduced for us at the tail end of a chapter entirely preoccupied with Pip's uncertainty about whether or not his gentlemanly self is still recognizable as the blacksmith's boy he once was, forges an important link between the instability of Pip's sense of identity and the instability of his narrative control. In reading this story, Pip suddenly finds his history publicly rewritten into a form that even he does not recognize. The convict's inability to recognize young Pip in older Pip has been replaced by his own inability to recognize his story in the story before him.

92 • CHAPTER 2

His change of fortune has done more than divide his low past from his high self. It has also divided his sense of self from the story he has become. As this newspaper article demonstrates, the "biography" of Pip is up for grabs.[17] By dividing his personal past from his public, gentlemanly image, by relishing and relying on his celebrity status, he has become public property to be fashioned as the public pleases. Magwitch's instrumental role in fabricating a gent ready-made (along with Miss Havisham's admission that she "stole [Estella's] heart away, and put ice in its place" in order to "mould [the impressionable child] into the form that her wild resentment, spurned affection, and wounded pride found vengeance in") may be the novel's most overt demonstrations that Victor Frankenstein is alive and well in Dickensland, but Pip's sense that his life history has slipped from his control and could be resurrected by others into something unrecognizable is a far more chilling necromantic threat to his character (*GE* 399). The vulnerability of his history to the narrative machinations of others comes to its apotheosis toward the end of the novel, when Orlick, Pip's worst and most lasting critic, tricks Pip into meeting him and threatens to kill him. "Let people suppose what they may of you," Orlick says to him, "they shall never know nothing" (425). In Pip's panicked response to this threat of narrative recalcitrance, we find the origin point of the "autobiography" itself and its opening insistence that the stories written on tombstones might bear no relationship to the bodies buried beneath them: "The death close before me was terrible, but far more terrible than death was the dread of being misremembered after death. And so quick were my thoughts, that I saw myself despised by unborn generations" (425). To return, then, to the novel's initial epitaphs, the critique of mimetic realism that inheres in Pip's "unreasonable" assumption that epitaphic words themselves are transparently representational and have the capacity to conjure his fully fleshed parents from their skeletal bodies also serves to undermine the project of autobiography itself, inviting us to recognize that "misremembering" the dead is as much a narrative problem as it is a formal one.

The child Pip, so clearly distinguished from the adult Pip by the narrator's refusal to identify with "the small bundle of shivers growing afraid of it all" who "was Pip," is a narrative resurrection, a long-buried body as poorly conjured by the language of personal history as his parents are by the language of tombstones. Adult Pip, as he tells us in the Blue Boar, is "so changed in the course of nature" that the child Pip would be undiscoverable in him without "accidental help," and yet he is filled "with a dread" at the idea of being recognized (*GE* 229–30)—a dread that he is quick to link to "the *revival* for a few minutes of the terror of childhood," a strangely equivocal phrase that suggests both the revival of childhood fears and the terrifying revival of childhood itself, which he has worked so hard—and so unsuccessfully—to kill off (230; emphasis mine). Pip's self-memorializing narrative might ultimately try to serve an elegiac purpose, working to resurrect and create connections between the multiple versions of himself "that flit around him like revenants," but his dread throughout the text at the repercussions of the resuscitative operations that might be at work upon him makes the epitaph a much safer form for him (Lutz, *Relics* 89). He would much rather use language to reinforce his own deadness than allow someone else to bring him back to life.[18]

Beginning the text in an epitaphic rather than an elegiac mode allows Pip to distinguish between the elegy's consolatory reanimation of the dead and the epitaph's unsettling deanimation of the living: in Debra Fried's words, "the very act of reading an epitaph is almost like a curse, an unfailing omen of the reader's own death" (617). Pip may seem to be revitalizing his parents' bodies by reading their epitaphs, but the obvious foundering of this effort only makes it clearer to us that the young Pip of the graveyard, put "on a high tombstone" by Magwitch a few moments later, is as dead and overwritten in these opening pages as his parents are. The narrative as a whole demands young Pip's death in order for narrator Pip to elegize him back into useful life, but it won't let us forget that this fictional work of elegy can only begin once young Pip has been killed off by the representational violence of epitaphic language. What the epitaphic realism of *Great Expectations*' beginning reveals is not only the failure of language to be mimetically representational, but also the pure fictionality of any retrospective narrative resurrecting the past into whatever its "real" form might have been: a "bundle of shivers" doesn't even come close to a fully fleshed child. Pip may be trying to elegize himself, to keep the world from "misremembering" him after death, but his opening epitaphic gambit tells us to be wary of any language that tries to speak of and for the dead, even if—especially if—it tries to write over the gaps in history where the dead themselves once were.

Pip's reading of his parents' epitaphs may be unreasonable, and epitaphs themselves might be a kind of curse, but as Debra Fried has argued, "to be dead is to be read" (619). Deborah Lutz makes a similar claim about Dickens's investment in reading the dead, arguing that "death might make the loved one more readable (if only slightly), especially if he or she takes on the character of representation" (*Relics* 100). Lutz offers a more redemptive reading than I do of *Great Expectations*' preoccupation with the living dead (and the dead alive), seeing the novel's elegies, epitaphs, and effigies—both of the living and of the dead—as a didactic lesson in the vibrancy and multiplicity of matter, whether living or dead: "stilled material can be stirring, and can stir, even when dead," she writes (101). Her overarching claim about Dickens and other

94 • CHAPTER 2

Victorian writers is that death was more often the origin point of narrative than its endpoint in the nineteenth century. She argues that death makes a life readable: as the body that once enabled a life transforms into an object that instead represents that life, it becomes interpretable in the way text is interpretable, and equally malleable. This possibility—that even as death transforms a once-living subject into a representation susceptible to the readings of others, it also opens that representation to a narrative multiplicity and sustenance that no singular living subject can possess—leads Lutz to label *Great Expectations* "a book of the dead," a designation of what she sees as the novel's ultimately redemptive investment in the necessity of the many selves, many experiences, many endings (quite literally, in the case of this novel's two endings), and many readings of the self by others that ultimately comprise identity (101).

I describe Lutz's argument here because it encapsulates the dream of resuscitative reading that I propose in my introduction, a dream that the scene from *Sketches by Boz* I explore earlier in this chapter fully embraces. But in *Great Expectations,* Pip never quite manages to achieve this kind of redemption, ultimately refusing to give up his desire for narrative mastery and commit to a life constituted through the readings of others. In the novel's final chapter, he explicitly reproduces the epitaphic impulse with which he opens his autobiography, showing us that instead of leading to redemption, the path his narrative takes only leads him (and us) back into the churchyard, the tombstones, and the epitaphs that remain as insistently nonrepresentational as they were when he first introduced them. After years away from the forge, Pip returns and peers through the door of his old home, finding Joe "smoking his pipe in the old place by the kitchen firelight" and, to his surprise, "sitting on my own little stool looking at the fire, was—I again!" (*GE* 481). The child on the stool is, of course, Joe and Biddy's son, also named Pip, but in a direct inversion of the novel's beginning, when Pip can only describe his childhood self as a detached bundle of shivers called Pip, here he sees a child who is most definitely not him and can only call him "I." Again, the language Pip uses to represent "the identity of things" deliberately falters here, revealing an obvious gap between the word "I" and the identity of the person it's meant to describe, just as the first chapter's description of "Pip" opens a chasm between Pip's narrative identity and the child-self he's portraying. Pip's story appears to come full circle here, but rather than demonstrating a kind of narrative redemption in this return to his beginnings (I won't deny him his moral redemption—he's clearly less of an asshole in his middle age than he is in his youth), Pip instead reproduces the very desire to control someone else's story that he has been railing against throughout a novel whose entire purpose has been the desperate reclamation of his own story from the hands of others. "You must give

Pip to me one of these days," he says to Biddy, "or lend him, at all events," a strangely phrased request for a visit that calls to mind both Miss Havisham's twisted desire for "a little girl to rear and love" and Magwitch's crowing triumph that even if he himself can't be a gentleman, at least he's "the owner of such" (481, 400, 321).

If Pip's earlier allusion to *Frankenstein* transformed creator into misshapen creature in order to express his horror at being made, owned, and exhibited by Magwitch, by the end of the novel Pip positions *himself* as the creator of a child, aligned with the novel's other dismaying creators, rhetorically remaking the identity of a boy that doesn't belong to him and quite literally reproducing (if also defanging) Magwitch's terrifyingly epitaphic act of putting little Pip on a tombstone: "And I took him down to the churchyard, and set him on a certain tombstone there, and he showed me from that elevation which stone was sacred to the memory of Philip Pirrip, late of this Parish, and Also Georgiana, Wife of the Above" (481). While there are caveats to be made here—Magwitch turns out to be far from a monster, and this daytime churchyard seems to be cheerfully liberated from its dark, murky place in Pip's nightmares—the novel still returns at its end to its epitaphic beginnings, once again aligning a retreat into epitaphs with a struggle for narrative mastery, once again putting a child on a tombstone in order to reify his role in a story, once again offering us epitaphs as nonrepresentative language rather than as connective tissue to the bodies that lie beneath them. This churchyard scene produces a vertiginous sense that history is repeating itself, that Pip's narrative *needs* history to repeat itself in order to take possession of it. Among these tombstones he has finally found a way to resurrect his dead childhood self into the story he wishes he'd had, and he imagines this reanimated Pip as happy to be the object of someone else's narrative as Magwitch imagined the original Pip was. By putting the new Pip on a tombstone—making him into an epitaph—older Pip erases and overwrites the child's reality as surely as he does his parents' when he conjures their fictional bodies from the words on their tombstones, as surely as Magwitch does Pip's own when, by putting *him* on a tombstone, he catalyzes Pip's transformation from a real boy into a gent ready-made. If in the Blue Boar Pip dreaded someone else bringing his childhood to life, now he exercises the power to do it himself, apparently unconcerned that in doing so he's also making little Pip into something he isn't. Emphasizing the child's attentiveness to Pip's parents' epitaphs only reinforces this work of uncanny narrative resurrection: he wants new Pip to begin at older Pip's beginning, ceding his young voice to the same empty mimetic language that gave old Pip his first, and false, inkling of the identity of things. This, then, is the endpoint of the novel's epitaphic realism and its imbrication in *Frankenstein*'s necromantic story: not a

96 • CHAPTER 2

redemptive surrendering of the self into the manifold continuum between life and death, as Lutz suggests, but instead a benignly brutal act of narrative and rhetorical reanimation, the replacement of a live child with a newly created living dead one, and the clear impossibility of the child on the tombstone ever being Pip's elegy rather than his epitaph.

DICKENS'S ZOMBIE REALISM

As Dickens moves from *Great Expectations* to *Our Mutual Friend,* however, he begins to more fully explore the possibility that death can operate as a space of resistance to social and narrative rigidity, as well as the idea that the representational (i.e., the unreal) nature of the dead can function as an invitation to interpret and read resuscitatively instead of as an injunction to narrate epitaphically. A number of critics have addressed *Our Mutual Friend*'s preoccupations with dead bodies, the porousness of the life/death divide, and the liminal or alternative states that pay allegiance to neither, like suspended animation, reanimation, vitalization, and recycling.[19] Several focus especially (although not solely) on the relationship between death and money in the novel. In Catherine Gallagher's words, "the transmission of life into inorganic matter and thence into money" bespeaks the novel's investment in "put[ting] the human body at the center of economic concerns," in ultimately "separating value from flesh and blood and relocating it in a state of suspended animation or apparent death" ("Bioeconomics" 93, 87, 88). That such relocation is a business of "death commodification," as Claire Wood argues, seems patently clear in the novel's opening scene of river-dredging, in which Gaffer Hexam's reminder to his daughter Lizzie that the river from which they're pulling corpses is her "living" sends her momentarily into a "deadly faint" (133; *OMF* 15). As the dead body they tow behind them takes on an apparent vitality of its own, "lung[ing]" and "wrench[ing]" ("though for the most part. . . . follow[ing] submissively"), the double meaning of the word "living" becomes horrifyingly literal (17). The economic value of the dead thing animates it into sentience at the expense of a girl who can only feel "deadly" at the idea that this rotting corpse should allow her "living."[20] Money is the currency of transformation in this movement from death to life and back again, even if Gaffer's famous rhetorical question—"How can money be a corpse's?" (16)— reveals that while the novel animates the dead as a repository of economic value, money is both the enabler and the limit of the text's metaphoric slippage between the lunging dead and the "living." A corpse can *be* money but it can't *use* money, and "living" can only be a noun when it ceases to be a verb.

Yet the relocation of value that Gallagher identifies in the novel, from flesh and blood to apparent death, isn't only monetary value, and the business these early pages of the novel transact isn't only economic. The text's mobile vacillation between living and dead, reanimation and deanimation, begins an appraisal of representational verisimilitude that anticipates the realist economy through which critics have measured Dickens's literary value for more than a century. George Henry Lewes lays out the evaluative terms in his 1872 essay, "Dickens in Relation to Criticism," when he writes that Dickens's "many cultivated readers and critics" see in Dickens's writing "human character and ordinary events pourtrayed with a mingled verisimilitude and falsity altogether unexampled. The drawing is so vivid yet so incorrect . . . that the doubt arises how an observer so remarkably keen could make observations so remarkably false" (148). A few sentences later, he identifies the nature of this falsity more specifically as representation that feels more mechanical than lifelike: "And the critic is distressed to observe the substitution of mechanisms for minds, puppets for characters . . . if one studies the successful figures one finds even in them only touches of verisimilitude" (148). That Dickens's characters, whether "monstrous failures" or "successful," bear more similarity to toys than to people comes up earlier in the essay as well, when Lewes writes that it "may be said of Dickens's characters that they are too wooden, and run on wheels; but these are details which scarcely disturb the belief of his admirers . . . when they are puppets of a drama every incident of which appeals to the sympathies" (146). Where a critic's evaluative terms identify "falsity" in the distance between Dickensian representation and verisimilitude, an admiring reader's affective experience of the novels finds only emotional truth. Where the "vividness" of Dickensian representation fails in its appeal to our rational minds, it succeeds in engaging our sympathetic imaginations, even if such engagement bears a striking similarity to "being affected, as it were, by [Dickens's] hallucination[s]" (144, 145).

Lewes's essay ostensibly sets out to rescue Dickens from criticism that skirts the affective pleasure his work produces and focuses on his myriad technical "defects" (143)—defects, Lewes freely admits, that emerge at least as much from measuring Dickens's novels "by an academic or conventional standard derived from other works" as from the novels themselves (141)—but he takes protracted pleasure in scrutinizing these defects and readers' willingness to overlook them. Ian Duncan has suggested that while Lewes's tone is "deprecating," this essay nonetheless "recognizes the distinction of Dickens's art from realist aims and techniques" ("Mutual" 295). However, the disparity Lewes identifies between Dickens's apparently hallucinatory-*cum*-puppet-show aesthetic and the realist "precedent" against which critics negatively judge his work doesn't actually free Dickens from the evaluative system of this precedent (141). Lewes only *pretends* to rescue him from it. Instead, Lewes gleefully describes both Dickens's divergence from the apparently organic representational aesthetic of realism[21]—Lewes's substitution of mechanism for mind and puppet for character is a scathing ascription of inorganicism to Dickensian technique[22]—and the ways in which this aesthetic stirs readers' base bodily and emotional instincts rather than their intellects: it produces "revulsion[s] of feeling" and "burst[s] of laughter, . . . whether rational or not," it makes "our pulses quicken," and "we enjoy [the novels] like children at play, laughing and crying at the images that pass before us" (144, 147, 154). These delighted descriptions articulate the terms by which Dickens fails far more clearly than they promote the novel techniques in which he may be succeeding. "Dickens had powers that enabled him to triumph in spite of the weaknesses that clogged them," Lewes writes at the essay's beginning, yet "powers" and "weaknesses" become indistinguishable from one another as the essay unfolds (143). By its end, the novels have far more in common with insane hallucinations, unsophisticated toys, poorly wrought automata, and regressions into overemotional childhood than they do with good novels (novels that display "thought, delicate psychological observation, grace of style, charm of composition"), and Lewes has taken his comfortable place with the same critics he berates for "preferring rather to dwell on [Dickens's] shortcomings and exaggerations" than on his genius (154, 142).

As the essay's conceit of rescuing Dickens from critics who denounce his lack of "technical skill" demonstrates, Lewes is hardly alone in the nineteenth century and beyond in criticizing Dickens's lack of representational verisimilitude.[23] I focus on Lewes's essay at some length, however, because he mobilizes the same porous life/death, animate/inanimate, organic/inorganic imagery for his realist critique that Dickens himself does in *Our Mutual Friend* to push back against the very pre-eminence of realist representation that Lewes celebrates. Lewes doesn't *quite* suggest that Dickens's characters are zombies that we, his hallucinating and overemotional readers, foolishly think are human until they eat our brains and leave us only with our unappetizing childlike feelings. But he does present the realism Dickens fails at as at once an aesthetic of life and of lifelikeness, with little distinction between them. All his machine metaphors, with their wheels and springs and repetitive motions so unlike what we find "in life," insist to us that the problem with Dickens is that no matter how well he manipulates the sympathies and beliefs of his readers, he hasn't the intellectual or technical skill to forge "organic" characters: characters that are somehow both alive and lifelike (146).

The casual synonymy between these two fundamentally different states emerges most fully when Lewes slips from describing Dickens's characters as mechanical puppets to describing them as the twitching dead frogs made famous in Luigi Galvani's late eighteenth-century experiments with electricity, and then back again. When one reads Dickens, Lewes writes, one is "reminded of the frogs whose brains have been taken out for physiological purposes, and whose actions henceforth want the distinctive peculiarity of organic action, that of fluctuating spontaneity" (148–49). The frog's artificially stimulated movements might seem like the movements of a living frog, but they lack the expansive extemporaneity of a creature driven by its own natural needs and desires. Instead, "they are as uniform and calculable as the movements of a machine," and, like Dickens's wooden characters, their lack of organic complexity makes it impossible to "believe them to be like reality" (149).[24] The comparison Lewes offers here suggests that puppets' poor imitations of real people are akin to galvanized dead frogs' poor imitations of life, and while this makes superficial sense on its own, as a combined analogy for Dickens's aesthetic failure it strangely and distortedly conflates the mimetic work of realism (lifelike representation) with its impossible vanishing point (life itself).[25]

As the opening scene of *Our Mutual Friend* shows us, Dickens himself was intensely interested in the ways that language could lurch and wrench this conflation of life and lifelikeness into being, as well as in the possibility that death could be a valuable alternative to both of these lively-ish conditions: Lizzie's "deadly faint" offers a temporary respite from all the filth of the river's "living." Lewes may insist that Dickens is a technical failure because he fails at creating life, but in his final novel Dickens finds far more aesthetic purchase in willfully and wistfully experimenting with ways of being dead than he does in the myriad returns to life that drive the novel's plot. Despite the pretend-happy marital endings that we get in this novel when certain characters come back to life—like John Harmon and Eugene Wrayburn—*Our Mutual Friend* sees far more potential—generic potential and social potential—in being dead than it does in coming to life, or being brought back to life, or tending toward life, or striving toward life at all. Although the novel demonstrates a clear obsession with animating and reanimating characters and things, it just as obsessively resists the restrictions that life—and its attendant and slightly uncanny realist variant, lifelikeness—places on fiction. And it is precisely through the same galvanic metaphor Lewes uses to criticize Dickens's failed realism that Dickens refuses realism as a measure of literary value in the text.

The specter of galvanism haunts the novel. As Lewes's essay suggests (and as I discuss at length in the following chapter on Robert Browning's

The Ring and the Book), galvanism often operated as rhetorical shorthand in the mid-nineteenth century for not-quite-real life: as a metaphor for vitality that *seemed* lifelike but just wasn't quite the same as actual life force. Like Lewes, Dickens borrows galvanism's associations with animation, vitality, and lifelikeness—as well as its inevitable association with deadness—to reflect on the merits and aspirations of realist representation. Yet where Lewes's galvanism is antithetical to realism's organicism, Dickens's galvanism is a perfect analogy for realism's *in*organicism. What Lewes sees as Dickens's aesthetic failure is really a form of immanent critique on Dickens's part, a staged and self-reflexive "failure" to make characters lifelike that critically exposes how flawed a goal lifelikeness is in the first place. Unlike Lewes, for whom galvanism serves as a prime metaphor for Dickens's failure to achieve a truly lifelike realist aesthetic, Dickens uses galvanism as a metaphor for the failure of this realist aesthetic itself.

The remainder of this chapter teases out the galvanic rhetoric that's so loudly *almost* present in *Our Mutual Friend,* in combination with analyzing moments in the novel that privilege a state of being dead over attempts at coming to life. In the interplay between galvanic life and being dead, Dickens writes insistently against the aesthetic expectations of realism's mirroring of "Life and Nature," as Lewes says, and imagines alternatives to the mechanics of social cohesion and domestic telos that are so often realism's primary goals (142). The lull of Lizzie's "deadly faint" in the midst of the grotesquerie of the river's life hints at what being dead might allow characters to escape: not only the novel's cannibalistic economy in which the river's corpses can be "meat and drink" and its morbid developmental logic in which the detritus of its dead becomes the fires, baskets, and cradles of the nursery, but also the tricks of language that can animate even corpses into lifelike characters. "A neophyte might have fancied that the ripples passing over [the corpse] were dreadfully like faint changes of expression on a sightless face," the narrator tells us after describing the body's lunges and wrenches, a description fully indebted to early nineteenth-century galvanic exhibitions in which electrical charges passing through the heads of corpses would produce "horrid grimaces; so that the spectators, who had no suspicion of such a result, were actually frightened" (*OMF* 17; Aldini 71). Like these exhibition spectators, Dickens's "neophyte" might be easily conned into believing that dead things can be brought to life by external forces. The river is a "living," after all, just as "electricity is life," according to 1860s advertisements for galvanic medical devices, but neither Lizzie, whose voice drops from the chapter after her deadly faint, nor her father, who aggressively asserts that the dead belong "t'other world" rather than this one, fall for such sleights of hand (16).

Although Lewes accuses Dickens's adoring fans of being drawn so deeply into Dickens's hallucinatory imagination that they mistake a brainless electrified frog for a living creature, Dickens clearly identifies such "neophyte" readers as *mis*readers, fooled into believing that galvanic fancies are the equivalent of real life. Gaffer, the narrator tells us in the last sentence of chapter 1, "was no neophyte and had no fancies" (*OMF* 17). This opening chapter ends not with the uncanny image of a lifelike corpse that has come to be the novel's most emblematic figure but with an omniscient dismissal both of its lifelikeness and of readers who can't tell the fancies of lifelikeness from the fact of life. The novel is full of "incapable" readers who read "mechanically," having the ability neither to "locate nor convey the Life in the text" they read, but this opening salvo explicitly attacks the sort of reader who *believes* in the life that a text fictionally creates, who mistakes the representation of real life for life itself (Gallagher, "Bioeconomics" 112). As Freedgood has argued, the nineteenth-century "realistic novel creates an open circuit between fictionality and factuality," allowing readers to move freely between belief in the worlds that novels create through their references to recognizable truths and a suspension of such belief when these truths get unpleasant ("Fictional" 408). As Dickens suggests in his critique of "neophyte[s]," however, it is precisely realism's willful coupling of fictionality with factuality that produces bad readers (and perhaps bad writers) who make no distinction between life and meager lifelikeness, and who can't recognize the artifice of a novelist's language as mere waves—aquatic or electric—manipulating the faces of dead men.

GALVANIC FICTIONS AND BEING DEAD

Dickens specifically uses the word *galvanic* as a fuzzy, maybe even incoherent, metaphor for the fantasy of lifelikeness, and for the slippage between life and lifelikeness, that both characters and readers seek in realist fiction. In contrast to this galvanic artifice—both aesthetic and social—of realist lifelikeness, Dickens presents being dead in the novel as a liberating, communal condition outside of the economic, gendered, and generic systems and limitations of realism's insistence on characters coming to life. Unlike other Victorian writers—like Lewes, Robert Browning, Carlyle, and even Dickens himself in some of his earlier novels[26]—who present "galvanic" life in opposition to "real" life, Dickens's slippery galvanic metaphors in *Our Mutual Friend* present these two kinds of life nearly indistinguishable from one another. In this novel, being dead is the only emancipatory alternative to life, galvanic, "real," or both. Although Dickens doesn't use the word *galvanic* often in the novel,

102 • CHAPTER 2

his usage is weighted with galvanism's long history of not-quite-real-life: the history of miraculous science, of quackery, of horror, of hope, and of farce that I describe in the "Galvanic History" section of my introduction. Although by the 1870s several British and American writers, including Edward Bulwer Lytton, were writing utopian novels about the heights to which society could rise if it learned to tap electricity's forces within and without the body to their highest potential, the middle decades of the century with their dubious galvanic chains, suspect electric cookers, and dreadful "galvanized Dilettant[es]" had a more fraught sense of the ways in which electricity could and should be marshaled in material, therapeutic, and rhetorical forms (Carlyle, *Past* 65).[27] Whether using galvanism as a positive metaphor for aesthetic power, as I argue in the next chapter Browning does, or as a negative metaphor for historiographical and cultural failure, as Carlyle does, early to mid-nineteenth-century writers' turns to the rhetoric of galvanism brought scientific debates about the differences between life and electrified "lifelikeness" to bear on literary forms and aesthetic judgments. To metaphorize art as electricity was simultaneously to embody and disembody vitality, to both naturalize and denaturalize the association between character and reality, to foreground the ways that "life" might be manipulated and instrumentalized in potentially grotesque as well as potentially spectacular ways.

How real was the realist writer's power to make—or failure to make—living beings out of things, be they bits of bodies, rags of paper, or scraps of language? In *Our Mutual Friend*, Dickens tests the rhetorical value of thinking about his fictional project in the terms of galvanic electricity: in terms, that is, of uncanny imitation, of nearly lifelikeness, of material into which an animating principle artificially introduced wakes to seemingly recognizable life. Galvanism is briefly mentioned, and more often loudly unspoken in the novel—there and not there, present in concept even when the words aren't explicitly used. Galvanic animation for Carlyle makes for bad history, because it falls short of true life; galvanic animation for Browning makes for good poetry, for the exact same reason. But galvanic animation for Dickens is the path of realism not taken, because it is *too close* to true life. Galvanism, both spoken and unspoken in the novel, implies a vocabulary of imitative life to which Dickens seeks an alternative. Reanimation is always galvanic in this novel, even when Dickens doesn't use the word *galvanism,* and it's always bad, despite reanimation seeming to be the novel's primary desire. The only possible end for galvanic reanimation is the reinforcement of deeply disturbing, and deeply conventional, marital and familial bonds: as Bella says to her father when she tells him that Rokesmith has proposed to her, "[This] will electrify you" (*OMF* 453). The parts of the novel in which coming to life becomes a galvanic process are the very places in the novel where life becomes a restrictive aesthetic mode. The haunting galvanic presence in *Our Mutual Friend* makes life, and the return to life, a suspect formal and domestic phenomenon in the novel.

There are only two explicit mentions of galvanism in *Our Mutual Friend.* Dickens compares the eight volumes of Gibbon's *Decline and Fall of the Roman Empire*, "ranged flat, in a row," on a table in Boffin's Bower, to a "galvanic battery," and he describes a melancholy Twemlow, lonely because he has no "Adorable" to keep him company, dropping asleep and having "galvanic starts all over him" (*OMF* 62, 122). My edition of the novel footnotes the latter of these, saying, "'Galvanism' was an important metaphor, much brandished by Carlyle, for forms of 'inhuman' vitality, dead flesh made to twitch" (811). This is certainly accurate, as I show in my introduction's discussion of Carlyle, but it's also noticeable that Twemlow's restless sleeping doesn't seem to be a moment in which this metaphor is particularly applicable. Are we supposed to understand from this description that Twemlow is somehow inhuman, or that his restlessness is unnatural? Or that the fictions about his "Adorable" that he's imagining to be true, and that are disturbing his sleep, are in fact nothing more than artificial stimulations? This latter may be true, but it requires some interpretive gymnastics to imagine that labeling his starts "galvanic" tells us anything more about the pathetic fictionality of his longings than the narration itself already does, with all of its parenthetical contradictions of poor Twemlow's notions: "and he thinks the adorable bridesmaid is like the fancy as she was then (which she is not at all), and that if the fancy had . . . married him for love, he and she would have been happy (which they wouldn't have been)," and so on (*OMF* 121–22). If galvanism is meant to be a metaphor for artificiality in this instance it doesn't accomplish much, except that the metaphor in combination with the narrator's clear skepticism reveals how entirely galvanism and skepticism are entwined with one another. In describing Twemlow's agitation as "galvanic," Dickens forces his readers to imagine the poor man being jolted with electric wires, maybe to associate his disturbed "starts" with macabre memories of Aldini's electrified and twitching corpses. But—and this is an important but—this association makes no sense in the context of this passage. The "important metaphor" to which the footnote directs us reveals nothing about Twemlow or his fantasy life.

The word *galvanic* here provides us a superficial visual image—we can all close our eyes and imagine Twemlow twitching in agitated sleep—but the *metaphor* of galvanism and the allusion to Carlyle embedded in the visual image of a "galvanic start" is more complicated than that. It leads us to seek certain kinds of meaning in the passage that aren't there. It draws attention to

104 • CHAPTER 2

itself *as a metaphor*, and to its insufficiency and incoherence as a metaphor. Twemlow—who, the novel's end confirms, is one of the few characters in the novel that actually has a living, human soul—suffers galvanic starts when he dreams a fiction for himself that the narrator insists never had a chance at being real. The galvanism doesn't jolt him back to reality but rather suggests that he's fallen into an uncomfortable, dreamy belief in his fiction. If anything, what the word *galvanic* suggests in this moment is that galvanism in the novel metaphorizes *not* artificial life, as it does for Carlyle, but an inability to distinguish *between* artifice and reality. Galvanism here is a metaphor not for zombie realism but for quack figuration, for our willingness to believe in the efficacy of fictional language to create something real.

The word *galvanic* is a kind of quackery in both of its instances in the novel, not only failing to provide metaphoric legibility but also testing our credulity about the power of art to enable any sort of genuine life. The other use of *galvanic* occurs, as I said, when Dickens compares the volumes of *Decline and Fall* that Boffin has "ranged flat in a row" to a "galvanic battery." This is an easy simile to just skip over, but if you stop on it, it's a deeply weird visual comparison. How could these books possibly look like a galvanic battery? A galvanic battery looks like two cups of water with metal rods sticking out of them, connected to each other by a wire and a salty piece of paper. Even a voltaic battery, if Dickens got his batteries mixed up, looks like a vertical pile of metallic discs, and it demands an awkward kind of mental contortion to visualize in relation to these books. Maybe Dickens was imagining some earlier version of a Boyd's battery, with its flat metal discs arranged in a row instead of in a circle? I'm not entirely sure that such a thing even existed. But whether this simile invokes a real, cure-all quack battery or just a set of rhetorical associations with artificial vitality, once again the comparison draws attention to its own insufficiency, even as it brings galvanism into the novel as a figure for the belief in fictional vitality. Mr. Boffin imagines that these galvanic books will help "begin to lead [him] a new life," and Mrs. Boffin hopes they will "do you both [Boffin and Wegg] good" (60, 62). In describing this most famous of histories as a galvanic battery, Dickens here—far more than when he describes Twemlow's twitchy sleep as galvanic—presents galvanism as a nodal point of vitality, artificiality, and artistic practice: the chance for "a new life" that we know the books won't actually provide. Gibbon's *Decline and Fall* exemplifies exactly the kind of history that Carlyle had in mind when he lamented the "dead ashes, wreck and burnt bone" that "assiduous Pedantry" has dug up from the past and labeled History—no life to be found there (*Past* 46). While Carlyle often praised Gibbon's talent, he also found Gibbon's desire for objectivity and his meticulous references endlessly tedious.[28] Dickens describes as a galvanic battery precisely the kind of history that Carlyle would label galvanic rather than alive (if he didn't just call it a dead wreck): a history that strives to be as true to its sources and as objectively real as possible but that (for Carlyle at least), in striving to be objectively true, in choosing fidelity over aesthetic energy, falls short of actual life.

But Dickens doesn't exactly describe *Decline and Fall* as possessing galvanic energy. Instead he describes it as a battery, meant to provide galvanic energy to its recipients: in this case, jolting Mr. Boffin into his new life. And the novel makes no bones about the absurdity of this proposition. Between Boffin's misrecognizing "Roman" as "Rooshan" and Wegg's "wooden conceit" in body, reading style, and comprehension of the text, the novel dismisses any synonymy between reading and bringing a text or a person to life (*OMF* 64). Gallagher's argument that the novel's "incapable readers can neither locate nor convey the Life in any text" suggests that a text might still be a storage vessel for a life force, even if readers can't find it ("Bioeconomics" 112). But what if there isn't any life force stored in a text at all? Comparing *Decline and Fall* to a galvanic battery both presents and resists the idea that a text has life, or the idea that we should think about a text in those terms at all. A text may *seem* to be full of life waiting to rejuvenate its readers, but whatever energy a text has is, at best, only an imitation of life. And even that imitation—if Boyd's batteries are any indication—might be nothing more than ineffective quackery. Our desire to find lives, or "new life," in texts, our willingness to believe that life is what a text will show us or that life is what a text will give us (as Mr. Boffin wanted)—this desire makes us gullible fools.

In the cases of both Twemlow's uneasy rest and *The Decline and Fall,* galvanism becomes, if it becomes anything at all, a metaphor for the *belief* in artifice, for the willful misconstrual of fiction for life. In these minor, easily forgettable uses of the word *galvanic,* Dickens presents galvanism as the ultimate, fallacious dream of what realist fiction is supposed to accomplish. Galvanism is shorthand for the fantasy that fake life can be indistinguishable from real life, the fantasy that the gap between representation and reality can be erased. Galvanic energy is artificial vitality that *looks like real life.* As Dickens presents it in these two brief references, galvanism as an aesthetic metaphor is an acknowledgment of mimetic desire, desire that the novel in these moments, and at large, refuses to endorse. Dickens drops the word *galvanic* into the text in these minor but scathing moments so we have it in the back of our minds. Without explicitly labeling the novel's many reanimated lives galvanic fictions or predicating the narrative form of the novel as a whole on the production of an inauthentic life (as he does in *Great Expectations*), Dickens's crackling galvanism in *Our Mutual Friend*'s margins nonetheless makes palpable the fictionality of the lives unfolding in its main plot.

Our Mutual Friend wants its characters to stay dead. Or to be dead. Or to die again. This impulse toward death is a liberatory impulse, and different from the "suspended animation" that Gallagher and others have described as the novel's primary obsession.[29] These critics focus on the text's investments in the potentiality of the lingering state between life and death: disembodied vitality possesses energy, value, and meaning not yet expended or circumscribed, and thus it is endlessly useful, desirable, redeeming and redeemable. As Nicholas Royle has argued, "This novel is about living on, not as the triumph of continuing to live but as a movement of return or haunting which comes back, folds back from the beginning on what one might have wanted to call 'life' itself. There is . . . only the spectral elusiveness of living on" (49). "Living on," "death-in-life," "life-in-abeyance," "suspended animation": while indicating a state of not-quite-aliveness, these familiar characterizations nonetheless privilege life in the novel, or at least the striving toward life, over death. They may hover somewhere in the middle of the life–death continuum, but they face in the direction of life, and expect that life, or life again, will be the eventual outcome of the inevitably temporary state of suspended animation that so many characters in the novel experience. But what *Our Mutual Friend* suggests over and over again is that "life," in a novel, is a set of binding restrictions, a state of sheer artifice, a reduction of imaginative possibility. And god help these poor characters, all they want is to be allowed to be dead. How many times in the novel does a character make this express wish? From Jenny Wren's call to "Come up and be dead," to John Harmon's declaration that he "shall come back no more," to Rogue Riderhood's instinctive unwillingness, "like us all, every day of our lives, . . . to be restored to the consciousness of this existence," to Eugene's insistence to Lizzie that he "ought to die," "being dead" in this novel (an active condition diametrically opposed to the inactive state of "life-in-abeyance"[30]) seems like a nonconsummation devoutly to be wished (*OMF* 280, 367, 440, 735).

There are two particular scenes in the novel that dangle the prospect of "being dead" in front of us. One is the scene of Jenny inviting Riah to "come up and be dead" on the rooftop of Pubsey and Co., and the other is Rogue Riderhood's near-drowning scene. The Jenny Wren scene presents being dead in all of its utopian possibility, but I'll focus first on the Rogue Riderhood scene, even though it comes later in the novel. This scene, with its primary focus on "life-in-abeyance" rather than on actually being dead, reveals the inevitable failure of imaginative possibility that inheres in the striving toward life that the term *life-in-abeyance* (and the scene as a whole) implies. This is a scene of literal reanimation, one in which galvanic energy is writ large, if invisibly. Its lyrical musing on the disembodied spark of life is tied inextricably to the potential for modernity (whether in the form of medical science, technology, or even Dickens's narrator) to artificially maintain, return, or reproduce life. By contrast, the Jenny scene hovers quite literally above the realm of modernity, away from human action, beyond the desire for life. The respite it provides from the novel's constant need to reanimate its dead offers a brief glimpse of alternative narrative and social possibilities free from the telos, and the aesthetic demands, of coming to life, even if its brevity and earliness in the novel suggest that such respites will always give way to the galvanic lifelikeness that drives the novel's plot.

The Riderhood scene's interest in "sparks" of life, its mention that "all the best means are at once in action" to work on Riderhood, and the doctor's use of "this or that" apparatus to try to resuscitate him show that this is the place in the novel where the idea of galvanic animation has its most palpable presence, both literally and figuratively (*OMF* 439, 440, 442, 439, 441). In many newspaper reports of drownings and near-drownings in the mid-nineteenth century, articles refer to specific ways that doctors attempt to restore animation to seemingly lifeless bodies, and galvanism is often mentioned, if not always used. For instance, according to one article about an accidental drowning in Cambridge: "Every means were taken to achieve resuscitation, but without effect . . . artificial inhalation was attempted. Galvanic apparatus was sent for, but could not be procured" ("Lamentable Accident" 10). The lack of proper galvanic equipment at the time of this accident was met with outrage: "If a galvanic apparatus be an important aid in restoring animation, it ought not to have been wanting at the critical moment," a letter to the editor says with regard to the incident ("Few Occurrences" 8). Galvanic devices were a regular part of the apparatus of reanimating the drowned, as this report of an inquest suggests by its surprise at how poorly galvanism worked in the instance it investigates: "It was a remarkable circumstance that not the least of any of the *usual* symptoms produced by galvanism upon persons after being even a quarter of an hour or 20 minutes in the water could be produced in this case, showing that Captain Harrison must have been under the water several minutes, and perfectly suffocated, or had died from apoplexy" ("Inquest" 10).

Whether or not we're meant to assume that galvanism is one of the tools that brings Riderhood back to life, this scene operates in the realm of galvanism and galvanic metaphor, fetishizing the idea of "life" itself, that sparky, magical, disembodied force, but disgusted by the body that has life in it. The "spark of life" out and about in the world enables a nearly mystical utopian

108 • CHAPTER 2

fellowship to form within the gritty spaces of the Six Jolly Fellowship Porters pub: "everybody present lends a hand, and a heart and soul," not to Riderhood but to the spark of life that's now outside of Riderhood, precisely *because* it's now "curiously separable" from the man (*OMF* 439). In his unwillingness to be restored to consciousness, to reunite spark with body, Riderhood is, briefly, the narrator tells us, "like us all," part of a fellowship of feeling from which he is usually banished.

In this extended moment of suspended animation, of life-in-abeyance, enmities, social roles, and familial dynamics break down into a communal effort to keep life from slipping away. There's a moment of ecstatic possibility here, for life to be detached from gritty reality, from lifelikeness, and for relationships to therefore come into being across and beyond the categories that reality usually dictates. But this collective desire to preserve life can't be detached from the desire to bring Riderhood *back* to life: we see the paradox of Victorian electricity at work here, glorious as a force in and of itself, corrupt and spiritually vacuous when embodied. These two desires, for life and for reanimation, are inextricable from one another in this scene. Disembodied life is a temporary state of being. Either it finds a body again, or it vanishes, and thus the possibility for utopian fellowship forged around the fascination with disembodied life is also inevitably temporary. However much the language of this scene revels in suspended animation, the action of the scene has a definite narrative objective. Its aim is to reanimate Riderhood, and reanimate Riderhood it does, explicitly showing the dissolution of the communal soul as the life around which it formed once again takes root inside Riderhood's body. Just as both the medical apparatus and the obsession with life in this scene lead inevitably to reanimation, so too does the lyrical dream of a fellowship forged around a desire for life inevitably dissolve upon Riderhood's waking up and living. Fellowship, it seems, as John Harmon suggests when he tells us that "dead, I have discovered the true friends of my lifetime," flourishes much better among the dead than among the living (367).

Being dead allows characters to opt out of the systems, the desires, and the relationships that form and constrain realist plots. It allows them to escape narration and to adopt the position of omniscient narrator, instead. Jenny Wren's description of being dead on the rooftop of Pubsey and Co. emphasizes its freedom from the restrictions of everyday experience, freedom from the ways in which geographies of the city and rehearsed human interactions and modes of survival dictate the forms that living must take. As one of Dickens's reviewers wrote, "we are almost oppressed by the fulness of life which pervades the pages of this novel," and Jenny seems to share this feeling of the oppression of life from which being dead frees her.[31] "You see the clouds rushing on above the narrow streets, not minding them. . . . And you hear the people who are alive, crying, and working, and calling to one another down in the close dark streets, and you seem to pity them so! And such a chain has fallen from you, and such a strange good sorrowful happiness comes upon you!" Jenny says (279). Life requires one to be fettered by necessities of living, just as lifelikeness, according to another of Dickens's reviewers, is bound by "the hindrances and incongruities which in actual life would be so likely to hang about [ideal human nature] and cramp its actions" (Stott 207). Dickens, this reviewer argues, with his "minuteness and elaborateness of detail," his scenes "in places familiar to everyone," and his apparent desire to "reproduce that which *is* as nearly *as* it is possible," makes it seem as though he aspires to *vraisemblance*, to realism—but "the realism is illusory," the reviewer tells us, and what Dickens really puts before us is "a state of things quite inconsistent with fact" (208, 207).

As "a state of things quite inconsistent with fact," "being dead" is the condition the novel offers as most profoundly antithetical to the *vraisemblance*, the lifelike aims, of realism. As Diana Fuss writes in *Dying Modern*, the idea of "being dead" is a "powerful oxymoron," stretching "the limits of ontology beyond the point of reason," and this brief rooftop interlude, set high above the crowded, constraining streets of the city, acts as more than just an idealized moment of escapist urban fantasy for the characters involved (45). It's also a moment of generic fantasy, what Elisha Cohn would call an atemporal "lyrical moment," described initially like a still life painting, later as a vision, and as a whole outside of the progress of plot, romance, economics, and domesticity that comprise the realist novel's "narratives of struggle or failure" (5). It is "a rest," as Jenny calls it, from lifelikeness: a moment of suspended animation, technically, but only in the sense of "animation" as rote, mechanized, galvanic movement (*OMF* 279). Being dead doesn't demand movement. It has no aims, no beginning or end. To *be*, without having to live, means that you can just *be* anything at all.

Gallagher has suggested that the "power of suspension" in the novel is "given only to men"—by which she means that the "state of suspended animation" and the ability "to be retrieved from apparent death" are "exclusively masculine in *Our Mutual Friend*," because the ability to control value in the text is an exclusively masculine privilege ("Bioeconomics" 115–16). But the power to be dead, without the onus of having to return to life—the ability to occupy a state of fact-defying, ontological confusion without agonistic debate about its value and permanence à la John Harmon—in this scene is rendered an exclusively female privilege, and one that liberates femininity from the constraints of genre as much as it liberates genre itself from the demands of

110 • CHAPTER 2

gender constraint. Jenny herself embodies ontological uncertainty. To borrow from Hilary Schor, Jenny is "a sign for Dickens's fiction because she is a sign for social fact, [but also] because she is linked to all sorts of 'fancies' in the novel" (198–99). She's certainly feminine, but her femininity is deliberately unmoored from singular identity: she is described as "a child—a dwarf—a girl—a something," a "whatever it is," a "Miss What-is-it" (*OMF* 222, 228, 278).[32] Although her "fancies" often follow the outlines of domestic reality—they're fancies of friendship, of courtship, of marriage, of motherhood, of punishment or retribution for misbehaving children or traitorous "friends"—they illuminate the conventions of these socially cohesive strictures instead of enmeshing her within them. Jenny's imagination and her status as "a whatever," "a something," a liminal figure, exempt her from her own neatly vacuous happy ending, even if they also make her a privileged conduit for the vacuous happy endings of others. It's her liminality, the narrator tells us, that allows her to know that the climactic word Eugene Wrayburn can't seem to say as he's lying on his deathbed is "wife" (720, 722).

Yet if Jenny's liminality is a conduit for marital bliss, it's equally a conduit for other potential forms of blissier bliss, and the rooftop scene presents an idealized moment of feminine fellowship unmoored from static gender roles and from the systems of exchange that dominate the novel's twin poles of economics and marriage. Jenny, the "whatever," Lizzie, the "female waterman," and Mr. Riah, the "godmother"—these are the characters who can be dead, characters whose very identities resist the restrictions of gender and lifelikeness alike, and whose communal state of being dead excludes anyone, like Mr. Fledgeby, who tries to write them back into a narrative of exchange. "*You* are not dead," Jenny tells Fledgeby, ordering him to "Get down to life" after he tries to inquire about Lizzie's business. "'And you,' said Fledgeby, turning to the other visitor, 'do you buy anything here, miss?' 'No, sir.' 'Nor sell anything here, miss?' 'No sir.' Looking askew at the questioner, Jenny stole her hand up to her friend's, and drew her friend down, so that she bent beside her on her knee. 'We are thankful to come here for rest, sir,' said Jenny" (278–79). Jenny's motions here physically draw Lizzie out of a conversation about buying and selling and into a space of "rest" that is also a space of female intimacy. In doing so, she creates a synonymy between "being dead" as an escape from the constraints of everyday life and "being dead" as a state of utopian community—female utopian community, specifically.

Henry James, in his dreadful review of *Our Mutual Friend*, insisted that "every character here put before us is a mere bundle of eccentricities, animated by no principle of nature whatever," and that "a community of eccentrics is impossible" (787). But it's precisely Jenny's resistance to an animating principle—to the novel's galvanic impetus to bring everything to life—that enables this "impossible," intimate community, in all of its utopian queerness, to have space in a novel that's determined to force everyone into marriages, families, and conspiratorial domestic arrangements.

Jenny, Lizzie, and Riah obviously can't be dead on the rooftop forever. The plot continues, and they're in it. But they also don't get narrated back to life: this chapter ends instead with Jenny's call to come up and be dead. And in this narrative respite, not only from the constraints of the everyday but also from the novel's compulsive desire to reanimate its dead into domestic role-playing, Dickens suggests that being dead might just be the only life worth living.

CHAPTER 3

Robert Browning's Necropoetics

The same galvanic lifelikeness that Dickens's final completed novel finds so suspect and so coercively antithetical to the liberating possibilities of being dead, Robert Browning sees as the miraculous power of poetry to produce aesthetic artifice free from the constraints of historical fact, objectivity, and authenticity. When Browning published his 1868–69 book-length "murder poem," *The Ring and the Book,* his reputation as a poet "with special gifts of intellect and originality" that were at the same time put in the service of a poetics of great "crudity" and "jolting violence" seemed once again confirmed (review, *Times* 4).[1] "I felt . . . like a creature with one leg and one wing, half hopping, half flying," Browning's friend William Allingham told Thomas Carlyle after reading the poem's first volume, while others characterized the poem as "incongruous materials" incapable of forming a "harmonious whole," or as simultaneously "life-like" and a "morbid anatomy" (Allingham 207–8; review, *St. Paul's* 397; review, *Fortnightly* 125).[2] These friends and reviewers, torn as they were between awe at the poem's intellectual ambition and disgust at its aesthetic execution, envisioned their ambivalence as states of bodily transformation, and incomplete states at that: halfway from legs to wings, from parts to a whole, from life to death. Without acknowledging directly the grotesque corporeality so prevalent in many of Browning's most well-known dramatic monologues, these readers nonetheless see the almost-changed body as a metaphor for Browning's poetic strangeness. This strangeness was characterized by the formal tension, as Carlyle would have it, between "an Old Bailey story that might have been told in ten lines" and a long dramatic monologue, or as Browning himself wrote in his "Essay on Shelley," between poetry that "reproduces things external" and poetry that is the "radiance and aroma of [the poet's] personality" (qtd. in D. Rossetti, *Letters* 284; "Essay" 1243, 1244).[3]

In Browning's dramatic monologues, as in the responses above, the changing body—specifically, in the monologues, the once-dead body, the almost-alive-again body—is a locus for aesthetic experimentation that both critiques poetry's inevitably subjective relationship to facts (historical facts, observable facts, and the facts of literary influence) and uses that relationship as the basis for generic innovation. The reanimated body, whether appearing in poems like *The Ring and the Book* or in shorter dramatic monologues like "Porphyria's Lover" and "My Last Duchess," becomes a figure through which Browning considers the fraught relationship between unassailable historical materiality and original aesthetic practice: between the dictates of what has come before and the desire to create something new out of it. Functioning as critical and always-ironic foils to the multiple projects of aesthetic resurrection spread across the nineteenth century—nationalist cultural revivals in England, Scotland, and Ireland, the vogue for exhibiting relics and recreating ancient tombs (and the responsive museum poetry that I discuss in chapter 4), and spirit photography and other ghostly technologies, among them[4]—the dramatic monologues I examine in this chapter are both about reanimating the dead and acts of reanimation themselves. While critics have argued that we can see the dramatic monologue as "a form of verbal resuscitation of the dead, a quasi-Spiritualist voicing of dead men and women," and Victorian reviewers especially found in Tennyson's dramatic monologues "the secret of the transmigration of the soul," dramatic monologues in which the dead come to life call our attention to the limits of the poet's reanimating power (Faas 29). They expose the inherent subjectivity of any resuscitative poetic project, the fictive and necessarily inventive nature of aesthetic resuscitation. Nothing can come back from the dead unless the poet reanimates it, and such regeneration, as Viktoria Tchernichova argues, requires the poet to be "daringly inventive beyond the facts of his material" (113). Browning uses his dramatic monologues to draw an analogy between corporeal reanimation and poetic practice, and in doing so he probes, critiques, and reinvents the process by which new, "living" poetry can emerge from the intransigent bodies of the past.[5] His necropoetic form brings long-dead voices back to life, but not with the expectation that his monologists will speak truth. Rather, as Diana Fuss argues about corpse poems more generally, giving poetic voice to the dead makes "present a certain kind of absence," revaluing the deadness of the dead

114 • CHAPTER 3

(71). For Browning, the emphatic and inalterable fact of his speakers' deaths creates the condition necessary to scrutinize and to relish the imaginative truths his own poetics of aesthetic resurrection can reveal.

REANIMATING ELIZABETH

A twelve-book magnum opus, *The Ring and the Book* opens as the poet insists that his work is to "resuscitate" rather than to "create," to "start the dead alive" but not to "make" out of nothing as God can make (*RB* 1.719, 1.713, 1.733).[6] The poem, which uses a series of dramatic monologues in blank verse to recount the story of a seventeenth-century murder, trial, and execution, conceives poetry's relationship to history as an effort of reanimation. As the poem recasts this relationship in turn as the relationship between the living and the dead, between modern innovation and old forms, and between art and facts, the notion that poetry can do as much—but only just as much—as reanimating the dead becomes a way for Browning to theorize an imaginative modern poetics that remembers, but refuses to be bound by, the past: a modern poetics, lodged in the ironically resuscitative form of the dramatic monologue, that I'm calling *necropoetics*.[7] The "past," in *The Ring and the Book,* is threefold. It's Browning's conjugal past, incarnate in the poetic influence of his much-beloved dead wife. It's the literary past, manifest in the subjective poetics of the Shelleyan Romanticism with which the poem engages. And it's the past as nineteenth-century historians such as Michelet and Carlyle conceived it, resuscitated from historical facts into the vibrant testimony that forms *The Ring and the Book*'s structure.[8] By reanimating—rather than imitating, rejecting, or worshiping—these three embodiments of the past, Browning develops a necropoetic aesthetic that reflects upon and denaturalizes the connection between memory and creativity, between inheriting the dead and generating something lifelike. The task of the poet, as the poet-narrator of *The Ring and the Book* describes it in book 1, is to "enter, spark-like, put old powers to play, / Push out lines to the limit" (1.755–56). Poetry will emerge from the active fusion of the poet's orchestrating anima and the dead forms to which he has access. Rather than proposing a treatise of radical formal change, *The Ring and the Book* offers a galvanic theory of innovation (old body, new spark) in which poetry will always be a memorial project, both abolishing and obsessively remembering the dead in the resuscitative act of pushing old formal lines to new limits.

Adam Roberts has called *The Ring and the Book* "a poem explicitly figured as a séance," but one whose ultimate presiding spirit is the dead Elizabeth Barrett Browning rather than the dead seventeenth-century Florentines whose voices Browning resurrects: a poem both haunted by and incessantly mourning Browning's lost muse, a poem whose repeated "necromantic act" of giving voice to the dead constitutes Browning's limitless "gift to Elizabeth Barrett" (113, 121).[9] Indeed, the poem in some ways clearly memorializes Elizabeth.[10] The ring of its title belongs to her, she is the Muse to whom the poet addresses himself in the first and last books, and the tale of the murdered Pompilia, trapped in a smothering, deathlike marriage, clearly echoes Elizabeth's own memory of being trapped in her father's house before her elopement with Robert. As she told her friend Mrs. Martin, she looked "more dead than alive" on her wedding day, recalling her "morbid and desolate" years on Wimpole Street with "the sort of horror with which one would look to one's graveclothes, if one had been clothed in them by mistake during a trance" (*Correspondence* 14.35, 14.30).[11] "I was buried, and that was the whole," she wrote of her old life once she had escaped it (14.30).

Yet while Elizabeth may be the poem's presiding muse, she is only obliquely its chief object of mourning, and it is her absence, not her memory, that guides Browning's aesthetic choices. Just as the necropoetic art of Browning's dramatic monologues needs the deaths of its subjects, so too does the evolution of *The Ring and the Book* need the death of Elizabeth. Browning recognized *The Ring and the Book,* in part, as a monument to his isolation. His gripes about having to write the poem without help metaphorically dwell on Elizabeth's absence by explicitly recalling the language Browning used in his courtship letters to describe Elizabeth's muse-like role in his creative process. In 1862 Browning complained to his close friend Isa Blagden, who helped transcribe *Men and Women,* that he must "begin on [his] murder case" without her help as his amanuensis, repeating this line seven years later as a lament about solitude to another close friend, Julia Wedgwood, in response to her harsh criticism of *The Ring and the Book* (*DI* 134). "[I] pray you to observe that it has been a particularly weary business to write this whole long work by my dear self," Browning wrote, "I who used always to be helped by an amanuensis—for, I cannot clearly see what is done, or undone, so long as it is thru' the medium of my own hand-writing" (*RB and JW* 162). By "amanuensis" he refers here to Isa rather than to Elizabeth, but these frustrated words bleakly and directly echo the words Browning once lovingly wrote to his not-yet-wife: "And dearest, I mean to take your advice and be quiet awhile and let my mind get used to its new medium of sight—, seeing all things, as it does, thro' you: and then, let all I have done be the prelude and the real work begin" (*Correspondence* 11.70).[12] Over their sixteen-year courtship and marriage, Elizabeth's sensibility had come to be the metaphorical handwriting through which

Browning viewed his poetic project, but work on *The Ring and the Book*, in which Browning associated the sight of his own handwriting with his "weary" solitude, came to be marked by the dearth of this sensibility. The absent Elizabeth becomes the raison d'être for the obfuscating and deferred conditions of writing, so thematically prevalent in the text of *The Ring and the Book* itself, to which Browning alludes when he writes that he "cannot clearly see what is done, or undone, so long as it is thru' the medium of [his] own handwriting."

Even more concretely, Elizabeth, who *was* alive when Browning found the "Old Yellow Book" that would provide the "crude facts" of *The Ring and the Book,* was appalled by the contents of the book and indifferent to its creative possibilities. The book, full of testimony and details from Count Guido Franceschini's trial and execution for the murder of his child-bride Pompilia, fascinated Browning, yet as he admitted once to Wedgwood, "[my wife] never took the least interest in the story, so much as to wish to inspect the papers. It seems better so to me, but *is* it better?" (*RB and JW* 154). In the words of one of Browning's biographers, "Elizabeth took an instant dislike to the whole business. She was repelled by the sordidness of the tale and refused even to leaf through the papers. Bowing to the judgment of his flesh-and-blood Muse, Browning put aside his own ambitions for the Old Yellow Book" (Neville-Sington 97). Browning could bring *The Ring and the Book* into being only when Elizabeth was no longer there to stop him. When Browning finally returned to the Old Yellow Book, years after finding it, and produced what he clearly believed to be his magnum opus, Julia Wedgwood's first response to the poem is to see it as a poem determined—and fundamentally flawed—by Elizabeth's absence. In one 1868 letter she writes, "Do you remember once saying to me that your Wife was quite wanting in—I am not sure of the exact words, but the sense was, the scientific interest in evil?—I think you said, the physiology of wrong. I feel as if that interest were in you unduly predominant" (*RB and JW* 137). In another, more succinctly, "I felt as if I were reading what you had lost in your wife" (150). This comment is oddly phrased, for what Browning lost in his wife certainly wasn't a love for the grotesque. As Elizabeth wrote, she watched with "horror" the "ghastly" funeral processions that Browning so loved to watch, and was disgusted when he brought home a human skeleton and started gleefully disarticulating its bones.[13] "My wife would have subscribed to every one of your bad opinions of the book," Browning replied resignedly to Wedgwood, recognizing that Elizabeth had never shared his interest in what he called "morbid cases" (*RB to JW* 154, 143).

As these exchanges between Browning and Wedgwood demonstrate, by the time Browning had completed writing *The Ring and the Book,* he had recognized that his masterpiece ran wholly contrary to Elizabeth's aesthetic sensibility and would, in fact, have offended her. Browning began his "murder poem" as an homage to his dead wife and muse, only to realize when it was done that the pleasure it displays in "morbid cases" would have resulted in nothing but Elizabeth's "bad opinions."[14] Yet even at its beginning, *The Ring and the Book* revises one of the most well-known passages of *Aurora Leigh*—its meditation on form in book 5—drawing attention to the grotesque morbidity that would mark Robert's departure from Elizabeth's influence.[15] The famous question Elizabeth Barrett Browning poses in *Aurora Leigh*—"What form is best for poems?"—and her answer,

> Let me think
> Of forms less, and the external. Trust the spirit,
> As sovran nature does, to make the form;
> For otherwise we only imprison spirit
> And not embody (5.223–27)

returns in the sense and meter of one of the most important passages in book 1 of *The Ring and the Book*:

> No less, man, bounded, yearning to be free,
> May so project his surplusage of soul
> In search of body, so add self to self
> By owning what lay ownerless before,—
> So find, so fill full, so appropriate forms. (1.722–26)

These two passages attempt to answer the same question about how poetic form develops, but while Barrett Browning's answer in *Aurora Leigh* resists any finality of form, seeing form as a natural, living, emerging order—"we want new *forms*. . . . Let us all aspire rather to *Life*," she wrote to Robert (*Correspondence* 10.135)[16]—Browning's answer in *The Ring and the Book* suggests that form is an inert, pre-existing entity to be inhabited and reawakened. Barrett Browning's lines are written in almost regular iambic pentameter, broken only by the two hypercatalectic lines with the word "spirit" in them. We can hear in these overflowing but still metrical lines the work of the spirit acting upon form: embodiment without imprisonment and freedom compassed by nature. Barrett Browning makes it clear in *Aurora Leigh* that form should always be simultaneously organic and bounded, and should emerge from the present moment, as demonstrated by her famous diatribe against historical poetics that directly precedes her lines on the natural emergence of form:

> Nay, if there's room for poets in this world
> A little overgrown (I think there is),

> *Their sole work is to represent the age,*
> Their age, not Charlemagne's,—this live, throbbing age,
> That brawls, cheats, maddens, calculates, aspires
> . . . .
> To flinch from modern varnish, coat or flounce,
> Cry out for togas and the picturesque,
> Is fatal. (5.200–210; emphasis mine)

These lines avow a desire for form to emerge from the living—"living art, / Which thus presents and thus records true life," she calls it—not as a reinvention of what is dead and past (5.221–22). To "cry out for togas and the picturesque," to seek after the distant past, is "fatal" to poetry that Barrett Browning wants to be as "live" and "throbbing" as the age in which it is written.

In *Aurora Leigh*, "death inherits death" (5.199). In *The Ring and the Book*, "something dead may get to live again" (1.729). Robert, in stark opposition to Elizabeth's acerbic dismissal of poems made out of five-hundred-year-old "chivalric bones," imagines such "bones in dim disuse" rife with aesthetic potential, waiting for a poet's vitality to resuscitate them to new life (5.198; 1.753).[17] While Browning, too, writes his passage (reproduced again here for ease) in mostly regular iambic pentameter, punctuated by an occasional spondee or trochee—

> No less, man, bounded, yearning to be free,
> May so project his surplusage of souls
> In search of body, so add self to self
> By owning what lay ownerless before

—his breaks from an almost hypnotic meter wake us at moments in which the poem specifically addresses form. The last line of the passage, "So *find*, so *fill full*, so *appropriate forms*—" (emphasis mine), in which I count six rather than five stresses in a line almost indivisible into feet, calls our attention to form by dismantling it, enacting the phrase "fill full" while also forcing us to pause on each verb and fully absorb the contemporary poet's formal project: finding, filling, and appropriating old forms.

This project becomes more complex as the passage continues and the vague language of bodies and souls morphs into language specifically about bringing the dead back to life:

> That, although nothing which had never life
> Shall get life from him, be, not having been,
> *Yet something dead may get to live again,*

> Something with too much life or not enough,
> Which either way imperfect, ended once:
> An end whereat man's impulse intervenes,
> Makes new beginning, starts the dead alive,
> Completes the incomplete and saves the thing. (1.727–34; emphasis mine)

Reanimation in this poem is an artistic power defined by its limitations. In these lines, the limitations are its material requirements—"Something with too much life or not enough / Which either way imperfect, ended once"—and its distance from the creative power of God: "although nothing which had never life / Shall get life from him, be, not having been." Carol Christ has suggested that "the question for Browning is whether the animation of bodies is bringing the dead back to life or robbing graves to create phantoms," but the anxiety of reanimation in *The Ring and the Book* is less about the moral implications of what a poet *can* do than about the aesthetic implications of what a poet *can't* do ("Browning's" 395). As a statement of creative power, the negatives in these lines—although, nothing, never, not—all distinguish the work of the poet from "God's process" while simultaneously lodging the poet within a closed aesthetic system of "find[ing]" and "appropriat[ing] forms" (1.717). The bodies of the dead become a compulsory basis for poetry as well as figures for the constraints of poetic tradition ("the appropriation of forms"). That is, they are both essential and delimiting, both the bones of possibility and the precinct of impossibility. While Matthew Campbell argues that this passage is about the "artistic will" that "can find form for something which had lived but is now in need of a completion," about "giving life through the technique of the artist," these lines care less about resuscitating *through* form than about resuscitating form itself (116).[18] "I enter, spark-like, put old powers to play, / Push lines out to the limit," the poet says a few lines later, suggesting that somewhere in the world is a pre-existing body (a form) into which the artist projects his life-giving impulse.

REANIMATING SHELLEY

This language of animation as aesthetic limitation is strongly reminiscent of Browning's famous "Essay on Shelley," written seventeen years before *The Ring and the Book*.[19] In this essay on Shelley, an introduction to a collection of letters, Browning compares galvanic energy to the likeliness of the "lower incitements" of a poet's soul "stimulating the nobler inspiration," to achieve great poetry. "As soon will the galvanism that provokes to violent action the muscles

120 • CHAPTER 3

of a corpse, induce it to cross the chamber steadily: sooner," Browning writes disparagingly ("Essay" 1246). This comparison, overtly recollected in *The Ring and the Book* as the poet's feat to "mimic creation, galvanism for life," reminds us that the poem's obsession with the limitations of poetic form, and with its own relationship to the literary past, is often an explicit negotiation between subjective Romanticism and objective dramatic poetry as Browning defines them in his "Essay on Shelley" (1.740).

Browning's strong affinity for Shelley, whom he read first at age fourteen when his mother gave him a book of Shelley's poems, has been well documented by more than a century of critics.[20] Even by 1891, when his friend Alexandra Orr wrote *The Life and Letters of Robert Browning,* she notes that "it is almost a commonplace that some measure of Shelleyan fancy is recognizable in 'Pauline,'" and while she insists on Browning's "poetic individuality" being stronger than any set of influences, she also admits that Shelley remained for Browning "the greatest poet of his age" because "beyond all others, [Browning] believed [Shelley's poetic] exercise to have been prompted by the truest spiritual inspiration" (Orr 39). While critics like Harold Bloom have classically seen Shelley in Browning's later work as a "repression," a "hidden God" whom Browning resists only in order to emulate—"[This] is Browning as he wished to have been, locked in a solitary struggle against the precursor-principle, but struggling *in* the visionary world of the precursor," Bloom says of "Childe Roland" (204)—later critics have been less interested in Shelley's Godlike place in Browning's imagination than in how Browning conceived the aims of the Romantic poets in relation to his own work.[21] "Whether factual or mythified, alive or dead, human or immortal, the Romantic epipsyche became an increasingly problematic emblem that allegorized the male's unsatisfied desire for fusion," U. C. Knoepflmacher has argued, suggesting that Browning's early dramatic monologues engage with the problem of finding an "'objective counterpart' for his subjective will and feelings" (144). Others have painted Browning's poetic trajectory as one that progresses smoothly "from self-conscious Romantic digressions to a more dramatic presentation of the story," from subjective poetry to objective poetry (to borrow Browning's terms from his "Essay on Shelley") (Martens 39). To understand Browning's work as a progression from one of these terms to the other, however, is to suggest, first, that *he* considered objective and subjective poetics to be wholly distinct from one another—a suggestion that his "Essay on Shelley" does not entirely support—and second, that his consciousness of the distinction mapped onto an evolution away from Romantic influence and dependence. Instead, the relationship Browning articulates between Shelley's poetics and his own is something closer to what Tom Mole describes as a "renovation project," one in which Browning reimagines Shelley's subjective poetics in terms that intimately connect to his own objective poetic project (3).

The "objective poet," Browning tells us at the beginning of the "Essay on Shelley," endeavors to "reproduce things external . . . with an immediate reference, in every case, to the common eye and apprehension of his fellow man" (1243). The "thing fashioned" in this way, his poetry, "will of necessity by substantive, projected from himself and distinct" (1243). Browning offers Shakespeare as the highest example of the objective poet (although he makes it quite clear that he is also referring to himself) and argues that from Shakespeare's work, as from all objective poets, "we learn only what he intended we should learn by that particular exercise of his power,—the fact itself,—which . . . each of us receives for the first time as a creation" (1244).[22] The objective poem is fact: a discrete, unmediated creation. The subjective poet, by contrast, "is impelled to embody the thing he perceives, not so much with reference to the many below, as to the one above him," a poet of Divine interiority rather than worldly exteriority whose work is "the very radiance and aroma of his personality, projected from it but not separated" (1244–45). Shelley, of course, is Browning's subjective poet par excellence, and the essay both praises Shelley and insists that his letters are key to understanding his poetry: to understand the subjective poet in any fundamental way, "we must look deep into his human eyes" (1244). Yet despite this appeal to Shelley's humanity, the essay suggests that subjective poetry is close to the Divine, while objective poetry is closer to man.

But the essay also wants to posit objective poetry, poetry that "speaks for itself" (i.e., Browning's own dramatic monologues) as equal in value to poetry steeped in personality (1244). "It would be idle to inquire," he writes of the two poetic faculties, "which is the higher or even rarer endowment" (1245). Even if the essay stands as "a tribute to the genius of Shelley," a "memorial of a very touching affection" to "a divinely inspired man," as Alexandra Orr describes it, it also rolls the task of homage into the simultaneous task of self-tribute (Orr 178, 182, 180). "If the subjective might seem to be the ultimate requirement of every age," Browning writes, "the objective, in the strictest state, must still retain its original value. For it is with this world, as starting point and basis alike, that we shall always have to concern ourselves" ("Essay" 1245). He reiterates this celebration of objectivity in a letter about *The Ring and the Book,* when he writes that the "business" of the poem has been "to explain *fact*"—for "this is God's world, as he made it for reasons of his own, and . . . to change its conditions is not to account for them" (*RB and JW* 144). Yet just as Browning imagines the classic contrast between Romantic subjective poetry and objective poetry in his essay as a cyclic process—each kind of poetry ultimately leading into the other[23]—so too does *The Ring and the Book* ultimately use its metaphor of objective reanimation to acknowledge and define an inherently subjective relationship between poetry and its historical bones: bones both of fact and of form. Browning's initial presentation of an absolute distinction between objective and subjective poetics, followed by his inability to wholly articulate—perhaps even to wholly believe in—this binary, provides a useful, if troubling, tool for examining both his thinking about aesthetic matters in *The Ring and the Book* and his actual practice in the historical monologues.

Browning's essay becomes a literary memorial to Shelley at the same time that it obsessively enacts a poet's desire to resist dissolving into his memorial object, to maintain the faltering fiction of a work of art "projected from himself and distinct." Yet his definition of the "objective poet" cannot be disentangled from the way he defines the "subjective poet," and his sense that the two "may issue hereafter from the same poet in successive perfect works" accounts for his own path from "Pauline" forward, as well as for his concession that only rarely does either objectivity or subjectivity in a poet manifest itself so prominently "as to be pronounced comparatively pure" ("Essay" 1245). Browning's exaggerated defensiveness when confronted by Julia Wedgwood's accusations of subjectivity—she once accuses Browning of "lending [too] much of yourself to your contemptible characters" (*RB and JW* 136)—makes sense in light of his own attempt to excuse what he sees as Shelley's greatest Romantic flaw, as well as the defining quality of the subjective poet: writing out of a state of mind (and Browning quotes Shelley directly here) "in which ideas may be supposed to assume the force of sensation, through the confusion of thought with the objects of thought, and excess of passion animating the creations of the imagination" ("Essay" 1252). When Wedgwood thus identifies the same tendency in *The Ring and the Book*—"I should have thought that very detachment of attention from sympathy would have implied a filtering away of your own thoughts from your own representations, which is the very opposite of what I find with you" (*RB and JW* 158)—she aligns Browning with the Romantic impulse about which he was most anxious.

Browning's Romantic proclivities—as well as his critiques of Romanticism—show themselves most clearly in his earlier poetry, where he engages more overtly with the play between Romantic subjectivity and dramatic objectivity than he does in *The Ring and the Book*. Many of his dramatic monologues, particularly "Porphyria's Lover" and "My Last Duchess," obsessed as they are with murdering, memorializing, and reanimating, dramatize the failure of the poet to preserve an objective distance from his aesthetic creation, attempting in their staging to critique but not to repudiate the structures of subjective poetry.[24] Other poems, like "Memorabilia," which explicitly uses

Shelley and his "To a Skylark" as antitheses to its speaker's poetic sensibility, endeavor to wholly disengage representation from subjectivity—to actually create the kind of pure "objective" poetry of which Browning's essay admits "there has yet been no instance" (1245). In all three of these specific poems, a memorial object—a body, a painting, or a feather—becomes the site for a crisis of subjectivity, although each poem memorializes, and thus registers the crisis, in different ways. "Porphyria's Lover" and "My Last Duchess" violently display the ethical and aesthetic repercussions of using language to bring the dead back to life. "Memorabilia," in contrast, refuses to memorialize at all, but in the ramifications of its refusal reveals the same impossibility of categorically "pure" poetry as do the monologues that bask in poetry's impurity. While these poems come long before *The Ring and the Book,* they refract Browning's agitation about aesthetics and Romanticism through the conceit of returning the dead to life, and in doing so provide models for reading the later poem's obsession with reanimation as a fraught engagement with both poetic history and poetic possibility.

The objective poet, in Browning's essay, maintains the integrity of "the world" that the subjective poet necessarily destabilizes by integrating the world with his personality. "There may be no end of the poets who communicate to us what they see in an object with reference to their own individuality," he writes early in the essay, but "what it was before they saw it, in reference to the aggregate human mind, will be as desirable to know as ever" (1245). Although the implicit self-referentiality of this comment suggests the dramatic monologue as the poetic form most proficient in divorcing itself from the poet's "individuality," at the same time the maniacal aesthetic projections of the narrators of monologues like "Porphyria's Lover" and "My Last Duchess" stage the violent impossibility of a poetry beyond subjectivity—the impossibility of a poetry in which a skylark (in Thomas Hardy's words) really could be just "a little ball of feather and bone" ("Shelley's Skylark," line 10). Although Browning maintains an ironic distance from the speakers of these poems, the speakers' aesthetic conceits nonetheless reflect a concern that the objectivity of dramatic projection—the speakers' projections in the poems, and Browning's own projections of the speakers—might be implicitly subjective, as well. In these monologues, Shelley's skylark has been replaced with female corpses, but the psychopathy of the poems lies not in the corpses themselves but in poetry's capacity, its need, to keep these corpses unnaturally alive, to reimagine Shelley's "Divine" ecstasy as the most abject of poetic undertakings.[25]

The aberrant animation of these corpses by their lovers manifests the very problem that objective "dramatic poetry" should contravene ("Essay" 1245): the contamination of the object, "the world," by an infusion of individual sub-

124 • CHAPTER 3

jectivity—the "pathetic fallacy" revamped for the modern necrophiliac—a phenomenon manifested to the utmost at the end of "Porphyria's Lover":

> The smiling, rosy little head,
> So glad it has its utmost will,
> That all it scorned at once is fled,
> And I, its love, am gained instead! (52–55)[26]

Objectivity and subjectivity crumble into one another when the poem's narrator forces his own thoughts onto the corpse, for at the same moment in which he wholly objectifies Porphyria by transforming the corpse from a "she" to an "it," he also breathes into it the deviant spark of (what Browning in a very different context would have to call) his own "inner light and power" by investing the dead body with a spirit beyond its own form ("Essay" 1245). This animating move sounds rapturous in Browning's Shelleyan terms, but the terms of his poem reveal its gleeful sadism: "And I untightened next the tress / About her neck; her cheek once more / blushed bright beneath my burning kiss," the narrator tells us, clearly delighting in his strangulation (46–48).

The narrator derives a sense of self, a self-conscious (and an uncertain) "I," only from his creation of the corpse's self-awareness—"No pain felt she; / *I am quite sure* she felt no pain" ("Porphyria" 42–43; emphasis mine). Browning implicates his own aesthetic project, and his doubts about that project, in this displacement and projection of subjectivity, which is wound into the pathology the monologue encapsulates. For, although the poet and the speaker of the poem are expressly distinct from one another, methodologically the speaker's projection of fictional subjectivity precisely mimics the poet's task of creating a fictional subjectivity in the dramatic monologue. The animated corpse becomes a grotesque amplification of the dramatic poem's forged poetic persona.[27] The subjectivity Browning fingers in Shelley as the ascendant potential to see "what God sees" is resurrected in "Porphyria's Lover" as the height of perversity ("Essay" 1244): a violent, unnatural, inauthentic literary construction, a living corpse. In this monologue, "subjectivity" constitutes not a pathway to the divine but a profane poetic convention that refuses to let the dead stay dead yet lacks the capacity to actually bring anything except artifice back to life.

"My Last Duchess," in contrast, has no dead body to revivify, but this monologue uses the aesthetic representation of the body as a substitute through which to renew the violent pleasure of subjection. "There's my last Duchess, painted on the wall," the Duke begins, recreating the once-woman as pure representation, a projection of his own aesthetic and narrative desires.

The dead Duchess, voided of all subjectivity, embodies the culmination of his desire for control, a climactic moment, discrete and frozen ("I gave commands; / Then all smiles stopped together") (45–46). A singular satisfaction, however, will not suffice. The dead Duchess may be the climax of the story, but the Duchess "looking as if she were alive" far more potently enables the Duke's fantasy of her ongoing capitulation to his will and to his language: the continuous reanimation of her form with his subjectivity (2). The lines "Even had you skill / In speech—(which I have not)—to make your will / Quite clear to such an one" equate the "speech" at hand with the violent way in which the Duke did make his will "quite clear," but the brutality, and the pleasure, of language lies in its imposition rather than its evacuation of subjectivity (35–37). The Duke's story of the Duchess reiterates the violence of his murder by resuscitating her in his own image. His language memorializes both his desire and her subjection.

As the poem's rhythm and prosody enmesh our own reading pleasure within the Duke's commingled murdering and memorializing instincts, it becomes increasingly clear that the aestheticization of violence displayed in the Duke's monologue has wider implications for poetry itself and the way it functions in its memorial capacity as an instrument of subjective violence. As Elisabeth Bronfen has written, the violence of aestheticizing the dead body lies in its displacement of pain "onto a formal level"—the pain of a dying woman "is subordinated to notions of artistic ability and aesthetic effect" (51). "My Last Duchess" (and "Porphyria's Lover," as well) deliberately and depravedly makes grotesque violence beautiful. Its language colludes with its psychopathic narrator by creating a gorgeous, painted corpse, by aesthetically entering into a psychology that savors memorialization as a constant re-enactment of death's initial violence. It does so in the ironic form of the dramatic monologue, however, which suggests that the pleasure the poem seems to take in this literary violence is not actually its primary interest. Rather, the poem's lovely brutality invites us to reflect upon the aesthetic and ethical quandary of binding together poetry and violence in the act of representation. To the extent that the portrait of the Duchess can be considered a stand-in for poetry as a whole, or more specifically for memorial poetry, "My Last Duchess" hyperbolically insists that the object of remembrance in the poem can never do more than *look* as if alive. Anything beyond the bare outlines of its form must be the projections of the poet. The memorial poem becomes a performance of violence by draining and forcibly reconstructing the subjectivity of a silenced body. Yet as the poet enmeshes himself in the fictive reconstitution of this subjectivity, the memorial poem also comes to deny the distinction between poet and object that Browning in his Shelley essay so adamantly desires, although falls short of entirely achieving. Memorial poetry will always be about its remembering poet.[28]

"Memorabilia," published more than a dozen years after "My Last Duchess," thus posits remembering as the fundamental opposition to objective poetry, and memory as a derisory rather than a formative phenomenon: "And the memory I started at— / My starting moves your laughter" (7–8). The poem begins by recording the poet's awe at meeting a man who had met Shelley, but it quickly deflates the transformative value of the Shelley-encounter by showing the man's total lack of transformation. "But you were living before that. / And also you are living after," the poet recognizes, expressing in the singsong repetition of these lines a sardonic acknowledgment that the value of such an encounter lies in poetic convention rather than in actuality—that the spiritual significance (or in this case, the lack of spiritual significance) of the moment of encounter exists only in the poet's literary revision of the moment (5–8). The only place where Browning's idea of "subjectivity" could ever come to fruition, these lines suggest, is in the memorial poem, by which I mean, quite literally here, the poem predicated on memory or commemoration. "Memorabilia" (as its title ironically implies) thus seamlessly transitions from a rejection of Shelleyan subjectivity in the first two stanzas into a rejection of memory itself in the stanzas that follow.[29] "I crossed a moor, with a name of its own, / And a certain use in the world no doubt," the poet tells us in the third stanza, perhaps alluding to and undermining the literary aura of Emily Brontë's famous landscape, but more importantly, reveling in forgetting it (9–10): forgetting the aura, the name of the moor, its use in the world, and even the near-ballad form of the preceding stanzas. Forgetting becomes the poem's means to objectivity, its method of setting up the potential for subjective Shelleyan poetry and then mercilessly, unambiguously, dismissing it:

> For there I picked up on the heather
> And there I put inside my breast
> A moulted feather, an eagle feather!
> Well, I forget the rest. (13–16)

Parodying Romantic ecstasy with the exclamation point in the third line, this final stanza shows that Shelley's "Divine" eye, with all its so-called power to turn a bird into a "blithe spirit," must first be enabled by literary memory. And the objective poet, therefore, must and does forget.

But in this willful forgetting, which allows a moor to remain a moor, and a feather, a feather, the poet cannot help but extinguish his own project. Forgetting denies not only subjectivity but the very possibility for poetry, and in this nihilistic gesture lies the crux of the antimemorial poem. Poetry cannot cease remembering, and, in remembering, reanimating. Language itself is a memorial phenomenon, each word, to borrow from Giorgio Agamben, "a dead language handed down to us by the dead," and to forget is fundamentally to reject its signifying capacity (74). Browning's notion of objective poetry in its most ideal form—"the fact itself" ("Essay" 1244)—negates not only subjectivity but also its own linguistic condition as a medium through which the world can be "reverted to and relearned" (1245). "Memorabilia" thus finally belies any firm distinction between objective and subjective poetry theorized in Browning's essay, projecting in its "objective" self-annihilation a death beyond the reanimating reach of the memorial, a death of poetry itself.

REANIMATING POMPILIA

To wholly reject Romanticism, then, is to attempt a poetics that refuses to engage with, remember, or memorialize its past, a poetics that Browning clearly finds neither tenable nor desirable. *The Ring and the Book* instead offers a memorial poetics that interrogates the mechanisms by which we remember and that sees the process of remembrance as one inextricable both from revision and from invention: as a process of reanimation, with all of its contingent possibilities and limitations. The testimonial structure of the poem, its multiple "complete" versions of one story of a woman's death, works to make the distance between the illusion of fact and the imperfection of memory transparent. The whole story of the poem is not a series of facts but a conglomeration of memories, bits of "fact" transformed by time and subjectivity into something new.[30] The dead Pompilia is reanimated again and again, but always imperfectly.

The transformation of Pompilia's death into something other than itself becomes the project of each of the "voices" of the poem. For each voice, including Pompilia's own, death enables the possibility for revision or redaction, yet its own fundamentally representational nature makes transparent the aesthetic mechanisms by which this rescripting takes place. As Elisabeth Bronfen and Sarah Webster Goodwin have suggested, representing something dead "is in a sense to return it to life: the voice represents not so much the dead as the once living, juxtaposed with the needs of the yet living" (7). Diana Fuss describes this resuscitative representational act slightly differently when she writes that "speaking in the voices of the dead provides a way for poetry to make present a certain kind of absence," to remind us of all that has been lost rather than to console us for it (71). In both cases, however, poetically reanimating the dead doesn't aim to produce a living voice but to emphasize the artifice of the poet's own ventriloquizing, the gaping silences of the dead that the poet can speak over with his own desires but never fill. By expressing *The Ring and the Book*'s ars poetica using the language of reanimation, Browning demonstrates how vested his text is in the aesthetic possibilities buried in these deathly silences. The corpses in this poem all enable Browning to consider what poetry can and can't do in the absence between the "once" of the dead past and the "yet" of the living artist. Giving voice to the dead Pompilia in book 7, especially, allows Browning to put book 1's metaphorical reflections on resuscitative representationality into practice, for Pompilia's is the poem's primary metapoetic voice, the voice that most clearly reveals not only how little authenticity lingers in a resuscitated body but also how aesthetically vital such inauthentic bodies can be for poetry that longs to make art rather than history.

The comparison that Browning makes in his essay on Shelley between poetry and galvanizing a corpse, and that he makes again in *The Ring and the Book* when he describes the poet's attempt to "mimic creation, galvanism for life," infuses the relationship between poetry and reanimation with several layers of self-reflexive irony (1.740). In the essay on Shelley, Browning draws a comparison between successful galvanic movement and successful poetry inspired by the "lower incitements" of a poet's soul—the two are equivalent, and equally impossible—yet in *The Ring and the Book*, successful galvanism has become a wholly possible metaphor for the entire poetic project at hand. Where failed galvanic movement in the essay becomes a disparaging point of comparison for poetry of a low order, in *The Ring and the Book*, galvanism becomes the fully attainable aspiration of Browning's poetic project. By yoking the idea of galvanism to the "simulation," or forgery, of "noble inspiration," the structure of the comparison in the essay implies the *impossibility* of galvanism generating any kind of authentic movement (or authentic poetry) ("Essay" 1246): neither trying to find poetic inspiration in the lower incitements of the soul nor trying to galvanize a corpse into genuine mobility will produce any kind of success. Yet this same inauthentic simulation becomes the entire task of the poet who "mimic[s] creation" in *The Ring and the Book*.

The Ring and the Book locates the impossibility of originality and the vanishing point of historical truth in the interchangeability of written document and dead body, both "texts" that the poem brings to life. Although the validity (or invalidity) of actual documentation plays a central role in the poem's mediation of fact and fiction, the Count's forgery of letters is described as an "infiltration flavoured with himself," a strangely sensual, even violent, bodily image (3.1361).[31] The narrator renders body and document transposable in the poem's first book when he describes the object of his "spark-like" powers as a "rag of flesh, scrap of bone in dim disuse, / Smoking flax that fed fire once" (1.753–54).[32] The body, the "rag," the "scrap," becomes a thing to be written, a figurative page on which the poet will "push lines out to the limit" even as it remains a corpse to be animated and led out "through a ruin of a crypt" (1.756–57). Similarly, the penetrative bodily image of an "infiltrated" document, with its implication of self-projection, strongly recalls book 1's vocabulary of resuscitation, in which the poet "project[s] his surplusage of soul / In search of body, so add[s] self to self" (1.723–24). The forging of documents is reframed as a masculine casting of the self, as an imposition of subjectivity equal to the narrator's poetic entrance into "rags of flesh." The Count's written "infiltration" and the poet-narrator's act of reanimation become forms of the same representational duplicity, the poem and the body sites for the same evacuation of objective historical fact.

The poem's central body—the murdered Pompilia—is the poem's primary site of fraudulence, not only in its catalytic status for the poem's collection of conflicting truths but also in its own very identity. "Pompilia was a fable not a fact," half of Rome tells us in book 2, alluding to the lies Pompilia's "mother" told in claiming the child as her own (2.550). The revelation of this parental duplicity casts as much doubt on Pompilia's corporeal humanity as it does call her parentage into question. The grammatical confusion in this passage is highly suggestive: "She it was, bought and paid for, passed the thing / Off as the flesh and blood and child of her," the crowd narrates, "She" and "it" referring to Pompilia's mother but also, as the referent of "bought and paid for," to Pompilia, the "thing," the "flesh," the "blood," and only lastly "the child" (2.574–75). Pompilia's status as a dying and dead body in this poem, simultaneously a "she" and an "it" throughout, seems to originate in this moment of doubtful identity, as though Pompilia's very form has become "all lie, no touch of truth at all" (2.555). Both her birth and her death contravene any possibility of an authentic story. Her birth transforms her into an indecipherable "thing," and her equally indecipherable death animates a series of voices whose truth-value the poet-narrator dismisses as "the world's guess" (1.842).

Yet Pompilia has been called "a pearly image," the one "snowdrop growing out of that dunghill" of a book, Browning's memorial tribute to "the angel [who] had hallowed his life" and the single trustworthy voice in *The Ring and the Book* (RB and JW 158, 156; Gaylord 27).[33] The desire to trust one voice out of the cacophony defies the testimonial logic of the poem as a whole, in which the experience of each voice revises the finale that precedes it and proleptically negates the story that will follow. However, to situate Pompilia as the poem's primary memorial figure is to understand that her voice is also the poem's most literally epitaphic voice: the voice that foregrounds the rupture

130 • CHAPTER 3

between past and present, as well as the tenuous bands of memory, subjectivity, and creativity that necessarily stretch across it.[34] Unique among Browning's women, Pompilia speaks for herself from the grave. She is neither posthumous portrait nor blushing cadaver filtered through the voice of a psychopath but an almost-corpse, liminally dead, who argues against masculine projection and objectification even as she calls her own objectivity and historical sensibility into question. She antithesizes the ironized "Romantic" impulses of the poem's villainous forgers who try to project their stories onto hers, yet she is also the poem's most historically unstable and literarily incapacitated character. In all the different visions and revisions of the murder that Browning provides us, Pompilia's character remains the only one whose testimony acknowledges the aesthetic and historical complexity of trying to tell such a story, post-facto and drawing from only her own point of view. Pompilia, in fact, is the single character for whom Browning had no testimony to draw out of the Yellow Book. She was dead and couldn't actually speak at the trial the Yellow Book records, so her testimony is his aesthetic invention, and in this it becomes a vanishing point at the intersection between poetry and history. As a dead woman, she occasions the poem's consideration of the relationship between historical truth and aesthetic truth, but as a speaking corpse she gives voice to the poem's ultimate suggestion that the two need not—*must* not—have anything to do with one another.

Pompilia is a dead woman with a voice and a story: an impossible figure within Browning's oeuvre who thus takes her place beyond it and offers a reflection on its strategies. As a meta-character, she seems trustworthy not because she is inherently pure but because her story *is* the story of the poem's form. In recognizing her own subjectivity and the "difference in minds" and "in eyes" that allow people to "misinterpret and misprise" truth, she acknowledges the impossibility of accessing historical fact that the poem's series of monologues sets out to ironically demonstrate (7.918–20). Her monologue speaks as much about the poem's confrontation with its own conventions as it does about the events leading to her murder, and although critics have suggested that her death "authorizes the truthfulness of her speech and the idea that truth can be found," the "truth" she speaks is an aesthetic rather than a historical one, full of subjectivity, shifting memories, and silences (Bronfen 292). She positions herself as one of Browning's dead women. She concedes her own objectified state as simultaneously a sexual object ("I was the chattel that had caused a crime") and a corpse ("do you want the victim by / While you discuss the value of her blood?"), and she acknowledges that both of these objectified states render her "mute" (7.520, 524–25, 521). Yet, in voicing her own muteness, she contravenes both the silence and the objectification of her dead, "stone-like," female body, little more than someone else's subjective representation "shimmer[ing] through the gloom o' the grave," as Guido says (7.1005; 11.1680). Pompilia's testimony demonstrates the dual-edged capacity of written language to be both a vehicle of historical truth and a means of counterfeit. "How happy are those who know how to write! Such could write what their son should read in time," she exclaims, imagining writing as a mode of historical preservation, only to retreat into the opposite position later in the monologue—"I was glad, / Then, for the first time, that I could not write"—as she acknowledges that written documents can just as easily be false as true (7.82–83, 1489–90). History itself is little more than something that "someone dreamed / And get[s] to disbelieve it at the last" (7.109–10). She may recall her history from a place beyond the grave, yet by her own admission she recalls a series of blank spots, cleaned parchments, and colored truths.

It is marriage, not her husband's actual act of murder, that Pompilia imagines as the thing that killed her. On her miraculous deathbed, she describes herself as a revenant, killed into marriage and resurrected through her escape.

> Up the aisle
> My mother keeping hold of me so tight,
> I fancied we were coming to see a corpse
> Before the altar which she pulled me toward,

she tells us of her wedding day four years earlier, and recalls her father saying that by marrying Pompilia to Guido, her mother has "murdered . . . Me and yourself and this child besides" (7.430–34, 492–93). "Murdered or not / Be it enough that your child is now my wife!," Guido replies, revealing an intrinsic confusion of marriage and funeral, bride and corpse, spectator and spectacle in the act of taking a child-bride (7.494–95). Pompilia has no idea where she stands in this ceremonial transition from subject to object, "coin," "chattel." She imagines herself as funeral guest instead of wedding participant, and her recollection of this uncertainty of position demonstrates the same desire to resist masculine projection as does her speaking through death. As a bride, she sees herself simultaneously inscribed in a story of someone else's choosing and entirely vacant of any story, recalling a prophetic moment in childhood when a friend identifies her in a picture of Daphne, "such green leaves / Flourishing out of your finger-ends," the recollection of which sparks the melancholy lament that "all my life . . . Looks old, fantastic, and impossible" (7.193–94, 198–200). She insists now that she is not Daphne, with all the incipient resistance to objectification that goes along with rejecting the myth of a woman transformed into a tree to avoid sexual advances of a god, but she has nothing with which to replace this overdetermined story. "All since is one blank," she says of her years with Guido. "Had I been dead?" she asks of this blankness—"How right to be alive!," she says of her escape from the marriage, her resurrection from the blankness of death (7.1247): "I know I wake,—but from what? Blank, I say!" she insists again (7.594).

Reanimation, in all of its incarnations—the seemingly literal, in that Pompilia speaks despite Guido's murder of her; the metaphorical, in her resuscitative escape from marriage; and the literary, in Browning's necromantic dramatic monologue—allows Pompilia a voice to tell her own story, but the condition of her reanimation is her recognition of the distance between subjectivity and truth in memory, in storytelling, and in temporality. As Guido laments, "Had she been found dead as I left her dead / I should have told a tale brooked no reply," but her miraculous life instead turns his "plausibility into nothingness" (11.1702–3, 1687). Rather than subjectivity transforming into an act of violent projection, however, as it does in Guido's "plausible" story, for Pompilia subjectivity and revision become forms of salvation. "By special grace perhaps, / Between that first calm and this last, four years / Vanish," she tells us, like "Memorabilia" suggesting that forgetting history can sometimes be as important a means of accessing truth as remembering is (7.600–602). Yet, again like "Memorabilia," forgetting can only be a temporary kind of grace, ultimately rejected in favor of subjective, inventive remembering: "I review / And comprehend much and imagine more, / And have little to forgive at last" (7.635–37). While her ultimate desire is the revelation of truth, Pompilia's death places her outside of written chronicle ("this blood of mine . . . Washes the parchment white") and her reanimation, beyond historical chronology—"thence comes such confusion of what was / With what will be"—such that her voice, despite the clear fact of its writtenness, refuses any implicit connection between truth, writing, and history (7.1716–18, 210–11). Instead, truth lies in acknowledging subjectivity: in acknowledging the distance between "truth" as an objective ideal and truth as a representational phenomenon, "sheer dreaming and impossibility" (7.112).

Like our frame narrator's arguments about creativity, Pompilia sees truth as a platonic ideal, of which humans can only create shadow versions. "Marriage on earth seems such a counterfeit," she says at the end of her monologue, "mere imitation of the inimitable: / In heaven we have the real and true and sure," echoing the narrator's thoughts about the limitations of poetry's counterfeit creative powers in book 1 (7.1824–26). For Pompilia, killed by "marriage on earth," the revelation of earthly limitation is a liberating reach toward heavenly possibility. Yet this association of Pompilia's sham marriage with the poet's own resuscitative imitation of God's creative power—poetry—

makes it clear that the relationship between language, violence, and death that Pompilia's monologue exposes (and that the Count's monologues, like "My Last Duchess" and "Porphyria's Lover," perpetrate) is implicit in *The Ring and the Book*'s structure, its endless repetition of the story of her murder. As the most self-reflexive monologue in the poem, besides the framing narrative of the first and last books, Pompilia's obsessions with subjectivity, violations of teleology, and the damaging potential of language remind us that the poem itself kills Pompilia over and over again, exploring all the different nuances of language with which this murder can be committed. Yet, by bringing her back to life in equal measure, the poem also demonstrates that revision is as much a method of resuscitative memorializing as it is a killing-off of the past.

REANIMATING THE RENAISSANCE

Although Browning deliberated the distinction between objectivity and subjectivity, he had no illusions about the dead as a source of truth. However, as evidenced in *The Ring and the Book,* he credited the imaginative truth of his resuscitating art. The self-consciously subjective, necropoetic revision we see in the form of *The Ring and the Book*—its series of dramatic monologues, each of which revises the story told before—offers us a model for the way that poetry effectively can engage both with the past as a subject for art and with literary history as a fount of poetic method. The final book of *The Ring and the Book* returns to the metaphor of reanimation that the poet introduces in the first book but this time uses it more explicitly to negotiate the relationship between historical truth, art, and memory. The book introduces the metaphor by attempting to make a distinction between "human testimony" and "Art" with a capital "A," ascribing truth to the latter and calling the former inherently false. Yet, by pitting testimony and art against one another to conclude a poem that throughout renders the two fundamentally indistinguishable, the poet only draws attention to the impossibility of historical truth outside of subjective self-reflection. "There, would you disbelieve stern History / Trust rather to the babble of a bard?" the poet-narrator asks sardonically, then uses his image of reanimation to inflate the power of this "babble":

> So did this old woe fade from memory,
> Till after, in the fullness of the days,
> I needs must find an ember yet unquenched,
> And, breathing, blow the spark to flame. It lives. (12.826–30)

134 • CHAPTER 3

More explicitly than in the first book, the resuscitative task of the poet here becomes one of generative remembering, salvaging what has been forgotten by breathing the dead back to life.

In this, the echoes of resuscitative historians like Michelet are unmistakable, and we see Browning engaging not only with the history of literary influence but also with the ways in which his contemporaries conceived and composed history itself. As Philip Harwood wrote in an 1842 essay entitled "The Modern Art and Science of History," modern historians should aim to "recreate worlds out of the loose, chaotic elements furnished by chroniclers and bards" (188)—a phrase that, like Browning's appeal to galvanism, brings Mary Shelley as much as Percy to mind, especially her resuscitative insistence in the 1831 introduction to *Frankenstein* that "invention . . . does not consist in creating out of void, but out of chaos" (350). As Harwood's description of historiographic work continues, the task of the historian sounds more and more Frankensteinian. The historian must have the skill to "reconstruct the skeleton from the single bone," Harwood writes, "and clothe that skeleton with flesh and blood, and breathe into it a living soul" (188–89). He lays out not just an end goal of living history but a meticulous reanimation process that Victor himself would have to appreciate.[35] Harwood's sense of the historian as resurrectionist shares much with Michelet, with whose "speculative thinking" the Brownings were familiar.[36] As I describe in my introduction, Michelet succinctly sets out a historicist methodology of "resuscitat[ing] the living reality from the dead facts" (Jann xiii): "Yes, each dead man leaves a small property, his memory, and asks that it be cared for. . . . [History] gives life to these dead men, resuscitates them" (Barthes 101–2).

In her study of the Italian Renaissance in the Victorian imagination, Hilary Fraser points out the parallel between Michelet's claim that history is a mode of "resurrection" rather than "narration" or "analysis," and Browning's own resurrectionist metaphor for the work of poetry. "Browning's poet is, like Michelet's historian, Promethean," she argues, capable of breathing life and heat, in Michelet's words, into "so many forgotten, unrecognized men" (Fraser 17).[37] She details at length the resuscitative impulse of nineteenth-century history, particularly the Victorian passion for using tombs, funerary monuments, and effigies as ways of accessing the past, and the Victorians' sense of the Renaissance itself as culturally modeling the "archaeological, necromantic metaphor of *disinterment,* a digging up that was also a resuscitation or a reincarnation" (40).[38] Yet Fraser argues that the aim of this resuscitative project of history for the Victorians "was to resurrect the past in such a way that it should appear to be both authentic and autonomous, even though the complementary demand for relevance to the present actually militated against the desired authenticity and autonomy" (38). Fraser describes resurrection for historians like Michelet or even Carlyle as a task of excavatory truth, an effort of objectivity, and she makes no distinction between this historiographic ideal and the apparently equivalent ideal of poetry in *The Ring and the Book*, which, she reminds us, aspires to "transform 'dead truth' into 'live truth'" (17). But this appeal to authenticity is precisely what Browning ironizes in *The Ring and the Book*, not only in the very sections of the poem's introduction from which Fraser draws her parallels but in the multiply narrated structure of the poem as a whole, which in repeating the same story from so many different points of view demonstrates the absurd impossibility of either "authenticity" or "autonomy."

Critics who have noted the relationship between historicism and the resuscitative metaphor for poetry in the opening of *The Ring and the Book* often seem inclined to ignore its ironies: "Such miracles [referring to resurrection]," one critic argues, "are analogous to the artist's work, which must be morally serious since it re-enacts at a lower level the creation of man by God" (Gent 26). Although Browning certainly considered great poetry a morally rigorous endeavor, the lines in *The Ring and the Book* in which he claims that the poet "Repeats God's process in man's due degree, / . . . / Creates, no, but resuscitates, perhaps" are far more interested in critically delimiting the artist's work than in touting its triumphant Godlike success (1.719). While contemporary critics see the critical and aesthetic success of *The Ring in the Book* as synonymous with the poem's own wholehearted assertion of success, the poem itself refuses to bear out this collapse of terms, interested as it is in the gaps between language and truth, and in showing that success from one perspective is often poignant failure from another.[39]

Although Browning seems to present an ideal of objectivity equivalent to Michelet's in *The Ring and the Book*, the poem in fact denies the validity of what Michelet sees as the natural extension, the ultimate goal, of this resuscitative ideal of history: the possibility that forgotten human voices, once resuscitated, can tell their true stories. Browning instead sees human testimony as the antithesis to the truth of art. "Our human speech is naught, / Our human testimony false, our fame / And human estimation words and wind," the narrator says, before insisting that "Art remains the one way possible / Of speaking truth" (12.834–36, 839–40). The contradictions in these few lines self-consciously encapsulate the generic irony inherent in the dramatic monologue. The lines first claim that the poet's art is an act both of memorialization and of resuscitation, implying that it can bring forgotten human voices back to life. They then deny that these human voices can speak truth. And, finally, they argue that Art is the one avenue to truth. How are we to

136 • CHAPTER 3

reconcile the truth of resuscitative art with the falsity of human testimony? The reconciliation lies in the irony of the dramatic monologue: "Why take the artistic way to prove so much?" the narrator asks, "so much" referring to the untrustworthiness of human testimony (12.841). Because art, as he says, "speaks truth." But in characterizing art as the means of speaking the truth of human falsity, Browning underscores the fissure between the aims of his art and the objective rendering of the human voice, between the subjective nature of the dramatic monologue and the fiction of a "dramatic poetry" that "speaks for itself" (as the "Essay on Shelley" would have it). This final book insists that truth lies beyond and between language—"between the lines," in Herbert Tucker's words ("Dramatic" 231). "Art may tell a truth / Obliquely, do the thing shall breed the thought, / Nor wrong the thought, missing the mediate word," the poet says in the poem's penultimate stanza, pointing us explicitly to the imaginative rather than the conscriptive task of poetry, suggesting that art is a vehicle for subjective knowledge instead of an end in itself, and insisting that we recognize the ironic sensibility of the book as a whole (12.855–57). We are, after all, being instructed to glorify poetry's capacity to "miss the mediate word" and, thus, to appreciate the distance poetry creates between language and meaning.

To see, then, a direct parallel between the resuscitative historical sensibility of a historian like Michelet and Browning's poetic sensibility in *The Ring and the Book* would be to wholly ignore the ironic capacity built into the resuscitative form of the dramatic monologue that Browning chooses to use. Furthermore, the ultimate aim of the resuscitative historian, to quote Roland Barthes on Michelet, is to "reverse Time, [to] turn back to the place of the dead and recommenc[e] their life in a clear and useful direction," to restore a life "fresh and virgin of death" (83–84). Death is the necessary condition of history but also what resuscitative history sets out to erase completely. Yet, as Browning makes most clear in the first and final books of *The Ring and the Book*, resuscitative poetry will always be a memorial gesture, one that remembers and aestheticizes death instead of striving to eradicate it. In book 1, when the poet says "The life in me abolished the death of things," this resurrection of the past immediately metamorphoses into a theatrical metaphor, one used repeatedly throughout the poem, continuing with "as then and there / Acted itself over again once more / The tragic piece" (1.520–23). The life the poet raises before our eyes gleams with the dramatic artificiality suggested by the words "acted," "tragic," and "piece," and what we see most clearly in these obsessively first-person lines is the poet's revivifying rhetorical power: the scene playing out through his literary eyes, not an unmediated view of the past. We see, in other words, the aesthetic process of reanimating what has been dead instead of the flawless substitution of life for death. We see what has been lost as much as what can be returned.

The poem registers an intense confusion between the remnants of the past out of which the poet makes his art and the resulting art itself. "Is fiction which makes fact alive, fact too?" the poet muses, drawing our attention to the malleability of both terms as well as grammatically destabilizing the distinction between life and death (1.706). If fact needs the life of fiction, or art, to make it live, then how could living art and dead fact be the same? The living art, grammatically as well as conceptually, always carries the dead past with it. When the poem returns to its metaphor of reanimation in its final book, this metaphor has been explicitly bound to memory, or to the absence of memory, as the passage that I already quoted demonstrates: "So did this old woe fade from memory, / Till after, in the fullness of the days, / I needs must find an ember yet unquenched." The word "need" reminds us that the poet is bound by his mortal limitations. He does not have God's power to create something out of nothing, and thus he must always seek out the dead in order to reanimate it into art.

As Browning wrote exasperatedly to Wedgwood in response to her criticism of the poem, "Before I die, I hope to purely invent something,—here my pride was concerned to invent nothing" (*RB and JW* 144). *The Ring and the Book* celebrates poetry as a historically contingent art rather than one originating beyond the bounds either of the past or of literary tradition. At the same time, however, Browning uses the metaphor of reanimation to resist any teleological model that would place him in an uncomplicated or unbroken timeline with his poetic history. Necropoetics require death, a rupture in time, in order to bring anything back to life. By compulsively reanimating a story of death, the poem insistently demonstrates that art does indeed make itself out of the bones of the past. These lines—"I needs must find an ember yet unquenched, / And, breathing, blow the spark to flame"—in which life can only spark if there is a dead memory to flame to life, not only make reanimation a fundamentally memorial act, contingent on the passage of time, the loss of a story, and the death of its actors, but also turn our attention to the poet's aesthetic "need" to materially remember—not to mourn what is lost, but to make a work of art by scavenging among the remnants of the lost, reanimating them in his own poetic image.

CHAPTER 4

W. B. Yeats and the
Necromantic Museum

For Robert Browning in *The Ring and the Book*, Renaissance Italy is what Jonah Siegel calls a "haunted museum," a historical space in which Browning can express the uncanny gap between artistic representation and historical reality as an act of poetic necromancy (4). For many other nineteenth-century English poets, the haunted museum that aroused necromantic fantasies was an actual museum: the British Museum, an imperial institution that inspired poets like Dante Gabriel Rossetti, John Keats, and Thomas Hardy to think about the national collection as an ethically problematic fusion of art and history. For these poets, who see the British Museum seeking to collect and make into British art the historical relics of other cultures, the museum becomes an imaginative site of cultural death and colonial reanimation alike.

Whether killing off culture or appropriating and recreating the past, the British Museum is an emblem through which English poets consider the relationship between aesthetics, mortality, and history, and, in doing so, the relationship between their own art and its unstable place in an inevitably political history. The collections in the museum provide poets like Rossetti, Keats, and Hardy with objects through which to consider how divorcing—or failing to divorce—the aesthetic from the historical alters the ethical and structural integrity of art. The artifacts of ancient cultures, like the winged bull of Nineveh and the Parthenon Marbles, that comprise the subjects of much museum poetry are remnants whose resuscitated lives in English poems catalyze the poets' anxiety about the inherently imperial, and thus destructive, nature of their own art. As an English institution dating back to 1753, the British Museum was for these poets a fundamental and inescapable symbol of material history and the politically flawed transformation of history into art.

Irish poets of the nineteenth century, however, had no such national emblem, as Ireland in the 1880s was just beginning to institutionalize the idea of a "national collection." W. B. Yeats, who began his poetic career in the 1880s, had a different, less gothic sense of the relationship between collecting, history, and art than did the English poets around him. Although he lived in London surrounded by—and much enamored with—its museums, he did not share the museum-inspired imperial guilt of his English counterparts, nor did he have an equivalent Irish institution to occupy a similar position in his early poetry. What is now the Irish National Museum, once the Dublin Museum of Science and Art, only broke ground in 1885, and Yeats began writing at a moment in Irish history when the structure, contents, political purpose, and social function of a national collection were all hotly under debate. While Yeats spent his later decades mired in frustrated controversies about Dublin's museums and art collections, the Victorian Yeats had faith in the political, aesthetic, and historical efficacy of the collection as a site for the synthesis of a national sense of self.

My aim in this chapter is, first, to show how Yeats's first folklore collections and critically overlooked early work, "The Wanderings of Oisin," are instrumental in forming his theories of aesthetic revivalism; and, second, to think about Yeats as an important bridge between Victorian studies and Irish studies, a writer whose particularly Irish idiom emerged as an engagement with Victorian literary and cultural phenomena, despite his professed hostility to Victorian ideals. It's well-trodden critical ground to suggest that Yeats derived much of his aesthetic theory from Victorian critics like Walter Pater and Matthew Arnold, even if he would deny it.[1] My point is that Victorian culture itself—Victorian institutions like the museum—offered up the same fertile ground to Yeats that it did to British poets like Rossetti, Keats, and Hardy, although the poetry that grew out of it became part of a different national dialogue.

With plans for an institutional museum of ancient artifacts still nascent and unformed in Dublin, Yeats's early work creates textual museums out of historical fragments, stories, and poetic forms. Born just as Victorian England was feeling flush with an influx of new museums in the wake of the Great Exhibition of 1851—between 1850 and 1882 the number of museums in Britain expanded from fewer than 60 to more than 250—Yeats emerged onto the literary scene three decades later amid a waning Victorian sense that national identity could be developed and displayed in public collections of the past. Yet the young Yeats, inspired by the revivalist historicism of Standish O'Grady—whose *History of Ireland* (1878–80) I discuss in my introduction and who Yeats identified as the writer who "started us all"[2]—maintains a belief in the poetic power of history collected and repurposed for the modern moment.[3] Yeats's early work retrenches mid-century Victorian optimism about the political and aesthetic power of the historical collection, reimagining the alienating act of collecting as a process of national revitalization.[4] In doing so, Yeats writes against the notion, increasingly prevalent in the later nineteenth century, that the museum was a space of death instead of a space of life. His *Fairy and Folk Tales of the Irish Peasanty*, especially, demonstrates a fascination with the possibility that a national collection could make the dead past live again, and "The Wanderings of Oisin" explicitly theorizes modern national poetic life emerging in the aftermath of collecting ancient legends. Although Yeats's later poems that deal explicitly with national collections excoriate what he sees as their institutionalization of mortality, in the last decades of the nineteenth century his efforts of literary collecting reveal an idealistic captivation with the poetic and political potential of collecting the past in order to bring a national future to life.

THE MUNICIPAL GALLERY, ADORNO, AND THE POSSIBILITY OF CULTURAL REVIVIFICATION

In May 1887, lately removed from Dublin to London, the twenty-four-year-old William Butler Yeats wrote to his friend Katharine Tynan that every day in this English city was "much like any other day" but that finally he had found a spot in which to begin work on the essays on Irish literature he had been commissioned to write: the South Kensington Museum, which he grouchily described as "a very pleasant place, the air blowing through the open windows from the chestnut trees, the most tolerable spot London has yet revealed to me" (*Letters* 39).[5] Throughout his first few years feeling "like a Robinson Crusoe in this dreadful London," both the South Kensington Museum and the British Museum were Yeats's workplaces of choice for the essays, poems, and stories that connected him to the world of Irish literature. He fell into black moods whenever the rain meant that he "lost [a] day" at the museum (*Letters* 59, 78).[6] In these first months, the city's museums offered Yeats a space of animated salvation from the dreary London streets where he imagined "the souls of the lost are compelled to walk . . . perpetually" (81–82).[7]

It was during these months of 1887 and 1888 that Yeats began to write a long poem entitled "The Wanderings of Oisin." During these months as well, he began the first of several anthologies of Irish writing that he would compile over the next five years, a collection of Irish fairy- and folktales that emerged from melancholic visits to his native Sligo and a sense that Ireland was losing touch with its native past. In the introduction to this anthology, he describes its composition with a semblance (tongue-in-cheek though it may be) of anthropological sensibility. "Yet, be it noticed, if you are a stranger," he writes, "you will not readily get ghost and fairy legends, even in a western village. You must go adroitly to work, and make friends with the children, and the old men. . . . The old women are most learned, but will not so readily be got to talk, for the fairies are very secretive, and much resent being talked of" (FFT 4). Both "Oisin" and the collection of folktales mark Yeats's attempt to create an ongoing collection of Irishness in the midst of London's "dead souls"—to construct an aesthetic, anthropological, and literary museum of the Celtic past at the same moment when Ireland was itself in the midst of building and debating the contents of its first National Museum, when poets whom Yeats admired like Dante Gabriel Rossetti and Thomas Hardy were thinking about the relationship between museum objects and the artistic process, and when Yeats himself was beginning to consider the most "workable" relationship between modern poetry and the ancient past.[8] Although most writing about Yeats and museums focuses on his 1937 poem "The Municipal Gallery Re-visited," it is in his earliest published books that Yeats develops a theory of "museographic" poetics that imagines the collection not as an object-mausoleum or a place of mortal ruins—as did many of his nineteenth-century contemporaries—but as a space that allowed poetry, both ancient and modern, to come to life.[9]

Nearly fifty years later, Yeats would again turn to a museum—this time Ireland's Municipal Gallery—and find in that "hallowed place" Ireland's "spiritual freedom" (CP 321, STP 5). Here, he said in a speech to the Irish Academy of Letters in 1937, "there were pictures painted by men, now dead, who were once my intimate friends," but here also Yeats found himself "restored to many friends," twisting his grammar to envision simultaneously the restoration of his dead compatriots and his own return from the dead (STP 4). Although Yeats revised and reimagined his speech about the Municipal Gallery into his far more melancholic poem "The Municipal Gallery Re-visited," to which I return at the end of this chapter, the speech, while in many instances lifted directly into the lines of the poem, sees the museum not as an epitaph but as a space of revivification.[10] During his visit to the Municipal Gallery, Yeats

142 · CHAPTER 4

says in his speech, he saw "the events of the last thirty years in fine pictures: a peasant ambush, the trial of Roger Casement, a pilgrimage to Lough Derg, event after event" (*STP* 4). These words, reproduced in the poem as static and fragmented images, in the speech have a progressive energy, calling to mind a film reel projecting a series of moving images. The Gallery of the speech is emphatically not the place of a stagnant, persistent present—this is "Ireland *not* as she is displayed in guide book or history," Yeats says—but a space of "magnificent vitality," where the work of artists has rendered Ireland "in the glory of her passions" (*STP* 4). His words about the Gallery in his speech (in contrast to the poem itself) imply that the museum, though full of images of his dead friends, has somehow managed to bring him back to life.[11]

The museum may thus be a place where things seem to go to die and also a place where things come to life. Theodor Adorno has outlined these two interrelated, if antithetical, theories of the museum in his essay "Valéry Proust Museum," which famously begins by likening the museum to a mausoleum. "Museum and mausoleum are connected by more than phonetic association. Museums are like the family sepulchers of works of art. They testify to the neutralization of culture" (175). Adorno's essay offers two different understandings of how this neutralization of culture relates to mortality. Reading Paul Valéry's discomfort with museums in "The Problem with Museums" and Marcel Proust's meditations on the afterlife of art in *À la recherche du temps perdu,* Adorno argues that an understanding of the museum as a space of death emerges from Valéry's sense of art as a "pure thing" that loses its "expressive realization"—is put to death—when it becomes part of the chaotic cultural jumble of a museum (181, 182). Proust, by contrast, according to Adorno, sees works of art as "from the outset something more than their specific aesthetic qualities[—]they are part of the life of the person who observes them" (181). Whereas Valéry, as he writes in "The Problem of Museums," thinks that the "juxtaposition of dead visions" in the museum "has something insane about it," for Proust, Adorno says, "only the death of the work of art in the museum [can] bring it back to life," for only when art is "severed from the living order in which it functioned" will its "true spontaneity" be released (Valéry 203, Adorno 182).

Adorno's essay traces not only two notions of the museum's relationship to mortality but also two notions of the relationship between art and observer within the space of the museum. To Valéry, the very fact of seeing artworks out of context sounds their death knell, but to Proust, the presence of viewers allows objects to live again, to have an ongoing, active place in an ever-changing culture. Adorno, with reservations, ultimately comes down on Proust's side, concluding that the "natural-history collections of the spirit have actually transformed works of art into the hieroglyphics of history and brought them a new content while the old one shrivelled up," but he, too, recognizes that maintaining the museum as an afterlife requires a particular kind of dynamic between art and viewer. Only the visitor who "leaves his naïveté outside" and who concentrates on two or three paintings "as fixedly as if they really were idols" can keep art from the catastrophe of museum-death (185).

Yeats would seem to share Proust's ecstasy at the revivifying power of decontextualization, but for Yeats the museum is less a place of historical dismemberment than a space in which the multiplicity of world history swirls together in synergistic recombination. Like Walter Pater, in whose vampirically reborn Mona Lisa the experiences of humanity are collected and regenerated, Yeats accorded the museum a culturally reanimating power, a power to give the dead a new, exciting, and culturally weighty life rather than a denigrated or monstrous one. Yeats's late nineteenth-century museum is not Adorno's space of neutralized culture, or Valéry's insane juxtaposition of dead visions, or Proust's elated severing of art from function. Instead, Yeats imagined the museum as a model for the culturally revivifying power of poetry, for the ways in which fragments of history could be resuscitated—and rehistoricized—by the modern aesthetic imagination. Adorno, Valéry, and Proust all have in common a sense that the museum, as a space of contextual and historical dismemberment, relies on the way its visitors experience its collections to re-establish (or destroy) the life force of the objects within them. Yeats's poem and speech about the Municipal Gallery share this view that the way in which one looks at the art in a collection—with a critical eye in the poem and with "overwhelming emotion" in the speech—can either kill or restore to life, although in Yeats's case it is his own mortality, rather than the mortality of works of art, at stake in the act of looking.

BRITISH MUSEUM POETRY AND THE
GUILT OF NECROMANCY

For Dante Gabriel Rossetti, by contrast, works of art themselves, as well as nations and cultures as a whole, come under threat in the modern museum. In "The Burden of Nineveh," one of the most famous museum poems of the nineteenth century, Rossetti sees England's own future ruin in the statue of a "wingéd beast" being brought into a room in the British Museum:

> For as that Bull-god once did stand
> And watched the burial-clouds of sand,

144 • CHAPTER 4

> Till these at last without a hand
> Rose o'er his eyes, another land,
>   And blinded him with destiny:—
> So may he stand again; till now,
> In ships of unknown sail and prow,
> Some tribe of the Australian plough
> Bear him afar,—a relic now
>   Of London, not of Nineveh! (Rossetti 350)[12]

Rossetti imagines the museum not only as a sepulcher of mixed ancient cultures—"dead Greece" and "the corpse of Nineveh" stand side by side—but also as a kind of slaughterhouse. The statue, itself a mythical hybrid of man, bull, and winged lion, becomes a "dead disbowelled mystery," a "mummy of a buried faith / Stark from the charnel": not just a monument brought to its final resting place but a jumbled body disgorged and left amid a jumble of other bodies. This strange dead creature occasions Rossetti's imaginative recreation of ancient Nineveh, but his regeneration of the ancient world never escapes the mortality from which it emerges. "From their dead Past thou liv'st alone," Rossetti writes of the priests of Nineveh, and his wonder at the sculpture's shadow, cast alike by the sun of Nineveh and the sun of London, suggests not a revelatory persistence or rebirth of the past but instead the persistence of cultural doom and destruction (48).[13] Time and distance have disintegrated in the space of the museum, such that "home" and "alien" sit on top of one another, and the very idea of "antiquity," with all it suggests of history and the passage of time, can only be referred to between quotation marks that imply that antiquity is nothing more than what can be collected from the past:

> Why, of those mummies in the room
> Above, there might indeed have come
> One out of Egypt to thy home,
> An alien. Nay, but were not some
>   Of these thine own "antiquity"? (101–5)

The collapse of these ancient cultures at the beginning of this stanza portends a similar danger for Rossetti's present moment, leading in the second half of the stanza into an attendant dissolution of the elegant grammar that has thus far characterized the poem. Rossetti's speaker, though maintaining the poem's regular tetrameter lines, seems to lose track of sentence structure in a series of both run-on and befuddled incomplete questions about the evacuation of meaning suffered by these lingering cultural artifacts:

And now,—they and their gods and thou
All relics here together,—now
Whose profit? whether bull or cow,
Isis or Ibis, who or how,
    Whether of Thebes or Nineveh? (106–10)

The shift in this stanza from a lament about the tendency of the museum to flatten, diminish, and dehistoricize its objects—Valéry's "domain of incoherence" in which the "juxtaposition of dead visions has something insane about it"—to a stanza in which that diminishment bleeds into the aesthetic process of poetry itself models the shift in the poem as a whole from Rossetti's dream vision of the dead Nineveh to his waking fear that Victorian London, too, will go the way of the dead museum artifact (Valéry 203). Barbara Black has suggested that the repetition of "and" in the second half of the stanza "mimic[s] the museum's heaping effect" (144). More importantly, however, these lines transform the confusion of the museum's historical juxtapositions into a muddle of language. The verbless lines, which grammatically suffer the same lack of temporal development as the objects on display, show the museum to be a morass as much for English poetry as for the collection and exhibition of history. Borrowing the iambic tetrameter of much of Tennyson's "In Memoriam," "The Burden of Nineveh" is ultimately a poem of mourning, not for the lost culture of which only a sculpture remains but for the art of England, proleptically buried and misunderstood by excavators.[14] Rossetti envisions England's imperial archaeological practices getting their comeuppance when "some tribe of the Australian plough" plunders the sculpture as a relic of English culture (178), or when some future archaeologist,

finding in this desert place
This form, shall hold us for some race
That walked not in Christ's lowly ways,
But bowed its pride and vowed its praise
    Unto the God of Nineveh. (186–90)

The pathos of this anticipatory destruction of England, however—an empire whose fall the museum predicts in its collection of relics from other fallen empires—lies not in the demise of England itself but in the resultant indecipherability of its relics: the inability of art to retain its historical, spiritual, and aesthetic sensibility across time. By the poem's end, the sculpture comes to represent a series of interpretive errors, and Rossetti's final description of the piece focuses on its stasis, its blindness, its incurable weight:

146 • CHAPTER 4

> Those heavy wings spread high
> So sure of flight, which do not fly;
> That set gaze never on the sky;
>   Those scriptured flanks it cannot see;
> Its crown, a brow-contracting load;
> Its planted feet which trust the sod: . . .
> (So grew the image as I trod:)
> O Nineveh, was this thy God,—
>   Thine also, mighty Nineveh? (192–200)

Yet this description also seems rapturous at the idea of a sculpture that is not *meant* to fly, or see, or read—a sculpture, in other words, that has no purpose beyond its own aesthetic presence. Rossetti, like those future archaeologists of England, does not know what the statue represented for Nineveh, but this final stanza transforms the sculpture from a site of cultural representation into a pure aesthetic object, divorced from meaning, time, and space. Art, not history, becomes the poem's final presiding deity, and the question that ends the poem—"O Nineveh, was this thy God,— / Thine also, mighty Nineveh?"— creates an aesthetic continuum between ancient Nineveh and modern Britain that tries to compensate for the absence of any kind of historical or cultural continuum.

For Rossetti, the only way out of the cultural bind of the British Museum is in recourse to pure aestheticism. But the aesthetic stagnancy of this sculpture—wings that "do not fly," eyes that "cannot see" either scripture or the sky, a "brow-contracting crown," and "planted feet"—recalls the poem's initial images of the museum as a space of death, where "dead Greece" and "the corpse of Nineveh" stand in stark contrast to the "living eyes" of museum-goers there to consume them. The imaginative reanimation of scenes from ancient Nineveh that compose the poem's middle vanish in a turn to a Gothic darkness at odds with the poem's beginning. The sunshine seems "to shiver off the day" and the "callous wind . . . swept the shadows off the ground," leaving death and art fused as the mutual and unassailable conditions of the statue. Where Proust sees "the death of the work of art in a museum" as the release "which brings it back to life," in Rossetti's poem this release into pure aesthetics becomes an ecstatic death sentence (Adorno 182). The poem's end, so much more passionate in tone than its beginning—

> In our Museum galleries
> To-day I lingered o'er the prize

Dead Greece vouchsafes to living eyes,—
Her Art for ever in fresh wise
From hour to hour rejoicing me (1–5)

—tests the possibility of art as a spur for historical and cultural reanimation, before finally, and far more fervently, returning to the sense of pleasure in aesthetic death put forth so coldly in these first lines.[15]

"The Burden of Nineveh" presents two possible paths for the ancient objects collected in the British Museum: either they can be the relics of history, providing an access point for modern eyes to regenerate the past, or they can be transhistorical works of art, maintained in an eternal present tense by their aesthetic value. The poem ultimately falls on the side of the latter, the side of transhistorical aesthetics, because the former, the side of historical artifact, leaves no viable place for art to persist. To see the work of art as a cultural relic is ultimately to imagine its destruction and cultural appropriation, its subjective revivification by imperial imaginations and its attendant loss of meaning. By setting his poem in the British Museum, the imperial collection par excellence, Rossetti allows his own artistic effort to become a participant in the power struggle between aesthetics and the political subjugation inherent in the collecting practices of the British Empire. The British Museum forces a choice between the aesthetic and the historical, between a beautiful death and an imperial reanimation.

In recreating a world of Nineveh within its own poetic strictures, the poem re-enacts the violent appropriation by which the statue came to be enclosed within the walls of the museum. Rossetti deliberately "wakes" the poem from this imperial dream—"Here woke my thought"—when he ceases to imagine Nineveh and begins instead to project the same fate for England. Imaginative reanimation becomes a cycle of imperial violence, and in this act of self-reflection the poem recognizes itself as its own imperial museum, collecting, decontextualizing, and recontextualizing the statue beyond any kind of historical recognition. Rossetti's turn to aesthetics in the poem's last stanza thus has a profoundly political implication. Instead of perpetuating the aggression of colonial necromancy, Rossetti chooses instead to allow Nineveh to be killed into art. In doing so, he attempts to create a literary space beyond the reach of politics and historical necessity.

As I discuss at greater length later in this chapter, the young W. B. Yeats, wandering through the British Museum nearly thirty years after his much-admired predecessor wrote "The Burden of Nineveh," also found in the ancient statues there an occasion to probe the relationship between cultural

148 • CHAPTER 4

displacement, aesthetic power, and historical revivification. Yet unlike Rossetti, for whom the aesthetics of the museum could offer nothing but death, Yeats found in the aesthetic conundrum of the museum the possibility for new life—and for new *Irish* life, in particular. As the much older Yeats recalled, his younger self was fascinated with national museums and with the ways in which old artifacts collected in new places acquired, as he called it, a certain kind of "joyous energy" (*TV* 38). He translated this excitement about the second life of museum objects into a theory of Irish cultural revivalism predicated on a full process of excavating, displacing, and refashioning old Irish legends into modern poetry.

As "The Burden of Nineveh" suggests, however, for many English poets, unlike for Yeats, the aesthetic and political implications of the British Museum as a space of revival were deeply unnerving throughout the nineteenth and early twentieth centuries. In *Time Flies: A Reading Diary,* a book of religious meditations published in 1885, Christina Rossetti recalls how a friend "shrank from entering the Mummy Room at the British Museum under a vivid realisation of how the general resurrection might occur even as one stood among those solemn corpses turned into a sight for sightseers. And at that great and awful day, what will be thought of supposititious heads and members?" (128). The day's entry, which caustically critiques the "scandalous multiplicity of relics" of St. Martin that have proliferated across churches, begins its consideration of spiritual inauthenticity by suggesting that it would be "most pious and most reverential" overall "to leave the dead at rest in their graves," and ends with this gothic image of the British Museum's mummies coming back to life. Rossetti's dismay at the practice of collecting relics reaches its apogee in the British Museum's collection of Egyptian mummies, for in the very act of collecting, the museum has irreverently transformed what once were "solemn corpses" into an entertaining "sight for sightseers" (128).

Rossetti cannot help but imagine, with some fear, this gruesome spectacle coming to life out of place and out of time, for the mummies' conversion from authentic bodies into inauthentic exhibition invites the anxious fancy of an analogical conversion from truly dead to dreadfully alive again. When the museum creates as false and spiritually vacuous an identity for these mummies as churches do for the "supposititious heads and members" of false religious relics, it enables these bodies to have a new and threatening life beyond the bounds of their "solemn" deaths—one in which Rossetti and her friend, at least, "shr[i]nk" from participating (128). Like her brother's "The Burden of Nineveh," Christina Rossetti's meditation envisions the British Museum's collection not as a stagnant "ossuary that house[d] the dead" but as a dangerously transformative enterprise, although in her case it is the spiritual, rather than the cultural, appropriation of objects that morphs into an irreverent and impious horror of dead bodies coming to life (Black 135).

Decades earlier, John Keats addressed the museum's transformative danger in a sonnet about the British Museum's other famously fraught collection. His 1819 sonnet "On Seeing the Elgin Marbles" captures a similarly destabilizing, almost gothic experience of the museum metamorphosing these famous symbols of idealized Hellenism into material "monument[s] of National glory" (qtd. in G. Wood 133).[16] The British Museum's acquisition of the Parthenon ruins from Lord Elgin in 1816 followed a lengthy debate in Parliament about the legality of removing the marbles from Athens, and the presence of the marbles in the museum, as Gillen D'Arcy Wood has written, "generated a concern that the political motivations behind their institutionalization . . . would destroy their aura of ideality" (133). In putting the marbles on display in its national museum, Britain was both remaking the world of ancient Greece as a fundamentally *British* fascination with Hellenism and fetishizing the imperial power that could acquire and display these foreign treasures for the pleasure of its citizens.

Wood has described the entrance of the marbles into the museum as inaugurating a new phase in Britain's relationship to ancient Greece: "If sentimental Hellenism is a work of mourning, as Schiller had suggested two decades before, then the arrival of the Elgin Marbles at the British Museum symbolized nothing less than antiquity's return from the grave" (133). By describing the shift in this way, Wood emphasizes the materiality of the past that the Parthenon Marbles forced museum-goers to confront, in contrast to the idealized beauty of a lost ancient culture that could be imagined in the distant ruins of Greece. Whereas the energy of "sentimental Hellenism" arose from wishing after an unattainable beauty, the shock of the marbles forced both the physical reality of the ancient world and the processes of time, acquisition, and politics to the forefront of Hellenic interest. Yet his metaphor also suggests that the marbles, once put on display in London and at the mercy of their new British owners, were inappropriately disturbed from their rest and fittingly uncanny to the Londoners who saw them there.[17]

Keats's sonnet on the marbles, which begins with a reminder of death that, by its end, has rendered its speaker "dizzy" with pain and in the midst of a lyric breakdown, reflects in both its subject and its structure the uncanniness that Freud says is experienced in the highest degree in "anything to do with death, dead bodies, revenants, spirits, and ghosts" (148). Rather than address the marbles specifically (neither of Keats's Elgin sonnets do so), Keats focuses

150 • CHAPTER 4

instead on the disturbing superimposition of real life atop the familiar images of his imagination, a double vision that generates, for Keats, a feeling like a confrontation with death:

My spirit is too weak—mortality
Weighs heavily on me like unwilling sleep,
And each imagin'd pinnacle and steep
Of godlike hardship, tells me I must die
Like a sick Eagle looking at the sky.
Yet 'tis a gentle luxury to weep
That I have not the cloudy winds to keep,
Fresh for the opening of the morning's eye.
Such dim-conceived glories of the brain
Bring round the heart an undescribable feud;
So do these wonders a most dizzy pain,
That mingles Grecian grandeur with the rude
Wasting of old Time—with a billowy main—
A sun—a shadow of a magnitude. (73)

Wood has suggested that this poem runs "the full gamut of melodramatic effect," to end in a "serious case of the shock of the real" (137). Barbara Black contends that the emotive confusion in the poem stems from the marbles representing "in equal measure atemporal grandeur and time-wasted ruins" (135). I would argue instead that the poem's lyrical dissolution is the inevitable outcome of its "feud" between death and life, between the material ravages of history and an imagined vision of the living past. The image of Keats's living death at the poem's beginning—the weight of mortality bearing down on the living poet—iterates his distress at seeing the living death of the marbles where he expected to see the life of ancient Greece, and the collapse of grammar into a series of dashes at the poem's end suggests that the lyric voice, like the museum, cannot maintain its aesthetic idealism in confrontation with material relics of the past. The sonnet form itself is degraded at the end of the poem, for the contrast between the poem's strict meter and the faltering grammar and image in the last two lines foregrounds the inability of the form to sustain coherence when reality and fantasy fail to coincide. Material history interferes with the Romantic imagination, and this sonnet—a familiar form for meditating on antique ruins[18]—loses its hold on the distinction between its form and its object, becoming its own strange "shadow of a magnitude" and a model of the relic's degraded second life in the museum.

When Thomas Hardy, in his 1905 poem "Christmas in the Elgin Room, British Museum: Early Last Century," fantasizes that the marbles actually have come to life, the museum space becomes not a spur to uncanny language but an uncanny space itself, full of animated bodies who see the museum not as a collection of history but as a place of "exile" where they are "captives." These newly alive voices lament their transformation from gods into commodities, remaking the emblematic sounds of Christmas into a reflection on the British Museum as an emblem of political violence:

> We are those whom Christmas overthrew
> . . . .
> O it is sad now we are sold—
> We gods! for Borean people's gold
> And brought to the gloom
> Of this gaunt room. (885)

The poem that gives life to these voices ultimately silences them, as well, for by its final stanza the marbles have been reduced to nodding heads and throbbing torsos, dismembered bodies "whose limbs were shards beneath some Acropolitan clod." What begins as an apparent attempt to give political voice to these relics ends by diminishing them to animated, terrified bits of bodies, "shook . . . to the core" by the Christmas bells clanging in celebration. Hardy's poem opposes any notion that the public museum's dedication "to preservation, and to those objects of the past whose useful life is in effect over," might, as Philip Fisher has suggested, allow it to be a "storage area for authenticity" (453). The poem suggests instead that these objects were ripped from useful life and made into something they are not, still longing for their place "radiant on Athenai's hill" (885).

The poem reveals the uncanniness of the museum in two ways. First, by transforming the marbles into speaking, feeling victims, Hardy makes both literal and ethically fraught the notion that the museum gives new life to relics of the ancient past. And second, by then stripping these beings even of their imagined voices, Hardy enacts the violence that the British Museum's decontextualization of art objects perpetrated on ancient cultures. The poem pulls in two directions, both reanimating the dead and deanimating the living, forcing readers to hover in an unstable museum space that simultaneously resurrects and destroys the past. Hardy's political stance in "Christmas in the Elgin Room" gives an ethical weight to the gothic sensibility that pervades all of his museum poems: the "mould of a dead bird" whose "coo . . . has perished not" in "In a Museum," the voice of Paul seeming to echo from a stone in "In the British Museum," and the "dead fingers . . . shrunk in the tomb" that play the old instruments in "A Phantasy in a Museum of Musical Instruments" all imagine the museum as a place in which the work of art must necessarily be a revenant, not simply retaining the traces of its past but relying on the poet to assist in its active struggle to resurrect them (404, 358, 559).

Other British Museum poems from the nineteenth century share this sense that poetry must step into the aesthetic and spiritual gap left by the museum's cold, institutional collection, regenerating a living past from the museum's deadening effect. Sir Edwin Arnold's 1853 "To the Statue of Eumousia in the British Museum," for instance, fantasizes about the "honey-voice" of a statue throwing "off its long, long sleep" (10).[19] "And with the witching song rose the dim Past, / And the dull present faded!" the poet exclaims, but all too quickly the past dies again (19–20):

> This might not last: and soon that beaming eye
> Froze to cold death again; thy dulcet tongue
> Was locked in marble, and no more the sigh
> Of silver music from that rich lyre rung;
> . . . .
> And then the vision past—the spell was flown,
> And all the Goddess gone—save that most living stone. (28–36)

For Arnold, the museum cannot sustain the imagined rebirth of the past. It enables the fantastical possibility of new life but almost immediately shuts it down again, leaving the poet in the last stanza to offer his own art as the only possible means of reinvigorating the spirit of the past:

> May I the high tale of my heart believe
> That thou didst bid me sing? then will I weave
> Thy praises, Goddess, in my lowly line,
> So thou wilt ne'er thy faithful votary leave. (40–43)

The final stanza's string of questions is plagued by doubt. The young poet, now shaken from the museum fantasy, seems uncertain about the performative task he has assigned his own lyric voice, but his recourse in this last stanza to a particularly archaic language and apostrophe nonetheless offers poetry both as a model and as a substitute venue for revivifying the past.

Laurence Binyon, an English poet who worked in the British Museum in the early 1890s, offers a similar contrast between the work of the museum and the work of poetry in his 1908 poem "In the British Museum." The poem, which begins in the same room of the museum as Rossetti's "The Burden of Nineveh," starts by describing a girl hurrying through the gothic gallery full of "monstrous visions of ages past," sculptures with "strange motionless features," and "sombre monuments," until she finally settles beneath "the darkest shade" of a statue and goes to sleep (60). The poem then becomes a dream vision, transporting the girl from the museum into "an unknown land," "far from home," and conjuring "Immense Forms" that "grave[ly]" smile down on her as she begs them to "Speak, speak, or crush me!" (61). The monumental statues exist simultaneously in two worlds, the gallery and the dream—the museum and poetry—but only the imaginative power of the latter can transform them from uncanny stones into animate ecclesiastics. Again, the museum catalyzes a dream vision of an animate past, but the art of poetry must act as a supplement for what is spiritually lacking in the museum room, and in doing so, stands in contrast to the museum's deadening force. Yet, even in Binyon's hands, the museum poem cannot make the museum objects speak, as Hardy's "Christmas in the Elgin Room" briefly does. Hardy's poem, more profoundly than these other or even his own other museum poems, struggles with both its responsibility to the museum's antiquities and its failure to bring back to life what they have lost. The poem ultimately becomes an elegy not just for the useful life of museum objects but also for the efficacy of poetry as an alternative means of animating the past.

THE IRISH TEXTUAL MUSEUM AND THE
DREAM OF CELTIC REVIVAL

W. B. Yeats viewed the power of poetic art in a far more efficacious light. In 1903 he compared the imagination to the centuries-old entombed body of Father Christian Rosencrux: "It seems to me that the imagination has had no very different history during the last two hundred years, but has laid in a great tomb of criticism, and had set over it inextinguishable magical lamps of wisdom and romance, and has been altogether so nobly housed and apparelled that we have forgotten that its wizard lips are closed, or but opened for the complaining of some melancholy and ghostly voice," he wrote, suggesting that *only* the "wise comments" and the "criticism of life" engendered by contemporary poetry could wake the buried and robed imagination of the past (*BFCR* 308–9). Even at the earliest stages of his career, Yeats imagined that modern poetry and historical legend belonged in a symbiotic relationship to one another, the former drawing a power of expression from the latter and the

154 • CHAPTER 4

latter thus persisting in contemporary national culture. "I am not very fond of retrospective art," he wrote to Katharine Tynan in 1888: "I do not mean we should go to old ballads and poems for inspiration, but we should search them for new methods of expressing ourselves" (*Letters* 98).[20] Stories and tales of the Irish national past were *meant* to be excavated and given new life through modern expression. To borrow Gregory Castle's description of J. M. Synge's revivalist ethos, "what disappears . . . was only ever preparing for a (re)appearance, subject to change and renewal, in the world of art" ("Synge" 226). As did Browning in *The Ring and the Book,* Yeats imagined the past as a scattering of literary remnants, but remnants, he wrote, that had to be gathered into collections of "workable subjects," specifically "meant for Irish poets" to draw on (*Letters* 88).[21]

Yeats began his own work with Irish relics in several anthologies of Irish stories he collected between 1887 and 1892: two collections of Irish fairy- and folktales, a collection of William Carleton's stories, and a collection of "prose tales of modern Irish life," called *Representative Irish Tales,* meant to "illustrate as far as possible the kind of witness they bear to Irish character" (*RIT* 25). Although he certainly reprinted some already published work in these collections, he aimed, particularly in the folklore collections, to unearth "*original matter of value which no one else could have got*" from beyond the urban realm of the Irish intelligentsia (*Letters* 90; original italics).[22] Leah Price has argued generally about anthologies that "the anthology's ambition to represent a whole through its parts is always undermined by readers' awareness that the parts have been chosen for their difference from those left out," but Yeats's own ambition for these anthologies had more to do with gathering and displaying material that had not yet been gathered than it did with excerpting and excising already popular fiction (6). Rather than "textual mutilation," Yeats's work was an act of textual re-memberment, piecing together, reorienting, and giving new life to the scattered pieces of Irish national literature that the Irish nation, it seemed, had not yet accessed (49). Like that of any nineteenth-century curator of a "national" collection, however, Yeats's sense of purpose shared the colonial sensibility that reimagined educational value as an act of cultural dissemination, as the prefatory poem to his 1892 fairy-tale anthology, "Where My Books Go," makes clear:

> All the words that I gather,
>   And all the words that I write,
> Must spread out their wings untiring,
>   And never rest in their flight,
> Till they come where your sad, sad heart is,

> And sing to you in the night,
> Beyond where the waters are moving,
> Storm darkened or starry bright. (*IFT* n. pag.)

This poem brings the act of collecting and the act of creating into parallel with one another, but here it gives them a single, romantically missionary purpose that does not entirely make sense as the preface to an anthology whose fairy tales were collected *from* the peasantry in order to be presented *to* Irish educated classes. Yeats disseminates tradition, not modernity, but in envisioning his books flying out "Beyond where the waters are moving"—a phrase that implies a distinctly mythic, distinctly non-urban destination—he casts his project in an imperial light that recalls both the bringing of civilization to the colonies and the appropriation of colonial cultures for British educative purposes. Although Yeats viewed his anthologizing process as one that excavated and regenerated the past of the peasantry in order to render it available to the present-day intelligentsia, he seemed unable to divorce this process from the same colonial associations that so disturbed Dante Gabriel Rossetti when he was confronted by antiquities in the British Museum.[23] And, indeed, the British Museums Association in the early twentieth century had the same idea that Yeats had, as Henry Balfour made clear in his 1909 presidential address when he identified western Ireland as a wealth of primitive cultural artifacts that would be "useful to the student of the evolution of our national characteristics, since they are survivals from stages long since past in the history of the Higher Culture of Great Britain" and are "of the greater value by reason of the persistence of some of their old-time culture-environment" (257–58). Where Yeats saw the raw material for a modern revival of Celtic culture, Balfour saw the missing links in British evolution, but both maintained the same anthropological and acquisitive interest in the enduring primitivism of the Irish West.

If the collecting of Celtic heritage by an Irishman was less of an imperial act than was the collecting of the same antiquities by an Englishman, it nonetheless shared a structure in which repossessing a past Other became the key to gaining contemporary knowledge and forging a national identity. "Museums are as selective as literary anthologies, which in many respects they greatly resemble," Declan Kiberd has argued in an essay called "Museums and Learning," "because they are often the result of a colonial encounter, and are based on the notion that a native culture need not be known whole and entire" (225). These two analogous venues, Kiberd suggests, both represent an imperial ideology in which "colonialists felt that they alone could construe the natives who might never be expected to construe themselves" (225). Kiberd seems surprised that postcolonial scholars in Ireland and India would perpetuate the tradition of anthologizing their own literature, despite the colonial overtones in the practice of anthology, but he paraphrases Seamus Deane's justification of the Irish Field Day Anthology as an explanation: "if people are going to have to live in enclaves and ghettoes, they might at least be enclaves and ghettoes of their own making, as opposed to sites constructed by others" (226). In the case of Yeats and other Irish anthologists who set about collecting their own native heritage, the anthology was, at least in theory, less an act of historical appropriation than an exercise in cultural self-creation, and one that, for Yeats in particular, was meant to allow for a fluid movement between past and present instead of the Darwinist teleology that structured most nineteenth-century British anthropological museums.[24] In his essay, Kiberd fantasizes about what a museum created by Yeats might look like: "In Yeats's museum, the visitor would first have confronted the present moment, and then gone back over time, to the period of primitive man, who had so much more to teach us. He would have had his visitors walk in straight lines but in the opposite directions of most" (221–22). The Yeatsian museum would thus not be Balfour's museum of cultural evolution—a collection that could show how the present emerged from the past—but rather a museum of cultural revival, a collection that brings the past back to life in order to reshape the present.

Just as Kiberd's imaginary Yeatsian museum follows a revisionary temporal logic, proposing the ancient as the pinnacle of development and the modern as a degraded state of being ("There would be no Darwin had there been no book of Genesis," Yeats once wrote [qtd. in Kiberd, "Museums" 222]), so are Yeats's museographic texts—his first collection of folklore and "The Wanderings of Oisin"—occupied with problems of temporal progression, with the relationship between primitive and contemporary, and with the ways in which national identity can and cannot be shaped by contact with the past. I call these texts "museographic" because both, in different ways, struggle with principles of collection and display that are driven by Yeats's Romantic anthropological instincts and nationalist loyalty to his material history. Yeats's ascription to a Romantic school of folklore that privileged the "imaginative" possibilities of the old stories over the "merely scientific" cataloging of comparative anthropology bears itself out in these texts that refute the synonymy between imaginative production and the act of collecting in and of itself.[25] As Yeats wrote in 1890, "when [the man of science] captures a folk-tale, nothing remains with him for all his trouble but a wretched lifeless thing."[26] Outspoken in his distaste for Victorian scientific rationalism, Yeats describes his own collecting as an imaginative, resuscitative alternative to this violent scientific "capturing," even as his *Fairy and Folk Tales of the Irish Peasantry*, which began in a trip to Sligo to gather old stories from the peasantry there, seemed to imitate it. "The Wanderings of Oisin," which Yeats finished writing during this same trip, presents the act of collecting more metaphorically—yet equally imperially—as the poem gathers Celtic legend, Homeric epic, Romantic themes, Victorian allusions, and the art of Irish resistance into a single "national" narrative that Yeats hoped would "make a few friends, perhaps, among people of my own sort—that is the most" (*Letters* 88).[27] The poem, about a man going to and returning from faeryland, offers a metareflection on Yeats's own trips back and forth to Sligo collecting tales of Irish fairies. "Oisin" allegorizes the act of folklore-collecting as an immersion in the land of the dead, and the process of shaping that folklore into modern poetry as the far-more-important return. Its obsession with the return from states of suspended animation, particularly apparent in its third book, which is the focus of the final section of this chapter, expresses Yeats's radical realization that retrospection and revival can never be synonymous—that cultural revival does not derive from the simple excavation of old stories but rather from a heroic act of aesthetic transformation that can reanimate those legends into bodies of modern poetry.

Old Ireland for Yeats was a spur to modernity rather than a miring history, and thus his enthusiasm throughout the 1880s and '90s for excavating and collecting the Irish past lay in the possibility that it could both be remade by, and itself remake, modern Irish literary culture. But at the same time, Yeats maintained an anthropological sensibility and a socially conscious rationale alike in his desire to collect the old Irish folklore and literature that he believed were the "body and soul" of Ireland (*RIT* 25). "This book differs also from some of its kind," Yeats wrote in 1894 of an anthology of Irish poetry he had collected, "in being intended only a little for English readers, and not at all for Irish peasants, but almost wholly for the small beginning of that educated and national public, which is our greatest need and perhaps our vainest hope" (*BIV* xxvii). Yeats hoped his anthologies, as collections of the Irish character, could serve an educational purpose not simply by making literary artifacts available to the general public but by coalescing a particular class of the national public that had "been through the mould of Trinity College or of English Universities" and had far less knowledge of their own Irish heritage than they had of their learned English one (*BIV* xxvi).

At the same moment, across the Irish Sea, Dublin itself was working to institutionalize the same desire in the form of a newly established Irish national museum. The Science and Art Museum Act, which passed in 1877, authorized the construction of a new museum in Dublin, under the control of the Department of Science and Art in London, to house and expand the collections of art and antiquities then privately held by the Royal Irish Academy. The shift in ownership of this collection from an Irish institution to the British imperial sector caused some outrage among Irish antiquarians, who saw the move, as Elizabeth Crooke has written, "symbolically . . . placing the control of the material remains of the Irish past in the hands of a London department" (114). While Irish officials imagined the museum as an "important national institution" and a repository of the treasures of the Irish past, the Department of Science and Art saw the museum as "part of a system developed for the mutual benefit of all members of the Union," and, like the South Kensington Museum in London, expressly intended as a tool to educate the public in the industrial arts, not in their national history (Crooke 114). Upon its initial selection of a non-Irish architect to design the building in 1882, the Department of Science and Art seemed to be fulfilling Ireland's initial dismay about London's objectives for its national museum. "We candidly say," wrote the editor of the *Irish Builder*, "we have not much faith in the good intentions of the South Kensington officials respecting Ireland or matters Irish" (qtd. in Crooke 117). The MP for Yeats's beloved Sligo declared that the project was "condemned and protested against by men of all political parties, and . . . not a single voice was raised in its favour," leading a successful campaign to have the design competition reopened and the design granted in 1883 to an Irish architectural firm (Sexton n. pag.).

Even more important than the debates about what, precisely, should make up the collections in the new museum was an ongoing concern about who the museum's intended audience really should be, and how Ireland's antiquities could be retained and displayed for nationalist purposes while under an English administration. When the museum opened in 1890, its antiquities collection was relegated to a far-from-prominent position on the museum's first floor. The bulk of its space, exhibitions, and lectures was devoted to the industrial arts of other nations, which, as one report on antique lace said, although "mostly foreign," was intended to be "highly suggestive to the lace workers of Ireland" (Crooke 124). Instead of cultivating and expanding the national antiquities collection that would provide the Irish public a material connection to its own history, the early Dublin Museum of Science and Industry became a small reproduction of the South Kensington Museum. It was devoted to providing foreign and imperial examples that could, in theory, improve the industrial production of its Irish audience. In 1892 the Irish nationalist journalist and MP William O'Brien lamented that the Royal Irish Academy had given up to the "South Kensington cabinet of curiosities, the inestimable relics of Celtic antiquity bequeathed to them by the pious patriotism of generations of Hudsons, Hardimans, and Wildes."[28] What had begun as a wish to make Ireland's treasures more publicly available, and to allow these antiquities to be an educational hub for nationalism and patriotism, had become instead an exercise in "the imperializing of Ireland" (Crooke 109).

In his 1849 *Beauties of the Boyne*, William Wilde, husband to Speranza, father of the famous Oscar, and eventual compiler of the first catalog to accompany the Royal Irish Academy's collection, bemoans the Irish National Education Board's willingness to teach their students about every other country "but [to] never once allude, in their system of education, to the national history of the people they are employed to teach" (vi). That "the ordinarily educated—and above all, that the learned of any country—should be unacquainted with the materials of our Irish history, is a lamentable fact," he writes, insisting that in writing this book that describes the landscape, history, and archaeological remains of the most famous river in Ireland, one of his main objects has been "to popularize [the great mass of Irish historic manuscripts]—to render my countrymen familiar with facts and names of Irish history" (vi–vii). Wilde's preface to this book praises the antiquarian work being done by George Petrie and others, as well as the Royal Irish Academy's newly awakened "zeal and enthusiasm . . . [in] creating a museum of Celtic and early Christian antiquities unexampled in the British Isles" (ix). But the preface also laments the gap between the private work of these antiquarians and the Irish public's awareness of their national heritage. "Why has the catalogue of this, our national collection, been so long delayed? Why is not each new specimen of interest figured in the Proceedings of the Academy, and its description thus widely distributed among the public?" (x).[29]

Wilde, like Yeats forty years later, felt hugely the absence of knowledge about the Irish past, even in the educated Irish classes, who, as Yeats also realized, were suffering from a British imperial education that veered toward cosmopolitanism and away from Irish cultural and national heritage. The wish of Wilde and others for more public funding for the Royal Irish Academy—"even fifty pounds a year," Wilde argued, would allow for public projects untenable under the "miserable pittance which is doled out to this noble institution by Parliament" (*Beauties* x)—which eventually led to its collection coming under the control of the Department of Arts and Sciences, was fundamentally a wish for an Irish cultural revival via the material remains of Ireland's rich Celtic history. Midway through the nineteenth century, Wilde's excitement that the Royal Irish Academy had finally "awoke from the apathetic slumber in which it remained during the early part of [the] century" was tempered by the widespread belief, expressed even by noted Irish historians, "that there exist in the Irish annals no materials for the civil history of the country."[30] Bringing the newly woken Academy's collection of Irish antiquities into the purview of public education would be, Wilde hoped, a giant step toward waking the Irish population as a whole to its almost-lost past.

If Irish history could be institutionally relegated to the margins by a museum right in the heart of the Irish metropolis, then it was up to Irish writers like Yeats, who himself felt marginalized in that other, bigger, British metropolis, to imagine an Irish past that could flourish right in the heart of Victorian modernity. He wanted an Irish past that could move fluidly *between* margin and metropole, between Sligo and London, between landscape and museum. When Yeats, in his *Book of Irish Verse,* echoes Wilde's dream that a national collection could be a tool of historical education for the Irish middle classes, he also expresses his faith in the power of the Irish past to persist and reinvent itself in the contemporary Irish imagination. "How strong a wind blows from the ancient legends of Ireland," he writes in the book's introduction, and "how vigorous an impulse to create is in her heart to-day" (xxvi-xxvii). These two phenomena—the active spirit of the past and the energetic creativity of the present—flourish concurrently and co-dependently for Yeats. When in 1887 he embarked on his trip to Sligo to finish "The Wanderings of Oisin" and to begin collecting folktales from the people there, he wrote an excited letter to Katharine Tynan in which he enclosed "the first fruit of [his] fairy-hunting": a set of "trivial verses" *he* had written called "The Fairy Doctor" (*Letters* 49):[31]

> The fairy doctor comes our way
> Over the sorrel-coloured wold;
> Now sadly, now unearthly gay!
> A little withered man, and old. (*Letters* 50)[32]

"Trivial" though the poem may be, it demonstrates Yeats's sense that the act of collecting was a process simultaneously of gathering and of reimagining. He models in this literary artifact the quality of temporal simultaneity that museologist Susan Pearse assigns particularly to the material museum object. "Objects have the capacity to be perpetually reinterpreted, re-formed within a desired contemporary context. But they also, always, carry with them the characters they acquired in their original and subsequent contexts. . . . Objects are therefore both content and interpretation, both past and present; in semiotic language they are, always, both signifier and signified" (236). So, too, does the old Irish folktale for Yeats become at the same time both national heirloom and creative fodder. "The Fairy Doctor" is a singsong parable of the ways in which modern times can benefit from the collection of old traditions, as well as of the danger in not treating these old traditions with enough respect. The poem warns of the "glamour he may fold / Closely round us body and mind," for the only thing the fairy doctor cannot heal, Yeats tells us, is "he who pining fell / Glamoured by fairies for their own." The poem's sole threat is the seductive lure of the past, but its solution seems to be *using* the past to heal the present rather than either fetishizing or dismissing the power of "the little withered man and old."

Yeats's act of collecting was an effort of cultural recuperation, these filled notebooks acting as what Stephen Greenblatt might call "a monument to the fragility of cultures" at the same time that Yeats believed, as he wrote rather gleefully in his introduction to *Fairy and Folk Tales of the Irish Peasantry,* that "the Spirit of the Age ha[d] in no manner made his voice heard" in Sligo, nor would "troops of [its] like . . . change the Celt much" (Greenblatt 546–47, *FFT* 3). Yeats's elegiac tone in describing his forays through Sligo searching for folklore contrast sharply with his faith in the immutability of the old culture, and his own personal melancholy enables his greater revivalist instinct. As Germain Bazin wrote in his foreword to *The Museum Age,* describing the museum collection simultaneously paying tribute to time passing and clinging to time's endurance, "Only when men sense the waning of a civilization do they suddenly become interested in its history, and, probing, become aware of the force and uniqueness of the ideas it has fostered" (19). If Bazin here describes the essential condition of any historical museum collection, he equally describes a folklore collection that simultaneously aimed to preserve the remnants of the local Irish past and to recreate them for a modern urban readership.[33]

Sligo and the idea of a museum were, in fact, strangely entwined for Yeats. In his 1922 autobiography, thoughts of Sligo become a frame for Yeats's recollections of the time he spent in the British Museum in the late 1880s, and for the joy that he imagined in the presence of some of the sculptures there:

> The statues of Mausolus and Artemisia at the British Museum, private, half-animal, half-divine figures, all unlike the Grecian athletes and Egyptian kings in their near neighbourhood, that stand in the middle of the crowd's applause, or sit above measuring it out unpersuadable justice, became to me, now or later, images of an unpremeditated joyous energy, that neither I nor any man, racked by doubt and inquiry, can achieve; and that yet, if once achieved, might seem to men and women of Connemara or of Galway their very soul. (*Autobiographies* 137)

162 • CHAPTER 4

These statues, taken from the Ottoman Empire by a British archaeologist in the 1850s, had decorated the pinnacle of the famous Mausoleum of Mausolus. They are funerary monuments, literally part of a mausoleum, and yet displaced into a museum Yeats imagines them as ideal representations of "joyous energy," not as the bearers of death that Keats and Hardy imagined the Parthenon Marbles to be.

In the brief ekphrasis of this passage, Yeats reflects not only on the museum statues themselves but also on his relationship to the whole tradition of nineteenth-century museum poetry that has come before him: Shelley's "Ozymandias," Keats's "On Seeing the Elgin Marbles," Rossetti's "The Burden of Nineveh," and the other poems I discussed earlier in the chapter.[34] By focusing his attention on the Mausoleum statues rather than on these other Egyptian and Greek antiquities that had already gotten so much play in English poetry, Yeats presents an alternative narrative of the museum's relationship to its antiquities than the dire one that poets like Rossetti had already put forward. The subtext of this passage suggests that a poet's alternative focal point in the museum will generate poetry with a far more optimistic narrative of the intersection between the museum collection and poetic genesis. Instead of experiencing the lively displaced funerary statues as uncanny reminders of mortality, Yeats identifies a kind of life force in these figures. More specifically, and more strangely, Yeats recognizes a distinctively *Irish* life force in them—the ideal energy these statues embody, could it be somehow bottled, "might seem to men and women of Connemara or of Galway their very soul." Yeats finds in the British Museum neither the materialization of imperial violence—like Rossetti does—nor art reduced to a hollow corpse, but rather clear evidence of an ancient and great culture experiencing an energized second life—one only *enhanced* by its presence in a modern British Museum.

To Yeats, these statues become the superlative figures for the revival of the Irish West—Connemara and Galway, the Celtic heart of Ireland: figures embodying not only the true soul of the Irish but also the capacity to represent that soul in a way, "if once achieved," that could render it recognizable to itself (*Autobiographies* 137). In other words, these statues, displaced and on display in a wholly new context, are examples of how the spirit of a culture might be even more available and recognizable in new forms than in old ones—models for the reanimation of the Irish past via formal recontextualization. It is telling that this recollection of a foray into the British Museum, which comes in the midst of a paragraph in Yeats's autobiography about the need to root modern poetry in a specific national landscape, does not appear wrongly placed to Yeats, although it would seem both digressive and paradoxical to praise the Persian antiquities in an English museum collection in the midst of arguing for the importance of embedding art in its native ground. Yeats himself, however, imagines that he is similarly displaced, and in imagining himself displaced in a way analogous to the statues, he also implicitly imagines that he is particularly suited to represent native Irish energy. The paragraph about the statues begins, "Though I went to Sligo every summer, I was compelled to live out of Ireland the greater part of every year, and was but keeping my mind upon what I knew must be the subject-matter of my poetry" (*Autobiographies* 137). By beginning this way, the paragraph instinctively entwines the plight of dislocation with the necessity of Celtic subject matter. Yeats continues by lamenting the absence of Welsh or Scottish landscapes in the work of William Morris and Percy Bysshe Shelley, whom he also imagines displaced from Celtic heritages but nonetheless accountable to them. "I believed that if Morris had set his stories amid the scenery of his own Wales, for I knew him to be of Welsh extraction and supposed wrongly that he had spent his childhood there, that if Shelley had nailed his Prometheus, or some equal symbol, upon some Welsh or Scottish rock, their art would have entered more intimately . . . into our thought" (137). Yeats argues here for the concrete nationalizing of art, yet at the same time makes the relationship between art and its native soil one based on imaginative cultural memory, not one predicated on actual presence. Art and artists need not *be* in their native land as long as their work remembers and expresses the energy of that land. And perhaps—perhaps—this energy will be best expressed in non-native contexts, or through non-native forms. The associative process of Yeats's logic provides the statues standing in the British Museum with the symbolic resonance of this kind of cultural memory. No longer in their native mausoleum but emerging in a British context full of "unpremeditated joyous energy," the statues become models for the rebirth of antiquity, and the British Museum itself—like poetry—the aesthetic vehicle for this new, energetic life.

Yeats returns several pages later in his autobiography to the same meditation on the relationship between poetry and native landscape—again invoking Shelley[35]—that introduces this British Museum passage, but here he instead introduces his musing on the composition of "The Wanderings of Oisin." "Might I not, with health and good luck to aid me, create some new *Prometheus Unbound*; Patrick or Columbkil, Oisin or Fion, in Prometheus' stead; and instead of Caucasus, Cro-Patric or Ben Bulben? Have not all races had their first unity from a mythology, that marries them to rock and hill?" (*Autobiographies* 166). Again, Yeats gestures toward the importance of native soil. But, as with the Persian statues finding a joyous energy in the British Museum, and like Standish O'Grady's Promethean version of Cuculain, Yeats dreams of the old Irish lands and legends finding a new life in *British* Romantic poetic form, Shelley's *Prometheus Unbound*. Without acknowledging the influence of O'Grady, George Bornstein has suggested that in conceiving "The Wanderings of Oisin" as a kind of *Prometheus Unbound,* Yeats imagined that the poem could "rais[e] nationalistic feeling above party cabals and materialistic goals" by reimagining the heroic Irish past in a context of "Shelleyan beautiful idealisms of moral excellence" (24). Even more than this, however, Yeats fantasized that recasting an Irish story in a British poetic form would serve a concrete social, educative purpose, as well as a Romantic nationalist one. As with his anthologies, and as with O'Grady's *History* and the Irish antiquarians' aspirations for an Irish national museum, Yeats hoped that "The Wanderings of Oisin" would bring the tales of ancient Ireland out of the peasant West and into the purview of the modern Irish reader.

Irish poetry was already a kind of bardic museum, an oral space in which the past was collected and preserved, but Yeats envisioned a poetics that could be simultaneously museographical, pedagogical, and political. "We had in Ireland imaginative stories," he continues in his autobiography, "which the uneducated classes knew and even sang, and might we not make those stories current among the educated classes . . . and at last, it might be, so deepen the political passion of the nation[?]" (*Autobiographies* 167). In recontextualizing the legend of the Fenian hero Oisin, Yeats longed to unite the educated Irish with the mythology of the Irish landscape and to extract the mythology *from* the landscape in order to annex it to a political desire. And, as with the statues of Artemisia and Mausolus, full of "joyous energy" in the British Museum, the imaginative result of this social and political recontextualization would be the reanimation of these ancient Celtic tales: tales which, displayed in new forms, "might move of themselves and with some powerful, even turbulent life" (167). Despite beginning both the British Museum passage and the "Oisin" passage with the necessity of the Irish landscape, and tied as he feels to that landscape—"the very feel of the familiar Sligo earth puts me in good spirits. I should like to live here always, not so much out of liking for the people as for the earth and the sky here, though I like the people too," he wrote during one of his trips there (*Letters* 49)[36]—Yeats nonetheless accords the mystic power of reanimation not to the magic of the native mythical soil but to a fundamentally imperial act of cultural appropriation. If the British Museum can bring a mausoleum to life, then what might the forms of British poetry be able to do for Irish legend?[37]

"THE WANDERINGS OF OISIN" AND THE NECESSITY OF RETURN

In asking this question, I do not mean to suggest that Yeats found a definitive answer in "The Wanderings of Oisin," only that this question was percolating both as he wrote it and when he reflected on writing it thirty years later (in the passages from his autobiographies discussed above). "Oisin" experiments with everything from ballad form and Shelleyan pentameter to the long, Anglo-Saxon verse form of Beowulf, but Yeats was never happy with the result. He revised the 1889 version significantly for its 1892 reprint, disappointed, as he wrote, that "only shadows have got themselves onto paper" (*Letters* 87).[38] The question of where, precisely, Irish nationalism should locate Irish history—and, in Yeats's case, Irish poetry—becomes one of the fundamental concerns of "The Wanderings of Oisin," which in its reimagination of a traditional Irish story both revels in and carefully brackets the mythic Irish landscape of fairies and folktales. In the introduction to *Fairy and Folk Tales of the Irish Peasantry*, Yeats romanticizes the land of faery as a primordial, changeless space, a space in which tradition and experience are naturally understood and conveyed through a poetic, symbolic idiom. Yet in "The Wanderings of Oisin," the land of faery becomes a place where poetry ceases to exist. The poem pushes us to consider the formal mechanisms of Celtic Revivalism: the ways in which Yeats was beginning to theorize the balance between a full immersion in Celticism and the need for a modern poetic form that could bring Celtic myth into the land of the living. The poem ultimately pays homage not to faeryland but instead to the world beyond Irish legend, creating a fairy tale of cosmopolitan creativity that backs away from the Celticism that so enamored Yeats during his fairy-tale hunts. It becomes a tribute to the textual museum, locating the artistic usefulness of folkloric "artifacts" not in their native lands but in their extraction to, and literary revival in, the less mythic but more generative world of modern Ireland. A parable of Yeats's own project of collecting Celtic stories, "The Wanderings of Oisin" proposes a system of Irish literature in which the collected past becomes the inspiration for, but not the endpoint of, the creation of a national identity: a system that offers a literary correlative to calls from museum curators in the 1890s for "living museums" rather than static collections of dead history, as well as a validation of Yeats's own sense that the Irish past should be "interwoven with one's life" and made part of modernity (*Letters* 104).[39]

This three-book, 915-line poem is the story of the Fenian hero Oisin and the Immortal Niamh, who falls in love with him and convinces him to come with her to her home of Tír na nÓg, "the Country of Youth" in some legends, the land of the dead in others. In this poem, although not in the most often-told versions of the story, Oisin follows Niamh to three different islands (the Island of Dancing, the Island of Victory, and the Island of Forgetfulness), on each one temporarily surrendering to its hypnotic charms before shaking himself awake and begging to move on (both to a new island and to a new verse form). After three islands, Oisin gets homesick and begs Niamh to let

166 • CHAPTER 4

him go back to Ireland, even if only for twelve hours, to see and hear his old friends again. She agrees but warns him that he must stay on the white horse that will carry him back, for if his feet even brush the earth he will never be able to return to Tír na nÓg and all of his three hundred years will descend upon him. He agrees and gallops home, but when he arrives he discovers that though he remains young, his clan has passed away and Ireland has been converted to Christianity and changed beyond recognition. Disappointed and longing to return to Niamh, he begins his journey "home," stopping along the way to help some old men carrying heavy bags of sand. As he bends to help them, his saddle breaks and he falls to the earth. The horse vanishes, and he instantly becomes a crippled old man, wanting nothing more than to die.

Yeats's poem tells the story as a dialogue between Oisin and St. Patrick soon upon Oisin's return, and it acknowledges an eighteenth-century narrative poem by Michael Comyn called "Lay of Oisin on the Land of Youth" as a primary source. The events of the poem, Yeats writes in his note to it, "are supposed to have taken place rather in the indefinite period, made up of many periods, described by the folktales, than in any particular century; it therefore, like the later Fenian stories themselves, mixes much that is mediaeval with much that is ancient" (*Collected Poems* 493). Yet Yeats also acknowledges that while he used Comyn's poem and "suggestions from various ballad Dialogues of Oisin and Patrick, published by the Ossianic Society," most of the poem is "wholly [his] own, having no further root in tradition than the Irish peasant's notion that Tir-n-an-oge (the Country of the Young) is made up of three phantom islands" (*Letters* 132).[40] "The Wanderings of Oisin" is thus not a poem about the things, or stories, it collects—this is the dominion of the folklore collections—but about how material remnants can be interpreted and reconstituted as national history. That Yeats presents this reconstitution as a poem about a man coming back from the land of faery to rediscover his poetic voice suggests, however, that he envisions this process as both a return *from* history and a return *to* history—a return *from* the primordial land of myth and *to* the world of the historical imagination, an act of revival that escapes the past but always requires its lingering traces to remain.[41] The poem's structure of loss and return is the inevitable structure of a forged national poetry, which demands the double-consciousness of returning the dead to life.[42]

Yeats writes in the introduction to *Fairy and Folk Tales of the Irish Peasantry* that the "various collectors of Irish folk-lore have, from one point of view, one great merit, and from the point of view of others, one great fault. They have made their work literature rather than science . . . [and] have caught the very voice of the people, the very pulse of life" (6). In contrast to the anthropological and philological interests of eighteenth-century Irish antiquarians, who, in Yeats's mind, expropriated the idiosyncrasies of the peasantry to reconstruct "the primitive religion of mankind or whatever else" such people "are on the gad after," Yeats believes the company of nineteenth-century folklorists into which he projects himself recognizes in the peasantry a depth of imagination, an authenticity to be revered and tapped instead of conscripted for stultifying anthropological purposes (6). But although Yeats dismisses what he sees as the reductive end products of academic folklorists who "tabulated all their tales in forms like grocer's bills," he still acknowledges that there is a deliberate method to proper folklore-collecting (6). "You must go adroitly to work, and make friends with the children, and the old men," he writes instructively, casting folklore-collecting not as a science but as a preservative art requiring both skill as a hunter and a certain ear for accuracy (4).

He rejects anthropologists not for their impulse to collect but for their calculated interpretations of their fodder. He abuses anthropologists' "tabulated tales" and, while delighting over a manuscript of the Deirdre story held by the Royal Dublin Society that allows for an "almost word for word" contemporary knowledge of the tale, suggests that it is not the art of collecting but rather the science of analysis with which he quibbles (*FFT* 4). Properly collecting and properly—aesthetically—reconstructing these peasant tales are equal parts of the folkloric process for Yeats, and he criticizes even literary folklorists for falling short on one or both of these elements. Thomas Crofton Croker (*Fairy legends and traditions in the south of Ireland* [1825]) and Samuel Lover (*Legends and stories of Ireland* [1831], *Popular tales and legends of the Irish peasantry* [1834]), for instance, "did not—mainly for political reasons— take the populace seriously," in all the "shallowness of an ascendant and idle class" imagining "the country as a humorist's Arcadia" and creating "the stage Irishman" out of it (*FFT* 7). And Patrick Kennedy (*Legends of Mount Leinster* [1855], *Fictions of our forefathers* [1859]), "who seems to have had something of a genuine belief in the fairies," related stories accurately but had "far less literary faculty" than would be desirable (7). These folklorists could collect stories with ease, but their ability to interpret them—for Yeats, a process synonymous with transforming them into literary products—fell sadly short. Only Lady Jane Wilde, the fiery poet "Speranza" of the *Nation*, a "perambulating family mausoleum" of a person and the writer with whom I begin this book, earns high praise from Yeats for revealing in her own folklore collection the "innermost heart of the Celt, . . . cushioning himself about with dreams, and hearing fairy songs in the twilight, [and pondering] on the soul and on the dead" (qtd. in Friedman 23; *FFT* 7).[43] Here, finally, is the depth of imagination that Yeats's

"Introduction" seeks in the land of faery: neither a nymph-filled woods nor a primitivist Disneyland but instead his Celtic Twilight, a veritable museum of poetic intensity.

Yeats describes the land of faery as simultaneously atemporal and steeped in historical sensibility:

> These folk tales are full of simplicity and musical occurrences, for they are the literature of a class for whom every incident in the old rut of birth, love, pain, and death has cropped up unchanged for centuries: who have steeped everything in the heart: to whom everything is a symbol. They have the spade over which man has learnt from the beginning. The people of the cities have the machine, which is prose and a *parvenu*. (*FFT* 5)

Faery is timeless, yet ancient, and separated from "the cities" not only by a different sense of history but also by different language formations. The "symbolic," musical, and heartfelt realm of the peasants is the realm of poetry (Yeats's admiration for the Symbolist poets seems implicit in this), while the material world of the cities can only speak in prose. To truly interpret, to truly represent, the stories of the peasants is to be able to hear them as poetry, even if not necessarily rendering them in verse. The project of folklore is bound up with the idea that, if collected and represented honestly, these peasant stories will be simultaneously a space of national history and a space of poetry. When Yeats himself begins to craft his own version of the Irish fairy tale of Tír na nÓg in "The Wanderings of Oisin," however, the land of faery becomes precisely the opposite of this realm. He conceives a place, instead, where impossible temporality, a kind of frozen animation, disrupts all attempts at making poetry. Exile to the land of faery becomes exile to the land of the dead and is simultaneously a crisis of historical positioning and a crisis of poetic genesis.

The poem uses a language of intense temporal confusion to insist that these two crises are implicitly intertwined. Much like the story of Odysseus, to which "The Wanderings of Oisin" has been often compared, Yeats's long poem begins in a state of "afterwards."[44] In fact, it begins in several states of "afterwards," a condition Yeats chose to particularly emphasize in his 1892 revision of the poem.[45] We see the poem's "post-ness" first in the retrospective narration of Oisin, now "bent, and bald, and blind," and in the post-pagan Ireland of St. Patrick, where faeries have become "demon thing[s]" amid the "burial-mounds" of Oisin's Fenian friends (1.1, 4). We see it in the aftermath of the battle of Ghabra (the "great battle," according to Yeats, "where the power of the Fenians was broken") (1.6, 18). Even Niamh, an Immortal from Tír na nÓg, the Country of Youth, in the poem's opening stanzas comes under the weight of its melancholic post-ness. At least, in Oisin's recollection of her, she comes aesthetically to embody an end rather than a beginning, her lips not just "like a sunset," but like a "stormy sunset on doomed ships," and a fiery color "gloom[ing]" instead of blooming in her hair (1.21–23). These descriptors stand in marked contrast to Niamh's own picture of Tír na nÓg as a land from which "the blushes of first love never have flown" (1.85): a land of eternal dawn, not of preserved twilight. By beginning "after," the poem immediately pitches its own composition in opposition to the world of faery it describes, "far / Beyond the tumbling of this tide," a country outside of time, that *has* no after (1.48–49). As Yeats writes in his introduction to the Tír na nÓg section of *Fairy and Folk Tales of the Irish Peasantry,* "age and death have not found it" (179). On one hand, it seems perfectly obvious to say that Oisin's story happens afterward: as the only mortal to have gone to Tír na nÓg and returned, his legend is more about the return *from* than the journey *to,* the end of a three-hundred-year absence rather than its beginning. And yet, to suggest that the poem posits its essential condition as one that requires the world of faery to have been experienced and lost is also to suggest that this timeless, apolitical realm of legend can be a space of inspiration but not a space of poetry.

This poetic suppression emerges most profoundly in book 3 of the poem, on the Island of Forgetfulness, where giant, monstrous creatures live in a blissful state of thoughtless slumber; but even in book 1, poetic composition by the bard Oisin is noticeably blocked. Poetry is both Oisin's ticket to Tír na nÓg and the reason he leaves it, but in between going and coming back there is unexpected silence. As Niamh tells the Fenians at the beginning of the poem, explaining her desire to take Oisin with her,

> I loved no man, though kings besought,
> Until the Danaan poets brought
> Rhyme that rhymed upon Oisin's name,
> And now I am dizzy with the thought
> Of all that wisdom and the fame
> Of battles broken by his hands,
> Of stories builded by his words. (1.62–68)

Desire and aesthetic adulation blend in her "dizzy" fantasies of Oisin's Fenian tales, as do desire and poetic inspiration in his response:

> There was no limb of mine but fell
> Into a desperate gulph of love!
> "You only will I wed," I cried,

170 • CHAPTER 4

> "And I will make a thousand songs,
> And set your name all names above." (1.72–76)

Just as Niamh falls in love not with the man himself but with the way in which he has poeticized Irish legend—"stories builded by his words"—so Oisin imagines his marriage to Niamh as an act of rendering her into poetry. "You only will I wed . . . And I will make a thousand songs," he says, suggesting that his marriage will be synonymous with the generation of poetry. But while this marriage is certainly an entrance into legend ("mount by me and ride / To shores by the wash of the tremulous tide," Niamh says), the emphasis of this stanza describing the marriage is not on where Oisin will go but on what Oisin will collect when he gets there (1.80–81). As her wedding gift, Niamh offers Oisin "a hundred hounds . . . And a hundred robes of murmuring silk . . . a hundred youths, mighty of limb, / But knowing nor tumult nor hate nor strife, / And a hundred ladies, merry as birds" (1.86–96). The list of legends Oisin will receive when he is wed goes on and on, its rhythmic iambic pentameter drawing attention to the intrinsic relationship between possessing legend and making song that the poem ultimately bears out. Oisin may imagine marriage to Niamh as a bardic apotheosis, but his true "song" can only be built out of the material faery tales to which she gives him access.

Oisin's famed rhymes of battles broken and stories built, with all of their implied change, teleology, and oscillation, stand at odds with Niamh's world, "Where men have heaped no burial mounds, / And the days pass by like a wayward tune" (1.82–83). And Oisin's promise to make a thousand songs, while ultimately fulfilled by the poem itself, comes to no fruition on the Islands of Dancing, Victories, and Forgetfulness. His single attempt to sing, amid the dancers on the Island of Dancing in book 1 of the poem, fails completely.

> But when I sang of human joy
> A sorrow wrapped each merry face,
> And, Patrick! by your beard, they wept,
> Until one came, a tearful boy;
> "A sadder creature never stept
> Than this strange human bard," he cried;
> And caught the silver harp away,
> And, weeping over the white strings, hurled
> It down in a leaf-hid, hollow place. (1.234–42)

This section of the poem is much taken up by the songs of Aengus and the dancers of Tír na nÓg, who several times repeat a refrain vilifying "the grey wandering osprey Sorrow" (1.303, 319, 342). Oisin, the wandering bard with a silver harp, embodies the very "wandering" gray Sorrow that the dancers' song so despises, and his literal silencing by the child who takes his harp is only magnified by the suppression of his actual song. The child snatches the harp after Oisin has begun to sing, but Oisin, our narrator, never provides us any of those "sorrowful" poetic words he sang to the dancers. Oisin thus both aligns himself with and sets himself against the faery folk: aligns himself with them in the narrative act of self-silencing that parallels the boy's burying of the harp (Oisin is, of course, the teller of the tale, so any suppression of language is his own) and sets himself against them with the sorrow-inducing poetry of "human joy" so wholly antithetical to their sorrow-denying insistence that "God is joy and joy is God" (1.300). Oisin can be part of the world of faery in silence but will always be exiled from it in poetry.

We see this poetic isolation reiterated in book 3, on the Island of Forgetfulness, both in Oisin's initial resistance to the "unhuman sleep" of the islanders and in his waking from it after he capitulates. In this book Yeats retreats from contemporary verse forms and writes in a version of the long, caesuraed lines of Anglo-Saxon poetry, suggesting that modern poetry and immersion in this land of deathly sleep are incompatible. When Oisin first arrives on the island, he attempts to wake the "huge white" sleepers in order to hear their stories, certain that whatever forgotten stories they have just need to be recollected:

Snatching the horn of Niam, I blew a long lingering note.
Came sound from those monstrous sleepers, a sound like the stirring of flies.
He, shaking the fold of his lips, and heaving the pillar of his throat,
Watched me with mournful wonder out of the wells of his eyes.

I cried, "Come out of the shadow, king of the nails of gold!
And tell of your goodly household and the goodly works of your hands,
That we may muse in the starlight and talk of the battles of old;
Your questioner, Oisin, is worthy, he comes from the Fenian lands." (3.748–55)

Oisin's "long lingering note" interrupts the silent coma of the monstrous sleepers, but his call to bardic camaraderie earns only a wordless response from the sleeper: "His lips moved slowly in answer, no answer out of them came." Instead, there's only a sound, "soft" but "piercing," that washes away bardic memory "like a sea-covered stone" and lulls Oisin into the same silent sleep that his horn's note briefly disrupted. Stories and names and histories are lost on the Island of Forgetfulness, irretrievable through language, and Oisin's failed appeals to memory and poetry mark his essential difference from the

172 • CHAPTER 4

inhabitants of this island. Again, in memory and poetry he is divided from his surroundings, in forgetfulness and silence, part of the community. And though he is lulled to sleep with the huge white creatures, "a century . . . forgot," still "the ancient sadness of man" rises in him, and he wakes, begging to return to the world of the living:

> I cried, "O Niam! O white one! if only a twelve-houred day,
> I must gaze on the beard of Finn, and move where the old men and young
> In the Fenians' dwellings of wattle lean on the chessboards and play,
> Ah, sweet to me now were even bald Conan's slanderous tongue!" (3.804–7)

Oisin again breaks the forgetful silence of the sleepers, articulating the most plaintive part of his desire to leave the island as a wish to hear the language of his own people, even in slanderous version: to return from the exile of faery to the world of words.

Seamus Deane has claimed that the exilic position of the human in the faery world "is one of the most effective" poetic positions, for he "remains within Ireland as part of its true and permanent history and yet in exile from all that in Ireland is part of its transient and yet actual existence" (113). However, in positing these islands of Tír na nÓg not only as places to which Oisin has been exiled (or has exiled himself) but also as places *from* which poetic language exiles him, Yeats suggests instead that the human in the world of faery cannot occupy any kind of poetic position at all. He can witness, he can immerse himself, and he can remember, but he cannot create. He can be a collector but not, in the moment of immersion, an artist. Deane proposes that Yeats uses the trope of the child/woman/man gone with the *sidhe* to create a space for poetry that was bound to Ireland's Celtic identity but divorced from the "greasy till" banality of modern Ireland that we see in a poem like "September 1913." But in contrast to these claims that the mythical realm of faery is the realm of a particularly symbolic, particularly authentic, particularly Yeatsian Irish poetry, exile to Tír na nÓg in "The Wanderings of Oisin" presents a far more muddled relationship between poetry, memory, and nationality than the one Deane (and Yeats, too, in the introduction *to Fairy and Folk Tales*) packages so neatly. The poem implies that while poetry can *eventually* synthesize the materials of immersion, be they fairy stories or literary traditions, into a national mythology, it can only do so afterward— this poetic mythology can *only* be an afterword. Oisin describes his years of forgetful sleep as an impossible stasis. "So lived I and lived not, so wrought I and wrought not, with creatures of dreams," he says, stuck in this moment between life and death, between creation and absence, caught in the land of faery but unable to generate anything out of it (3.786). The poet here is mired in a "dream" tradition from which he, in order to remain a bardic poet, has no choice but to wake.

The tradition of Yeats's Island of Forgetting in book 3 is twofold, for it is as much Tennyson's 1832 island of "The Lotos-Eaters" as it is a locale of Irish folklore. Oisin's linguistic displacement from the island, which echoes both his physical displacement from the battle-torn Ireland of his youth and his spiritual displacement from St. Patrick's Christian Ireland upon his return, represents the impossible lyrical position of a poet mired in multiple traditions. This compound dislocation certainly expresses the fraught condition of Yeats's own Anglo-Irish identity, which pushed him into a complex dilemma of simultaneous identification with and distance from both the Sligo peasantry and the London/Dublin literary aristocracy. The process of folklore-collecting, which required immersion in an Irish landscape that was both Yeats's home and very much not his home, was in many senses an expression of just this kind of national dislocation. Just as significantly, however, the third book of "Oisin" functions in a similarly complex relationship to English poetic tradition, paying homage to Victorian British obsessions with classicism—Homericism more particularly—and with Tennyson himself as Poet Laureate, at the same time that it virulently contravenes the ahistorical somnolence with which Tennyson ends his famous poem. Yeats embraces the English canon while refuting it by writing an alternative ending—a historical ending, an Irish ending—to Tennyson's English story. As much as "Oisin" is about an immersion in and a return from Irish folklore, so too is it a poem about the return from English poetry and the reconstruction of its remnants into an Irish national tradition.

Like the last section of "Oisin," "The Lotos-Eaters" tells the story of an island populated by a somnolent race drugged with the fruit of the lotus (the "bell-branch" that produces "unhuman sleep" in "Oisin"), who tempt Odysseus's men to lie down with them and forget their home, "far beyond the wave" (Tennyson 45).[46] Besides the parallel scene-setting and the repeated attention in both poems to the word "wander," in several key moments Yeats's language explicitly echoes Tennyson. The first stanza of the Choric Song in Tennyson's poem, with its "sweet music" that "softer falls" than "night dews," its "sleep brought down from blissful skies," and its creeping ivy, clearly resonates in Yeats's own description of enchanted sleep:[47]

> Then he swayed in his fingers the bell-branch, slow dropping a sound in
>> faint streams
> Softer than snow-flakes in April and piercing the marrow like flame.

174 • CHAPTER 4

> Wrapt in the wave of that music, with weariness more than of earth,
> The moil of my centuries filled me; and gone like a sea-covered stone
> Were the memories of the whole of my sorrow and the memories of the
>   whole of my mirth,
> And a softness came from the starlight and filled me full to the bone.
>
> In the roots of the grasses, the sorrels, I laid my body as low;
> And the pearl-pale Niamh lay by me, her brow on the midst of my breast;
> And the horse was gone in the distance, and years after years 'gan flow;
> Square leaves of the ivy moved over us, binding us down to our rest.
> (3.758–67)

The lotos-eaters' island is "a land / In which it seemed always afternoon," a land "where all things seem'd always the same." The "seem'd always" in these lines indicates that the island is a place, like Yeats's island, without history or memory, a constant present tense that serves as an escape from the ongoing formation of cultural heritage in the mariners' "Fatherland" (Tennyson 39). This "Fatherland," the mariners' distant Ithaca, has become a place where "the minstrel sings / Before them of the ten years' war in Troy, / And our great deeds, as half-forgotten things," a realm to which they could only return "like ghosts," killed into national memory (120–24). When the mariners insist on remaining on the island, they reject the bardic songs that transform their actions into tradition, even disavowing their fundamental identities, their essential place in the "*race* of men" (165; emphasis mine). "The Wanderings of Oisin," like "The Lotos-Eaters," locates the creation of national heritage at home, in the world of battles, toil, death, and memory, not in the faery land of forgetfulness and eternity. It is this that Yeats borrows most poignantly from Tennyson, but while Tennyson's English mariners end the poem by dismissing the importance of bardic tradition and insisting that they "will not wander more," Yeats's Irish Oisin wakes and follows the "keen[ing]" of "Remembrance" off the island and back to the homeland from which he can tell his story (Tennyson 173; 3.843). This call of poetry—for what phrase could more perfectly encapsulate Yeats's sense of Irish poetry than the "keening of Remembrance"?—brings Oisin back from the land of the dead, in part because he believes so wholeheartedly in the power of his own poetry to wake the dead. Upon his return to Ireland, Oisin, little more than a singing corpse walking on the graves of his dead friends, insists to St. Patrick that he can "go to the Fenians, O cleric, to chaunt / The war-songs that roused them of old; they will rise" (3.892–93). He imagines that his poetry will reanimate the friends and history so many years gone. Yet only belatedly does he recognize that *he* is the dead that poetry, or the desire for poetry, has brought back to life. The historical imagination, for this Yeats poem, *does* reside in "greasy till" Ireland, in national, bardic language—in the return from the land of forgetting and the land of the dead.

There are many ways to read Oisin's return to Ireland and to poetry: as a dismissal of the Celtic periphery as a locus of national tradition; as the literal and literary revival ("they will rise. . . . innumerable, singing, exultant") of Fenian history; as a recognition that cultural identity emerges out of the ragged remains of history rather than in a Tennysonian distance from it; as a voice of resistance to the mundane forces of colonization embodied by St. Patrick; as a melancholy understanding that poetry lives in the aftermath of irretrievable loss; or as some combination of all of these (3.893–94). The ambiguous intertwining of melancholy and transformative potential seems to be Yeats's point; for poetry, in Yeats's oeuvre, can never and should never provide an unequivocal theory of how literature relates to its historical rags and bones. Once home, Oisin can "dwell in the house of the Fenians, be they in flames or at feast" (3.915). He can both tell his tale and imagine his re-entrance into history, whether that history be something to celebrate or something to lament. However, he has been gone too long, and his return to life is also a return to death. "I rose, and walked on the earth. / A creeping old man," he tells us, and the state of "afterwards" that makes poetry possible proves to be a profoundly isolating condition (3.883). "Ah me! to be shaken with coughing and broken with old age and pain, / Without laughter, a show unto children, alone with remembrance and fear," the last section of the poem begins, suggesting that in this liminal moment between faery tale and history, even poetry can be a state of exile (3.908–9).

This exile is, essentially, the exile of the collector, "alone with remembrance," who has moved outside of time instead of transforming remembrance (as Yeats does) into a synthetic anthology of legends, traditions, and identities (3.909). "The Wanderings of Oisin" finally presents the folklorist in a fundamentally alienating relationship to history. While Rossetti, Keats, and Hardy align poetry with collecting as destructive acts of colonial necromancy, reinscribing the death of ancient cultures by trying to unnaturally reanimate them, Yeats imagines that the collected past can be revivified *by* poetry's capacity to bring it forward into the present moment. In "The Wanderings of Oisin," however, Oisin tries to inhabit the present and the past simultaneously, and, in this attempt, discovers that he is dead to both. The poem bears out Yeats's sense that Irish identity is far less about retreating into the Celtic past than it is about seeking to gather that past as a foundation for modern poetry—less about making the dead speak than about giving them a new kind of life. Yeats's folklore collection, as Susan Stewart has suggested more generally of collections, "does not displace attention to the past; rather, the past is at the service of the collection [and] time is not something to be restored to an origin" (158). Oisin is ultimately destroyed by his desire to go back to his origins—back to Fenian Ireland and back to Tír na nÓg. Yeats rescues Irish poetry only by reconceiving Oisin's path as a path of revision—both historical and literary—rather than as a path of regression, but he cannot rescue Oisin himself, who remains lost in longing for a time that is gone.[48] For Yeats, the Celtic past must be, but can *only* be, substance for the literary development of modern Irish identity.

The character Oisin stands as Yeats's youthful warning—perhaps a forgotten warning—against the immersive lure of Celticism. In his letters from the late 1880s, Yeats may describe London as a land of the dead, but he describes Sligo that way even more forcefully: "Going for a walk is a continual meeting with ghosts. For Sligo for me has no flesh and blood attractions—only memories" (*Letters* 54–55).[49] Fifty years later, however, it is neither London nor Sligo but a museum—once the sort of place where Yeats would have found a life force—that Yeats imagines as the land of the dead. In "The Municipal Gallery Re-visited," Yeats stands among the portraits of dead friends and recalls with melancholy his youthful belief that "All that we did, all that we said or sang / Must come from contact with the soil, from that / Contact everything Antaeus-like grew strong" (*Poems* 326). Now, the museum and the possibility of native poetry stand at odds with one another, and instead of offering a space of productive formal revival, the museum and poetry together offer a bureaucratically aestheticized version of Ireland: "'This is not,' I say, / 'The dead Ireland of my youth, but an Ireland / The poets have imagined, terrible and gay'" (326).[50] If the Irish Municipal Gallery represents not the reanimation of dead Ireland but an imaginary Ireland disconnected from its spirit, it also embodies precisely Dante Gabriel Rossetti's Victorian sense of a politically deadening museum that the younger Yeats resisted so strongly. In reading "The Wanderings of Oisin" as a version of the Victorian museum poem— one that valorizes rather than decries the aesthetically transformative power of collecting old things in new places—we can see in a later poem like "The Municipal Gallery Re-visited" Yeats returning to his Victorian roots and finding them bent, and bald, and blind.

CHAPTER 5

Bram Stoker's
Irish Mummy Gothic

Written in 1903, just as the Irish Literary Revival was gathering speed and Anglo-Irish writers were frantically mining Celtic history for nationalist inspiration, Bram Stoker's mummy novel *The Jewel of Seven Stars* offers a (quite literal) counterversion of the young Yeats's historical revivalism. In this novel, the artistic imagination becomes a tool for the violent acquisition of power instead of a means to create new cultural identity, and "sav[ing] the thing," as Robert Browning would have it (the rag of flesh and scrap of bone, the corpse, the mummy, the history), becomes a dangerous act of possession, not an ecstatic work of restoration. If Yeats's early work posited reviving old legends and stories as fodder for producing a collective Irish identity that could supersede the sectarian and colonial violence tearing Ireland apart, Stoker's mid-career work asks how damaging a work of Irish art can become if the historical bones it refleshes aren't actually an artist's to bring back to life. Resurrecting *Jewel*'s gothic synthesis of Irish and Egyptian nationalist movements at the turn of the twentieth century, I argue in this final chapter that Stoker's contribution to the proliferating European imperial genre of mummy fiction is also a story of Ireland's own appropriations and misappropriations of historical knowledge. Reading against the grain of a novel that—like *Dracula*—seems to be about the dangerous repercussions of British imperial aggression, this chapter asks how much structurally similar aggression inheres in the most

178 • CHAPTER 5

apparently idealistic, most seemingly redemptive acts of imagining the past to life. . . . and how unwilling these pasts are to take such revivals lying down.

Drawing its plot from the nineteenth-century European fad for bringing treasures of the colonies home to put on display in the metropolis, *Jewel*'s characters become obsessed with resurrecting an ancient Egyptian queen, as well as all the knowledge she possesses, for modern use. A young lawyer named Malcolm Ross narrates the novel. He is only tangentially connected to the unfolding events, drawn in by his love for Margaret Trelawny, the daughter of the Egyptologist who brings the Egyptian queen Tera's mummy back to Britain to resurrect her. The first half of the book reads like a standard locked-room whodunit. Malcolm receives a desperate note from Margaret saying that there has been a murder attempt on her father and that she has no idea who the attacker could be. Malcolm rushes to her aid and, with the help of a police sergeant and a doctor, spends a good portion of the book trying to figure out who committed this violent crime. Suspicion falls both on Margaret, who always appears first on the scene of the attacks (there are several of them), and on a man named Corbeck, another Egyptologist working with Mr. Trelawny. Meanwhile, Mr. Trelawny remains in a curious, trancelike state of unconsciousness, and through Corbeck, Malcolm begins to learn the history of Queen Tera, to whom Mr. Trelawny has devoted his life's work. After three days of anxious watching on the parts of the house's conscious inhabitants, Mr. Trelawny mysteriously wakes up and sets in motion his "Great Experiment," an attempt to resurrect Queen Tera using all the provisions she had laid out thousands of years before to do it herself.

The group—Mr. Trelawny, Margaret (who happens to look exactly like Queen Tera), Malcolm, Corbeck, and the doctor—recreate Tera's tomb in the tunnel of the Trelawnys' remote country home in Cornwall and succeed in bringing her back to life—with devastating results.[1] They see their project as an effort of salvation—for the mummy and for themselves—and yet the novel is rife with violence (both physical and aesthetic) as the characters, including the dead queen, attempt to maintain aesthetic and political control over all that she has the potential to represent. The primary antagonist in *Jewel* isn't really its revenant—Queen Tera doesn't actually become ambulatory until the last page—but rather the *process* of reanimation itself, along with its complicated ethical relationship to aesthetic power and historical ownership. *The Jewel of Seven Stars* presents the idea of collective history—history that seems stable, open, and available for the artistic taking—as a catalyst for violence, spinning a story about the resurrection of an Egyptian mummy into a gothic lesson about the instability and recalcitrance of resuscitated history.

FROM REVIVAL TO REANIMATION

We began to see stirrings of this recalcitrance at the end of the last chapter, in Yeats's "The Municipal Gallery Re-visited." In this late poem, the once-inspirational possibility of historical artifacts revitalized by museums into new aesthetic forms collapses into disappointed certainty that the museum no longer has the power to properly animate the latent spirit and energy of the dead past. This transition represents more than a melancholic reversal by a poet who would be dead before the decade's end. It also reveals the clear disparity between a European seeing a museum collection of distant Persian or Celtic antiquities that he imagines he has the right to revive in his own modern image and one pensively encountering his *own* intimate past—"my friends' portraits"—collected and displayed for others to imagine to life in the same appropriative way. When Yeats confronts the museum's spectacle of his own dead compatriots, he can't bear to let other disconnected and ahistorical imaginations revivify them into new forms. His descriptions instead tell viewers exactly how he wants them to interpret the movements, the expressions, the scenes, and the very souls that are arrayed across the walls. Yeats insists that these painted remnants be forever etched with the "lineaments" of Irish history, embalmed in a "hallowed place" and remembered only in the full fledge of a contextual splendor shaped around his own Irish past: "And say my glory was I had such friends." For a poet who once transubstantiated Persian funerary monuments into new life force for the Irish soul, this funereal endpoint for the lively Irish portraits in "The Municipal Gallery Re-visited" becomes a tacit indictment of the imperial violence underlying such revivals, as well as a Rossetti-esque admission that the museum makes a far kinder mausoleum than it does a necromancer.

Yeats's museum writings refract the complicated coloniality of late nineteenth- and early twentieth-century Irish cultural nationalism as it both mined the ancient Irish past for forms of Irishness beyond the reach of British imperial rule and subjected that past to the same kinds of ideological revival that Rossetti presents as such an insidious form of colonial violence in "The Burden of Nineveh." As Amy Martin puts it, in the nineteenth century, "Irish and British nationalisms and national identities not only existed in intimate relation, but emerged as an endless, inextricable series of reflections and refractions," in their rhetorical and aesthetic strategies as well as in their mutual, if oppositional, dependence on one another (*Alter-Nations* 2). Like Mary Shelley in her "Reanimated" stories, like Robert Browning with his Yellow Book, Yeats's impulse to euphorically reimagine fragments of other pasts

180 · CHAPTER 5

into forms that express his own present moment can't help but also erase any traces of cultural specificity that linger in those fragments. In "The Municipal Gallery Re-visited," Yeats writes desperately against this imperial erasure, but to do so he must make sure that his dead stay dead. The reanimated bodies that rise through the nineteenth century, even those that rise in anticolonial resistance, will always share a form with colonized bodies: instrumentalized, essentialized, and sometimes electrified, their new aesthetic lives never escape the shadows of the other lives lost in their remaking.

Writing in the last decades of more than three centuries of British colonialism, Irish Literary Revival writers like Yeats couldn't escape the ideological contradiction of a literary project looking to the Celtic past to erase the scars of colonialism's own erasures (of Irish land, Irish communities, Irish culture, and even the Irish language itself).[2] Gregory Castle, borrowing from Walter Benjamin to describe what he calls the "transfigurative artistic temperament" of the Revival, argues that writers like Yeats and J. M. Synge worked not to "salvage culture" that had been lost but rather "to redeem it by brokering anew the 'secret agreement between past generations and the present one'" ("Synge" 214). Neither authentically reproducing a past that has vanished nor attempting to rescue whatever tattered scraps of it might linger in the present, the revivalist imagination instead engages in an act of deliberate "cultural misrecognition" that makes an idea of the past available for "new grounds of recognisability in the present" (225, 226). Castle insists that this aesthetic misrecognition is neither a form of cultural appropriation nor an act of cultural erasure. Instead, reviving the past in images that provide the Irish present a vision of its longed-for liberated future is a form of "elegiac summoning," always encapsulating both a mourning for what has been lost and a dream of what might come (212).

And yet, many late nineteenth- and early twentieth-century Irish writers viewed the cultural nationalism of the Irish Literary Revival with deep skepticism, specifically *because* they saw it as a form of cultural appropriation. As the journalist D. P. Moran scathingly wrote of Yeats in 1899, "A certain number of Irish literary men have 'made a market'—just as stockjobbers do in another commodity—in a certain vague thing, which is indistinctly known as 'the Celtic note' in English literature, and they earn their fame and livelihood by supplying the demand which they have honourably and with much advertising created" (qtd. in Smyth 347). James Joyce, described as the Revival's "chief rebel," famously lambasted one of Lady Gregory's folklore collections as a record of "sorrow and senility" that would be better viewed with "delicate scepticism" than as a blueprint for an Irish national future (Flanagan 51; Joyce, "Soul" 74, 75).[3] For Joyce, the problem with the Revival wasn't that it longed for an Irish identity liberated from colonial oppression but that in inventing a model for a unified Irish identity out of the world of peasants and fairies, the Revival did nothing either to represent or to mitigate the multiple political and social forces shackling Ireland firmly to its subjugation: as Stephen Dedalus says in the first chapter of *Ulysses,* "I am the servant of two masters . . . an English and an Italian. . . . And a third, Stephen said, there is who wants me for odd jobs" (Joyce 20).[4] Joyce's well-known and scathing critiques of the Revival and the Romantic nationalist sensibility underpinning it don't argue against the Celtic and peasant history from which these movements draw their energy. His critiques instead lambast the movements' idealization of what he sees as a miserable past that has little bearing on the modern imperial and social politics from which a new and liberated Ireland would have to somehow extract itself. "History, Stephen said, is a nightmare from which I'm trying to awake" (34).

But waking from history might be exactly what's *most* dangerous about the Literary Revival's appeals to the Celtic past. This chapter turns from Revival writers like Yeats (and their more conventional critics like Joyce) to Stoker's *The Jewel of Seven Stars,* an Irish gothic novel in which historical awakening is nothing short of monstrous. *Jewel* appears at first glance to be an archetypal tale of gothic reanimation gone awry, with antecedents as early as Jane Webb Loudon's novel *The Mummy!* (1827), with its "galvanic battery of fifty surgeon power . . . surely enough to reanimate the dead" (15), and visible descendants in the absurd colonialist plots of movies from Hammer's 1932 *The Mummy!* to the late twentieth- / early twenty-first-century Universal *Mummy* franchise. Instead of reading *Jewel* only in this British colonialist context, however, this chapter recontextualizes Stoker's now-classic mummy tale as an engagement with the aesthetic and political strategies of Irish cultural nationalism at the end of the nineteenth century. The critique mounted in the novel doesn't reproduce Joyce's frustration with the Literary Revival's substitution of Romantic history for the oppressions of modern political reality but instead attacks the oppressive modern politics that inhere in the appropriative mechanisms of historical revival itself. As the characters in the novel work frantically to reanimate a five-thousand-year-old mummy, the text constantly asks what dire consequences might arise from reanimating a past that isn't really yours to bring back from the dead, even if you believe wholeheartedly that the reanimation will serve the greater national good. At what point does the desire to recuperate the past through art—the desire to "save the thing"—become a violence perpetrated on that thing rather than a revitalization of it? And how harshly will that violence be revisited on the saviors?

182 · CHAPTER 5

A VAMPIRIC HISTORY OF IRELAND

Stoker's "second most famous" novel may seem as distant from Irish interests as is Egypt itself, but *Jewel*'s Egyptian context (which I explore in the next section), as well as the violent relationship the novel constructs between art, history, and cultural possession, all resonate with the dynamics of the Irish political and aesthetic landscape at the beginning of the twentieth century. Although *Jewel* has received far less attention from Irish studies critics than Stoker's vampire novel has, Irish studies' unwavering devotion to *Dracula* helps create a critical context through which to see *Jewel*'s mummy as a sustained engagement with the mechanisms and toxicities of Irish revivalism. At the same time, reading *Jewel* as a novel trading in the dangers of the Irish historical imagination illuminates *Dracula*'s own seemingly tangential forays into the perils of resuscitative history, showing them to be rife with the monstrous political potential that *Jewel*'s mummy ultimately fulfills.

Since the late 1990s, Stoker's most famous book has become the poster novel of the Irish gothic, with critics reading its vampire as an Irish Catholic monster, an evil Anglo-Irish Protestant landlord, and a vicious incarnation of the colonial structures that created and demonized such distinctions in the first place.[5] Early criticism of the "Irish" *Dracula*, which began as a debate about which side of the imperial battle—British or Irish, Anglo-Irish or Catholic Irish—the evil vampire was meant to represent, ultimately abandoned such singular allegorical readings in the face of the novel's seemingly endless capacity to undercut its own apparent symbolic systems.[6] The problem with reading *Dracula* for allegory, as Jack Halberstam baldly puts it, is that "attempts to consume *Dracula* and vampirism within one interpretive model inevitably produce vampirism," reifying as monstrous the very traits they critique the novel for associating with its monster (88). In Halberstam's stead, later Irish studies criticism turned its attention away from *Dracula*'s many potential Others and toward the text's representation of the ideological production of otherness itself, arguing that the novel aims less to take sides in the eternally ideological battle for the Irish soul than it does to critique the structure of the battle itself. Joseph Valente offers the most sustained of these interpretive interventions, reading against the grain of prior *Dracula* criticism that ultimately sees the novel reinscribing the conservative racial and political anxieties of British imperialism. Valente instead understands *Dracula* as an engagement with hybridity, not as a nightmare of miscegenation, arguing that *Dracula* ironizes rather than fears the threat of racial degeneration and thus depicts not a monstrous racial Other but the destructive power of obsessions with racial purity. The primary import of Valente's argument inheres in its assertion that *Dracula* offers a critique of colonial systems, not an anxious reproduction of these systems, and it invites further readings of *Dracula* as a metapolitical text about the creation and cultural repercussions of ideologically determined narratives.

Dracula makes clear from the very start that the "how" of narrative form will be one of the novel's primary preoccupations. "How these papers will be placed in sequence will be made clear in the reading of them," the text's brief preface begins, priming us to pay as much attention to the intricate formations of the novel's structure as to the plot that builds across its pages. Most often in the novel, the question of "how" seems answered with "modernity": narrative form emerges from typewriting, from journalism, from anthologizing, from suspicious subjectivity, from new gender norms, from decolonization. But there is one strange, easily overlooked scene in the novel—just before the sensationally famous scene in which three vampiric women take sexual advantage of the confused but highly aroused Jonathan Harker—in which the "how" of narrative becomes intimately entwined with the historical imagination. This scene is about the creative conjuring of the past to life and about the sympathetic ties that writing produces between past and present, and it stands in sharp contrast to the novel's larger pitched battle between history's haunting power and the uncanny forces of modern technology. It encompasses several key concerns that I draw together across the whole of this book to argue that the undead monsters scattered across nineteenth-century British and Irish literature—stitched-together creatures, speaking corpses, zombified characters, dead men walking, and wrathful mummies, among them—are historicist monsters, resuscitated by writers experimenting with the possibilities and the consequences of instrumentalizing the past for modern use. As an Irish novel filled with English characters, haunted by a vampire who dreams of stealing English lives that don't belong to him to remake them in his own image, *Dracula* takes the threat of cultural appropriation to its most literal extreme. Yet it's neither just a novel about fears of "reverse colonization," as Stephen Arata has argued, nor a novel about what Valente calls "the metrocolonial condition" of Ireland's hybrid position within the British Empire. It's also a novel whose complicated coloniality produces multiple, and often conflicting, versions of historical life. Against the ever-present threat of intractable historical persistence, the characters in *Dracula* remember, revive, return, and reproduce in attempts to find narrative and political alternatives to Dracula's always haunting presence. And yet, as this odd, forgettable scene demonstrates, such alternatives bear their own vampiric imprints, inescapably shaped by ideology, desire, and the violence of the conquest they struggle to hold at bay.

Jonathan has begun to wander Dracula's castle, seeking an escape from the vampire's oppressive aura, and describes himself venturing into a forbidden area he hasn't seen before. Upon seeing the rooms' comfortable furniture, he

184 • CHAPTER 5

immediately decides that "this was evidently the portion of the castle occupied by ladies in bygone days," and while he initially feels a "dread loneliness" in these rooms, his unease quickly transforms into a "soft quietude" as he imagines past inhabitants of the room into being:

> Here I am, sitting at a little oak table where in old times possibly some fair lady sat to pen, with much thought and many blushes, her ill-spelt love letter, and writing in my diary in shorthand all that has happened since I closed it last. It is the nineteenth century up to date with a vengeance. And yet, unless my senses deceive me, the old centuries had, and have, powers of their own which mere "modernity" cannot kill. (41)

History works differently in this part of the castle than it does in the parts where Count Dracula holds sway. If the centuries-old vampire embodies a past that seems to live dangerously and irrepressibly on, as Jonathan suggests when he earlier describes Dracula as a living incarnation of history—"In his speaking of things and people, and especially of battles, he spoke as if he had been present at them all" (33)—whatever old "powers" linger in these rooms offer Jonathan an escape from Dracula's insidious haunting and allow him to experience the past in a different way.[7] Although this diary entry doesn't dismiss the contrast between "old centuries" and "modernity," the language itself works far harder to synthesize the two than it does to pit them against one another. "Some fair lady" doesn't haunt Jonathan. Instead, as the word "possibly" indicates, Jonathan imagines her to life, writing her into a thinking and blushing existence in the present.

In this bizarre flight of fancy, Jonathan engages something akin to William Godwin's "romantic invention" or Michelet's resuscitative historiography (464). If Dracula's undead body manifests history as a life-sucking force to be defeated, this diary entry presents history as a generative, sympathetic mode of engagement with the dead. Jonathan resurrects the past by collapsing the distance between then and now, by using an act of writing in the present to conjure an act of writing from the past. As he stumbles between past and present tense in this passage, he seems to recognize that his resuscitative imagination has created an unstable historical simultaneity that grammar can neither entirely express nor contain. The woman that Jonathan describes writing her love letter—thinking, blushing, and misspelling as she pours out her heart on paper—becomes a fleshed and blooded character as he projects himself into her psyche, and his image of himself writing can't be disentangled from his image of her writing.

The passage's grammar is unsettling. It seems at first that "nineteenth century up to date with a vengeance" refers to Jonathan's shorthand diary, but in fact it refers to the entire sentence that precedes it. It isn't the shorthand itself that's modern but this process of historical invention, of superimposing one history atop another (or history atop the present), of modern language generating a history to suit its needs, whether or not such a past ever existed. Jonathan clearly sees this set of rooms, so full of female presence, as a pleasant antithesis to "living alone in the rooms which [he] had come to hate from the presence of the Count" (41). These are not just different rooms but rooms in which Jonathan, having escaped from the Count's haunting aura, recognizes a different kind of historical energy. Given that the novel's whole narrative aims to use modernity to kill off Dracula's powerful embodiment of the "old centuries," Jonathan's pleasurable feeling that in this part of the castle "the old centuries had, and have, powers of their own which mere 'modernity' cannot kill" tells us, again, that this space offers him an alternative to the vampire's haunting threat. As gothic novels since the eighteenth century have demonstrated, when the past refuses to stop haunting the present, it falls to the present to put the past to rest if it can. Yet the tone and tenses of Jonathan's reflection in this passage present the past not as a threat that he, with all his modernity, wants to obliterate, but as a source of creative inspiration. Instead of an antagonistic relationship, the past and the present co-exist and mutually inform one another.[8]

Among the strangest dissolutions in this act of creative resuscitation is the dissolution of gender distinctions. As Jonathan imagines himself in the woman's chair, mimicking her actions, the boundary between feminine and masculine energies softens, but not in the frantically violent, vampiric way that gender-bending happens later the novel. Jonathan thinks he's found a safe haven from Dracula in the act of writing himself into women's history. He emphasizes the room's status as at once a space of historical empathy, a space of safety, and a space of femininity: "I determined not to return to-night to the gloom-haunted rooms, but to sleep here, where of old ladies had sat and sung and lived sweet lives whilst their gentle breasts were sad for their menfolk away in the midst of remorseless wars" (42). His imagination happily produces a history for these women who may or may not have existed—he happily fancies that this resurrected past makes a more comfortable environment than the vampirically "gloom-haunted" present and happily believes that he is as welcome in these women's space as he would be if he were one of them. For Jonathan, identifying across gender lines—empathizing and sharing intimacy with women—enables him to bring history to life.

186 • CHAPTER 5

Yet this momentary (and imaginary) utopian gender fluidity can't quite suppress the fact that Jonathan maintains his masculine privilege throughout this scene. Even as he takes comfort in participating in what he believes to be a welcoming feminine past, the patriarchal force of his historical sensibility can only produce these ancient women as passive, gentle, timid, and longing for their menfolk. In his mind, they desire his presence as much as he desires theirs. He isn't writing *their* history in any authentic sense. Instead, he's claiming them for his own historical fantasy, bringing them to life in the way that brings *him* the most succor. The diary entry in which Jonathan enacts this historical fantasy begins with a fervent wish that while he remains in Dracula's castle he "may not go mad" and an assertion that writing in his diary is the only thing that could possibly "soothe" his frantic mind (41–42). Writing the history of these women to life fulfills these two needs, serving as an alternative to the maddening horror of Dracula both in its creative historical form and in its gentle phantasmic content. Within the frame of this particular diary entry, however, it becomes especially clear that the new life Jonathan breathes into these old, decorated rooms is a life he needs for himself—that no matter how much he claims to value the "habit of entering accurately" his observations into his diary, in this instance he jettisons accuracy in favor of resurrecting the past into an imagined story that best suits his needs.

Soon after Jonathan drifts into a tranquil sleep on the strength of his resuscitative experiment, he wakes to discover that his utopian fantasy of ancient women welcoming him into their intimate circle has been little more than an exercise in historical fabrication and appropriation. Because, of course, there really *are* ancient women in this part of the castle, and they have their own agenda. There's no way they're going to let Jonathan write their history and their desires for them, nor will they assume the passive role he has scripted for the ancient women of his imagination. While he sleeps and dreams of blushing ladies, his imaginary feminine community shudders and dissolves into the reality of bygone women reanimated by a vampire's bite rather than by a historical imagination. In place of his singing, blushing companions rises a living nightmare of dangerous, voluptuous, vampiric women who materialize within the room in dreadful parallel to the "gentle" women that Jonathan has tried to materialize through his writing. The women he imagined "lived sweet lives" are still "sweet in one sense, honey sweet," but now "with a bitter underlying the sweet": women that he "somehow" recognizes "in connection with some dreamy fear," women longing for a taste of the man who has, indeed, come home to them (42, 43, 42).

With the appearance of these actual women, the control of history that Jonathan *thought* he had slips away, and instead of his gentle women he's confronted with three sexy, bloodthirsty vampires. Instead of scripting their story, he describes himself as the passive recipient of their sexual aggression. He just lies there, as he says, with a "wicked, burning desire that they would kiss me with those red lips" and watches as they move on top of him (42). "Lower and lower went her head as the lips went below the range of my mouth and chin and seemed about to fasten on my throat . . . I could feel the soft, shivering touch of the lips on the super-sensitive skin of my throat, and the hard dents of two sharp teeth, touching and pausing there" (43). No matter how gentle or soothing your historicist intentions may be, *Dracula* shows us nothing if not the sharp teeth your resurrected past can use to bite you. Right on the heels of Jonathan's attempt to imagine to life a group of ancient women to commune with, this dangerous vampiric seduction becomes as much a referendum on the perils of resuscitative history as it is a denial of Jonathan's masculine authority: the past you dream back to life won't always be as amenable to your story as you want it to be. If the composition of *Dracula* as a whole purports to stitch pieces of the past into a coherent narrative that consolidates the power of its writers against the forces of the vampire—as the preface says, "All needless matters have been eliminated, so that a history almost at variance with the possibilities of latter-day belief may stand forth as simple fact"— Jonathan's fantasy-turned-reality of the castle's bygone ladies anticipates the realization he has in his end-note that such "simple fact" won't ever be anything but a figment of the historical imagination. "It was almost impossible to believe that the things which we had seen with our own eyes and heard with our own ears were living truths . . . there is hardly one authentic document" (377). In a text in which writing and vamping so often metaphorically stand in for one another, this diary entry's specific juxtaposition of historical writing and historical vamping suggests that what's at stake in both is control over a story, with bodies and journals simply different mediums through which that control is exercised.

Unexpectedly for a vampire novel, Stoker introduces this dangerous potential of resuscitative history long before he introduces the novel's most visibly reanimated body: "Lucy Westenra, but yet how changed. The sweetness was turned to adamantine, heartless cruelty, and the purity to voluptuous wantonness" (215). Lucy's transformation from dead to undead underscores the text's investment in what Patrick O'Malley describes as "tableaux of spectacular gender and sexual anxiety," centering a particularly "male experience" of female sexuality ("She" n. pag.). Like Jonathan's vamping at the hands of Dracula's brides, Lucy's sensational rise from the grave as the dangerous "bloofer lady" transfigures female desire into a threat to masculine authority and renders the allure of such desire intrinsically monstrous. Yet, as O'Malley also suggests,

188 • CHAPTER 5

focusing on such graphically sexual scenes in isolation draws our attention away from the more subtle ways that *Dracula* embeds complex gender and power dynamics in questions of history, narrative, and self-determination. While countless critics have tied Lucy's apparent vampiric availability to her flirtatious affect and desire for multiple men early in the novel—to borrow Christopher Craft's words, she "flaunts the encasements of gender norms" long before Dracula attacks her (121)—they are less likely to recognize that the path from Lucy's history of flirtation to her emergence as a vampire is mediated by her own attempts to narrate herself out of Dracula's control.[9] Over and over in her diary she insists that she feels peaceful, has emerged from her illness, and has been revitalized, even as her body falls prey to Dracula's visits: "[I] am full of life, and sleep well," she writes, and am "quite restored" (114). Lucy tries to resist being resurrected in Dracula's image by writing herself to life in her *own* image. The novel creates space for her to imagine herself as a different story with a far less punishing ending, even if it ultimately denies her this agency and subjects her monstrously resuscitated body to the "violent correction" of a wooden stake (Craft 116).

Dracula's most lurid attentions to female vampires thus both follow on the heels of meditations on gendered writing practice and narrative authority, but I focus particularly on the sequence in Dracula's castle rather than on Lucy's resurrection because as the novel moves from Dracula's castle to the English shores, it also moves from its early preoccupation with the dangers of a persistent past to a battle for the coming fate of the British Empire. "Time is on my side," Dracula sneers at the men trying to hunt him down in London, "Your girls that you all love are mine already, and through them you and others shall *yet* be mine" (308; emphasis mine). The scenes of writing that undergird the novel's two confrontations with vampiric women explicitly mark its shift from depicting the vampire as aggressive historical haunting to suggesting that vampirism is everyone's modern future. The vampiric brides who rise from their graves in Dracula's castle do so in energetic retaliation for Jonathan attempting to write their history for them, while Lucy's rising represents the failure of her efforts to write her own nonvampiric future. It is the latter failure that the second half of the novel focuses its energies on remediating. As Jennifer Wicke, Daniel Martin, and others have clearly demonstrated, Stoker's synthesis of vampire and of-the-moment technologies of reproduction signals the novel's far more profound interest in the colonizing forces of modernity than in Dracula's literal historicism. The novel's final admission that its story is nothing but "a mass of type-writing" rewrites its preface's unbelievable "history" as a reflection not on past events but on the modern mediating forms through which such events have been recorded and compiled (377). By

Dracula's final page, on which we learn that "every trace of all that had been was blotted out" (save one baby with secret vampiric blood in his veins), it has become clear that modernity's most potent effect is its ability to overwrite historical presence with technological absence, and that history stands at odds with belief not because we don't believe in monsters but because we can no longer believe in history itself (377).

In this light, Jonathan's almost forgettable foray into history-writing in the novel's first section, matched as it is by the novel's first real scene of vampiric attack, brings into sharp relief the possibility that in "the nineteenth century up to date with a vengeance," imaginatively resuscitating the past might have far more in common with vampiric reproduction than Jonathan realizes. As his shorthand simultaneously conjures and overwrites the ill-spelt love letters of bygone days—as his technological mediation both brings to life and kills off any authentic version of the past—the vampires that rise in response to his efforts seem as inevitable as Lucy's rise from her mausoleum after Dracula's attacks. Jonathan's reanimation of the past, which at first seems like a soothing and idyllic alternative to the vampiric history that Dracula embodies, turns out to be little more than vampiric history in different form. For the real danger of Dracula lies not in the fact that he comes bearing centuries of history with him—he's no ghost, come to right the wrongs of the past—but in his power to remake the present in his own image. As Van Helsing warns everyone, the risk in confronting Dracula is "that we become *as him*; that we henceforward become foul things of the night *like him*—without heart or conscience, preying on the bodies and the souls of those we love best" (240; emphasis mine). Vampiric history transforms as it resurrects. Even Dracula's own ecstatic recitation of Szekely history demonstrates this, as the freedom-fighting "story of his race" becomes enfleshed in the heart, blood, and brains of an imperialist vampire body (35). Vampiric history animates the past with its own blood to make it useful in the present. Just as Dracula's victims return from the dead *like him* instead of like themselves and are meant to serve his needs ("to do my bidding and to be my jackals"), Jonathan's bygone ladies come back from the dead as materializations of his own desires instead of as themselves, first as gentle companions and then as seductresses whose red lips he longs for (308). The vampire brides aren't Jonathan's to control, but they embody the most extreme consequence of making history out of one's own "wicked, burning desire" (42). They represent both the possibility and the peril of resuscitative history. Imaginations like Jonathan's may be able to bring the dead to life, but what comes out of the grave rarely bears any resemblance to what went into it, nor does it always want to act out the story it's been resurrected into.

190 • CHAPTER 5

In *The Jewel of Seven Stars,* this brief flicker of *Dracula*'s attention to the dangers of the resuscitative historical imagination, suppressed by the novel's more pressing concerns about the reproductive dangers of its monster, flares into an entire plot in which the resuscitative imagination *is* the monster. By contextualizing *Jewel* within the mechanics of the Irish Literary Revival, we can look back at this scene in *Dracula* and see it underwritten not only by imperial and gendered power dynamics but also by the Revival's longing for an imagined communal past that could efface the damage of ongoing colonial maneuvering in the present. *Jewel* has always shivered in Dracula's long critical shadow, occasionally examined in its own right as a key artifact of the late Victorian Egyptomania craze but more often read as Stoker's lesser (although not his worst) effort to reproduce the qualities that made *Dracula* so compelling: an insidious but strangely absent monster, an unsettling mishmash of history and of-the-moment modernity, unreliable narrators, a preoccupation with psychological breakdown, and a heavy-handed, if also disordered, imperial allegory, among others.[10] But *Jewel* isn't *Dracula*'s more buttoned-up late Victorian gothic heir. *Dracula* is *Jewel*'s Irish political precursor, seeding an unexplored and metaphorical possibility that the resuscitative historical imagination might be monstrous that *Jewel* then cultivates into a reanimated monster whose embodied history can destroy the world. Unlike *Dracula,* whose primary danger (and potential salvation) is modernity's capacity to overwrite the past, *Jewel*'s ultimate danger is a past that refuses to be overwritten, no matter how desperately the technologies, desires, and ideologies of modernity beat against its sarcophagus.

Valente begins his analysis of *Dracula* with Stoker's biography, reminding us, as earlier biographers have not, that Stoker came from both native Irish and British blood, and thus could not be writing from a wholly "Anglo-Irish" perspective: "That Stoker himself came partly from Celtic stock, that he was an Anglo-Celtic rather than a traditionally Anglo-Irish subject, surely undercuts the popular position that Stoker substantially shared the anxiety of Anglo-Irish intellectuals . . . at the prospect of Celtic racial pollution, atavism, or degeneration" (Valente, *Dracula's* 16). While this broad, biographically revisionist beginning narrows its focus to an argument primarily about only two of Stoker's several novels—*Dracula,* of course, and Stoker's first novel, *Snake's Pass,* his only novel with an actual Irish setting—it reminds us that Stoker, in writing all his novels, always embodied the Irish colonial condition, was always both Anglo and Celtic, as well as being always both a "Londoner of . . . standing" and "a big, red-bearded, untidy Irishman" (Glover 26). *The Jewel of Seven Stars,* written by this same English, red-bearded Anglo-Celtic Irishman, functions similarly as a metatext about the formation of Irish national narratives, but instead of yearning after some kind of generative cultural hybridity,

as Valente argues *Dracula* does, *Jewel* sees the collapsing of cultural categories as a dangerously flattening cultural homogenization. The Irish gothic has
always been defined as a genre emerging from the racial and religious anxieties
of a culture split between creeds, languages, and national affiliations, a genre
"maintaining a series of deep-seated, troubled connections with wider systems
of prejudice, paranoia, and bigotry" in which both Catholics and Protestants,
as Luke Gibbons has written, "provided their own revenants, as entire societ-
ies and various 'doomed races' became the anthropological equivalents of the
architectural ruins that scarred the landscape" (10–11). *Dracula,* whether falling victim to anxieties about imperial power, race, and xenophobia or standing apart from these anxieties to point out their absurdity, remains the urtext
of this genre, predicating its idea of monstrosity on the incontrovertible presence of racial and imperial strife, even if only to deny it any validity.

Six years after *Dracula,* however, and just after Yeats and Lady Gregory
brought the Irish Literary Revival movement into full public swing with their
famous Irish nationalist play *Cathleen ni Houlihan,* Stoker introduced a new
kind of Irish gothic in *The Jewel of Seven Stars*: a gothic that abandons sectarian difference,[11] relying instead on the genre's transnational fluidities to medi-
tate on the violent and inauthentic smoothing of cultural difference inherent
in Irish nationalist "revivals," or recreations, of Irish history. As Stoker scathingly wrote in his journal in 1873, while he was still living in Dublin, "The
people—who are the People? When we talk of them in such a general way, we
cease in our minds to deal with living, thinking, feeling entities and regard
only abstract forms of thought. . . . The past ye cannot bring back or recreate" (*Dublin Years* 290–91). His new Irish gothic abjures anxieties about the
dangers of national rupture to instead imagine the dangerous repercussions
of inventing national cohesion, especially by bringing back the past. The belief
in reanimation is precisely the belief that the ultimate rupture—that between
life and death—can be healed through some superhuman effort, be it scientific, aesthetic, or mystical. But as anyone who has seen any mummy movie
ever made knows, mending this rift can have unpredictable consequences.
The act of reanimation at the center of *Jewel* functions as a gothic instrument
for pushing the aesthetic mechanisms and politically homogenizing desires
of early twentieth-century Irish cultural nationalism to their most destructive
imaginative limits.

EGYPT AND IRISH NATIONALISM

While *The Jewel of Seven Stars* has been called the best of the mummy fiction
that poured into Europe at the fin-de-siècle, the novel overthrows many of the

192 • CHAPTER 5

generic conventions that define this then-new category of gothic romance.[12] The formulaic mummy story is familiar: an Egyptian mummy accidentally comes to life in the nineteenth-century (or twentieth-century, or twenty-first-century) West and creates chaos there until the brave efforts of a Western hero (insert Brendan Fraser here) lay it to rest. Sometimes, there are small twists: the mummy is a woman and the hero falls in love with her before bravely laying her to rest, or the hero uses his intellect rather than his muscle to lay the mummy to rest, but, like all good "imperial gothic" or "reverse colonization" fiction from the end of the nineteenth century, the formulaic mummy story introduces Eastern disorder into the West, panics, and as quickly as possible re-establishes order and Western supremacy.[13] In *The Jewel of Seven Stars,* however, Western order never returns, as East and West become dangerously interchangeable doubles of one another and throw the very ideology of Western colonialism into doubt. The imperial exhibition suddenly becomes a means for acquisitions to control their owners, feminine virtue merges seamlessly with sexual voraciousness, and the language of the supernatural subsumes the power of modern technology. Reviews of the novel, while primarily favorable, couldn't help but notice the disconcerting effect of the novel's turn from its genre's reliance on the West always winning: "All through the story the reader is *bewildered* and tantalized by the strange and *bewildering* turn of events which cannot even be hinted at in a brief notice of Mr. Stoker's *extraordinary* story," wrote one reviewer in February 1904. "Mr. Stoker has very successfully surrounded his story with an atmosphere that impresses the mind and warms the imagination of the reader to the *unusual* and *extraordinary* character of the tale he is telling."[14] Strange, bewildering, extraordinary, unusual: *Jewel* just isn't your everyday basement mummy reanimation.

Critics have never recognized *The Jewel of Seven Stars* as a particularly Irish novel. Like *Dracula,* its characters are English instead of Irish, but unlike its more famous predecessor, *Jewel* lacks the allusions to now-conventional markers of Irishness (blood, Catholicism, coffin ships) that give critics of the Irish *Dracula* a foothold. It was only after decades of critical rigor, however, that *Dracula,* "at first glance among the least Irish of all Stoker's texts," came to be seen as his most Irish text (Glover 25). Stoker's only novel *actually* set in Ireland was his first one, *Snake's Pass,* but the lack of explicit reference to Ireland in the other novels, including *Dracula,* rather than proving Stoker's loss of interest in an Irish political register, has instead signaled to critics "the refractoriness of the Irish question" in the novels, demonstrating that "time and again, Ireland's condition proved [too] difficult [for Stoker] to name" (Glover 25)—but not too difficult to think about. *Jewel* relies on the same muddled racial and gender dynamics, fixation with doubling, and schism between history and modernity that critics have identified in *Dracula* as indications, in Valente's words, that "the writing of Ireland . . . is in itself a writing across or between—not within—distinct . . . political logics" (*Dracula's* 4). The Irish colonial condition, in other words, which critics now so willingly see as integral to an understanding of *Dracula*, reveals itself in the thematic structures of Stoker's novels rather than in Irish characters or settings—thematic structures which constantly posit epistemologically impossible positions (both white and nonwhite, both male and female, both old and young, both English and not English, both historical and modern) akin to the position the Irish occupied in the Empire as both peripheral imperialist subjects and colonized imperial objects. "Irishness" in *The Jewel of Seven Stars* reveals itself in the multiple and contradictory colonial positions the novel simultaneously embraces, as well as in its ambitious attempt to resolve these contradictions through old mythologies made flesh in the present.

But why write a mummy novel to probe the complexities of a colonized Ireland and the wishfully reparative aims of the Irish Literary Revival? Mummies were certainly a popular fascination in London during the early nineteenth century, when looting Egypt for European pleasure was all the rage. Loudon's popular 1827 novel *The Mummy!* capitalized on the novelty of private parlor mummy unrollings in the 1820s and 1830s, the ever-growing Egyptian collections at the British museums, the gaudy Egyptian décor of William Bullock's Egyptian Hall (designed by a Scotsman), and the vogue for Egyptian motifs on funerary monuments.[15] By the 1880s, however, Egypt had come to occupy a different place in the British imagination and political landscape. In its struggle to gain independence from the Ottoman Empire, Egypt found itself falling into bankruptcy, selling its shares of the Suez Canal to Benjamin Disraeli in the 1870s. As Europe's gateway to the Middle East and India, Egypt's canal was of great strategic and financial value to the British, and they kept a close eye on it. When a new nationalist movement, under the leadership of Colonel Ahmed Arabi, came to the forefront in Egypt in the early 1880s, England felt that their interests were under siege and so bombarded Alexandria, beginning a protective, "temporary occupation" in 1882 that lasted well into the first decades of the twentieth century.[16]

The specific nature of Egypt's position in the British Empire by the time Stoker wrote *Jewel*, as well as Egypt's and Ireland's mutual involvement in a global network of nationalist resistance movements, ties the novel's Egyptianness to a specific and fraught contemporary international politics.[17] For both political and economic reasons at the end of the century, Egypt came to represent for the British the cracks and crevices of their imperial power.[18] Though beneficial to the empire on the surface, Britain's uncontested assumption of

194 • CHAPTER 5

power over Egypt in the 1880s prompted moral, political, and economic backlash at home, eventually leading to what Samuel Clark calls a wider "crisis of empire" after World War I.[19] Britain could "safeguard imperial communication, trade and power across its far-flung empire" only when Egypt and its Suez Canal were in British hands, but focusing energy on Egypt made the empire vulnerable in other places (Gifford 1). Britain refused to turn Egypt over to the Egyptians because, in the eyes of the British, there was no one who could properly govern, as an 1898 article in *The Spectator* makes clear: "Have we brought forward, or are we bringing forward, any body of men who are fit to rule? . . . There does not at present exist any body of educated natives into whose hands the administration could be placed without the certainty of its immediate deterioration and ultimate ruin."[20] By the 1890s the British Empire had outgrown its resources, and while it seemed that its enormous size was synonymous with strength, its amplitude only meant that there were more open spaces to defend and more lines to supply. John Morley in 1906 insisted that Britain's "vast, sprawling empire" presented "more vulnerable surface than any empire of the world ever saw" (qtd. in Porter 123). It was difficult to defend places like Egypt, informally occupied in the 1880s and 1890s, because anticolonial sentiment in the native population both gained from and added steam to nationalist uprisings elsewhere in the empire. Furthermore, Britain chose to concentrate its imperial energy in North Africa not only because it was "a vital piece of the strategic puzzle in the Middle East" but also because British naval power could be utilized more fully there than in Asia and other places (Gifford 7). However, the empire was growing larger than its armaments, and by the early 1890s the British navy was far below par. All in all, by the end of the century, despite the patriotic touting of poets like W. E. Henley ("We are not one of the 'dying nations,' we! Our tradition is alive once more; our capacities are infinite," he wrote in 1899), the British Empire was on the cusp of crisis, and the "fatal disgust with Egyptian matters into which England ha[d] fallen" strained the island nearly to its breaking point (qtd. in Porter 29).[21]

This is the most obvious colonial context for *The Jewel of Seven Stars* (and for the larger canon of fin-de-siècle British mummy fiction), and *Jewel*, like many other mummy texts, relies on the uncanny doubling of British and Egyptian characters to emphasize the fragility of British colonial power in the face of Egypt's monolithic ancient history and contemporary political complexity. But *Jewel*'s obsessive doubling of characters does more than simply indicate that "British" and "colonial other" are too indistinguishable for comfort in an Egyptian context. It also invites doubled readings in which overlapping referents are implicit in the text's insistence that its characters have shadow lives in different times, places, and cultures. If the novel presents Britain and Egypt as obvious doubles of one another in the figures of Margaret and Queen Tera, it also uses these characters' names (the British Margaret and the queen named after the Irish Hill of Tara, ancient seat of the Irish High Kings), their mutual non-British coloring, and their absolute refusal to be governed to introduce Ireland as a shadow double in the novel's more overt British/Egyptian dyad. Signals in the text like the queen's name and coloring that seem to be both Egyptian and Celtic, as well as Irish/Egyptian political affiliations throughout the late nineteenth / early twentieth century, allow us to see a fear of growing Irish power in this text in which the British self begins to crumble in confrontation with an exotic Other.[22] Furthermore, the doubling of Margaret and the queen specifically collapses any *visible* physical distinction between the British characters and their supposed Other, reminding us that while the British might have caricatured their nearest and most pervasive colonial problem as monkeys, Calibans, and Frankensteins, the racial distinction between British colonizer and Irish colonized was based on religious, economic, and social distinctions, not on skin color, rendering the colonial power differential between Britain and Ireland less stable and visually identifiable than Britain wished it to be.[23]

Historians have argued that Irish nationalist uprisings were at the root of Britain's decision to occupy Egypt in 1882, as "the deteriorating situation in Ireland" at the time "predisposed" the British government to distrust Egyptian self-rule after riots broke out in Alexandria (Gifford 9). Egypt and Ireland followed a similar early twentieth-century timeline toward eventual decolonization in 1922, calling each other "sister nations" in the fight for independence from Britain and mutually straining the resources of the empire from both near and far.[24] The Irish had long maintained an intense political and aesthetic kinship to this culture in which they saw profound parallels to their own situation. They had, in fact, even fabricated an origin story that traced their race and language back to the ancient Egyptians.[25] In 1790, for instance, John Whittley Boswell published a pamphlet entitled *Syllegomena of the Antiquities of Killmackumpshaugh, in the County of Roscommon, and Kingdom of Ireland, in which It Is Clearly Proved that Ireland Was Originally Peopled by Egyptians.* In the pamphlet, Boswell uses the discovery of an ancient souterrain and cave to spin a spurious and absurd archaeological and philological web that traces the Irish people and language back to the ancient Egyptians. Using everything from the hardness of the bones he finds in the cave to a sketchy analysis of Phoenician commerce, Boswell at one point concludes triumphantly that "it is therefore the highest probability, indeed almost a certainty" that a lost Egyptian fleet mentioned by Herodotus came to Ireland, because Ireland "was so unknown at the time" (38–39). Whether Boswell was, as has been suggested, misinterpreting the old Irish legends that gave the Irish Scythian origins and had them residing in Egypt for a time before the Exodus or whether (more likely) he is making elaborate fun of the Royal Irish Academy is open to debate. But farcical or not, his pamphlet represents the eighteenth-century culmination of a line of legend, antiquarianism, and philology tracing Ireland's prehistory to ancient Egypt. Tying Irish ancestry to Egypt meant connecting Irishness both to the monumental pharaonic tradition and to the biblical tradition of Exodus, connections that imbued a small, shaky Ireland with authoritative historical consequence and continued to reverberate throughout the corpus of nineteenth- and twentieth-century Irish literature.[26]

In the nineteenth century, however, with Napoleon's invasion of Egypt in 1798, a subsequent short British occupation, and a decades-long struggle between the Egyptian nationalist leader, Mohammed Ali, and the Ottoman Empire, Egypt became more than a symbol of ancient grandeur. A new playground for the European imperial game, it was now seen as a nation marked by nationalist movements, struggles for independence, and the ashes of colonialism. From the British occupation in the 1880s forward, Egypt particularly attracted the attention of Irish writers and nationalists, who regarded the country's oppressed position as a reflection of Ireland's own status in the empire. Thus, for instance, Lady Gregory emerged into the politico-literary arena in 1882 with a long defense in the *Times* of Colonel Ahmed Arabi, whose attempts to stave off British and Ottoman rule in Egypt had led to the British bombardment of Alexandria. As she writes in her autobiography, it was in Egypt, on the cusp of "a revolution," that she "first felt the real excitement of politics" that would eventually lead her into the Irish nationalist fight for passage of the Home Rule Bill (Gregory 58). Others, like Michael Davitt (founder of the Irish National Land League), visited Egypt to show support for its nationalist agitators, hoping, as James Joyce's schoolmate Francis Sheehy-Skeffington put it, "that [the Egyptian imbroglio] might involve England in difficulties and enable a semi-revolutionary movement in Ireland to compel concessions of at least autonomy" (Sheehy-Skeffington 110).

Irish nationalists thus saw the fates of the Irish and Egyptian Home Rule movements intertwined practically as well as ideologically, and a few well-known Irish journalists wrote vociferously in defense of both national movements. Frederick Ryan, the first secretary/treasurer of the Abbey Theatre and the best-known among these journalists, wrote for both Egyptian and Irish nationalist newspapers, asserting over and over again the "many points of resemblance between the political struggle in Ireland and that in Egypt," as well as the "deeper economic resemblances between the two nations" and the links between "the fortunes of the national cause in Ireland and the national cause in Egypt" ("Ireland" 26). His articles strongly emphasize the likenesses in temperament and culture between the people of the two nations, and he argues that "there are many reasons why an Irishman should be interested in [the Egyptian] problem" ("Spoil" 25). Wilfred Scawen Blunt, who encouraged Lady Gregory's interest in Egypt, wrote endlessly in support of the Egyptian free state at the turn of the twentieth century, as did James Connelly, head of the Irish Socialist Party. In 1920 Susan Mitchell, a poet of the Irish Literary Revival, took great interest in a young Egyptian nationalist traveling through Ireland, writing that he possessed "a spirit of true understanding" for the Irish cause (ix).[27]

As manager of the Lyceum Theatre in London and Henry Irving's eyes and ears into the theatre world throughout the first decades of the Irish National Theatre and Literary Revival, Stoker would have known these writers (Lady Gregory and Frederick Ryan, in particular). Furthermore, his own ambivalent interest in the idea of a state-sponsored national theatre in London, which he discussed at length in an essay in 1908, makes it apparent that he was keeping an eye on the new Irish National Theater and its political and economic tribulations.[28] Even from London, the concerns of the nationalist Irish Revival were in his purview. While Stoker's own biography and politics are "notoriously elusive," as one critic has put it, Stoker was clearly (as his novels demonstrate) invested in the political landscape, and at least in his youth spoke vociferously of the need for political activism of an internationalist rather than an insular, nationalist kind (Glover 1). As he insisted in an address to Trinity College called "The Necessity of Political Honesty," "As truth broadens out from individuals to nations, we should have in view its teaching, not only to persons, but to the world at large" (37). Internationalism, he says, is "the dawning of truth—the broadening out of justice from the nations to the world at large—the casting off of the petty chains of local prejudice," and in this broadly conceived world, "the Ireland of the future is a subject for ambitious dreams" (43, 46).

Even more than internationalism in general, though, Stoker was interested in Egypt, in particular, and in Egypt's relationship to Ireland. *Jewel* may use Egypt as its primary referent for staging intertwined dramas of imperial subversion and nationalist revival, but Ireland is politically implicit in this referent as a model for Egyptian rebellion against the empire, as a source for Egyptian nationalist strategies, and as a resource drain compounding Britain's struggle to maintain its more far-flung colonies and protectorates (Rast 487).[29] Although no working notes for *The Jewel of Seven Stars* seem to have survived, the novel's scholarly detail demonstrates that it was extensively, even lovingly, researched. Stoker's mother Charlotte, although in most respects an ordinary middle-class parent, was fascinated by other cultures and introduced Stoker at

198 • CHAPTER 5

a young age to works like Abbé Everiste Huc's writings on China and Richard Francis Burton's tales of African adventures. As an adult, Stoker kept his own library stocked with books on Egyptology (including Sir E. A. Wallis Budge's study of Egyptian funerary practices, *The Mummy*), along with Babylonian lore, astrology, and alchemy. Perhaps his preoccupations with the occult ideas of the East stemmed from his mother's interest, or from his father's talk of travels in Asiatic Turkey (which Barbara Belford, one of Stoker's biographers, suggests strongly influenced the setting of *Dracula*).

More likely, though, Stoker's introduction to Egyptian history and politics came from listening to Sir William Wilde, who Stoker frequently visited during and after his years at Trinity College. Stoker's imagination was piqued by Sir William's multiple Egyptian enthusiasms: his instrumental participation in the campaign to bring to England Cleopatra's Needle, the magnificent obelisk then lying (as it had for centuries) beside Pompey's Pillar (a campaign that finally saw success in 1878, two years after Sir William's death); his favorite Egyptian acquisition, a prized mummy he found outside of a tomb at Saqqara, which he packed up and brought back to his home in Merrion Square in Dublin[30]; and his political interests in Egyptian independence. One biographer of Stoker's suggests that Stoker "borrowed" the plot of *Jewel* from Wilde's tales of acquisition, but the novel is at least equally invested in the politics of Wilde's writing about Egypt, and how this politics becomes a politics of Ireland. In 1840, at a turbulent moment in the fight for Irish Home Rule, Sir William, then a mild Unionist living in Dublin, published a travelogue in which he discusses at length the political state of Egypt, arguing fervently (despite his Irish Unionist inclinations) for Egyptian self-government and independence from the Ottoman Empire. "Were this vast country to be returned into the hands of Turkey," he writes, "it would but increase the difficulties under which that tottering state labours," while recognizing "the independence of Mohammed Ali" would offer a mutual advantage for both Egypt and Europe (*Narrative* 23, 27). The Anglo-Irish Wilde finds in the plight of Ottoman-ruled Egypt a political theatre in which he can express nationalist sympathies without anti-British sentiment: a sanitized, distant theatre in which Wilde's only overt political writing appears. However, rather than an anomaly in Wilde's oeuvre, this popular Egyptian travel narrative is a point of origin for Wilde's later books about Ireland, and its political lexicon makes its way into his later so-called apolitical work by binding Ireland to a global idiom of colonial struggle.[31]

Touring Egypt in 1838 during its "pre-archaeological period," Sir William might have told his Merrion Square guests, he became fascinated with the grandeur of the country's ancient monuments—a fascination that was quickly transformed into a desire to possess them for Britain and for himself (Belford 63). The young Stoker used to linger in the corner of Wilde's study and hang on Wilde's stories of Egypt, in which bringing a mummy back to Ireland represented, impossibly, both an act of European appropriation and a gesture of transnational political solidarity. Sir William's mummy in Ireland embodied an uncanny point of intersection between imperial violence and nationalist sentiment, one that Stoker clearly took to heart. Decades later, Stoker's choice to write a mummy novel didn't divorce his gothic fantasy from Irish politics. Rather, it emphasized the global network of Irish politics even as it transformed these associative connections into a story about the self-destructive consequences of cultural appropriation.

REANIMATED OBJECTS, AESTHETICIZED HISTORY: THE PROBLEM WITH WOMEN

In a short story, called "The Burial of the Rats," published in 1914, Stoker describes the great, mysterious dust heaps on the outskirts of Paris both as "a country as little known as that round the source of the White Nile," and as a landscape "such as may be met with in the remote parts of the Bog of Allen" (95). In this story, Egypt and Ireland synonymously evoke for Stoker an image of the marginal "social wilderness" into which his protagonist, a reckless pseudo-imperialist soon to be under siege, "determine[s] to penetrate" in order to "trace the dust to its ultimate location" (95–96). Stoker's imperial sensibility, then, could happen interchangeably in both Irish- and Egyptian-style settings, or could, overtly, by 1914. Even by 1903, however, when Stoker wrote *Jewel,* Yeats was already invested in the Egyptian mysticism of the Hermetic Order of the Golden Dawn, Oscar Wilde had published his poem "The Sphinx," and Irish nationalism had become infused with cross-colonial fervor. Stoker clearly had a solid associative foundation for naming his Egyptian mummy in *Jewel of the Seven Stars* after the Hill of Tara, still today one of the symbolic centers of Irish national identity.[32] That is to say, we must recognize that at the turn of the twentieth century, Stoker's focus on ancient Egypt and Egyptology in *Jewel* would have been enveloped in Ireland's empathetic fascination and identification with Egypt's political, spiritual, and historical place in the British Empire. The Egyptian subject matter of this novel, as the Queen Tera / Hill of Tara echo makes resoundingly clear, signals rather than obscures the Irish context of the novel's obsessions with doubling, androgyny, and historical revival. The resurrection of Queen Tera represents the crisis of Irish colonial identity as a crisis of the historical imagination, as the breakdown of

200 · CHAPTER 5

an illusory belief that a mythical past can or should be resurrected to sanitize or circumvent the violence of an imperial present.

The novel begins neither in city nor in country but in a dream, Malcolm's dream of the day he first met Margaret Trelawny. "It was all so real that I could hardly imagine that it had ever occurred before," the book begins, instantly throwing us into a world that employs the diction of reason and logic ("I could hardly imagine," Malcolm says) to characterize the blurring distinction between dream and reality (*Jewel* 1). We do not immediately understand the setting of the scene into which we have wandered, and although the content of this first sentence indicates that something is amiss—"so real" and "occurred before" both suggest the world of fantasy—its voice seems that of a clear-headed, outside observer. Malcolm can "hardly imagine" that he is in the mantle of his unconscious, but at the same time his dream has obviously displaced the rational real world that gives rise to a phrase like "hardly imagine." In acknowledging both his imagination and the real occurrence from which this dream arises, Malcolm conflates the two on both linguistic and psychological levels, and we can't be sure if we're in Malcolm's reality or in his mind. Malcolm describes the dream scene, his first meeting with Margaret, as deliberately as one would summarize a movie one is watching for a second time: "Again, the light skiff . . . glided out of the fierce July sunlight . . . Again, the water looked golden brown . . . Again, we sat in the cool shade . . . And so memory swooned, again and again, in sleep" (1). The passive connotations of the repeated "again" carve a distance between these events and their seemingly conscious, narrating observer, but we know he is dreaming. We're in Malcolm's mind and there's no space at all between the environment of the events and the site of the narrative consciousness. From this very first baffling sentence, we thus become privy to a world in which dreams and logical analysis, memory and experience fuse together into what Phyllis Roth describes as a "magical space" (113). Only in such blurred arenas can the fusions of identities in this story take place: "in the arcana of dreams . . . existences merge and renew themselves, change and yet keep the same" (*Jewel* 1). The replay of Malcolm's memories, Roth points out, "shadow[s] forth . . . the resurrection motif" that will become central to the novel's action (113). In Malcolm's insistence on dreams as necessary mediums for the renewal of memory, this opening scene foreshadows the blurry and supernatural physical spaces that will be essential for the "merging" and "renewal" of lives later in the novel.

As the novel moves out of Malcolm's dream into the conscious world, thematic echoes of Jonathan Harker's trip to Transylvania introduce what seems like a supernatural landscape. Beyond Jonathan's carriage window in *Dracula*, trees and hills appear "so far off that big things and little things are mixed" and "were themselves lost in the distance" (10). The same effect arises in "the dim grey light of the morning, which tends to diminish the size of things" that guides Malcolm's first hurried carriage-ride to the Trelawny house (*Jewel* 4). The two journeys have their similarities, though the former is in Eastern Europe and the latter in London, for both Jonathan and Malcolm travel out of comfortable domestic spaces into fantastic landscapes of preserved time. Castle Dracula, full of "centuries old" furniture in "excellent order" (not to mention a centuries-old vampire in excellent order), envelops Jonathan in an atmosphere of "strange ways" which make him inexplicably "uneasy" (*Dracula* 19, 21, 25). He fears he is "the only living soul within the place" (25). In occupying a space on the geographical border between Eastern and Western Europe and on the apparent border between life and death, Jonathan must also exist in a nightmare limbo where anything, even the appearance of an immortal blood-sucking Transylvanian, is possible.

Although Stoker doesn't display the grotesquely supernatural forces at work in *Jewel* as quickly or as blatantly as in the earlier novel, the Trelawny house has an uncanniness all its own, one that recalls the Yeatsian museum as much as the vampiric castle. As Malcolm tells us upon looking around Mr. Trelawny's curio-filled bedroom, "There were so many ancient relics that unconsciously one was taken back to strange lands and strange times . . . so many mummies or mummy objects . . . that one was unable to forget the past" (*Jewel* 22). And yet the presence of these objects in a British home equally represents the nineteenth-century political forces that made Egyptian treasures so ripe for the taking. Just as William Wilde's "souvenir" shopping bespoke a conservative imperial politics at odds with his more radical calls for Egyptian independence, the widespread amateur and professional European tomb-raiding of Egypt in the nineteenth century epitomized the large-scale misappropriations of Western colonialism while also, contradictorily, providing "evidence" that there was little distinction between the ancient Egyptians and modern Europeans.[33] As Jasmine Day bluntly puts it, "Embodying Egypt, mummies represented one part of a world conquered by the British Empire. Their private possessors owned a microcosmic Egypt" (21). But at the same time, mummies were also valued as "exemplars of the racial evolutionary theory then prevalent, an ideology that portrayed Europeans as the Egyptians' genetic descendants" (23). Mr. Trelawny's own Egyptological research follows in these incongruous footsteps, his house filled to overflowing with curios and sarcophagi that simultaneously estrange and replicate the house's British inhabitants. Like Dracula's castle and Yeats's Municipal Gallery, the Trelawny house breeds unease because its collection of artifacts produces a less-than-real borderland between familiarity and alienation, present and past, modern empire and historical remnant, life and "the multitudinous presence of the dead" (22).

It doesn't make for the homiest of environments, as Margaret tells Malcolm: "I sometimes don't know whether I am in a private home or the British Museum" (*Jewel* 20–21). As many critics have noted, nineteenth-century museum displays deliberately separated viewers from objects on display, and the expectation and assurance of distance made the presence of foreignness unremarkable in these public spaces.[34] Conversely, the presence of the public eye, Nicholas Daly writes, prevented "the museum's transformation into a forbiddingly exotic, even Gothic space," for the constant influx of British observers—eyes, voices, knowledge—kept antiquities from planting their alien roots in Western soil (32). This detachment sanitized these uncanny objects for the Western eye (and rendered them available subjects for Western poems like "The Burden of Nineveh"). In the Trelawny house, however, this same distance only succeeds in alienating the house's occupants by forcing them to be detached observers instead of active participants in their domestic space— they look but they can't *live*. The curios "evoke the curiosity" of Malcolm as he looks around Mr. Trelawny's bedroom, a reaction at once impersonally phrased and odd. This is, after all, the first time he has entered the home of the woman he loves, and his clinical impulse to "tak[e] accurate note of all [he] saw" displaces more expected reactions: interest, perhaps, or excitement (*Jewel* 16). Margaret—and Malcolm—stand amid this wealth of treasures, yet these two people are so temporally and culturally distanced from the artifacts that the objects' foreign presence usurps the psychological space usually reserved for "home." Even the objects themselves, to borrow James Clifford's analysis of the relationship between objects and humans in a museum culture, evoke an aura of unreality, for "collecting—and most notably the museum—creates the illusion of adequate representation of a world by first cutting objects out of specific contexts . . . and making them 'stand for' abstract wholes" (239). In a museum, as "The Burden of Nineveh" makes especially clear, objects often "stand in" for the cultures from which they have been appropriated, but in the Trelawny house they go a step further, becoming active manifestations rather than controlled metonymic representations. The curios are powerful enough to be what Egyptian culture itself represents to the Trelawnys: a bizarre combination of death, magic, the past, science, and modernity.

The most significant of these curios is, of course, the mummy, the ancient Egyptian queen Tera who embodies all these qualities to such a degree that unsynthesizable contradictions pepper the narrative with grammatical confusion about what, precisely, the mummy is. When Mr. Corbeck tells us first of discovering the queen's tomb, his narrative carefully separates its pronouns, referring to Tera as "her" and "she" only when he talks about the story of her five-thousand-year-old life and using detached definite articles to describe her as a mummy: "the mummified breast," "the end of wrist," "the blood on the mummy's hand" (*Jewel* 91, 95). The grammatical division between woman and mummy, between a living historical character and a clinically described dead thing, becomes confused when Mr. Trelawny takes over the storytelling, explaining the purpose behind what he oddly phrases as "my hunt for the mummy and her belongings" (117). In his version of the tale, she is both a treasure to be hunted and possessed and a subject with possessions of her own, both an "it" and "she."

The problem of the mummy's femininity plagues the text. She is modeled after the real Egyptian queen Hatshepsut, who claimed all the rights of kingship in spite of her gender and whose name was scratched out of the historical record upon her death. Like this real queen, Tera, "though a Queen, claimed all the privileges of kingship and masculinity," wearing man's dress in some of the images the Egyptologists describe while in others, "the discarded male raiment lay at her feet" (*Jewel* 93). Her exceptionality as a historical subject lies in this simultaneous erasure and embrace of gender distinctions, and the novel inexplicably ties this disruption of gendered roles to her "power over Sleep and Will." The pictures in her tomb showing "that she had achieved a victory over Sleep" also show "everywhere a symbolism" of the queen in both male and female dress (92–93). The idea of the queen's resurrection, then, becomes an instantiation of her uncategorizable gender identity. This is true even on a nonsymbolic level, for we are told that the priests "would after her death try to suppress her name," to erase her conundrum from history, and this threat leads Queen Tera to prepare for her resurrection "after long time," when those who had suppressed her would themselves be history (93).

The project of resurrecting Queen Tera, the novel's "Great Experiment," becomes an effort—a failing effort—in assigning and categorizing the identity of a figure who, as a corpse (both a "she" and an "it"), as an androgynous ancient ruler (both a "she" and a "he"), and as a museum artifact (both "British" and "foreign") refuses singularity at every turn. Although the novel begins in London as a locked-room mystery, it shifts considerably when Mr. Trelawny decides to finally begin his Great Experiment. The experiment, we learn, requires isolation, and the novel's setting moves from the city to Mr. Trelawny's remote house in Cornwall, in a fictional, Celtic-named county called Kyllion. The geography of the region—the barren, rocky cliff on which the house stands, isolated on three sides by the crashing sea—reminds us that Cornwall, along with Scotland, Ireland, and Brittany, was considered one of the Celtic nations of Europe, and that we have moved out of the English metropolis into a markedly Celtic periphery. The house itself has a sectarian political history, as well: Mr. Trelawny tells Malcolm that "during the Bloody Assize, more than a few [Protestant] Cornishmen found refuge" in the secret cave beneath the house where he plans to conduct the Great Experiment (*Jewel* 143–44). The Bloody Assize, in which hundreds of Protestants were sentenced to death in a huge trial for supporting the Protestant Duke of Monmouth's march against the Catholic King James II in 1685, not only failed to maintain Catholic rule in Britain (three years later, William of Orange, the demon of Catholic Ireland, began his own successful campaign against James II) but became, in 1902, much-contested Liberal shorthand for how the British should *not* conduct themselves in the aftermath of the Boer War.[35]

Stoker thus explicitly locates this Great Experiment in the midst of both sectarian and imperial political strife, as well as in a place, Mr. Trelawny says, that has not "always been used according to law" (*Jewel* 143). From the London of the Sherlock Holmes mystery, in which the laws of logic will always reign supreme, the novel has moved for its Experiment into the politically heated, sectarian, Celtic margins of the empire, as though to suggest from the outset that the Queen's resurrection will be less an allegory of British metropolitan strength than an experiment in shifting power dynamics, in political multiplicity, and in the resonant energy of a particularly Celtic shadow-world. And yet this cave is also as close a reproduction of Tera's own Egyptian tomb as Mr. Trelawny has found in the British Isles. "Here we are, and shall be, as isolated as Queen Tera herself would have been in her rocky tomb in the Valley of the Sorcerer, and still in a rocky cavern," Mr. Trelawny tells Malcolm as they enter the cave, superimposing one politically fraught history on another and gesturing toward the geographical double-consciousness that underlies the project of the novel as a whole (144). The reanimation of Queen Tera will take place at the intersection of Egypt and the "Celtic fringe," where the historical resonances of two sundered nations fuse and come to signify one another.

Queen Tera herself, with her Egyptian past and her Celtic coloring ("great masses" of "glossy black hair" piled on an "ivory" white forehead), is an emblem of this conceptual national synthesis yet otherwise remains a figure marked by schismatic doubling (*Jewel* 171). The confusion between "she" and "it" that we see in the men's story of the queen's history progresses into a pervasive confusion not simply about the mummy's femininity but about the ethical relationship between art and history and between the living and the dead. Queen Tera's resurrection is the novel's site of uncertainty about historical ownership, about aesthetic privilege, about scientific aggression, about national identity, and about feminine subjectivity. In short, the queen's resurrection is set up as the ultimate imperial project, only to end as an ultimate imperial failure. Both a seemingly lifelike subject eager to share her ancient knowledge and power, and a dead "thing" that the novel's men allow themselves to see as a nonthreatening, protected object, Queen Tera represents, on the one hand, an essential tissue of connection between past and present and, on the other, a past already conquered and made into art.

Similarly, the language of her resurrection oscillates between scientific experiment and darkly occult aesthetic project, between a desire to acquire the queen's ancient knowledge and a desire to possess the queen herself, couched in the transformation of the mummy into a work of art.[36] Queen Tera is a physical incarnation of history and the possibility for historical continuity. Through her, Mr. Trelawny tells us, "we may learn things that have been hidden from the eyes and the knowledge of men for centuries; for scores of centuries" (*Jewel* 117). Such a being, he insists, "can link together Old and New, Earth and Heaven, and yield to the known worlds of thought and physical existence the mystery of the Unknown[!]" (155). The reanimation of the Queen, then, is not just the reanimation of a body but also the reanimation of a lost past, and of historical knowledge that can infuse the present with its once-dead grandeur. But for this to be the case, the Queen can be nothing more than a material vehicle for knowledge. For history to be recoverable and usable, rather than simply a haunting past, it must be objectified and revalued according to modern standards.

In this need for reanimation, the novel exposes the conventions of gender and nationality that would allow such a transformation—a transformation from "she" to "it"—to take place. But in exposing them, and in doubting them, *Jewel* calls into question not only the now-conventional critical truism that "death turns the woman into an object of sight—the dead feminine body comparable to an exhibited art object"—but also the notion that a national history can be extrapolated from or created out of a cultural artifact (Bronfen xiii). In *The Jewel of Seven Stars*, these two elements are inextricable from one another, for Queen Tera stands at the center of the text as an endlessly shifting, indefinable, and resistant object of the other characters' fused sexual and historical desires. Nicholas Daly has argued that nineteenth-century European mummy tales in which a female mummy is collected and privately owned both nationalize and sexualize the idea of the desire-driven commodity, the imperial desire for historical ownership reinforced by the erotic desire to possess and use the female body. However, while *Jewel* certainly engages with this expression of intellectual desire as a more literal sexual desire, the mummy's reanimation throughout the novel—she seems to come to life several times before the ultimate attempt to raise her from the sarcophagus—stridently disavows the efficacy of any kind of desire—sexual or imperial—in possessing, objectifying, or containing historical knowledge. Quite literally, the mummy comes to life to escape the captors who wish to possess her: when Mr. Trelawny and Corbeck first try to bring her to England, she breaks out of her packing case and mysteriously vanishes as they carry her from the desert, only to reappear in her tomb in precisely the position from which they took her. During the three days it takes the men to reclaim her, we are told, Mr. Trelawny's wife dies in childbirth, and the novel explicitly connects the repossession of the mummy with the loss of Mr. Trelawny's object of sexual desire. "It seemed to have become in some way associated with [Trelawny's] Egyptian Studies," Corbeck says of Mrs. Trelawny's death, "and more especially with the mysteries connected with the Queen" (*Jewel* 98). The queen herself, whom we are to understand as the mysterious agent both of her own replacement in the tomb and of the death of Trelawny's wife, recognizes the interchangeability of Trelawny's academic desires and his erotic desires, deliberately devastating the latter in order to warn against his indulgence of the former. By using episodes of reanimation to destabilize the objectifying power of masculine sexual desire, the novel also destabilizes the possibility that reanimation can or should become a form of historical possession. Stoker thus transforms the key element of mummy fiction—the mummy returning to life—from an exercise in masculine desire, inscription, and control into a feat of feminine agency with both political and aesthetic repercussions.

Mr. Trelawny *tries* to approach his Experiment and his queen with a coldly clinical eye, illuminating her body with a harshly modern electric light in order to firmly establish her as an object as the moment of actual resurrection approaches. In tandem with keeping what is really more of a Great Séance than a Great Experiment from falling into a pot of spiritualist conventions, it seems essential that this potentially powerful and exotic female figure be sanitized and constrained as a scientific discovery. "There, in the full glare of the [electric] light," Malcolm says as he looks down at the mummy's aged and ragged wrappings, "the whole material and sordid side of death seemed startlingly real" (169). But just as the glaring electric light that makes the queen seem to be a dead specimen is the same "glare of . . . electric light" that the group will use to catalyze her reanimation, their insistence on seeing her deadness becomes a path to her animation.[37] Their wish that she remain a lifeless artifact until the moment she becomes a living conduit of knowledge crumbles when the group unwraps Queen Tera's body in preparation for her resurrection, for this unwrapping scene confronts the men with their own critical sensibilities and forces them to back away. Margaret, the novel's token living woman, sums up the problem of Queen Tera's dual existence in a moment of outrage at the shockingly callous detachment with which the novel's men treat the mummy. "'Father, you are not going to unswathe her!'

she cries. "All you men . . . Just think, Father, a woman!'" "Not a woman, my dear; a mummy!'" her father replies, "'she has been dead nearly five thousand years!'" (*Jewel* 167).

Margaret sets the possibility of reanimation squarely in opposition to the men's rejection of female subjectivity, insisting that the female corpse is as much a subject as a living woman and refusing death's objectifying power in the face of her imminent return to life. "Sex is not a matter of years! A woman is a woman, if she has been dead five thousand centuries! And you expect her to arise out of that long sleep! It could not be real death, if she is to rise out of it! You have led me to believe that she will come alive . . . !" (167). This possibility—that the Queen will indeed come alive—thus engenders a theoretical schism in the novel over the relationship between reanimation and subjectivity. To Mr. Trelawny, Queen Tera's resurrection means access to "lost arts, lost learning, lost sciences": "What is a woman's life in the scale with what we hope for?" he asks, suggesting that reanimating the queen will strip her of her "woman's life" and leave instead a "scale" of knowledge, in female form, that he can possess and use (154). Margaret, on the other hand, sees reanimation as the return of life, and agency, to a woman "in hope of a new life in a new world" (162). For Mr. Trelawny, reanimation is an exercise in masculine domination, a dehumanizing act of aestheticization; for Margaret, it means the pure revival of female agency.

Almost immediately upon offering these two conflicting poles, however, the novel collapses them. This scene of unwrapping, in which scientific objectivity is paramount to maintaining the queen as a medium of history, marks the moment in which science collapses into aesthetic sensibility, and aesthetics, into sexual desire. As the group unrolls the mummy, they become more and more entranced with the beauty of her linens, the golden embroidery on the gown lying across her body, her "wondrous [jeweled] girdle, which shone and glowed with all the forms and phases and colours of the sky," and finally, her body itself, "that beautiful form," "something to dream of," "like a statue carven in ivory" (*Jewel* 170–71). At the moment of complete unwrapping, the mummy transforms from a purely scientific and historical body into a work of art. And yet the art has a vulgar edge, its revelation presented as a thinly veiled striptease, something "indecent," our narrator tells us, something "almost sacrilegious" (171). The text offers us a drawn-out, elaborate unwrapping, reveals that the garment lying across the queen is a wedding gown rather than a death shroud, and the watching men become "more and more excited." The unwrapping finally climaxes in a "rush of shame" that "sweep[s] over" them at the sight of her finally nude body, its flesh "full and round," its skin "as smooth as satin"—hardly scientific, and instead simultaneously aesthetic and erotic (171).

208 • CHAPTER 5

This vessel of pure history has become an art object to be possessed and aesthetically reimagined rather than a body of knowledge to bring to life. At the same time, the very act of aestheticizing awakens a desire in the men that strips them, the gazing artists, of control over the scene. The grammar of the sweeping shame renders them passive objects of the queen's carnal power. And all of a sudden, the body looks "not dead, but alive." The transformation of the queen from specimen to sculpture marks the transformation of the men's desire to resurrect her ancient historical knowledge into their desire for creative power over her, but the inescapably erotic nature of this transformation suggests that the novel—like the mummy—can and will deny them that power. The queen instead comes alive, emblematically if not yet literally, her sudden *appearance* of life resisting the representational nature that her status as a dead object has allowed.

But she does not simply look *alive*: she is also "the image of Margaret," an exact double for Mr. Trelawny's daughter (*Jewel* 171). As Mr. Trelawny looks longer at the queen's body, he hugs Margaret to him, and "murmur[s] brokenly, 'It looks as if you were dead, my child!'" To make the queen seem alive, Margaret must seem dead. The novel seeks to make visible the insufficiency and the violence of aesthetic recuperation by rendering one woman as an image of death at the moment that the other's image of life seems to refute death. This flash of a dead Margaret reveals the danger posed to everyone by the men's continuously shifting representations of the queen—as art, as erotic object, even as living woman—by showing us what the queen resists when she resists the pressing force of this desire to transform her into a vehicle for masculine sensibility: the destruction of individuality and of agency. Interconnected as Queen Tera and Margaret are, the queen's reanimation enacts Margaret's deanimation, amplifying and visiting upon the living Margaret the aesthetic violence that Tera's dead female body invites, and that its suddenly lifelike look repudiates.[38] History, this transference suggests, is not for these men to bring back to life and "set right" (154). Instead, their desire to collapse the gap between history and modernity, to access ancient knowledge through modern science, to use past grandeur as a way of inventing a glorious future, may just wreak its own violence on the present.

IRISH REVIVALS: REANIMATION AND NATIONALISM

There is no single colonial allegory at play in this scene, nor in the novel as a whole. For an Anglo-Celt oscillating between English and Irish national affiliations, this is part of the point of writing a novel that itself constantly oscillates between but never synthesizes old magic and modern science, English and not English, art and history, death and life. Many readings of *Jewel* see the queen's unwrapping as a destabilization of masculine, British authority in confrontation with a dangerous Oriental Other, in which conventional power dynamics turn inside out: the gaze becomes a locus of power for the object of the gaze rather than the one who gazes, logical science collapses into irrational desire, and aesthetic reanimation perpetrates violence on the animators, not on the animated body.[39] Historical knowledge, in this model, would be the prize of colonial power, Egyptian wisdom being beneficial only inasmuch as the British colonizers can possess and reorder it for their own use but threatening when it begins to possess and reorder their own modern selves and spaces. The novel's opening chapters, in which the smell exuding from the Egyptian curios hypnotizes all the characters into strange trance-states, stand as evidence of this phenomenon, for these appropriated colonial objects refuse their passive containment and begin to transform a London townhouse into an exotic, Egyptian space.[40] In such readings, Queen Tera's Egyptianness is little more than shorthand for any feminized, colonized Other slipping out of and threatening British control. Her Egyptian mummy body is simply the most extreme incarnation of a stolen colonial artifact resisting its museum confinement, just as any frustrated stolen colonial object would.

But, as I keep arguing, Ireland's complicated colonial position and the interplay between Ireland and Egypt in *Jewel* interferes with such singular allegorizing. Valente claims that Stoker experienced Ireland and Irishness as "an uneasy social and psychic space between authority, agency, and legitimacy on one side and abjection, heteronomy, and hybridity on the other" (*Dracula's* 4). As an Anglo-Celt, and "hence a member of a conquering and a conquered race, a ruling and a subject people, an imperial and an occupied nation," Stoker himself embodied a unique Irish racial position as well as the contradictory position of Ireland itself within the British Empire (4). Simultaneously colonized and colonizing, Ireland not only was populated by dual Irish populations—the Unionists fiercely loyal to the crown and the Nationalists fighting for independence—but also made up a disproportionate percentage of the British imperial army, despite what Nationalist MP John Dillon explicitly called the Irish "hatred of imperialism."[41] According to one historian, "Ireland helped to maintain the British Raj in India in a manner out of all proportion to her size," both as part of the ruling class and as a huge proportion of the army stationed there, while at the same time, much as with Egypt, the fight for Irish Home Rule overlapped with and encouraged India's own challenges to British rule (Fraser 77). As both oppressor and oppressed, a nation both moving against its fellow colonies and lamenting the "English domination" that cut

210 · CHAPTER 5

Ireland's contact "with her own past, her own language and her own culture," Ireland's colonial circumstances created a fractured national sensibility caught between metropole and margins, Occident and Orient, modern politics and a mythically lost past (Mitchell ix).

Jewel captures the anxiety of this dual consciousness with a precision lost in readings of the novel that see only versions of British political unease in the multiple power struggles that the novel displays. Unlike *Dracula* (or *Carmilla, She, Jekyll and Hyde, The Beetle,* and most other classic late nineteenth-century gothic novels), *Jewel* isn't governed by fear of a monster. Rather, the novel's plot, the scheme and danger of planning the queen's resurrection, emerges from both the desire for and the fear of a union between divided entities: most grandly, between "Old Forces" and "New Civilization," and more locally, between the living Margaret and the "'Ka' of the dead queen" that seems to be "animating" her (*Jewel* 133, 149). "If it was indeed that she had in her own person a dual existence, what might happen when the two existences become one?" Malcolm muses anxiously (157). The two problems this question concisely identifies—first, the impossibility of sustaining two separate identities in one space, and second, the danger of trying to synthesize them—not only constitute the novel's essential conflict but also sum up the fundamental conflict of Irish coloniality itself.

We need not dig to see the problem of Ireland—at the tail end of the Boer War, at the beginning of its famous Literary Revival, in the throes of its fight for Home Rule—implicit in the novel's structural concern with dual identities, with the efficacy of historical revival, and with successful unions between ancient and modern and between East and West. In this, *Jewel* is less a colonial allegory than an expression of the discordant polysemy of Irish identity, mediated through a gothic tale of split personality, reanimated bodies, and the resurrection of the past. In the doubling, even the interweaving, of Queen Tera and Margaret, the novel presents an Irish identity divided into colonized and colonizer, victim and aggressor, and, most importantly, past and present iterations. More significant to *Jewel* than the overt split between Irish colonizer and Irish colonized, the dual identity of the novel's female characters expresses a simultaneously aesthetic and political split between the suppressed grandeur of a Gaelic past (Queen Tera's name, again, recalls the Hill of Tara, seat of the old Irish kings) and a degraded contemporary moment trying to reclaim its "lore," to catapult itself into "the true world of human progress" by "set[ting] [history] right" (154).[42]

As Susan Mitchell writes in her 1920 preface to *An Egyptian in Ireland,* a manifesto of the Irish national revival, Ireland's "heroic past" is finally being "reincarnated" in Anglo-Irish literature, a literature in English that nonetheless "bear[s] witness to the vitality of a race accounted dead" (x–xi). "Whatever is living in our country to-day, was born out of that union of Ireland's present with her past," Mitchell writes, and "it is most certainly true . . . that Ireland in her contact with her Gaelic original has not been making a retrograde movement, but that the intuition of the race has guided it rightly to that which has revitalized its life" (xi–xii). Yet part of the crisis of Irish identity at the turn of the twentieth century was precisely the disconnect between Ireland as it then was and the "Gaelic original" from which nationalists and revivalists insisted that Ireland draw strength. As O'Grady wrote in the introduction to his *History of Ireland,* the Irish historian's most difficult task was "to make this heroic period *once again* a portion of the imagination of the country," indicating not only the current deadness of the past to the present but also the aesthetic labor necessary to transform the past into something imaginatively valuable to the present (2.17). The events and deeds of the past, as he writes, "are no more [a nation's] history than a skeleton is a man"—the accretive process of fleshing dry bones into meaningful national culture is implicitly nostalgic, an act of revitalization that takes its tissues entirely from the present instead of from the past (1.22). Declan Kiberd has argued that the "great burden of post-colonial national elites" was that "they must have an *idea* of Ireland," an intrinsically theatrical invention of identity that created a "disjunction between role and self" based almost solely on the invention and/ or appropriation of Irish tradition (*Inventing* 289). The "national culture" excavated and performed by the literary revival "must always be a nostalgia, visible only in eternal retrospect as the after-image on a retina"—a culture constantly reinterpreted, recreated, and revised to suit whatever future the present nation wants to develop (Kiberd 301).

Kiberd goes so far as to call Irish national history a "form of science fiction," but Yeats perhaps summed up the aesthetic problem of the Literary Revival best when he asked, "Is not all history but the coming of that conscious art which first makes articulate and then destroys that old wild energy?" (*Inventing* 293; "Edmund Spenser" 268). Irish cultural nationalism created an irresolvable double-bind for artists caught between a past that had very little to do with them and a future that they were trying to form out of those materials of distant tradition. Obsessed with questions of cultural and historical authenticity, as well as with modernism's call to "make it new" both aesthetically and politically, writers like Yeats, Synge, and Lady Gregory oscillated between invention and regression, trying, as Seamus Deane has said, to make "a claim for cultural exceptionalism through legend rather than through history" and depending on the "paradigm of rebirth, renaissance, recovery of which the modern becomes both the beneficiary and the culmination" (51).

212 • CHAPTER 5

The necessary co-existence of past and present in a single aesthetic moment resulted in a surfeit of "pseudo-couples" in the literature of the Irish Renaissance, co-dependent and often antagonistic doubles that seemed to emerge from writers seeking grounds on which to combine their imposed inheritance and their developing future (Kiberd, *Inventing* 299).[43] Published in the midst of the Irish Literary Revival's first surge, *The Jewel of Seven Stars* views such Revivalist impulses from a critical, almost an ironic, distance, making literal and gothic both the double-consciousness and the renaissance of the past that defined these early and most nationalist of works. Stoker's novel literalizes both the cultural gap between Revivalists and their objects of revival and the impossible idealism inherent in the idea that revival, in any sense of the word, could successfully bridge this gap.

The crisis point in the strange doubling of Queen Tera and Margaret, in which Tera looking alive only makes Margaret look dead, is thus a Revivalist crisis point, brought on by the ease with which the male characters wrongly believe they can imaginatively transform Queen Tera into an inanimate work of art.[44] What the novel reveals in this moment of intermingled life-like and deathlike female appearances is an essential and irreconcilable conflict between seeing the dead past as an aesthetic object and trying to revive it for modern use. The past can either be killed into art or resurrected on its own terms, but it cannot be brought back to life *through* art, cannot be simultaneously aestheticized and alive. The image of the dead female body has been classically understood as a repression both of cultural alterity and of the knowledge of death itself—a displaced stand-in for what a culture both desires and fears and a space for masculine inscription[45]—but in this novel that dreams of reanimation, the dead female body functions as the *expression*, rather than the *repression*, of masculine aesthetic failure: the failure to possess, to inscribe, or to rescue. The paired women in the text allow us to see the workings of aesthetic desire simultaneous with its insufficiency as an act either of individual or of cultural redemption. When the queen looks alive, Margaret looks dead; when aesthetic reanimation seems successful, actual life seems extinguished.[46] During the striptease in which Margaret and Tera are revealed to be identical, their pairing demonstrates that representation and death are inseparable from one another, while also making it clear that representation and reanimation are antithetical rather than synonymous impulses. "Conscious art" and "wild energy," to use Yeats's terms, will destroy one another.[47]

The ultimate fantasy of the novel's characters, however, is not to make the queen "look alive," as they do in this moment of profound aesthetic confusion and danger, but to bring the queen *actually* to life, acquiring both the proof that resurrection is possible and all of the queen's lost ancient knowledge. The desire to reanimate the queen becomes a gothic incarnation of the Literary Revival, not because it enacts a dark fantasy about the life-giving power of art—the aesthetic fantasy of the Revival's Anglo-Irish writers—but because it makes dangerous the desire to reanimate a past culture and assimilate it in the present moment to better the future. The weight of this danger is ethical rather than philosophical. By mapping the possessiveness and cultural appropriation of this act onto a clearly colonial power dynamic—the resurrection of an Egyptian woman by a group of British men—the novel exposes the inherently imperial structure of this kind of cultural nationalism, which assumes that a "new" Irish culture can be made through the custody and reinvention of the past, at the expense of suppressing the reality of the present.[48] "What is a woman's life in the scale with what we hope for!" Mr. Trelawny exclaims as he describes his Experiment, revealing that he has no interest in the perpetuation of individual lives (even "the dearest life to [him] in all the world," which he readily puts at risk) but is instead willing, even eager, to subsume individuals into the remaking of world history (*Jewel* 153–54).[49] Cultural distinction, the rupture between past and present, and the violence of dragging a legendary figure from her native soil in order to put her to use all vanish in the quasi-religious fervor with which Mr. Trelawny justifies his Great Experiment. He transforms the queen's reanimation into an effort of global proportions, an attempt to unify not simply a nation but the entire world (as well as "Worlds beyond our ken") through this "new" fount of historical knowledge.

And yet all this grandiosity seems grossly out of proportion with the efforts of a tiny band of mad intellectuals, hiding in a Celtic cavern with a mummified Cathleen ni Houlihan, hoping to bring the past back to life. This novel makes the desire for reanimation both gothic and camp by showing its characters unknowingly trapped between their belief that they can possess the past as a usable object and their awe at the dangerous agency of history, fantasizing that the queen's reanimation will synthesize these two impulses rather than prove them to be irreconcilable. But the reanimated body, neither still dead nor quite alive again, reveals instead the chasm between aesthetics and history—between representation and social reality—that comprised the crisis of a late nineteenth-century Irish nationalism predicated on the belief that these two versions of the past could be made synonymous.

The queen's reanimation, the final scene of the novel, takes place in ever-increasing visual obscurity, where image and reality, the dead and the living, the past and the nineteenth century up to date with a vengeance, blur together in darkness, mist, and dense, billowing smoke. "My own eyes were nearly blinded," Malcolm tells us as the rest of the group gathers around the queen's sarcophagus. He sees "something filmy like a white mist" rise from the coffin, something "cloudy and opaque." Then, almost immediately, black smoke begins to fill the cavern, growing "thicker and thicker" until "the whole cavern began to get obscure, and its outlines were lost" (*Jewel* 176). Malcolm finally wades into the darkness to rescue Margaret from whatever is happening and, feeling what he thinks is her unconscious body on the floor, carries her out of the cavern. Everything, however, has gone wrong: it isn't Margaret's body but Queen Tera's that he has carried upstairs. By the time the black smoke clears, Tera has escaped, and Malcolm finds the rest of the group, including Margaret, dead in the cavern, "gazing upward with fixed eyes of unspeakable terror" (178).

The attention this scene pays to vision, to what can and can't be seen, recalls the earlier mummy unwrapping, in which the novel's resistance to the aestheticization of history begins by disempowering the male gaze. At the novel's end, the defeated gaze not only has lost its aesthetic influence—"its outlines were lost"—but also, more horrifically, can no longer distinguish between Margaret and Tera, between life and death, between reanimation and deanimation. Only in this moment of complete blindness does the novel bring about the obfuscation of individuality, the synonymy of past and future, and the ultimate reanimation of history that was the Irish Revival's Romantic dream. Yet as a naked, five-thousand-year-old Egyptian queen runs off to wreak havoc on the world, and our narrator remains trapped in a houseful of corpses somewhere on the Celtic fringe, this ultimate "proof that resurrection can be accomplished" seems like little more than an order of execution for the revivalist dreams of Irish nationalism.

EPILOGUE

The Undead Reader, or the Perils of Resuscitative Reading

The revivalist impulse that ends so catastrophically in *The Jewel of Seven Stars* is as much a hermeneutic impulse as it is a creative one: the ancient mummy, resurrected by new electricity and modern colonialist ideology, embodies not only the aesthetics of the Literary Revival but also the implicit interpretive work that underpins this aesthetics. Queen Tera's linen-wrapped, hieroglyphic-printed corpse is as much a text to be read as a past to resurrect, and the inextricability of reading her body and resurrecting it shows how inherently reliant historical revivals are on practices of readings the past that are "*animated* by values, ideals, and principles" of the present (Felski, *Hooked* 32). If Stoker's novel condemns the colonial arrogance of overstepped artistic bounds, then it equally probes the dangerous transgressions of injudicious reading, reading in which (to borrow one of Rita Felski's descriptions of postcritical reading) "textual details vibrate and resonate with special force when they hook up with our passions and predilections, our affectively soaked histories and memories" (*Limits* 178). Such reading practices run rampant in *Jewel* as its contemporary characters delve into the mummy queen's history, interpreting it into justification for their Great Experiment. "We men sat silent as the young girl gave her powerful interpretation of the design or purpose of the woman of old," Malcolm tells us as Margaret spins out what she believes to be Queen Tera's story of love and longing and kindness, rapt as "her every word and tone carried with it the conviction of her own belief" (Stoker, *Jewel*

129). Margaret's reading of Tera offers us a touching vision of a tender woman, yet her interpretive practice perfectly encapsulates Felski's vision of details "resonat[ing] with special force when they hook up with our passions and predilections": "I know the [Queen's] feeling for I have shared it myself," Margaret says, unable to see how fundamentally her own emotions animate her reading of the mummy's past life (129).

Felski's dream of postcritical reading sees such animation as accretive rather than distorting, as joyful rather than obtruding. Yet, taken to its resuscitative extreme, as it is in Stoker's novel and in many monster-filled novels that follow his, this dream of vibrant postcritical reading takes an insidious turn, enabling a corpse's reanimation but refusing any of her readers a happily ever after. Margaret's loving interpretation of Queen Tera ultimately bears little resemblance to the Queen's real story, and by the novel's end the hazards of overzealous resuscitative reading have left Margaret (and nearly everyone else) dead at the mummy's hands, "the glassy stare of her eyes through her fingers . . . more terrible than an open glare" (Stoker, *Jewel* 178). Two centuries later, murderous mummies and other corpses are still coming to life in nineteenth-century novels, but twenty-first-century writers have transformed them from objects that are dangerously resuscitated by nineteenth-century readers into the dangerous contemporary readers of nineteenth-century fiction. The zombies, vampires, and mummies that populate Austen, Brontë, and Dickens novels in the twenty-first century embody the drastic impress of new readers on old texts, the extreme, absurd, bloodthirsty "life" that resuscitative reading has the potential to awaken. In monster "mash-ups" like *Pride and Prejudice and Zombies* and *Jane Slayre*, corpses come to life in classic British fiction not simply to remake the canon in the image of contemporary paranormal zeitgeist but also to parody the monstrous potential of rabid readers to reanimate texts into oblivion.[1]

These mash-ups make literal the language of animation and reanimation that has long been a metaphor for theorizing interactions between reader and text, especially interactions alternative to the penetrative disinterments of critique, what Felski describes as "the endless deflationary work of 'digging down'" that characterizes suspicious reading practices (*Limits* 182). In his 1972 essay "The Reading Process: A Phenomenological Approach," for instance, Wolfgang Iser claimed that the relationship between a text and its reader will always be one of generative interpretation, for the "the reader's imagination animates" the "outlines" of a text and contributes a full half of what becomes "the literary work" that lives in the world (281). Iser's essay describes reading as an interpretive balance between text and reader, one that is constantly changing but whose fluidity "imparts to the text [a] dynamic lifelikeness" that allows it to be an active participant in worlds beyond its own (294). Borrowing from Georges Poulet, Iser entertains the possibility that "books only take on their full existence in the reader," and quotes Poulet's claim that "so long as it is animated by this vital inbreathing inspired by the act of reading[,] a work of literature becomes . . . a sort of human being" (298, 299). Taking Poulet even further, one later overview of reader response theory goes so far as to argue that reading "transforms the book-as-object—the heavy, dead, material thing—into a subject," specifically figuring reading as a process of bringing a dead textual object to active, subjective life (Richter 926). Deborah Lutz makes a similar argument specifically about Victorian books, arguing that if books are the "commemorative markers" of their dead nineteenth-century authors, readers "en-skin (enflesh) these dead words again, enlivening the corpse of their narrative" as they move "from moribund author to animated reader" (*Relics* 99). Dead books, like dead bodies, invite a resuscitative reading practice that revitalizes and multiplies their stories.[2]

In the introduction to their special issue of *Representations* dedicated to surface reading, Stephen Best and Sharon Marcus describe the symptomatic reading they critique as a violent search for material buried so deeply that "it can only be detected by an extreme degree of penetration," identifying Fredric Jameson in particular as popularizing an "image of the critic as wresting meaning from a resisting text or inserting it into a lifeless one" (4, 5). By contrast, interpretive methods that resist such assaults have the potential to "endow books with consciousness," and critics can be "anatomists . . . rearranging texts into new forms" rather than Jamesonian necrophiliacs taking their pleasures from corpse-texts (Best and Marcus 8, 11). Such language recollects eighteenth-century satires of antiquarians, which mocked such scholars' peculiar passion for "digging through Gothic and Roman ruins, handling dry bones, and pondering dusty books and artifacts" (M. Goode 72–73). The antiquarians who relished excavating old texts to discover their secrets—excavating what George Crabbe in 1781 called "lasting mansions of the dead"—were caricatured as lascivious corpses, perversely tainted by the deadness of the materials in which they buried themselves (qtd. in M. Goode 74). Like Best and Marcus's prurient modern Marxist, the antiquarian's work killed off texts instead of enlivening them, reifying ghosts instead of reviving the dead.[3]

As should be obvious, I'm carefully cherry-picking rhetorical flourishes from critics who also use countless other metaphors and images to describe the actions of symptomatic reading and its varied alternatives. But while resuscitative language isn't the only or even the primary figure for theorizing new reading practices, it remains a persistent and provocative one, popping up again and again across decades as a generative and speculative way to characterize active and ongoing interactions between reader and text. The New Zealand writer H. G. Parry, thinking explicitly about the magical potential of such "literary interpretation and theory," even conceives an entire novel out of the speculative capacity of these metaphors (460). *The Unlikely Escape of Uriah Heep* (2019) imagines what would happen if the animating interaction between reader and text were completely literal: if at the moment of reading when "each sentence and metaphor and reference feeds into the other to illuminate something important," when there's an "explosion of discovery, of understanding . . . emotional, intellectual, aesthetic," a reader will "see [someone or something from the text] so clearly that they manifest" (22). And once a reader has given a fictional character genuine material form in the real world, putting them back into their text "feels, momentarily, like dying" (28). In Parry's novel, literary analysis is literally the stuff of life, with different readings of texts animating different versions of characters into the world. As Sherlock Holmes tells a young English professor named Charlie when the novel's villain sics a nightmarish, superficially analyzed version of the Hound of the Baskervilles on him, "You can argue with its interpretation. . . . Think of it as an academic dispute. . . . You know why this reading is wrong" (40–41). To transform the creature at the door from an immortal gothic monster—a poor reading of the Conan Doyle novel—into an ordinary bloodhound/mastiff-cross doctored with phosphorous—a better and less dangerous reading of the novel—Charlie has to use his skill at literary analysis to correct someone else's deliberate misreading, reanimating the monstrous creature into a harmless, misunderstood doggy by reinterpreting Conan Doyle's text into new life.

Competing readings of Uriah Heep, Mr. Darcy, David Copperfield, even entire Dickensian streets are animated and reanimated across Parry's novel as Charlie battles to be a stronger, more ethical reader than his nemesis: a hundred-year-old reading of Moriarty animated by a long-dead Victorian woman "who wanted to *be* him," and so brought to life a character who is "her exact doppelgänger, in many ways: in appearance, in knowledge, in skills. But also Moriarty. So much more ruthless and ambitious than she knew how to be" (366). Readers in this novel bring to life characters that are always both reader and text, and a vague-faced Implied Reader wandering around among the more recognizable nineteenth-century characters shows how deliberately Parry builds her imaginative world out of the metaphors of Iser's reader response theory. That she focuses particularly (although not exclusively) on Victorian fiction and characters populating and threatening to overwhelm the otherwise ordinary New Zealand city of Wellington suggests not the allegory of nineteenth-century British settler colonialism that one might expect but instead her investment and geeky pleasure in Iser's claim that the form of the nineteenth-century realist novel, in particular, produces its experience of reality by insisting that the reader "takes an active part in the animation of all characters' actions" ("Implied" 771). In Parry's novel, this directive doesn't just produce an *experience* of reality. It literally produces a new reality that can only be stopped by refusing to participate in reader response theory. "I didn't know how to close read, or interpret," Charlie's brother says as he dives into the new world "shifting with printed sentences," "but I knew . . . the feeling of a story being told. I told this one" (Parry 428). Only telling one's story of oneself—rather than allowing the readings of others to bring characters to life—can save the world from the dangers of resuscitative reading.

As Parry's novel suggests, trading out the gothic buried secrets of suspicious reading for the notion of reading as necromancy isn't ultimately a turn away from gothic reading. Bringing corpses to life is hardly less risky than digging up old skeletons, even if the former is couched in more celebratory language. Yet Felski's *The Limits of Critique* makes this trade-off unrepentantly, turning constantly to bodies and their afterlives to work its way from a hermeneutics of suspicion to new affective modes of postcritical reading that "do justice to the transtemporal liveliness of texts": modes that allow us to be "animated by the words we encounter" and that acknowledge how readily "words from the past may spring back to life, acquiring fresh vigor and vitality" (154, 12, 125). Felski describes postcritical reading as distinct from the explicitly exhumatory work of many critical approaches to interpretation, offering metaphors of reanimation in its place to describe the alternative interpretive modes she is proposing. For instance, paraphrasing from the French critic Yves Citton's *Lire, interpréter, actualiser: Pourquoi les études littéraires?* she writes, "Advocating what he calls '*une lecture actualisante*'—where *actualiser* means to realize, to bring to life, but also to make contemporary—Citton insists that interpretation is not a matter of exhumation but one of reinvention, that attention to past context should not overshadow questions of transtemporal resonance and how literary works speak to us now" (178). Such language not only fantasizes about an interpretive mode that can truly liberate text from context but also presents literary interpretation itself *as* fantasy: fantasy as ripe with hope but also as potentially imperiled by gothic repercussions as nineteenth-century necromantic texts like Stoker's, whose plots are literal realizations of Citton's transtemporal resonances and chatty old books. Such fantasies don't always end badly—Browning and Yeats both make the fantasy of resuscitative reading into ars poetica—but even the poets suffer niggling doubts about just how lively galvanized texts can truly be.

Stoker's novel is the most insidious proleptic shadow of Citton's and Felski's dreams of readers bringing texts to life so we can hear what they have to

220 • EPILOGUE

say to, and in, our own modern worlds. In *Jewel,* the desire to reanimate—at any cost—upsets the balance between text and the reader's imaginative anima such that the "literary work" produced by their synthesis ends up a living monster rather than an oracle. The characters in *Jewel* are almost *all* readers. Long before we modern readers arrive on the scene, or even before Margaret interprets the queen through her own experiences of love, the events of the novel are catalyzed by Mr. Trelawny's reading—or misreading—of *another* book, the memoir of the seventeenth-century Dutch explorer who discovered Queen Tera in her burial chamber and warns others away from her. The characters all pass around this text, such that the story of this memoir becomes Queen Tera's story whether she wants it to be or not, and she becomes as much a text to be read as the memoir is. To desire access to the queen—to desire her resurrection—is to want to interpret her, and we, as readers and literary critics, must reflect on how easily a generative reading practice can slide into a violent one as Stoker's novel shows us how our interpretive choices, as much as any political revivalism, might reanimate a text in unexpected or even dangerous ways.

The gothic potential of resuscitative reading, so chillingly anticipated by Stoker, has been parodically realized in the twenty-first century as contemporary writers fill the novels of the nineteenth-century canon with zombies, vampires, and mummies and pitch Austen's and Brontë's heroines as the slayers of these slavering corpses. Who wouldn't want Elizabeth Bennet to take up a sword against the brain-eating zombies that encroach upon and rewrite her story? What could be more satisfying than Jane "Slayre" looking out at the vampiric Reed family and thinking "I don't want to be an immortal" just before hurling one of the bloodsuckers across the room (Erwin 12)? Novels like *Pride and Prejudice and Zombies, Mansfield Park and Mummies, Jane Slayre,* and *Grave Expectations* quite literally turn acts of reading into acts of reanimation as their authors pay homage to the Victorians (and almost-Victorians) by reinventing their novels as monster stories. These new novels are plagued by reanimated corpses that represent most potently the phenomenon of fan fiction itself, and in the eternal battle between novels as their original authors intended them and these "dreadfuls" ("They're back! They're back after all these years!" Mrs. Bennet shrieks in anguish), even the fan fiction likes to see the heroines triumph and the nineteenth century restored to its proper, brain-eating-corpse-free state (Hockensmith 21). These "Frankenfictions" are both more and less than neo-Victorian fiction, for they aim to capture not "the contemporary gazing at the Victorian gazing at itself" (as Sarah Gamble has described the neo-Victorian novel) but the contemporary gazing (so to speak) at the fundamentally altering effect of reading on the object being read (Gamble 127).[4] If neo-Victorian novels "animate the past . . . from the perspective of the present," then these new novels, which far more literally reanimate nineteenth-century texts by lifting the bulk of their actual words into newly monstrous tales, farcically reflect on our seemingly insatiable desire to see these texts brought back to life again and again, in film, in comic book, in trashy mystery novel, even in literary criticism (127).

Yet, even more than that, these novels ask (good-naturedly but not entirely unseriously) what kinds of havoc we wreak when we, as eager and single-minded readers, attempt to give them new life through our own readings and in our own images. Other critics have suggested that the same language of penetration that Best and Marcus associate with symptomatic reading can provide one way of describing how these mash-ups figure the relationship between reader and original text. In Rebecca Soares's words, monster-filled Austen novels enact "a theory of reading that highlights the disruptive, penetrative, and often violent potential of the reader" who has not only methodologically inserted new material into an old text but has also, in the case of the most well-known of these mash-ups—male-authored *Pride and Prejudice and Zombies* and *Sense and Sensibility and Sea Monsters*—explicitly thrust a masculine energy into the core of female authorship (430). This model of reading as violation, however, renders nineteenth-century texts passive victims of contemporary incursion, static objects sucked dry by the piercing assaults of the campy undead. The point of these mash-ups was never to leave the crumbling husks of Austen and Brontë and Dickens in their wake but rather to imagine (and parody) the alchemical power of readerly desire. As the blurb on its back cover says, "*Pride and Prejudice and Zombies* transforms a masterpiece of world literature into something you'd actually want to read" (Grahame-Smith n. pag.).

The vast majority of these novels channel this transformative force explicitly into reanimated corpses of various kinds (zombies, vampires, mummies), suggesting that it's the resuscitative instead of the penetrative potential of contemporary reading that fuels these mash-ups. The fact that some of these creatures bite and eat brains is secondary to their larger function as literary revival run amok, as monstrous metaphors for collaboration between dead authors and their living fans. As Ben H. Winters, author of *Sense and Sensibility and Sea Monsters* wrote facetiously in a HuffPost blog called "I Write with Dead People: How to Collaborate with a Corpse," "authoring a book about the undead may no longer suffice—your smart move nowadays is to write in partnership with an actual dead person," a practice of "co-authoring from the grave," which, he reminds us, "is hardly new" (n. pag.). Winters might be one of the few mash-up authors whose monsters aren't the undead, but he's crystal clear in likening fanatical contemporary readers of nineteenth-century fiction to the zombies that populate other mash-ups: "Beware the hordes of the living," he writes, the "diehard fan[s]" who can't see "that a good satire (or sequel, or adaptation, or homage, or whatever) reminds us of the enduring power of the original" (n. pag.). Understanding these nineteenth-century mash-ups as resuscitative reading taken to its most parodic extreme gives credence to these texts as comic but genuine reflections on the complexities of agential reading and on the potential for new, transtemporal life that reading can bring to canonical texts.

One of the mash-ups that most clearly and deliberately presents its reanimated corpse as an engagement with theories of reading is Vera Nazarian's *Mansfield Park and Mummies,* a text that's strangely absent from the spate of criticism on nineteenth-century monster mash-ups.[5] Nazarian frames her "co-authored" novel specifically as a spoof of an academic edition, including (as the novel's cover tells us) "scholarly footnotes" with information like "The distasteful pastime of Acting . . . is the equal of holding a Mardi Gras in the drawing room, complete with bead tossing, pole dancing, topless floats. . . . It is not to be borne," and appendices that show drawings of the location of the appendix in both a regular human body and a mummy in a cartoon sarcophagus (170). Nazarian doesn't simply reanimate *Mansfield Park*—and an explicitly Victorian *Mansfield Park,* at that, complete with references to Egyptologists and Verdi operas that hadn't yet been imagined when Austen wrote her novel[6]—but comically foregrounds the way in which her resuscitative efforts are akin to a reading practice that "shade[s] in the many outlines suggested by the given situations" of the novel and "creat[es] something new in which the reader's role is as decisive as that of the text" (Iser, "Reading" 281; Felski, *Limits* 174). The novel's outlines are remarkably well shaded by its animated mummy, who seems uncannily to embody the desires of any attentive Austen reader but who, the novel tells us, is a "*creature undead,*" exhumed from his resting place "by some zealous doctorate-endowed idiot, and then somehow returned to life" (Nazarian 308). In other words, the mummy isn't just *any* Austen reader—he's a literary critic, aware of his potential as a reader to remake *Mansfield Park* in relation to his own sensibilities.

This mummy, a pharaoh who goes by the name of "Lord Eastwind" and who fixates on Fanny as the reincarnation of his lost love, uses mesmeric power to make himself entirely forgettable to all of the characters except Fanny, behind whose shoulder he often sits, whispering exactly the things about *Mansfield Park* that readers are thinking and literary critics are trying to untangle. "'What will you think, Miss Price, . . . What will Edmund Bertram do now?'" Lord Eastwind asks Fanny after Mary Crawford has agrees to act in the play that Edmund had been so vociferously denouncing. "'Whatever my cousin does I will not question his judgment,' replied Fanny. 'A pity,' said Lord Eastwind, 'For in such intentional blindness you might overlook something of importance'" (Nazarian 173). The mummy's response to Fanny in this moment is a *reader's* response—this is precisely what readers want to shout into the void as we watch the impending train wreck of the *Lover's Vows* performance approach in the original *Mansfield Park*. Lord Eastwind is us, whispering with his undead voice into the novel's silences. Our readerly desires have taken on a life force of their own in the body of a resurrected mummy, and in doing so, they fundamentally alter the emotional landscape of *Mansfield Park*.

Yet not until these desires begin to alter the *plot* irrevocably—rather than just whisper behind it—do the mummy and his minions truly turn into monsters. During the ball that Sir Thomas throws for Fanny at Mansfield, Lord Eastwind tries to convince Fanny to come away with him and be his eternal love. In this moment when *Mansfield Park* threatens to transform from a Regency novel into a grocery store romance, all mummy-hell breaks loose. "Ladies and gentlemen were being accosted by lumbering creatures who had seemed to be mere servants or dancing companions only moments ago, and now were revealed to be walking monsters. The mummies grabbed at throats . . . leaning in with wide, unhinged jaws to take the precious *breath of life* from the living" (329). Meanwhile, Fanny, trying to escape the grasping hands of Lord Eastwind, recognizes that he, too, is nothing more than a reanimated corpse: "You are being a *monster!* Exactly the monster that you now are!" she cries, cringing away from his maggot-filled face (330). Undead readers longing for a trashy romance have gone wild in the novel, and only after a heroic effort by Fanny and the Bertrams to blow up the monsters' heads are these undead life-suckers expelled from Mansfield and the order of the novel at least temporarily restored. Campy though this scene may be, and insistent though the author's after-note may be in calling *Mansfield Park* "Austen's deathless (but never *undead*)" novel, both the reanimated pharaoh and *Mansfield Park and Mummies* itself make monstrously literal Iser's claim that "the reader's imagination animates [the outlines of the novel]" into a hybrid thing that is neither text nor the reader's imagination but something "halfway between the two" ("Reading" 281, 279).

The reanimated reader can accomplish much in this novel. As Nazarian reminds us in the after-note, he can "control and indeed move through space and time itself," producing a transnational and transtemporal incarnation of *Mansfield Park* that refuses to be bound by the dictates of race, nation, or historical chronology (n. pag.) And yet, breaking down these boundaries also produces "literary mayhem" that even the undead reader himself recognizes has the potential to destroy *Mansfield Park* completely (n. pag.). "You know what must be done," the mummy says to Fanny at the novel's end. "You must destroy me. . . . Take back my *breath of life*," he begs, and she obligingly desiccates him, leaving the embodiment of resuscitative reading a lifeless husk behind her as she plods forward to become the married mistress of Mansfield that Austen's novel always intended her to be (543).

Monster-filled mash-ups like Nazarian's offer postmodern manifestations of resuscitative reading run amok, and in doing so they reveal that the reanimated corpses already traipsing through so much nineteenth-century literature function as reflections on how we read the past as much as on how we recreate it. All of the alive-again bodies I've discussed throughout this book metonymically stand in for texts that have been aggressively read and fundamentally altered in the reading: the theatrical Creatures so self-conscious about their relationship to *Frankenstein*, the Dickensian zombie characters who can't escape the form of realist novels, the poetic corpses that are all incarnations of Browning's Big Yellow Book, the Victorian Oisin who revivifies ancient Celtic folklore, and the resurrected Queen Tera who embodies Irish Revival literature. The act of reanimation in all these works is an attempt to discover where, precisely, to draw the line between interpretation and creativity: between *reading* the past and *writing* the present. For some writers, like young Yeats, reanimation perfectly encapsulates a productive synthesis of the two, a synthesis in which politicized reading will always be a source of literary innovation. For others, like Stoker, the act of reading the past into the service of contemporary political desires results in the resurrection of monsters. Yet all these writers share an awareness that texts, and bodies, are always subject to being read, and as their characters struggle with how to read and write old corpses into new life, the texts themselves can't help but suggest that any effective act of reading will always be an effort of reanimation. Whether these necromantic writers see the reanimating impulse as a fount of creative potential or as a dangerous artistic act, and in whatever forms they imagine the repercussions of breathing new sparks into still bones, they also always provide models for us, as readers, to make their textual corpses walk again in new and unexpected ways.

NOTES

NOTES TO INTRODUCTION

1. "Signs of the Times" 22.
2. For a full reading of Wilde's "zombie horde" poem, see Martin, "Skeleton."
3. See especially Castle, *Modernism* and "Synge"; Valente, *Myth*; Howes and Valente; Kennedy.
4. See Rudy for an extended discussion of "the complex interplay of poetic form and electrical epistemologies" in how nineteenth-century poetry conceived of its aesthetic force and its effects on readers (5); see Morus for a history of electricity and the body in Victorian England; see Gooday for an analysis of electricity's "domestication" in the last decades of the nineteenth century; see Doyle, "Los Amigos Fiasco," for the porous boundary between electricity as a life force and as a death force in the late nineteenth century.
5. See Morus, *Shocking,* especially chapter 11.
6. Quoted in Rudy 4; "A Remonstrance" 73.
7. See also "An Appeal to Ireland": "And as flash follows flash on the mountains, / When lightnings and thunders are hurled, / So would throb in electrical union / Her soul with the soul of the world" (181).
8. This isn't to say that necromantic writers, especially those of the Irish Literary Revival, didn't draw aesthetic inspiration from nineteenth-century medieval revivalism (see Howes and Valente).
9. For these arguments, see especially Bronfen; Christ.
10. See especially Norman; Bronfen; Christ.
11. See Goode, especially 150–55. See also Valente, *Myth,* for how nineteenth-century ideas of manliness shaped the Irish Literary Revival.
12. See Martin, "Skeleton," on the dramatic monologue and Wilde's Irish Famine zombies.
13. See especially Levine's introduction.
14. Derrida's *Spectres of Marx* and Freud's "The Uncanny" are at the center of many such studies; see especially Wolfreys; Bove on spectrality. On spiritualism and mediumship, see

225

226 • NOTES TO INTRODUCTION

especially Owen; Galvan; Smajic; Kontou and Wilburn; J. Miller; Tromp; Briefel, "Freaks" and "Spectral."

15. See also Bronfen; Christ; Wood.

16. Nick Freeman describes Victorian ghost stories as judicial narratives about "the voice from the grave exposing guilt" (105).

17. See also Punter; Lloyd-Smith; Goddu (the latter two working specifically in an American gothic context).

18. See C. Levine, "Preface" and "Introduction."

19. See the *Manifesto of the V21 Collective*; *Responses to the V21 Manifesto*.

20. See Puckett for V21's Victorian echoes.

21. See especially Griffiths, "Untimely"; Coriale. For books that focus especially on the effects of the natural sciences on historicist thought and writing across the nineteenth century, see Griffiths, *Age*; Duncan, *Human Forms*. See Crimmins for Romantic historicism's futurity and Fermanis on Romantic histories of feelings. See O'Malley, *Liffey*, on the presentism of Irish historical literature in the nineteenth century.

22. Critics who have addressed this language in nineteenth-century historicist methodology include M. Goode; Griffiths, *Age*; Crimmins; N. Freeman; Fermanis.

23. See Chemers, *Monster*, especially chapters 2 and 3; H. Fraser 17.

24. See Mary Shelley's preface to her revised edition of Percy Shelley's lyrical poetry.

25. The lines Stoker quotes from "Prometheus Unbound" are from act 1, lines 192–93: "The Magus Zoroaster, my dead child, / Met his own image walking in the garden" (*Jewel* 126).

26. I offer a more detailed argument about O'Grady's entwining of Irish history and English romanticism in my 2016 essay, "Fleshing Dry Bones: Standish O'Grady's Sensory Revivalism."

27. Ernest Boyd attributes this first paradoxical phrase to Lady Augusta Gregory in *Appreciations and Depreciations: Irish Literary Studies*. For prime examples of O'Grady's queer socialist unionism, see his articles in the *Peasant* in the 1910s, particularly "The Physical Activities" (Standish O'Grady papers, Trinity College Dublin, TCD MS 11534, p. 40).

28. "Friends and Comrades," TCD MS 11534, p. 107.

29. See Higgins, "Carlyle's."

30. See the introduction of Higgins, *Heroic*, for a discussion of the complex ways that Carlyle offered models for the cultural nationalism of the Revival, despite his anti-Irish politics.

31. "*The Irish Worker*," 26 Oct. 1912, in *To the Leaders* 26; in other places, however, O'Grady also criticizes Carlyle's "funereal imagination" ("Walt Whitman" 270).

32. O'Grady, "Making."

33. See Forry, chapter 2, for a detailed overview of *Frankenstein*'s circulation in nineteenth-century popular culture.

34. See Castle, "Wild"; Fox, "Fleshing."

35. See Fox, "Fleshing."

36. See chapter 3 of Elizabeth Freeman for an analysis of *Frankenstein*'s relationship to eighteenth-century sentimental historiography. See chapter 1 for my own engagement with and expansion of this argument.

37. Mary Shelley's preface to her novel *Perkins Warbeck* offers a similar reflection on romance and history; both the Godwin essay and the Shelley preface are discussed in more detail in chapter 1. See also McCray on Godwin's production of an intimate, sympathetic relationship between reader and historical character.

38. See Adam Smith, chapter 1; M. Goode, chapter 1.

39. See Goode, chapter 6, for a detailed discussion of this debate. See also earlier books on the disciplinary forms of history in the nineteenth century, including Bann; Jann; Brand; Culler; Dale.

40. See especially Lloyd; Cleary for postcolonial readings that demand a revaluing of peripheral literature from Ireland and other nonmetropolitan locales.

NOTES TO INTRODUCTION • 227

41. See Bresadola for a more detailed discussion of Galvani and medical electricity.

42. For more on the defecating duck and the ways it troubled the boundary between mechanistic and natural life, see Riskin; Kang, chapter 4.

43. See especially Morus, *Shocking*, chapter 1, for his discussion of the relationship between galvanism and radicalism in early nineteenth-century Britain.

44. See Gigante for an extended consideration of what constitutes life and vitality for the Romantics.

45. Occasionally, however, credulous articles lauding the resuscitative powers of galvanism appeared even into the 1840s. See, for example, "Wonderful and Horrible Effects of Galvanism," which describes in lurid detail the reanimation of a just-hanged murderer.

46. Robert Montgomery Bird's satirical 1836 novel *Sheppard Lee, Written by Himself* is a primary example of such satire.

47. For instance, a 1905 article called "A Horrible Experiment" describes Aldini's experiments but invents salacious details about viewers dropping dead with the shock.

48. "Galvanic Experiment: An Account of some Experiments . . ." is the *Penny Satirist's* unattributed reprint of Ure's original article from *Quarterly Journal of Science and the Arts.*

49. *Le Courrier de la Louisiane*, 12 June 1846, p. 3 (advertisement for Christie's "Galvanic Rings and Magnetic Fluid").

50. "Galvanic Rings—How to Apply Them."

51. "Christopher Caustic, M.D." is a pen name for Thomas Green Fessenden.

52. See Holmes 38 for an analysis of the rise and fall of Elisha Perkins's Metallic Tractors.

53. See Waits 234–36 for a description of the 1870 letters relating to Dickens's order of a Pulvermacher's chain and for Pulvermacher's ads that appeared in the serial version of *Bleak House* as well as in *All the Year Round.*

54. Leaflet advertising "Pulvermacher's patent portable hydro-electric chain for personal use: (inventor and patentee- J.L. Pulvermacher)," Charles Meinig, distributed in 1851 (https://wellcomelibrary.org/item/b17999753).

55. These advertisements alternate statements about the "miraculous" power of the chain with deliberately jargon-filled descriptions of its scientific operations: "The chain decomposes unacidulated water and precipitates metals from their solutions."

56. See especially Rudy. For such an ad, see the *Saturday Review*, 2 May 1885, p. 597.

57. See Rance, chapter 5.

58. See Waits 235.

59. In 1807 a lightning strike to a gunpowder factory in Luxembourg destroyed two city blocks and killed upward of three hundred people. The *Times* described the building "exploding in an instant" when the lightning struck, plunging the whole town into "the greatest consternation and distress" (Monday, 20 July 1807, p. 2).

60. As "Punch on the Galvanic Ring" (1845) succinctly puts the distinction between actual electrical force and galvanic medical devices, "the quantity of galvanism they [galvanic rings] generate is next to nothing; certainly much less than that produced by a sixpence and a half sovereign lying in contact in a gentleman's waistcoat pocket" (167).

61. "Wonders and Curiosities of the Electric Telegraph," from the early 1870s, describes the "congeries" of the telegraph's currents "ramifying in every direction like the fibres of the nervous system in the human body, and constituting a net-work which embraces within its reach every important point in nearly three millions of square miles" (225).

62. In 1890 W. T. Stead described electricity, "the thunderbolt of Jove," as "the most puissant of all the servants of man" (332). "The Electric Light" and "The Gifts of Science to Art" offer further examples. See Gooday for a more extended discussion of this rhetoric of domestication/enslavement.

63. *Punch*, in particular, often targeted electrical apparatuses as vehicles for social critique. See, for instance, "Voting by Electricity" and "Universality of Electricity."

228 • NOTES TO CHAPTER 1

64. The latter, especially, recalls a number of articles published in the 1840s about the useful-ness of galvanism in recalling asphyxiated persons from the brink of death. See Bell for a list of articles supporting his assertion that the "value of galvanism to rouse patients asphyxiated, seems too well established to be readily discarded" (415).

65. As Walter Benjamin argues in *The Arcades Project*, however, they were certainly on their way, standing both as an architectural manifestation of history as "an endless series of things" and as a "phantasmagoria of the market, where people appear only as types" (14).

NOTES TO CHAPTER 1

1. See Sutherland's discussion of the cultural "distortion of Shelley's original conception of Frankenstein" into a galvanic reanimation narrative (25).

2. Elizabeth Freeman makes a similar argument about the gothic genre more generally, writ-ing that "the gothic was a kind of historical novel *in extremis*" (98).

3. Brinkema reiterates Freeman's claims, writing that "Victor Frankenstein will make a mon-strous experiment of just this kind of embodied sympathy in 1818, only sixty years after Smith's treatise" (8).

4. See Halberstam 28–29.

5. Heffernan (144) makes a similar point in discussing the impulse in film adaptations of *Frankenstein* to present viewers with stitched-together monsters.

6. Critical studies of *Frankenstein* often forget that Victor's creation is not simply an agglom-eration of *human* parts: see Heffernan 141; Freeman 103. Halberstam, in contrast, insists that we remember that the creature has been formed "out of bits and pieces of life and death, of criminals and animals, animate and inanimate objects" (36–37).

7. Almost all of these uses of the word *animate* were added in Shelley's 1831 revisions to the novel.

8. Milner's 1826 theatrical adaptation voices Frankenstein's experiment in the precise lan-guage of Romantic vitalism and makes clear the ways in which he debases Coleridge's insistence that the true artistic imagination finds the living, organic forms within things rather than imposing static shapes from without.

9. Critics nonetheless persist in identifying Victor's work as project of reanimation, either unreflectively, as in Kang's repeated references to the creature as a "reanimated corpse," or borrowing from Shelley's own 1831 reflections on the potential of galvanism to reanimate corpses, as in Stiles's description of the novel's "eponymous scientist-antihero harness[ing] electricity to bring to life a reconstituted corpse" (Kang 195, 199, 218; Stiles 172). Reanima-tion is especially significant to Young, who argues that "amalgamation, reanimation, and revolt against a creator" are the three specific elements "distinctive to the Frankenstein story" (14).

10. Among the most transformative critical readings of Victor's horror when the monster wakes are Moers and Stryker. My argument here doesn't close down any of the potential explanations for *why* Victor might find his suddenly animate creature so disgusting or any of the theoretical interventions this disgust opens for critics. Instead I point out that our long-standing cultural assumption that the creature is ugly because he's basically a living corpse (with all of the attendant abject horror and uncanniness Kristeva and Freud might assign to such a figure) is an assumption retroactively produced for us by Victor's horror at his creature's life.

11. See Kakoudaki 298 for a similar point.

12. See especially Allen 22; Hurst 133.

13. See Benjamin, "Theses" 257–58.

14. See Freeman 100–103 for more on these two relationships to historical embodiment in *Frankenstein*.

NOTES TO CHAPTER 1 · 229

15. "We enter as it were into his body, and become in some measure the same person as him," writes Adam Smith in *The Theory of Moral Sentiments* (12).
16. See Allen 30–31 for an optimistic reading of the text's republican longings.
17. Also quoted in Goode 162.
18. See Robinson for a detailed overview of the British periodical press's interest in the story between July and November of 1826.
19. See Kasmer 26.
20. See especially Duncan, *Scott's* 183–214, for an extended psychoanalytic analysis of the "upright corpse" in Scott and James Hogg.
21. See Friedman and Kavey 82.
22. See Morus, *Shocking* 75–78.
23. Peake's play did inspire some public outrage, however, drawing crowds eager to see on stage what protesters called the novel's "immoral tendenc[ies]" and "dangerous doctrines" (protest leaflet, qtd. in Forry 5).
24. As Halberstam argues, "the book presents itself not as the making of a monster but as the making of a human" (32).
25. In this I argue against Halberstam's claim that because the creature has been composed of disparate pieces, "he is always in danger of breaking down into his constitutive parts" (37). The novel offers no support for such a claim, focused as it is on the creature's acquisition of an increasingly human, and an increasingly integrated, sense of himself and the world around him.
26. Advertisement for Parr's Pills were widespread in both British and US 1840s periodicals, and their popularity rested on the claim that their inventor, Thomas Parr, had lived to 152 years of age by taking his remarkable curative.
27. The term "self-made men" was coined by Henry Clay in a speech to the US Senate on February 2, 1832, when he said that "almost every manufactory is in the hands of enterprising self-made men" (Clay 100). The link Clay makes between the term "self-made men" and the manufacturing industry is explicit in *Model Man*, which pokes fun at the mid-century British cliché that "the pioneers of the Industrial Revolution and many nineteenth-century manufacturers were 'new' self-made men, of modest or even humble origins" (Çrouzet 274).
28. I refer to Frankenstein's creation as a "monster" in discussing this play because that is how the play identifies him in the stage directions and dialogue.
29. Nineteenth-century newspapers as well as more contemporary accounts use both "Harvey" and "Hervey," "Leech" and "Leach" when they discuss the actor; I am using "Harvey Leach" here as it seems to appear slightly more frequently. See Chemers, "Mortification," for a more detailed analysis of Leach's career.
30. This particular obituary wasn't actually Leach's obituary; it was the obituary of Leach's friend Mr. Potter, the doctor to whom Leach bequeathed his body for scientific study.
31. Cook makes a similar point about the whole range of "What Is It?" exhibitions across the nineteenth century when he suggests that "what we see in retrospect is a manufactured image—a *character* called 'What is It?'—rather than the actual human beings who embodied these fictions" (140).
32. An 1850 illustration of the play in the *Illustrated London News* suggests that when the play was staged, the monster bore far more physical resemblance to Victorian stereotypes of Black Africans than he did to conventional images of automata. The text of the play offers no clear reference to race, but the creature's body, overtly racially marked as it seems to be in the illustration, creates a continuum between the threat of automated labor, anxieties about changing Victorian class structures, and what Carolyn Betensky has called the "casual racism" of an era in which racism "is so pervasive as to be unremarkable" (731). For arguments about the master/slave vocabulary and tropes of blackness in *Frankenstein*, see Brantlinger, "*Frankenstein*"; A. L. Smith; Malchow; Young. See Atanasoski and Vora for the

230 • NOTES TO CHAPTER 2

relationship between factory automation and "the racial histories of human chattel slaveries" that I believe *Model Man* engages (34). See Mellor 113 for interconnection between workers, technologies of production, and race in the 1831 edition of Shelley's novel.

33. The final words from the creature were cut from the final film but can be found in a late-stage script (Lady and Darabont, 2nd revised draft 92). Heffernan has argued that "the film dialogue between Victor and the monster about memory and the recorder calls to mind the ugly philosopher [Socrates]whose theory of knowledge is based on recollection, on the silent recorder known as memory" (149).

NOTES TO CHAPTER 2

1. Peter Brooks asserts that "the tracing of the [parents'] name—which [Pip] has already distorted in its application to self—involves a misguided attempt to remotivate the graphic symbol, to make it directly mimetic" (*Reading* 115–16). See also Lutz, *Relics*, chapter 3; Mangham, chapter 4.

2. See Reed's introduction for a comprehensive overview of critics situating Dickens among the realists; see also Mangham's introduction.

3. For realism's intrinsic contradictions, see Gallagher, "George Eliot"; Jameson, "Antinomies" and *Antinomies*; Shaw. See also Brooks; Walton.

4. For challenges to the Anglocentric canon, see especially Fox, "Realism's"; Ingelbien; Mullen. For challenges to what constitutes "the real," see G. Levine's discussion of *Frankenstein* (24–35); Lavery.

5. Novak, especially 31–35, offers a particularly compelling re-evaluation of realism's relationship to nineteenth-century photography's reliance on dismemberment, exaggeration, and abstraction to create images that represent the real. See G. Levine for nineteenth-century fiction's ever-receding "quest for reality" (41). See also Mangham; Menke.

6. See especially G. Levine 40; Mullen 4, 12–17; Freedgood, *Worlds* (particularly the preface, introduction, and conclusion).

7. Bove describes Dickens's resistance to mimesis in terms of spectrality rather than theatricality.

8. See Zigarovich 142.

9. Dickens's novels, according to Miller, "are not *mimesis* of an externally existing reality, but the interpretation of that reality according to highly artificial schemas (143).

10. As Zigarovich argues about Wordsworth's reflections on epitaphs, "the epitaph vocalizes language, embodying the act of inscribing reality into structure" (143).

11. See Greiner, chapter 3, for an argument that language, for Dickens, is the conduit through which the sympathetic imagination takes "the feelings [that] are dead to the reality outside of us" and allows others to "reconstitute" them" (96).

12. For early versions of this claim (besides Miller's), see Van Ghent; G. Stewart; Baldick, especially chapter 5. More recently (besides Greiner), see Gallagher, "Bioeconomics"; Reed; Creaney; Mangham, especially chapter 4.

13. I don't mean to suggest here that *Sketches* falls naively for this revivifying metonymic imaginary but rather that the text allows its animist fantasies to play out with interest and humor rather than with the deep pessimism that marks the opening of *Great Expectations*.

14. Lutz makes a similar point about the memorial tone of the novel when she argues that "the plot of *Great Expectations* moves within a thick air of the elegiac" (*Relics* 80). Jordan has described Pip the character as "a haunted man" and Pip the "retrospective narrator" as the novel's most "active medium," calling up and giving voice to the ghosts of his past in order to reconstruct the story of his life to suit his own needs (77). My point here is slightly different in that I suggest that Pip-the-narrator is himself the undead voice of the text rather than the medium channeling pasts ghosts, one whose voice embodies the

unsettling temporality of the epitaph as "phantom-narrative, an inscription haunted by a presence it has created itself" (Zigarovich 143).

15. See especially Jordan; Reisner.

16. Baldick's interest in this allusion is what he calls its "double equivocal inversion of the Frankenstein myth," which he describes as the diffusion of characteristics of both creator and creation across both Pip and Magwitch (119).

17. There is an argument to be made here that *Great Expectations,* coming so soon after Dickens's separation from his wife and publication of his "Personal" letter in *Household Words* that attempted (and spectacularly failed) to wrest public control of the scandalous story back into his own hands, offers a reflection on the disempowerment of celebrities at the hands of their publics.

18. I draw an important distinction here between elegy and epitaph that I have made elsewhere: see Fox, "Epitaphs"; Fried. See also Taylor, who describes the elegy as an explicitly resuscitative form.

19. See especially Gallagher, "Bioeconomics"; Creaney; Zigarovich; Mangham; Wood (especially chapter 4); Zimmerman (especially 162–67); Simon; MacDuffie (especially 122–30).

20. As Gallagher writes of this scene, Lizzie "would rather turn her own body into the dead white thing than keep it alive on such carrion. This first suggestion of how death might be exchanged for life is the most primitive and horrific of bioeconomic possibilities encountered in the novel" ("Bioeconomics," 93).

21. Lewes describes Dickens's hallucinatory practice as explicitly distinct from representational verisimilitude: "The images may have the vividness of real objects but they have not the properties of real objects, they do not preserve consistent relations with other facts, they appear in contradiction to other beliefs" (145).

22. See Dames 182–84.

23. Famously, Henry James in 1865 described the characters in *Our Mutual Friend* as "lifeless" and "mechanical" (787).

24. Duncan also discusses this passage, arguing that Lewes's galvanic analogy "characterizes the impact of Dickens's fiction upon his readers: physiological rather than intellectual, short-circuiting cognition to press directly on our nerves and feelings" ("Mutual" 295). Although I agree with Duncan's point and capitalize on the slippage he both identifies and amplifies between Lewes describing Dickens's characters as galvanized frogs and Dickens's readers themselves becoming galvanized frogs, my interest in Lewes's deployment of this analogy is the distinct opposition between his presentation of galvanism as incompatible with realist lifelikeness and Dickens's sense that galvanism is the perfect metaphor for realism's fictionality.

25. Dames describes the problem of Lewes's frog analogy in terms of the false distinction it creates between organicism and mechanization (183).

26. Dickens uses the word *galvanic* or versions of it a few other times across his novels: in *Sketches by Boz* he describes Mr. Minns starting from a chair "as though he had received the discharge from a galvanic battery" (ch. 2) and Mr. Thomas Potter's forced laughter as "galvanic chuckles" (ch. 11); in *Oliver Twist,* a peddler includes a galvanic battery in the list of mechanical devices needed to produce his quack stain-remover as Bill Sikes flees after killing Nancy (book 3, ch. 10); in *David Copperfield,* Betsy Trotwood tells a jerky Uriah Heep not to "be galvanic, Sir!" (ch. 35); anticipating *Our Mutual Friend*'s description of Bradley Headstone acquiring "mechanically a great store of teacher's knowledge" (*OMF* 218), in *Hard Times* Thomas Gradgrind's terrible teaching is described as galvanic: "Indeed . . . he seemed a kind of cannon loaded to the muzzle with facts, and prepared to blow them clean out of the regions of childhood at one discharge. He seemed a galvanizing apparatus, too, charged with a grim mechanical substitute for the tender young imaginations that were to be stormed away" (ch. 2); and late in *Martin Chuzzlewit,* Mr. Pecksniff "started back as if he had received the charge of an electric battery" (ch. 52).

232 • NOTES TO CHAPTER 3

27. See especially Edward Bulwer Lytton's *The Coming Race* (1871); John Macnie's *The Diothas: or, A Far Look Ahead* (1883), excerpted and republished by W. T. Stead as "Looking Forward: A Romance of the Electric Age" (1890); and Edward Bellamy's *Looking Backward 2000–1887* (1888). Albert Bleunard's *Babylon Electrified* (1890), although not a utopian novel set in the future, also images electricity as the cure-all for cultural backwardness and social ills, although its plot utilizes electricity as an explicitly European colonial power that reinforces the imperial hierarchies that these other novels aim to supplant.

28. See Cummings 192.

29. See Creaney; Gallagher, "Novel" and "Bioeconomics"; Royle; Kuskey.

30. The "activity" of being dead is similar to the active forms of "suspension" that Elisha Cohn and Anne McCarthy describe in nineteenth-century novels and poetry, respectively. For Cohn, moments of suspension interrupt the forward motion of novelistic *bildung* with alternative, lyric possibilities—these motionless moments are rife with "static intensity— still life, vibrant in its absorptive movelessness" (5), while McCarthy, arguing that suspended animation in poetry "mediates the experience of a fundamental unstable reality," underscores this point by pointing out that in the body of work she studies, "doing nothing requires a surprising amount of intention" (14, 11).

31. Unsigned review, *London Review*, 28 Oct. 1865, pp. 467–68 (reprinted on pp. 454–58 in Collins).

32. Given this description of Jenny, it's important to note that the 1840s Barnum "What Is It?" exhibition that I discuss in chapter 1 reprised in London in the 1860s, with a new Black actor playing the role of the "missing link" character. Whether Dickens is explicitly alluding to this show or not, labeling Jenny "Miss What-is-it" imbricates her in the racial, gendered, and ableist liminality of this incredibly popular exhibition.

NOTES TO CHAPTER 3

1. Although this is a generally positive review of the single work, the reviewer is torn about Browning's work as a whole: Browning's "special gifts of intellect and originality" are constantly at war with his "obscurity; want of quality, or prosiness; [and] uncouthness, or almost absence of rhythm" (4).

2. This characterization follows Allingham's complaint to Carlyle that Browning "had neither given us the real story as he found it, nor, on the other hand, constructed a poem out of it" (207–8).

3. Carlyle made this comment to Dante Gabriel Rossetti, who himself said of the poem's "incoherence" that "the thing that makes Browning drunk is to give him a dram of prosaic reality" (D. Rossetti, *Letters* 284).

4. On technologies of spiritualism, see especially Galvan; Briefel, "Freaks" and "Spectral." See Helfield on Browning and spiritualism.

5. This is a version of Tucker's point that Browning's monologues allow "dry bones" to "live for modern minds" ("Wanted" 31).

6. Quotations from *The Ring and the Book* cited by book/line number.

7. See Helfield; Roberts; Haug; Christ, "Browning's" and "Painting," which all identify the dramatic monologue as a form of necromancy.

8. See Tucker ("Wanted") on Browning and historicism; both M. Goode and E. Freeman for modes of eighteenth- and nineteenth-century embodied historiography; Jann for Victorian "resuscitative" historiographical methods; White, chapter 3, on Michelet.

9. O'Gorman suggests that the absence of grief in Browning's resurrectionary monologues forces readers of these monologues to experience Browning's poetry as something beyond the familiar/everyday.

10. See Orr 270.

11. *Correspondence* cited in the text by volume and page number.

NOTES TO CHAPTER 3 • 233

12. Robert Browning to Elizabeth Barrett, Feb. 13, 1846.

13. Elizabeth best expressed this displeasure with funerals to her friend Mary Russell Mitford in 1854: "Now you will understand at once what ghastly flakes of death have changed the sense of Rome to me! . . . I am horribly weak about such things—I can't look on the earth-side of death—I flinch from corpses and graves, and never meet a common funeral without a sort of horror. When I look deathwards I look *over* death, and upwards, or I can't look any way at all" (Jan. 7, 1854, *Letters of EBB* 2.153–54).

14. Toward the end of his life, Browning wrote to Isa Blagden of Elizabeth's "limited experience of all kinds": "*One* such intimate knowledge as I have had with many a person would have taught her,—had she been inclined to learn: though I doubt if she would have dirtied her hands for any scientific purpose" (Aug. 19, 1871, *DI* 365).

15. The Brownings' courtship correspondence is peppered with references to critical notes and suggestions that Elizabeth made for Browning's work, as well as with his appreciation for and acceptance of her sensibility. For examples throughout 1845, see Jul. 25, Aug. 3, Aug. 12, Sept. 24, and Oct. 29. In the last of these, Browning expresses his "unsatisfaction" and "shame" at poems "written before [Elizabeth's] time" (11.146).

16. Markovits, who takes the subtitle of her book from this Barrett Browning quotation, considers how the aspiration to life produces a form that can mediate between lyric and narrative time, and in doing so can "bridge the gap between popular literature and more elevated forms" (5).

17. See Crandell 239–43, although her focus is transformation rather than resuscitation.

18. Despite *The Ring and the Book*'s obsession with the history of poetic form, Saintsbury's "Tennyson and Browning" chapter mentions it only twice: once, quoting a line from it amid other blank-verse lines of "perfectly sound and satisfactory equivalence," and once to tell us that "no more need to be said of the blank verse of [Browning's] later days from *The Ring and the Book* onward" (219, 236).

19. It's useful to also consider Shelley's "The Cenci" as a source text for Browning, given its similarity in subject and time period to Browning's poem, as well as Shelley's own experiments with galvanism. Browning was familiar with both Shelleys' interest in theories of galvanic energy, particularly those of the experimental chemist Humphry Davy, to whose rhetoric one could easily attribute the energy and language of book 1: "Science . . . has bestowed upon [man] powers which may be almost called creative; which have enabled him to change and modify the beings surrounding him" (Davy 247).

20. "In my last travel I put down on a slip of paper a few dates, that I might remember in England, on such a day I was on Vesuvius, in Pompeii, at Shelley's grave," Browning wrote to Elizabeth in 1845, making it clear (as does his Shelleyan elopement the following year) that Italian history, for him, was as much a history of and homage to Shelley as it was to anything else (11.188). See Neville-Sington 146–57; Woolford, "Browning" and "Romantic"; Knoepflmacher; Bloom.

21. In 1870 Browning's already-declining worship of Shelley spiraled sharply downward when he read William Rossetti's memoir of Shelley, which outlines the circumstances of Shelley's separation from his pregnant first wife, Harriet. As Browning wrote Blagden, "when I think how utterly different was the fancy I had of [Shelley] forty years ago from the facts as they front one to-day, I can only avoid despising myself by remembering that I judged in pure ignorance and according to the testimony of untruthful friends" (*DI* 328).

22. The objective poet writes "what we call dramatic poetry," poetry that "speaks for itself, as we say" ("Essay" 1245, 1244)—almost literally so, in the case of the dramatic monologue.

23. Browning admits that "of the perfect shield, with the gold and silver side set up for all comers to challenge, there has yet been no instance"; in other words, that a wholly pure version either of the subjective poet or of the objective poet has yet to be seen ("Essay" 1245).

24. See Knoepflmacher, who contends that "Porphyria's Lover" and "My Last Duchess" represent Browning's ironic "animations of a process of [Romantic] deanimation" by which a "devouring male ego reduces the Female Other to nothingness" (151).

234 • NOTES TO CHAPTER 4

25. See Fuss on speaking-corpse poems as "literary fictions that seek to revivify and reauthorize the dead, at the risk of contaminating and killing poetry" (44).

26. All quotations from "Porphyria's Lover," "My Last Duchess," and "Memorabilia" cited by line number.

27. I use the word *forged* here to invoke Blanton, whose discussion of Browning's essay on Shelley uses the forgery of the letters as a figure through which to unpack the collapsed opposition between "seer" and "fashioner" that Browning fails to comprehensibly articulate (see 5–8).

28. See Fuss 67–68 on the differences between the speaking-corpse poem and the elegy.

29. Tucker ("Memorabilia") makes an opposing argument that "Memorabilia" is devoted to remembering Shelley, but his argument doesn't register the poem's ironic tone or the incongruity of its title with the positive intensity of memory that he attributes to the poem.

30. See Addcox on the testimonial structure of *The Ring and the Book*.

31. The Count's charge of adultery against Pompilia hinges on a set of letters allegedly written by and passed between Pompilia and the priest with whom the Count accuses her of having an affair, but Pompilia claims illiteracy (7.81). The Count's "letters are the facts," we are told, and yet "the facts are lies," "forged and falsified" (3.1360, 1315).

32. The narrator makes even more transparent the conflation of body and written word when he asks at the end of this long passage, "How title I the dead alive once more?" (1.779).

33. Markovits's analysis of Pompilia focuses specifically on Pompilia's "pearl-like body" both as a figure for thinking about the trustworthiness of Pompilia's narrative and as a figure for the form of the poem as a whole (143).

34. On the epitaph, see Fried; Mills-Courts; the previous chapter.

35. See M. Goode; Jann; Brand; Dale for further discussions of Victorian historiography as a resuscitative practice.

36. The Brownings were in Paris during the 1850s when Michelet was stripped of his place at the Collège de France and were clearly familiar with his work. As Elizabeth writes of the scandal in an 1852 letter, "Victor Cousin and Villemain refuse to take the oath, and lose their situations in the Academy accordingly; but they retire on pensions, and it's their own fault of course. Michelet and Quinet should have an equivalent, I think, for what they have lost; they are worthy, as poets, orators, dreamers, speculative thinkers—as anything, in fact, but instructors of youth" (*Letters of EBB* 1.70–71).

37. See my introduction for further discussion of nineteenth-century Promethean history.

38. Fraser is quoting Greene 93.

39. See Gent; Fraser.

NOTES TO CHAPTER 4

1. See Watson's discussion of Yeats and Victorian philosophical sensibility.

2. "O'Grady was the first, and we had read him in our teens," Yeats recalled (*Autobiographies* 183). The Irish revival poet A.E. wrote in an article in the Irish theatre magazine *Samhain* (Oct. 1902) that "Mr. O'Grady in his youth had the epic imagination, and I think few people realize how great and heroic that imagination was," to which Yeats appended a note saying that O'Grady's *History* "started us all; it stirred others, too," including (at least according to Yeats) the pre-Raphaelites Edward Burne-Jones and William Morris (A.E. 12). See also Higgins, *Heroic* 12.

3. See "Promethean History, Irish Revival" in the introduction.

4. Hoberman 175 makes a related argument about the museological aesthetic of Yeats's later poetry.

5. May 31, 1887.

6. To Katharine Tynan, Feb. 12, 1888 (*Letters* 59); Summer 1888 (78).

7. To Katharine Tynan, Aug. 25, 1888 (*Letters* 81–82).

NOTES TO CHAPTER 4 · 235

8. To Katharine Tynan, Sept. 6, 1888: "You will have to read straight through my book of folklore. It was meant for Irish poets. They should draw on it for plots and atmosphere. You will find plenty of workable subjects" (*Letters* 88).

9. I borrow the term *museographic* from Carle Bonafous-Murat.

10. See Ramazani, *Yeats* 50, for an argument that "The Municipal Gallery Re-visited" expresses a struggle between the museum and the poetic imagination for elegiac primacy, one that ultimately (and triumphantly) subsumes the former into the latter. See also Bonafous-Murat 223.

11. "The poet magnanimously identifies himself with his dead friends," Ramazani writes of the poem, "but in doing so, he also bids us to see their portraits as signifiers of himself" (*Yeats* 50).

12. "The Burden of Nineveh" is cited hereafter by line number.

13. Barbara Black points out that in the 1856 version of this stanza, the Egyptian mummy is called a "pilgrim" rather than an "alien," and argues that this change indicates Rossetti's "increasingly more accurate understanding of the irreverent and hostile undertaking of museum acquisition" (144).

14. In this, the poem shares much with Shelley's "Ozymandias," although by bringing the statue into the British Museum instead of leaving it in the desert, it makes an even more insistently proleptic comparison between the ruin of Nineveh and the ruin of England.

15. See Bronfen on Rossetti's "dead lady" poems, 117–21 and 367–68.

16. Wood here is quoting Benjamin Haydon, *The Diary of Benjamin Robert Haydon* (1960, 2:520).

17. See Altick 155 for ways in which the marbles, once in the museum, were also "brought to life" in other London venues during the nineteenth century.

18. As Black writes, "Keats's choice of setting—the modern-day museum instead of the sands of native desert . . . [shows] how the romantic fragment poem can evolve into the Victorian museum poem" (135).

19. Quotes from Edwin Arnold's "To the Statue of Eumousia in the British Museum" cited by line number in the text.

20. To Katharine Tynan, Dec. 21, 1888.

21. To Katharine Tynan, Sept. 6, 1888.

22. To Ernest Rhys, Sept.–Oct. 1888.

23. Chris Brooks makes a similar claim about Sir Walter Scott's antiquarianism (2).

24. The Pitt Rivers Museum in Oxford is the most famous example of a Victorian sociocultural evolutionary anthropological museum. See Bowden 141–42.

25. See Pethica; Watson.

26. W. B. Yeats, letter published Oct. 11, 1890, in the *Academy*, reprinted in *Uncollected Prose* 174.

27. To Katharine Tynan, Sept. 6, 1888.

28. *Gaelic Journal*, July 1892, p. 164; also qtd. in Crooke 123.

29. Wilde continues, "We know that many valuable acquisitions have been gained by visitors calling accidentally at the museum; many more would, we feel convinced, find their way into this collection, if some general and popular means existed of giving an account of those which are there already" (*Beauties* x).

30. Wilde is here quoting the great Irish scholar John O'Donovan, who in the preface to his 1842 scholarly book *The Battle of Magh-Rath* criticizes Thomas Moore, who in his 1832 *History of Ireland* refuses to admit that his lack of historical source material comes from his inability to read Irish rather than from an actual absence of source material (vii).

31. To Katharine Tynan, Aug. 13, 1887.

32. To Katharine Tynan, Aug. 13, 1887.

33. Yeats reveals these two contradictory impulses—to preserve the lore of the Celtic peasantry and to disseminate it to a literary public wholly divorced from that peasantry—in

the way he structures his introduction to *Fairy and Folk Tales* by moving from modes of storytelling in the Irish West to Plato.

34. Yeats was an admirer of Laurence Binyon, in particular, whom he asked to succeed Hugh Lane as the director of the Irish National Gallery after Lane's death in 1915.

35. See Bornstein 23–27 for a discussion of Yeats's "The Wanderings of Oisin" as an attempt to rewrite Shelley's *Prometheus Unbound* on Irish soil.

36. To Katharine Tynan, Aug. 13, 1887.

37. Yeats reverses this question in "The Celtic Element in Literature" (1897), asking instead what Celtic legend might be able to do for British poetry: "[the Celtic] has again and again brought the 'vivifying spirit' 'of excess' into the arts of Europe (136–37).

38. To Katharine Tynan, Sept. 6, 1888.

39. To Elizabeth White, Jan. 30, 1889. In 1895 Sir William Henry Flower, the director of the Natural History Museum in London, delivered an address at the opening of the Perth Museum in which he quoted an 1889 essay by George Brown Goode, the director of the United States National Museum, saying that "a finished museum is a dead museum, and a dead museum is a useless museum," and said the same of libraries: "The underlying idea of a library and a museum is precisely the same. They are both instruments of intellectual culture, the one as much as the other" (Flower 57).

40. "To the Editor of the *Spectator*," July 29, 1889.

41. While "The Wanderings of Oisin" carries the classic elements of Irish revivalism—the retelling of Irish myth, the romanticization of nationalism, the hero who is lost and then returns—it also has its hero return not as a reborn youth but as a decrepit old man. The classic image of Irish revivalism, Yeats's and Lady Gregory's Cathleen ni Houlihan, who begins as an old woman but is transformed into a beautiful Irish maiden as soon as she has found men who will go out and fight for Ireland, has its counterpart in Oisin, who spends most of the poem as a young man but becomes old and broken as soon as he sets foot on Irish soil. "The Wanderings of Oisin" exemplifies a revivalism that revives not the past itself but the past as a source of artistic inspiration. See Leerssen 194–95 on Cathleen and revivalism.

42. See Ramazani, *Hybrid* 29, for a description of Yeats's sense of the work that Irish poets have done to infuse a beaten-down Ireland with new life.

43. Friedman attributes this description of Lady Wilde to the Irish writer Henriette Corkran.

44. See in particular McKinsey.

45. Unless otherwise stated, the quotes from "The Wanderings of Oisin" come from Yeats's original 1889 version, included in *The Poems, Second Edition*, not from his 1892 revision, which has become the standard anthologized version. The quotes in this paragraph, however, are from the revised version, and book and line numbers are taken from *The Collected Poems of W. B. Yeats*. I quote here from Yeats's revision because the later version offers a more concrete blending of the personal and national melancholy that the first version of the poem suggests. Quotes are cited by book and line number.

46. Cited parenthetically by line number.

47. "There is sweet music here that softer falls / Than petals from blown roses on the grass, / Or night-dews on still waters between walls / Of shadowy granite, in a gleaming pass; / Music that gentlier on the spirit lies, / Than tir'd eyelids upon tir'd eyes; / Music that brings sweet sleep down from the blissful skies. / Here are cool mosses deep, / And thro' the moss the ivies creep, / And in the stream the long-leaved flowers weep, / And from the craggy ledge the poppy hangs in sleep" (Tennyson, "Lotos-Eaters" 46–56).

48. Marjorie Howes and Joseph Valente make a similar argument about Yeats's career more largely, calling him both a "poetic angel of history" and an "angel of poetic history" (8).

49. To Katharine Tynan, Autumn 1887.

50. Yeats was outraged over the bureaucratic waffling surrounding the establishment of a permanent location for Hugh Lane's Municipal Gallery (it did not open in its permanent space in Parnell Square until 1933). See his letter to Ernest Boyd, Jan. 20, 1915 (*Letters* 591–92).

NOTES TO CHAPTER 5

1. The public was so disturbed by this unhappy ending that in 1906 Stoker's publisher made Stoker rewrite the ending so that everyone lives happily ever after.
2. See Smyth.
3. See Nolan; Castle, *Modernism*; Hutton for their nuanced examinations of Joyce's indebtedness to Revival sensibilities in his own aesthetic project.
4. See Castle, *Modernism*, chapter 5, for Joyce's critique of Revivalism in *Dubliners*.
5. See Gibbons, especially chapter 8, for an outline of this critical history.
6. See especially Arata; Schmidt; Morash; Moses.
7. See Gibbons, chapter 8, on Dracula as an incarnation of Ireland's haunting colonial memory.
8. I offer a related analysis of this scene and the novel's redemptive queer feminine intimacies in "Building Castles in the Air" 597–600.
9. See, for instance, Halberstam 89.
10. For *Jewel* and Egyptomania, see Briefel, *Racial Hand*; Daly; Dobson, "Gods" and *Writing*; Fleischhack; Glover; Ramirez. See Glover 19–20 for an impressive list of *Jewel*'s inherited preoccupations.
11. See Gibbons, chapter 1, for a discussion of Catholicism as a separate ethnicity in eighteenth- and nineteenth-century Ireland.
12. See Daly. The most well-known of these by the first decades of the twentieth century were H. Rider Haggard's 1913 short story "Smith and the Pharaohs" (one could also put his popular novels *She* and *Cleopatra* into this category), Arthur Conan Doyle's short stories "The Ring of Thoth" and "Lot No. 249," and Théophile Gautier's "La Roman de Momie."
13. See Daly; Brantlinger for their foundational work on imperial mummy fiction; see Dobson, *Writing* and *Victorian*; Colla for more recent work.
14. *Harper's* 48, Feb. 20, 1904, p. 276; emphasis mine.
15. For work on Egypt in the British literary imagination, see Dobson, *Victorian* and *Writing*; Fleischhack; Youngkin. For work more specifically focused on representations of the mummy in Western culture, see Day; Luckhurst. For the relationship between museum collecting, Egyptology, and colonialism, see Colla.
16. See Gifford, chapter 1, for a detailed overview of this history.
17. See Rast for an analysis of the relationship between Irish, Indian, and Egyptian nationalist movements in the early decades of the twentieth century.
18. See Gifford; Whidden for detailed analyses of British imperialism in Egypt in the late nineteenth and early twentieth centuries.
19. William Gladstone, for instance, worried that the Egyptian occupation would lead to "embroilments with France and other Powers" and "would end forever the realisation of that lofty aim, the founding not of a terrestrial but moral empire" (qtd. in Gifford 10).
20. *The Spectator*, vol. 80, Mar. 26, 1898, p. 433.
21. "Egypt," *Saturday Review*, vol. 66, no. 1714, Sept. 1, 1888, p. 260.
22. This is a familiar "Irish *Dracula*" argument: see Arata; Glover; S. Deane; Gibbons.
23. See Gibbons 80.
24. See Rast 486–87.
25. This desire to link the ancient kings of Ireland to the pharaohs of Egypt remains persistent, bolstered in the twenty-first century by DNA analysis. See a 2021 article in the *Irish Central*, "Could DNA Prove That Ancient Egyptians Visited Ireland?" and a 2020 article from the *Independent*, "Unearthing the Ancient 'Pharaohs' of the Emerald Isle" (Gorman).
26. See Bender on Irish Revival literature and the story of Exodus.
27. At the same moment that Ireland was looking to the Celtic past to produce modern Irish art, Egyptians were calling on "ancient Egypt to be the source of an authentically Egyptian corpus of modern art and literature" (Colla 213).

28. As Stoker writes in this essay, the arts "can be, and are, of great educational value, teaching the power and worth of organization in very high forms," yet it is "when we try to localize [them] that trouble begins" (75). He invites us to consider the "ethical values in the matter," as well as the kinds of choices the state may have to make in putting its stamp on a particular kind of public amusement, and then outlines at length the extreme financial and social obligations such a theatre would have to fulfill, suggesting implicitly that a functional, great national theatre is little more than a pipe dream.

29. To "celebrate" Queen Victoria's Diamond Jubilee in 1897, the staunch Irish nationalists and socialist party organized a funeral procession through Dublin with a coffin labeled "British Empire." See Murphy 272–93 for an analysis of this spectacle.

30. The Wildes and the Le Fanus both lived on Merrion Square at the same time, and Stoker was in Le Fanu's employ while he was paying regular visits to the Wildes. The same square was home in the early nineteenth century (1809–47) to famous Catholic emancipator Daniel O'Connell, and both W. B. Yeats and the Celtic Revival poet George Russell (A.E.) lived there in the 1920s.

31. The resonances of Wilde's writing about Egypt are particularly apparent in his second published book, *The Beauties of the Boyne, and Its Tributary, the Blackwater* (1849), in which the cadences and vocabulary of his descriptions of the Irish landscape strongly echo his descriptions of the Egyptian landscape. Although *The Beauties of the Boyne* seems to share little intent with *Narrative of a Voyage*, a close reading of the two texts reveals that the concerns and political posturings of the Egyptian portions of the travelogue are very much in evidence in Wilde's "merely descriptive" characterization of the Irish countryside.

32. There are unsubstantiated rumors that Stoker, too, was a member of the Order of the Golden Dawn.

33. See especially Fagan; Day; Luckhurst for analyses of Egyptian tomb raiding in the nineteenth century.

34. See Mitchell; Colla, chapter 1. See also Marsh 284–87; Bennett, chapter 2.

35. See Lord Rosebery's speech, Dec. 17, 1901, reprinted in the *Irish Times*, Dec. 17, 1901, pp. 5–6.

36. Stoker's "Great Experiment" emerges from a historical moment in which the study of supernatural phenomena was trying to move out of the realm of occult religion and into the realm of science. See the introduction of Grattan-Guinness for more on the Society for Psychical Research, and Budge's 1893 study of Egyptian funerary practices, *The Mummy*. An 1887 article in *The Open Court* insists that the Egyptian "magician" in the nineteenth-century Western imagination "*was the scientist of his time*" (Sept. 29, 1887, p. 472; original italics).

37. See Doyle's 1892 "The Los Amigos Fiasco," in which an expert electrician tries to convince enthusiastic executioners that electricity has the power to enliven just as much as to kill. For a detailed examination of electricity's simultaneously life-giving and death-giving capacities, see Morus, *Shocking* part 4.

38. Even before this revelation of exact likeness, the novel takes pains to suggest that Margaret and Queen Tera are forms of one another, that Margaret has privileged access to Queen Tera's mind and intentions, and that Queen Tera's astral body can possess Margaret with increasing frequency as the resurrection approaches.

39. This argument often arises in comparisons between Stoker's novel and H. Rider Haggard's 1887 novel *She*. See Brantlinger, chapter 8; Glover, chapter 2.

40. See especially Ramirez; Day; Luckhurst; S. Deane, chapter 6; Bulfin, chapter 2, for Jewel's "reverse colonization" narrative.

41. In 1830, 42 percent of the British Army was Irish, although the Irish made up only 32 percent of the population. By 1881 these figures had dropped to 21 percent and 15 percent. See Jeffery 95.

42. By "degraded," I mean to suggest a present marked by a feeling of loss (of family and of knowledge) rather than a morally degenerate present.

43. Among the pairings Kiberd identifies are Stephen and Bloom (Joyce, *Ulysses*), Doyle and Broadbent (Shaw, *John Bull's Other Island*), Joxer and Boyle (O'Casey, *Juno and the Paycock*), and Didi and Gogo (Beckett, *Waiting for Godot*).

44. One of the first Tera-Margaret "shock" moments of the novel occurs when Mr. Trelawny reveals a red birthmark on Margaret's wrist that matches exactly the jagged, bloody line on Queen Tera's wrist where her hand was torn off and carried away as a treasure by fifteenth-century Dutch explorers. This is a telling moment, for the violent damage done to the queen's body by men who considered it a curiosity and a jewel to be stolen expresses itself on Margaret's body as a kind of tattoo, a decorative mark "like drops of blood" that incontrovertibly binds the two women together (115). Their bodies thus reveal art and violence not only intertwined, even synonymous, with one another, but also this synthesis as one of the most visible ties between ancient queen and modern woman.

45. See Bronfen, especially the introduction.

46. Stoker fundamentally altered this structure when he rewrote the novel's ending in 1906 to have the resurrected spirit of Queen Tera fuse into Margaret, allowing everyone to live happily ever after.

47. In making this argument, I counter a Marxist argument made by Brown, which holds that reanimation is a mechanism for calling attention to the deanimating force of representation: essentially an amplification of, not an opposition to, the violence of representation.

48. Lloyd argues that the structural desires of Irish nationalism and British imperialism were almost indistinguishable, both seeking to "occlude troublesome and inassimilable manifestations of difference by positing a transcendent realm of essential identity" (*Nationalism* x).

49. See Lloyd again: "The nationalist is called to identify totally with the nation, evacuating himself of the subjectivism of an English civilization in order to be 'saturated' and 'filled' with the Irish spirit. . . . That spiritual identification serves to conceal—or to suture, as one's point of view may be—the gap that drives one artificially to 'make' a history, whether national or literary" (75).

NOTES TO EPILOGUE

1. See especially Mulvey-Roberts for introducing the scholarly discussion of nineteenth-century monster mash-up novels and de Bruin-Molé for the first book-length study of this genre.

2. This reading practice is not unlike Andrew Mangham's notion of forensic ventriloquism, in which an observer's "study of the dead allows . . . objects of analysis to take new life . . . but never in a way that is independent of [the observer's] involvement" (loc. 6410).

3. Peltz and Myrone lay out the formation of eighteenth-century antiquarians "as distinctive and grotesque characters . . . polluted by the fragments they studied" (2).

4. See especially de Bruin-Molé, *Gothic*, from whose book title I borrow the term "Frankenfictions."

5. See Mulvey-Roberts; de Bruin-Molé, "Now" and *Gothic*; Soares; S. Miller; Dew.

6. The presence of a mummy and the text's many Egyptological obsessions—"historically inconsisten[t] and deviat[ing] from the original timeline," as Nazarian freely admits in her after-note—bring postcolonial readings of *Mansfield Park* firmly into the foreground of the text. Edward Said's foundational assertion that in Austen's few references to Sir Thomas's trips to Antigua she "reveals herself to be assuming . . . the importance of an empire to the situation at home" takes literal form in Lord Eastwind, an embodiment of imperial plunder who refuses to stay hidden in the margins of the text (89).

WORKS CITED

A.E. "The Dramatic Treatment of Heroic Literature." *Samhain* (edited by W. B. Yeats), Oct. 1902, pp. 11–13; reprinted in *Samhain: October 1901–November 1908,* Routledge (Routledge Revivals), 1970, pp. 11–13.

Addcox, J. Stephen. "The Holistic Truth of Memory and Testimony in *The Ring and the Book.*" *Victorian Literature and Culture,* vol. 41, no. 2, 2013, pp. 329–42.

Adorno, Theodor W. "Valéry Proust Museum." *Prisms.* Translated by Samuel and Sherry Weber, Neville Spearman, 1967.

Agamben, Giorgio. *The End of the Poem: Studies in Poetics.* Translated by Daniel Heller-Roazen, Stanford UP, 1999.

Aldini, Giovanni (John). *An Account of the late Improvements in Galvanism; with a series of curious and interesting experiments performed before the Commissioners of the French National Institute, and repeated lately in the Anatomical Theatres of London . . . To which is added an appendix containing experiments on the body of a malefactor executed at Newgate, etc.* London: Cuthell and Martin, 1803.

Allen, Graham. "Reanimation or Reversibility in 'Valerius: The Reanimated Roman': A Response to Elena Anastasaki." *Connotations,* vol. 19, nos. 1–3, 2009/2010, pp. 21–33.

Allingham, William. *William Allingham's Diary.* Edited by Geoffrey Grigson, Centaur Press, 1967.

Altick, Richard. *The Shows of London.* Belknap Press of Harvard UP, 1978.

Anastasaki, Elena. "The Trials and Tribulations of the *Revenants*: Narrative Techniques and the Fragmented Hero in Mary Shelley and Théophile Gautier." *Connotations,* vol. 16, nos. 1–3, 2006/2007, pp. 26–46.

Arata, Stephen D. "The Occidental Tourist: Dracula and the Anxiety of Reverse Colonization." *Victorian Studies,* vol. 33, Summer 1990, pp. 621–45.

Arnold, Edwin. *Poems Narrative and Lyrical.* Oxford: F. Macpherson, 1853.

242 • WORKS CITED

Atanasoski, Neda, and Kalindi Vora. *Surrogate Humanity: Race, Robots, and the Politics of Technological Futures.* Duke UP, 2019.

Austen, Jane. *Northanger Abbey.* Edited by Marilyn Butler, Penguin Books, 2003.

Auyoung, Elaine. *When Fiction Feels Real: Representation and the Reading Mind.* Oxford UP, 2018.

Baldick, Chris. *In Frankenstein's Shadow: Myth, Monstrosity, and Nineteenth-century Writing.* Oxford UP, 1987.

Balfour, Henry. "Presidential Address to the Museums Association, Maidstone Meeting, July 13, 1909." *Museum Studies: An Anthology of Contexts,* edited by Bettina Messias Carbonell, Blackwell Publishing, 2004, pp. 252–59.

Bann, Stephen. *The Clothing of Clio: A Study of the Representation of History in Nineteenth-century Britain and France.* Cambridge UP, reissue ed., 2011.

Barthes, Roland. *Michelet.* Translated by Richard Howard, U of California P, 1987.

Bazin, Germain. "From *The Museum Age* / Foreword." *Museum Studies: An Anthology of Contexts,* edited by Bettina Messias Carbonell, Blackwell Publishing, 2004, pp. 18–22.

Beiner, Guy. "Irish Historical Studies *Avant la Lettre*: The Antiquarian Genealogy of Interdisciplinary Scholarship." *The Routledge International Handbook of Irish Studies,* edited by Renée Fox, Mike Cronin, and Brian O'Conchubhair, Routledge, 2021, pp. 47–58.

Belford, Barbara. *Bram Stoker: A Biography of the Author of Dracula.* Knopf, 1996.

Bell, Luther V. "Restoration of the Asphyxiated." *The College Journal of Medical Science,* vol. 1, no. 11, Nov. 1856, p. 415.

Bellamy, Edward. *Looking Backward, 2000–1887.* Houghton, Mifflin, 1888.

Bender, Abby. *Israelites in Erin: Exodus, Revolution, and the Irish Revival.* Syracuse UP, 2015.

Benjamin, Walter. *The Arcades Project.* Translated by Howard Eiland and Kevin McLaughlin, Belknap Press of Harvard UP, 1999.

———. "Theses on the Philosophy of History." *Illuminations,* translated by Harry Zohn, edited by Hannah Arendt, preface by Leon Wieseltier, Shocken Books, 2007, pp. 253–64.

———. "The Work of Art in the Age of Mechanical Reproduction." *Illuminations: Essays and Reflections,* edited and introduction by Hannah Arendt, Mariner Books, 2019, pp. 166–95.

Bennett, Tony. *The Birth of the Museum: History, Theory, Politics.* Routledge, 1995.

Best, Stephen, and Sharon Marcus. "Surface Reading: An Introduction." *Representations,* vol. 108, Fall 2009, pp. 1–21.

Betensky, Carolyn. "Casual Racism in Victorian Literature." *Victorian Literature and Culture,* vol. 47, no. 4, 2019, pp. 723–51.

Binyon, Laurence. *The Collected Poems of Laurence Binyon,* vol. 2. Macmillan, 1931.

Bird, Robert Montgomery. *Sheppard Lee, Written by Himself.* Introduction by Christopher Looby, New York Review of Books, 2008.

Black, Barbara. *On Exhibit: Victorians and Their Museums.* UP of Virginia, 2000.

Blanton, C. D. "Impostures: Robert Browning and the Poetics of Forgery." *Studies in the Literary Imagination,* vol. 35, no. 2, Fall 2002, pp. 1–25.

Bleunard, Albert. *Babylon Electrified: The History of an Expedition Undertaken to Restore Ancient Babylon by the Power of Electricity and How It Resulted.* Translated by Frank Linstow White, illustrated by Montader, London: Chapman & Hall, 1890.

Bloom, Harold. "Browning: Good Moments and Ruined Quests." *Poetry and Repression: Revisionism from Blake to Stevens,* Yale UP, 1976, pp. 175–204.

Bonafous-Murat, Carle. "Palaces of Art or Memory Palaces: Museographic Poetry from Tennyson to Auden." *Mémoires Perdues, Mémoires Vives,* edited by André Topia, Carle Bonafous Murat, and Marie-Christine Lemardley, Presses Sorbonne Nouvelle, 2016, pp. 213–29.

Bornstein, George. *Yeats and Shelley.* U of Chicago P, 1970.

Boswell, John Whittley. *Syllegomena of the Antiquities of Killmackumpshaugh, in the County of Roscommon, and Kingdom of Ireland, in which It Is Clearly Proved that Ireland Was Originally Peopled by Egyptians.* Dublin: Privately printed, 1790.

Bove, Alexander. *Spectral Dickens: The Uncanny Forms of Novelistic Characterization.* Manchester UP, 2021.

Bowden, Mark. *Pitt Rivers: The Life and Archaeological Work of Lieutenant-General Augustus Henry Lane Fox Pitt Rivers.* Cambridge UP, 1991.

Boyd, Ernest A. *Appreciations and Depreciations: Irish Literary Studies.* 1918. Books of Libraries Press, 1968.

———. "Introduction." *Standish O'Grady: Selected Essays and Passages,* Talbot Press, 1918, pp. 1–19.

Branagh, Kenneth. *Mary Shelley's Frankenstein.* Edited by Diana Landau, afterword and notes by Leonard Wolf, photographs by David Appleby, Newmarket Press, 1994.

Brand, Vanessa, editor. *The Study of the Past in the Victorian Age.* Oxbow Books for the British Archaeological Association and the Royal Archaeological Institute, 1998.

Brantlinger, Patrick. "*Frankenstein* and Race." *The Cambridge Companion to Frankenstein,* edited by Andrew Smith, Cambridge UP, 2016, pp. 128–42.

———. *Rule of Darkness: British Literature and Imperialism, 1830–1914.* Cornell UP, 1988.

Bresadola, Marco. "Early Galvanism as Technique and Medical Practice." *Electric Bodies: Episodes in the History of Medical Electricity,* edited by Paola Bertucci and Giuliano Pancaldi, U of Bologna P, 2001, pp. 157–80.

Briefel, Aviva. "'Freaks of Furniture': The Useless Energy of Haunted Things." *Victorian Studies,* vol. 59, no. 2, Winter 2017, pp. 209–34.

———. *The Racial Hand in the Victorian Imagination.* Cambridge UP, 2015.

———. "Spectral Matter: The Afterlife of Clothes in the Nineteenth-century Ghost Story." *Victorian Review,* vol. 41, no. 15, Spring 2015, pp. 67–88.

Brinkema, Eugenie. *The Forms of the Affects.* Duke UP, 2014.

The British Critic (review of *Frankenstein*). N.S. 9, Sept. 1818, pp. 432–38.

British Library. "Freak Show: What Is It? (1846)." https://www.bl.uk/learning/timeline/item106349.html.

Bronfen, Elisabeth. *Over Her Dead Body: Death, Femininity, and the Aesthetic.* Manchester UP, 1992.

Brooks, Chris. "Introduction: Historicism and the Nineteenth Century." *The Study of the Past in the Victorian Age,* edited by Vanessa Brand, Oxbow Books, 1998, pp. 1–19.

Brooks, Mel, et al. *Young Frankenstein.* 20th Century Fox, 1974.

Brooks, Peter. *Reading for the Plot: Design and Intention in Narrative.* Harvard UP, 1984.

———. *Realist Vision.* Yale UP, 2005.

Brough, William, and Robert Brough. *Frankenstein; or, the Model Man.* Reprinted in Forry, pp. 227–50.

Brown, Bill. "Reification, Reanimation, and the American Uncanny." *Critical Inquiry,* vol. 32, no. 2, Winter 2006, pp. 175–207.

Brown, Wendy. *Politics Out of History.* Princeton UP, 2001.

Browning, Elizabeth Barrett. *Aurora Leigh.* Edited by Kerry McSweeney, Oxford UP, 1993.

———. *The Letters of Elizabeth Barrett Browning.* Edited by Frederic Kenyon, Macmillan, 1898.

Browning, Elizabeth Barrett, and Robert Browning. *The Brownings' Correspondence.* Edited by Philip Kelley and Scott Lewis, Wedgestone Press, 1984.

Browning, Robert. *Dearest Isa: Robert Browning's Letters to Isabella Blagden.* Edited by Edward C. McAleer, U of Texas P, 1951.

———. "Introductory Essay [Essay on Shelley]." *The Broadview Anthology of Victorian Poetry and Poetic Theory,* edited by Thomas J. Collins and Vivienne J. Rundle, Broadview Press, 1999, pp. 1243–53.

———. *The Ring and the Book.* Edited by Richard D. Altick, Penguin Books, 1971.

———. *Robert Browning's Poetry.* Edited by James Loucks and Andrew Stauffer, W. W. Norton, 2006.

Browning, Robert, and Julia Wedgwood. *Robert Browning and Julia Wedgwood; A Broken Friendship as Revealed by Their Letters.* Edited by Richard Curle, Frederick A. Stokes, 1937.

Budge, Sir E. A. Wallis. *The Mummy: Chapters on Egyptian Funereal Archaeology.* Cambridge UP, 1893.

Bulfin, Ailise. *Gothic Invasions: Imperialism, War and Fin-de-Siècle Popular Fiction.* U of Wales P, 2018.

Bulwer Lytton, Edward. *The Coming Race.* Edited by Peter W. Sinnema, Broadview Press, 2008.

Campbell, Matthew. *Rhythm and Will in Victorian Poetry.* Cambridge UP, 1999.

Carlyle, Thomas. "On History." *The Norman and Charlotte Strouse Edition of the Writings of Thomas Carlyle: Historical Essays,* edited by Chris R. Vanden Bossche, U of California P, 2002, pp. 3–13.

———. *Past and Present.* Introduction by Douglas Jerrold, J. M. Dent, 1960.

Castle, Gregory. *Modernism and the Celtic Revival.* Cambridge UP, 2001.

———. "Nobler Forms: Standish O'Grady's *History of Ireland* and the Irish Literary Revival." *Reading Irish Histories: Texts, Contexts, and Memory in Modern Ireland,* edited by Lawrence W. McBride, Four Courts Press, 2003, pp. 156–77.

———. "Synge and Disappearing Ireland." *Irish Literature in Transition, 1880–1940,* edited by Marjorie Howes, Cambridge UP, 2020, pp. 212–28.

———. "Wild and Improbable Narratives: Standish O'Grady's *History of Ireland.*" *Standish O'Grady's Cuculain: A Critical Edition,* edited by Gregory Castle and Patrick Bixby, Syracuse UP, 2016, pp. 1–31.

Chemers, Michael. *The Monster in Theatre History: This Thing of Darkness.* Routledge, 2018.

———. "The Mortification of Harvey Leach: Humour and Horror in Nineteenth-Century Theatre of Disability." *Theatre and the Macabre,* edited by Meredith Conti and Kevin J. Wetmore Jr., U of Wales P, 2022, pp. 13–27.

Christ, Carol. "Browning's Corpses." *Victorian Poetry,* vol. 33, nos. 3–4, Autumn–Winter 1995, pp. 391–401.

———. "Painting the Dead: Portraiture and Necrophilia in Victorian Art and Poetry." *Death and Representation,* edited by Sarah Webster Goodwin and Elisabeth Bronfen, Johns Hopkins UP, 1993, pp. 133–51.

Clark, Samuel. "Review of *Britain in Egypt: Egyptian Nationalism and Imperial Strategy, 1919–1931,* by Jayne Gifford." *History,* 16 Mar. 2021, pp. 331–32.

WORKS CITED · 245

Clay, Henry. "The American System: February 2, 3, and 6, 1832 (In the Senate)." *The Senate (1789–1989) Classic Speeches (1830–1993)*, vol. 3, bicentennial ed., compiled by Robert C. Byrd, edited by Wendy Wolff, US Government Printing Office, 1994, pp. 83–116.

Cleary, Joe. "The Nineteenth-century Irish Novel: Notes and Speculations on Literary Historiography." *The Irish Novel in the Nineteenth Century: Facts and Fictions*, edited by Jacqueline Belanger, Four Courts Press, 2005, pp. 202–21.

Clifford, James. "Objects and Selves—an Afterword." *Objects and Others: Essays on Museums and Material Culture*, edited by George W. Stocking Jr., U of Wisconsin P, 1985, pp. 236–46.

Cohn, Elisha. *Still Life: Suspended Development in the Victorian Novel*. Oxford UP, 2016.

Coleridge, Samuel Taylor. *The Collected Works of Samuel Taylor Coleridge, Volume 7: Biographia Literaria*. Edited by James Engell and W. Jackson Bate, Princeton UP, 1983.

———. "Shakespeare, with Introductory Matter on Poetry, the Drama, and the Stage." *Coleridge's Essays and Lectures on Shakespeare and Other Poets and Dramatists*, J. M. Dent and Sons, 1907, pp. 9–177.

Colla, Elliott. *Conflicted Antiquities: Egyptology, Egyptomania, Egyptian Modernity*. Duke UP, 2007.

Collins, Philip, editor. *Dickens: The Critical Heritage*. Barnes and Noble, 1971.

Cook, James W., Jr. "Of Men, Missing Links, and Nondescripts: The Strange Case of P. T. Barnum's 'What is It?' Exhibition." *Freakery: Cultural Spectacles of the Extraordinary Body*, edited by Rosemarie Garland-Thomson, New York UP, 1996, pp. 139–57.

"Cooking by Electricity." *Punch, or the London Charivari*, vol. 33, 14 Nov. 1857, p. 198.

Coriale, Danielle. "Jamming the Historical Machine." *boundary2 online*, 4 Oct. 2016, https://www.boundary2.org/2016/10/danielle-coriale-jamming-the-historical-machine/.

"Could DNA Prove That Ancient Egyptians Visited Ireland?" *Irish Central*, 7 Dec. 2021, https://www.irishcentral.com/roots/history/dna-ancient-egyptians-ireland.

Craft, Christopher. "Kiss Me with Those Red Lips: Gender and Inversion in Bram Stoker's *Dracula*." *Representations*, no. 8, Autumn 1984, pp. 107–33.

Crandell, Caitlin. "Browning's Metaforms: Transformation and the Work of the Artist in *The Ring and the Book*." *Victorian Poetry*, vol. 58, no. 3, Fall 2020, pp. 237–68.

Creaney, Conor. "Paralytic Animation: The Anthropomorphic Taxidermy of Walter Potter." *Victorian Studies*, vol. 53, no. 1, Autumn 2010, pp. 7–35.

Crimmins, Jonathan. *The Romantic Historicism Yet to Come*. Bloomsbury Academic, 2018.

Crooke, Elizabeth. *Politics, Archaeology, and the Creation of a National Museum of Ireland*. Irish Academic Press, 2000.

Çrouzet, Francois. *The Victorian Economy*. Translated by Anthony Forster, Routledge, 1982.

Culler, Dwight A. *The Victorian Mirror of History*. Yale UP, 1985.

Cummings, Mark, editor. *The Carlyle Encyclopedia*. Fairleigh Dickinson UP, 2004.

Dale, Peter Allen. *The Victorian Critic and the Idea of History*. Harvard UP, 1977.

Daly, Nicholas. "That Obscure Object of Desire: Victorian Commodity Culture and Fictions of the Mummy." *Novel: A Forum on Fiction*, vol. 28, no. 1, Fall 1994, pp. 24–51.

Dames, Nicholas. *The Physiology of the Novel: Reading, Neural Science, and the Form of Victorian Fiction*. Oxford UP, 2007.

Davy, Sir Humphry. "Discourse 15–17." *Frankenstein*, by Mary Shelley, edited by D. L. Macdonald and Kathleen Scherf, Broadview Press, 2012, pp. 246–47.

246 • WORKS CITED

Day, Jasmine. *The Mummy's Curse: Mummymania in the English-Speaking World.* Routledge, 2006.

de Bruin-Molé, Megen. *Gothic Remixed: Monster Mashups and Frankenfictions in 21st-Century Culture.* Bloomsbury Academic, 2020.

———. "'Now with Ultraviolent Zombie Mayhem!': The Neo-Victorian Novel-as-Mashup and the Limits of Postmodern Irony." *Neo-Victorian Humour: Comic Subversions and Unlaughter in Contemporary Historical Re-Visions,* edited by Marie-Louise Kohlke and Christian Gutleben, Brill, 2017, pp. 249–76.

Deane, Bradley. *Masculinity and the New Imperialism: Rewriting Manhood in British Popular Literature, 1870–1914.* Cambridge UP, 2014.

Deane, Seamus. *Strange Country: Modernity and Nationhood in Irish Writing since 1790.* Clarendon Press, 1997.

"Death from Dissecting," *Daily News* (London), Tues., 25 May 1847, p. 3.

Dew, Ben. "Rewriting Popular Classics as Popular Fiction: Jane Austen, Zombies, Sex and Vampires." *The Bloomsbury Introduction to Popular Fiction,* edited by Christine Berberich, Bloomsbury Academic, 2015, pp. 282–95.

Dickens, Charles. *Bleak House.* Edited by Nicola Bradbury, Penguin Books, 1996.

———. *David Copperfield.* Edited by Jeremy Tambling, Penguin Books, 2004.

———. *Great Expectations.* Edited by Charlotte Mitchell, introduction by David Trotter, Penguin Books, 2003.

———. *Hard Times.* Edited by Kate Flint, Penguin Books, 2003.

———. *Martin Chuzzlewit.* Edited by Patricia Ingham, Penguin Books, 2004.

———. *Oliver Twist.* Edited by Kathleen Tillotson, Oxford UP, 1982.

———. *Our Mutual Friend.* Edited by Adrian Poole, Penguin Books, 1997.

———. "Personal." *Household Words,* vol. 17, no. 429, 12 June 1858, p. 429.

———. *Sketches by Boz.* Edited by Dennis Walder, Penguin Books, 1995.

Dobson, Eleanor. "Gods and Ghost-Light: Ancient Egypt, Electricity, and X-Rays." *Victorian Literature and Culture,* vol. 45, no. 1, 2017, pp. 119–35.

———, editor. *Victorian Literary Culture and Ancient Egypt.* Manchester UP, 2020.

———. *Writing the Sphinx: Literature, Culture, and Egyptology.* Edinburgh UP, 2020.

Doyle, Arthur Conan. "The Los Amigos Fiasco." *The Idler,* Dec. 1892, pp. 548–57.

Duncan, Ian. *Human Forms: The Novel in the Age of Evolution.* Princeton UP, 2019.

———. "Our Mutual Friend." *The Oxford Handbook of Charles Dickens,* edited by Robert L. Patten, John O. Jordan, and Catherine Waters, Oxford UP, 2018, pp. 285–98.

———. *Scott's Shadow: The Novel in Romantic Edinburgh.* Princeton UP, 2007.

Eagleton, Terry. "The Ryan Line." *Crazy John and the Bishop,* Cork UP, 1998, pp. 249–73.

The Edinburgh Magazine and Literary Miscellany; A New Series of "The Scots Magazine" (review of *Frankenstein*). vol. 81, N.S. vol. 2, Mar. 1818, pp. 249–53.

"The Electric Light." *The Bengal Catholic Herald,* Mar. 17, 1849, p. 154.

Erwin, Sherri Browning, and Charlotte Brontë. *Jane Slayre.* Gallery Books, 2010.

Faas, Ekbert. *Retreat into the Mind: Victorian Poetry and the Rise of Psychiatry.* Princeton UP, 1988.

Fagan, Brian. *The Rape of the Nile: Tomb Robbers, Tourists, and Archaeologists in Egypt.* Charles Scribner's Sons, 1975.

WORKS CITED • 247

Felski, Rita. *Hooked: Art and Attachment*. U of Chicago P, 2020.

———. *The Limits of Critique*. U of Chicago P, 2015.

Ferguson, Samuel. *The Lays of the Western Gael and Other Poems*. London: Bell and Daldy, 1865.

Fermanis, Porscha. *Romantic Pasts: History, Fiction and Feeling in Britain, 1790-1850*. Edinburgh UP, 2022.

Fessenden, Thomas Green (Christopher Caustic, M.D.). *Terrible Tractoration, and Other Poems*. 4th American ed., Boston: Samuel Colman, 1837.

"Few occurrences are so melancholy as those . . ." *The Times*, Weds., 20 Sept. 1865, p. 8.

Fielding, Henry. *The History of Tom Jones, a Foundling*. Edited by Fredson Bowers, Modern Library of America ed., Random House, 1994.

Fisch, Audrey A. *Frankenstein: Icon of Modern Culture*. Helm Information, 2009.

Fisher, Philip. "Art and the Future's Past." *Museum Studies: An Anthology of Contexts*, edited by Bettina Messias Carbonell, Blackwell Publishing, 2004, pp. 436–54.

Flanagan, Thomas. "Yeats, Joyce, and the Matter of Ireland." *Critical Inquiry*, vol. 2, no. 1, August 1975, pp. 43–67.

Fleischhack, Maria. "Possession, Trance, and Reincarnation: Confrontations with Ancient Egypt in Edwardian Fiction." *Victoriographies: A Journal of Nineteenth-century Writing, 1790-1914*, vol. 7, no. 3, Nov. 2017, pp. 257–70.

Flower, Sir William Henry. "Local Museums." *Essays on Museums and Other Subjects Connected with Natural History*, London: Macmillan, 1898, pp. 54–57.

Forry, Steven Earl. *Hideous Progenies: Dramatizations of "Frankenstein" from Mary Shelley to the Present*. U of Pennsylvania P, 1990.

Foucault, Michel. *Discipline and Punish: The Birth of the Prison*. Translated by Alan Sheridan, Penguin Books, 1977.

Fox, Renée. "Building Castles in the Air: Female Intimacy and Generative Queerness in *Dracula*." *Dracula: A Case Study in Contemporary Criticism*, 2nd ed., by Bram Stoker, edited by John Paul Riquelme, Bedford / St. Martin's, 2015, pp. 590–607.

———. "Fleshing Dry Bones: Standish O'Grady's Sensory Revivalism." *Standish O'Grady's Cuculain: A Critical Edition*, edited by Gregory Castle and Patrick Bixby, Syracuse UP, 2016, pp. 191–209.

———. "Michael Longley's Early Epitaphs." *New Hibernia Review*, vol. 13, no. 2, Summer 2009, pp. 125–40.

———. "Realism's Irish Forms: Queering the Fog in Charles Dickens's *Bleak House* and Emily Lawless's *Grania*." *Victorian Studies*, vol. 61, no. 4, Summer 2019, pp. 559–81.

———. "Robert Browning's Necropoetics." *Victorian Poetry*, vol. 49, no. 4, Winter 2011, pp. 463–83.

Franklin, Caroline, and Michael J. Franklin. "Victorian Gothic Poetry: The Corpse's [a] Text." *The Victorian Gothic: An Edinburgh Companion*, edited by Andrew Smith and William Hughes, Edinburgh UP, 2012, pp. 72–92.

Fraser, Hilary. *The Victorians and Renaissance Italy*. Blackwell, 1992.

Fraser, T. G. "Ireland and India." *'An Irish Empire'?: Aspects of Ireland and the British Empire*, edited by Keith Jeffery, Manchester UP, 1996, pp. 77–93.

Freccero, Carla. *Queer/Early/Modern*. Duke UP, 2006.

Freedgood, Elaine. "Fictional Settlements: Footnotes, Metalepsis, the Colonial Effect." *New Literary History*, vol. 41, 2010, pp. 393–411.

248 • WORKS CITED

——. *The Ideas in Things: Fugitive Meaning in the Victorian Novel.* U of Chicago P, 2006.

——. *Worlds Enough: The Invention of Realism in the Victorian Novel.* Princeton UP, 2019.

Freeman, Elizabeth. *Time Binds: Queer Temporalities, Queer Histories.* Duke UP, 2010.

Freeman, Nick. "The Victorian Ghost Story." *The Victorian Gothic: An Edinburgh Companion,* edited by Andrew Smith and William Hughes, Edinburgh UP, 2012, pp. 93–107.

Freud, Sigmund. *The Uncanny.* Translated by David McLintock and introduction by Hugh Haughton, Penguin Books, 2003, pp. 121–62.

Fried, Debra. "Repetition, Refrain, and Epitaph." *ELH,* vol. 53, no. 3, Autumn 1986, pp. 615–32.

Friedman, David M. *Wilde in America: Oscar Wilde and the Invention of Modern Celebrity.* W. W. Norton, 2014.

Friedman, Lester D., and Allison B. Kavey. *Monstrous Progeny: A History of Frankenstein Narratives.* Rutgers UP, 2016.

Fuss, Diana. *Dying Modern: A Meditation on Elegy.* Duke UP, 2013.

Gallagher, Catherine. "The Bioeconomics of *Our Mutual Friend.*" *The Body Economic: Life, Death, and Sensation in Political Economy and the Victorian Novel,* Princeton UP, 2006, pp. 86–117.

——. "George Eliot: Immanent Victorian." *Representations,* vol. 90, no. 1, Spring 2005, pp. 61–74.

——. "The Novel and Other Discourses of Suspended Disbelief." *Practicing New Historicism,* edited by Catherine Gallagher and Stephen Greenblatt, U of Chicago P, 2000, pp. 163–210.

Galvan, Jill. *The Sympathetic Medium: Feminine Channeling, The Occult, and Communication Technologies, 1859–1919.* Cornell UP, 2010.

"Galvanic Experiment: An Account of some Experiments made on the Body of a Criminal Immediately After Execution, with Physiological and Practical Observations. By Andrew Ure, M.D., M.G.S." *The Penny Satirist,* no. 305, 18 Feb. 1843, p. 1.

"Galvanic Rings—How to Apply Them." *The Satirist; or, The Censor of the Times,* no. 673, 9 Mar. 1845, p. 74.

Gamble, Sarah. "'You cannot impersonate what you are': Questions of Authenticity in the Neo-Victorian Novel." *Literature Interpretation Theory,* vol. 20, 2009, pp. 126–40.

Gaylord, Harriet. *Pompilia and Her Poet.* Literary Publications, 1931.

Gent, Margaret. "'To Flinch from Modern Varnish': The Appeal of the Past to the Victorian Imagination." *Victorian Poetry,* edited by Malcolm Bradbury and David Palmer, Stratford-Upon-Avon Studies 15, Edward Arnold Publishers, 1972, pp. 11–35.

Gibbons, Luke. *Gaelic Gothic: Race, Colonization, and Irish Culture.* Arlen House, 2003.

Gifford, Jayne. *Britain in Egypt: Egyptian Nationalism and Imperial Strategy, 1919–1931.* I. B. Taurus, 2020.

"The Gifts of Science to Art." *Dublin University Magazine,* vol. 36, no. 211, July 1850, pp. 1–20.

Gigante, Denise. *Life: Organic Form and Romanticism.* Yale UP, 2009.

Glover, David. *Vampires, Mummies, and Liberals: Bram Stoker and the Politics of Popular Fiction.* Duke UP, 1996.

Goddu, Teresa. *Gothic America: Narrative, History, and Nation.* Columbia UP, 1997.

Godwin, William. "Of History and Romance." *Caleb Williams,* edited by Gary Handwerk and A. A. Markley, Broadview Press, 2000, pp. 453–67.

Gooday, Graeme. *Domesticating Electricity: Technology, Uncertainty and Gender, 1880–1914.* Pickering & Chatto, 2008.

WORKS CITED · 249

Goode, George Brown. *The Museums of the Future.* Washington, DC: Government Printing Office, 1891.

Goode, Mike. *Sentimental Masculinity and the Rise of History, 1790–1890.* Cambridge UP, 2009.

Goodwin, Sarah Webster, and Elisabeth Bronfen. "Introduction." *Death and Representation,* edited by Sarah Webster Goodwin and Elisabeth Bronfen, Johns Hopkins UP, 1993, pp. 3–25.

Gorman, James. "Unearthing the Ancient 'Pharaohs' of the Emerald Isle." *Independent,* 2 July 2020, https://www.independent.co.uk/tech/ireland-pharaoh-dna-stone-age-tomb-egyptian-dublin-boyne-a9592091.html.

Grahame-Smith, Seth. *Pride and Prejudice and Zombies.* Quirk Books, 2009.

Grattan-Guinness, Ivor, editor. *Psychical Research: A Guide to Its History, Principles, and Practices.* Aquarian Press, 1982.

Graves, Alfred Perceval. "Foreword." *Standish James O'Grady, the Man and the Writer: A Memoir by His Son Hugh Art O'Grady, Litt.D., with a Foreword by Alfred Perceval Graves and Contributions by A.E. and Others.* Talbot Press, 1929.

Greenblatt, Stephen. "Resonance and Wonder." *Museum Studies: An Anthology of Contexts,* edited by Bettina Messias Carbonell, Blackwell Publishing, 2004, pp. 541–55.

Greene, Thomas. *The Light in Troy: Imitation and Discovery in Renaissance Poetry.* Yale UP, 1982.

Gregory, Lady Augusta. *Seventy Years: Being the Autobiography of Lady Augusta Gregory.* Macmillan, 1976.

Greiner, Rae. *Sympathetic Realism in Nineteenth-century British Fiction.* Johns Hopkins UP, 2012.

Griffiths, Devin. *The Age of Analogy: Science and Literature Between the Darwins.* Kindle ed., Johns Hopkins UP, 2016.

———. "Untimely Historicism." *boundary2 online,* 4 Oct. 2016, https://www.boundary2.org/2016/10/devin-griffiths-untimely-historicism/.

Halberstam, Jack [Judith]. *Skin Shows: Gothic Horror and the Technology of Monsters.* Duke UP, 1995.

Hansson, Heidi. "History in/of the Borderlands: Emily Lawless and the Story of Ireland." *Liminal Borderlands in Irish Literature and Culture,* edited by Irene Gilsenan Nordin and Elin Homsten, Peter Lang, 2009, pp. 51–68.

Hardy, Thomas. *The Collected Poems of Thomas Hardy.* Introduction by Michael Irwin, Wordsworth Editions, 1994.

Harwood, Philip. "The Modern Art and Science of History." *Westminster Review,* vol. 38, Oct. 1842, pp. 170–89.

Haug, Jochen. *Passions Without a Tongue: Dramatizations of the Body in Robert Browning's Poetry.* Peter Lang, 2004.

Heffernan, James A. W. "Looking at the Monster: *Frankenstein* and Film." *Critical Inquiry,* vol. 24, no. 1, Autumn 1997, pp. 133–58.

Helfield, Randa. "Dead Women Do Tell Tales: Spiritualism, Browning, and the Dramatic Monologue." *Studies in Browning and His Circle.* vol. 27, Dec. 2006, pp. 7–25.

"Hervio Nano." *The Times,* Tues., 12 Apr. 1847, p. 5.

Higgins, Geraldine. "Carlyle's Celtic Congregation: Reviving the Irish Hero." *Victorian Keats and Romantic Carlyle: The Fusions and Confusions of Literary Periods,* edited by C. C. Barfoot, Rodopi, 1999, pp. 205–22.

———. *Heroic Revivals from Carlyle to Yeats.* Palgrave Macmillan, 2012.

Hoberman, Ruth. *Museum Trouble: Edwardian Fiction and the Emergence of Modernism.* U of Virginia P, 2012.

WORKS CITED

Hockensmith, Steve. *Pride and Prejudice and Zombies: Dawn of the Dreadfuls.* Quirk Books, 2010.

Holmes, Oliver Wendell. "Homeopathy and Its Kindred Delusions." *Medical Essays, 1842–1882,* vol. 9 of *The Works of Oliver Wendell Holmes,* Houghton, Mifflin, 1892, pp. 1–102.

"A Horrible Experiment." *Famous Crimes: Past and Present,* vol. 5, no. 58, 1905 (?), p. 143.

Howes, Marjorie, and Joseph Valente. "Introduction." *Yeats and Afterwords: Christ, Culture, and Crisis,* edited by Marjorie Howes and Joseph Valente, U of Notre Dame P, 2014, pp. 1–12.

Hurst, Isobel. "Reanimating the Romans: Mary Shelley's Response to Roman Ruins." *Regarding Romantic Rome,* edited by Richard Wrigley, Peter Lang, 2007, pp. 125–36.

Hutton, Claire. "The Irish Revival." *James Joyce in Context,* edited by John McCourt, Cambridge UP, 2009, pp. 195–204.

"The Indestructibility of Force." *Macmillan's Magazine,* vol. 6, 1 May 1862, pp. 337–44.

"Infallible Physics," *All the Year Round,* vol. 2, no. 45, 3 Mar. 1860, pp. 448–52.

Ingelbien, Raphaël. "Realism, Allegory, Gothic: The Irish Victorian Novel." *Irish Literature in Transition, 1830–1880,* vol. 3, edited by Matthew Campbell, Cambridge UP, 2020, pp. 238–56.

"The Inquest." *Times,* Monday, 23 Jan. 1860, p. 10.

Iser, Wolfgang. "The Implied Reader." *An Anthology of Criticism and Theory 1900–2000,* edited by Dorothy J. Hale, Blackwell Publishing, 2006, pp. 765–78.

———. "The Reading Process: A Phenomenological Approach." *On Interpretation: I,* special issue of *New Literary History,* vol. 3, no. 2, Winter 1972, pp. 279–99.

James, Henry. "Our Mutual Friend." *The Nation,* vol. 1, no. 25, 21 Dec. 1865, pp. 786–87.

Jameson, Fredric. *The Antinomies of Realism.* Duke UP, 2013.

———. "Antinomies of the Realism-Modernism Debate." *Modern Language Quarterly,* vol. 73, no. 3, Sept. 2012, pp. 475–85.

Jamin (Doctor). "On the Therapeutical Employment of Electricity." *The Lady's Newspaper,* no. 477, 16 Feb. 1856, p. 108.

Jann, Rosemary. *The Art and Science of Victorian History.* The Ohio State UP, 1985.

Jeffery, Keith. "The Irish Military Tradition and the British Empire." *'An Irish Empire'?: Aspects of Ireland and the British Empire,* edited by Keith Jeffery, Manchester UP, 1996, pp. 94–122.

Jordan, John O. "The Medium of *Great Expectations.*" *Dickens Studies Annual,* vol. 11, 1983, pp. 73–88.

Joyce, James. "The Soul of Ireland." *Occasional, Critical, and Political Writing,* edited by Kevin Barry, Oxford UP, 2000, pp. 74–76.

———. *Ulysses.* Vintage Books, 1934.

Kakoudaki, Despina. "Unmaking People: The Politics of Negation in *Frankenstein* and *Ex Machina.*" *Science Fiction Studies,* vol. 25, no. 2, July 2018, pp. 289–307.

Kang, Minsoo. *Sublime Dreams of Living Machines: The Automaton in the European Imagination.* Harvard UP, 2011.

Kasmer, Lisa. *Novel Histories: British Women Writing History, 1760–1830.* Fairleigh Dickinson UP, 2012.

Keats, John. *Keats's Poetry and Prose: A Norton Critical Edition.* Edited by Jeffrey N. Cox, W. W. Norton, 2009.

Kelleher, Margaret. "'Wanted an Irish Novelist': The Critical Decline of the Nineteenth-century Novel." *The Irish Novel in the Nineteenth Century: Facts and Fictions,* edited by Jacqueline Belanger, Four Courts Press, 2005, pp. 187–201.

Kennedy, Seán. "'Echo's Bones': Samuel Beckett After Yeats." *Yeats and Afterwords,* edited by Marjorie Howes and Joseph Valente, U of Notre Dame P, 2014, pp. 235–53.

Kiberd, Declan. *Inventing Ireland.* Random House, 1995.

———. "Museums and Learning." *The Irish Writer and the World,* Cambridge UP, 2005, pp. 219–34.

Kingsley, Charles. *The Limits of Exact Science as Applied to History: An Inaugural Lecture Delivered before the University of Cambridge.* Cambridge: Macmillan, 1860.

Knoepflmacher, U. C. "Projection and the Female Other: Romanticism, Browning, and the Victorian Dramatic Monologue." *Victorian Poetry,* vol. 22, no. 2, Summer 1984, pp. 139–59.

Kontou, Tatiana, and Sarah Wilburn, editors. *The Ashgate Research Companion to Nineteenth-century Spiritualism and the Occult.* Ashgate, 2012.

Kornbluh, Anna, and Benjamin Morgan. "Introduction: Presentism, Form, and the Future of History." *boundary2 online,* 4 Oct. 2016, https://www.boundary2.org/2016/10/anna-kornbluh-and-benjamin-morgan-introduction-presentism-form-and-the-future-of-history/.

Kristeva, Julia. *Powers of Horror: An Essay on Abjection.* Translated by Leon S. Roudiez, Columbia UP, 1982.

Kuskey, Jessica. "Our Mutual Engine: The Economics of Victorian Thermodynamics." *Victorian Literature and Culture,* vol. 41, no. 1, 2013, pp. 75–89.

Lady, Steph, and Frank Darabont. "Screenplay." *Mary Shelley's Frankenstein,* by Kenneth Branagh, edited by Diana Landau, afterword and notes by Leonard Wolf, photographs by David Appleby, Newmarket Press, 1994, pp. 30–139; 2nd rev. draft, http://www.horrorlair.com/movies/scripts/frankenstein.html.

"Lamentable Accident at Cambridge." *The Times,* Tues., 19 Sept. 1865, p. 10.

Lang, Andrew. "Introduction." *The Antiquary,* by Sir Walter Scott (2 vols.), introductory essay and notes by Andrew Lang, Boston: Estes and Lauriat, 1893, pp. xix–xxxv.

Lavery, Grace. "*The Mikado's* Queer Realism: Law, Genre, Knowledge." *Novel: A Forum on Fiction,* vol. 49, no. 2, Aug. 2016, pp. 219–35.

"Leach V. Simpson and Another." *The Era,* Sun., 16 June 1839.

Lee, Vernon. "Preface to *Hauntings*." *Hauntings and Other Fantastic Tales,* edited by Catherine Maxwell and Patricia Pulham, Broadview Press, 2006, pp. 37–40.

Leerssen, Joep. *Remembrance and Imagination: Patterns in the Historical and Literary Representation of Ireland in the Nineteenth Century.* U of Notre Dame P, 1997.

Levine, Caroline. *Forms: Whole, Rhythm, Hierarchy, Network.* Princeton UP, 2015.

Levine, George. *The Realistic Imagination: English Fiction from Frankenstein to Lady Chatterley.* U of Chicago P, 1983.

Lewes, George Henry. "Dickens in Relation to Criticism." *Fortnightly Review,* vol. 11, no. 62, Feb. 1872, pp. 141–54.

The Literary Panorama, and National Register (review of *Frankenstein*). N.S. vol. 8, June 1818, pp. 411–14.

Loudon, Jane (Webb). *The Mummy! A Tale of the Twenty-Second Century.* Introduction and abridgement by Alan Rauch, U of Michigan P, 1994.

Lloyd-Smith, Allan. *American Gothic Fiction: An Introduction.* Continuum International Publishing, 2004.

Lloyd, David. "Afterword: Hardress Cregan's Dream—For Another History of the Irish Novel." *The Irish Novel in the Nineteenth Century: Facts and Fictions,* edited by Jacqueline Belanger, Four Courts Press, 2005, pp. 229–37.

———. *Nationalism and Minor Literature: James Clarence Mangan and the Emergence of Irish Cultural Nationalism.* U of California P, 1987.

Lowell, James Russell. "A Moosehead Journal." *Literary Essays,* vol. 1 of *The Writings of James Russell Lowell,* Cambridge, MA: Riverside Press, 1890, pp. 1–41.

Luckhurst, Roger. *The Mummy's Curse: The True History of a Dark Fantasy.* Oxford UP, 2012.

"The Lungs, a Galvanic Battery!" *John Bull,* no. 1194, Sat., 28 Oct. 1843, p. 685.

Lutz, Deborah. "Gothic Fictions in the Nineteenth Century." *The Nineteenth-century Novel, 1820–1860,* edited by John Kucich and Jenny Bourne Taylor, vol. 3 of *The Oxford History of the Novel in English,* Oxford UP, 2012, pp. 76–89.

———. *Relics of Death in Victorian Literature and Culture.* Cambridge UP, 2015.

MacDuffie, Allen. *Victorian Literature, Energy, and the Ecological Imagination.* Cambridge UP, 2014.

Macnie, John. *The Diothas: or, A Far Look Ahead.* New York: G. P. Putnam's Sons, 1883.

Malchow, H. L. "Frankenstein's Monster and Images of Race in Nineteenth-century Britain." *Past and Present,* no. 139, May 1993, pp. 90–130.

Mangham, Andrew. *Dickens's Forensic Realism: Truth, Bodies, Evidence.* Kindle ed., The Ohio State UP, 2016.

Manifesto of the V21 Collective. 2015. http://v21collective.org/manifesto-of-the-v21-collective-ten-theses/.

Markovits, Stefanie. *The Victorian Verse-Novel: Aspiring to Life.* Oxford UP, 2017.

Marsh, Joss. "Spectacle." *A Companion to Victorian Literature and Culture,* edited by Herbert F. Tucker, Blackwell Publishing, 1999, pp. 276–88.

Martens, Britta. "'Knight, Bard, Gallant': The Troubadour as a Critique of Romanticism in Browning's *Sordello.*" *Beyond Arthurian Romances: The Reach of Victorian Medievalism,* edited by Loretta M. Holloway and Jennifer A. Palmgren, Palgrave Macmillan, 2005, pp. 39–51.

Martin, Amy E. *Alter-Nations: Nationalisms, Terror, and the State in Nineteenth-century Britain and Ireland.* The Ohio State UP, 2012.

———. "'The Skeleton at the Feast': Lady Wilde's Famine Poetry and Irish Internationalist Critiques of Food Scarcity." *Women and the Great Hunger,* edited by Christine Kinealy, Jason King, and Ciarán Reilly, Cork UP, 2016, pp. 149–60.

Martin, Daniel. "'Some Trick of the Moonlight': Seduction and the Moving Image in Bram Stoker's *Dracula.*" *Victorian Literature and Culture,* vol. 40, 2012, pp. 523–47.

McAteer, Michael. *Standish O'Grady, A.E., and Yeats: History, Politics, Culture.* Irish Academic Press, 2002.

McCarthy, Anne C. *Awful Paralysis: Suspension and the Sublime in Romantic and Victorian Poetry.* U of Toronto P, 2018.

McCray, J. Louise. "Novel-Reading, Ethics, and William Godwin in the 1830s." *Studies in Romanticism,* vol. 59, no. 2, Summer 2020, pp. 209–30.

McKinsey, Martin. "Counter-Homericism in Yeats's 'The Wanderings of Oisin.'" *W. B. Yeats and Postcolonialism,* edited by Deborah Fleming, Locust Press, 2001, pp. 235–51.

Menke, Richard. *Telegraphic Realism: Victorian Fictions and Other Information Systems.* Stanford UP, 2008.

Mellor, Anne K. *Mary Shelley: Her Life, Her Fiction, Her Monsters.* Routledge, 1990.

Miller, J. Hillis. "The Fiction of Realism: *Sketches by Boz, Oliver Twist,* and Cruikshank's Illustrations," *Victorian Subjects,* Duke UP, 1991, pp. 119–78.

———. *The Medium Is the Maker: Browning, Freud, Derrida and the New Telepathic Ecotechnologies*. Sussex Academic Press, 2009.

Miller, Sidney. "How Not to Improve the Estate: Lopping and Cropping Jane Austen." *Studies in the Novel*, vol. 49, no. 4, Winter 2017, pp. 431–52.

Mills-Courts, Karen. *Poetry as Epitaph: Representation and Poetic Language*. Louisiana State UP, 1990.

Milner, H. M. *Frankenstein; or the Man and the Monster!* Reprinted in Forry, pp. 187–204.

Mitchell, Susan. "Preface." *An Egyptian in Ireland*, by Ibrahim Rashad, privately printed for the author, 1920, pp. ix–xii.

Mitchell, Timothy. *Colonising Egypt*. U of California P, 1991.

"Modern Discoveries—The Electric Light," *Leicester Chronicle / Leicester Mercury*, Sat., 26 Oct. 1878.

Moers, Ellen. "Female Gothic." *The Endurance of "Frankenstein": Essays on Mary Shelley's Novel*, edited by George Levine and U. C. Knoepflmacher, U of California P, 1979, pp. 77–87.

Mole, Tom. *What the Victorians Made of Romanticism: Material Artifacts, Cultural Practices, and Reception History*. Princeton UP, 2017.

Morash, Chris. "'Even Under Some Unnatural Condition': Bram Stoker and the Colonial Fantastic." *Literature and the Supernatural: Essays for the Maynooth Bicentenary*, edited by Brian Cosgrove, Columba Press, 1995, pp. 95–119.

Morus, Iwan Rhys. "Radicals, Romantics and Electrical Showmen: Placing Galvanism at the End of the English Enlightenment." *Notes and Records of the Royal Society*, vol. 63, 2009, pp. 263–75.

———. *Shocking Bodies: Life, Death and Electricity in Victorian England*. History Press, 2011.

Moses, Michael Valdez. "The Irish Vampire: Dracula, Parnell, and The Troubled Dreams of Nationhood." *Journal X*, vol. 2, no. 1, 1997, pp. 66–111.

Moynahan, Julian. *Anglo-Irish: The Literary Imagination in a Hyphenated Culture*. Princeton UP, 1995.

Mullen, Mary. *Novel Institutions: Anachronism, Irish Novels, and Nineteenth-century Realism*. Edinburgh UP, 2019.

Mulvey-Roberts, Marie. "Mashing Up Jane Austen: *Pride and Prejudice and Zombies* and the Limits of Adaptation." *The Irish Journal of Gothic and Horror Studies*, vol. 13, Summer 2014, pp. 17–37.

Murphy, James H. *Abject Loyalty: Nationalism and Loyalty in Ireland During the Reign of Queen Victoria*. Catholic U of America P, 2001.

Nazarian, Vera, and Jane Austen. *Mansfield Park and Mummies*. Norilana Books, 2009.

Neville-Sington, Pamela. *Robert Browning: A Life After Death*. Weidenfeld & Nicolson, 2004.

Niemann, Michelle. "Browning's Critique of Organic Form in *The Ring and the Book*." *Victorian Poetry*, vol. 52, no. 3, Fall 2014, pp. 445–64.

Nolan, Emer. *James Joyce and Nationalism*. Routledge, 1995.

Norman, Brian. *Dead Women Talking: Figures of Injustice in American Literature*. Johns Hopkins UP, 2013.

Novak, Daniel. *Realism, Photography, and Nineteenth-century Fiction*. Cambridge UP, 2008.

O'Gorman, Francis. "Browning, Grief, and the Strangeness of Dramatic Verse." *The Cambridge Quarterly*, vol. 36, no. 2, 2007, pp. 155–73.

O'Grady, Hugh Art. *Standish James O'Grady, the Man and the Writer*. Talbot Press, 1929.

O'Grady, Standish. *History of Ireland: Critical and Philosophical,* vol. 1. London: Sampson Low & Co., 1881.

———. *History of Ireland,* vols. 1 and 2. London: Sampson Low, Marston, Searle, & Rivington, 1878, 1880.

———. *"The Irish Worker,"* 26 Oct. 1912. *To the Leaders of Our Working People,* edited by Edward O'Hagan, U College Dublin P, 2002, pp. 23–28.

———. "The Making of Nations," MS p. 133, collection that would become *Render to Caesar—Social Essays,* Standish O'Grady Papers, TCD MS 11534.

———. "Nature." *Sun and Wind,* edited by Edward O'Hagan, U College Dublin P, 2004, pp. 37–52.

———. Papers, Trinity College Dublin, TCD MS 11534.

———. "Walt Whitman." *Standish O'Grady: Selected Essays and Passages,* introduction by Ernest A. Boyd, Talbot Press, 1918, pp. 269–90.

O'Malley, Patrick. *Liffey and Lethe: Paramnesiac History in Nineteenth-century Anglo-Ireland.* Oxford UP, 2017.

———. "'She interest me too': Teaching Gender and Sexuality in *Dracula.*" *MLA Approaches to Teaching World Literature: Approaches to Teaching Stoker's "Dracula,"* edited by William Thomas McBride, Modern Language Association, forthcoming 2024.

Open-Eye. "The Wild Man of the Prairies: To the Editor of the *Times.*" *The Times,* Tues., 1 Sept. 1846, p. 6.

Orr, Alexandra Sutherland. *Life and Letters of Robert Browning.* New ed., revised and in part rewritten by Frederic G. Kenyon, Smith, Elder & Co, 1908.

Owen, Alex. *The Darkened Room: Women, Power and Spiritualism in Late Victorian England.* U of Pennsylvania P, 1990.

Parry, H. G. *The Unlikely Escape of Uriah Heep.* Redhook Books, 2019.

Peake, Richard Brinsley. *Another Piece of Presumption.* 1823. Reprinted in Forry, pp. 161–76.

———. *Presumption; or, the Fate of Frankenstein.* 1823. Reprinted in Forry, pp. 135–60.

Pearse, Susan. *On Collecting: An Investigation into Collecting in the European Tradition.* Routledge, 1995.

Peltz, Lucy, and Martin Myrone, editors. *Producing the Past: Aspects of Antiquarian Culture and Practice 1700–1850.* Ashgate Press, 2018.

Pethica, James. "Yeats, Folklore, and Irish Legend." *The Cambridge Companion to W. B. Yeats,* edited by Marjorie Howes and John Kelly, Cambridge UP, 2006, pp. 129–43.

Porter, Bernard. *The Lion's Share: A Short History of British Imperialism 1850–1995.* Longman, 1996.

Price, Leah. *The Anthology and the Rise of the Novel: From Richardson to George Eliot.* Cambridge UP, 2000.

Puckett, Kent. "Response to the V21 Manifesto." 2015. http://v21collective.org/responses-to-the-v21-manifesto/#response1.

"Punch on the Galvanic Ring." *Punch, or the London Charivari,* vol. 8, Sat., 12 Apr. 1845, p. 167.

Punter, David. *The Literature of Terror: A History of Gothic Fictions from 1765 to the Present Day.* 2nd ed., Longman, 1996.

Ramazani, Jahan. *The Hybrid Muse: Postcolonial Poetry in English.* U of Chicago P, 2001.

———. *Yeats and the Death of Elegy.* Yale UP, 1990.

Ramirez, Luz Elena. "The Intelligibility of the Past in Bram Stoker's *The Jewel of Seven Stars.*" *Victorian Literary Culture and Ancient Egypt,* edited by Eleanor Dobson, Manchester UP, 2020, pp. 185–206.

Rance, Caroline. *The Quack Doctor: Historical Medical Remedies for All Your Ills.* History Press, 2013.

Rashad, Ibrahim. *An Egyptian in Ireland.* Privately printed for the author, 1920.

Rast, M. C. "'Ireland's Sister Nations': Internationalism and Sectarianism in the Irish Struggle for Independence, 1916–22." *Journal of Global History,* vol. 10, 2015, pp. 479–501.

Reed, John. R. *Dickens's Hyperrealism.* The Ohio State UP, 2010.

Reisner, Gavriel. "Ghosted Images to Ancestral Stories: Spectres and Narrators in Dickens' *Great Expectations.*" *American Imago,* vol. 76, no. 2, Summer 2019, pp. 223–49.

Responses to the V21 Manifesto. 2015. http://v21collective.org/responses-to-the-v21-manifesto/.

Review of *Frankenstein. The British Critic,* N.S., vol. 9, Apr. 1818, pp. 432–38.

Review of *Frankenstein. The Literary Panorama, and National Register,* N.S., vol. 8, 1 June 1818, pp. 411–14.

Review of *The Ring and the Book. St. Paul's Magazine,* vol. 7, Jan. 1871, p. 397.

Review of *The Ring and the Book. The Times,* Fri., 11 June 1869, p. 4.

Review of *The Ring and the Book. Fortnightly Review,* vol. 5, no. 25, Jan. 1869, p. 125.

Richards, Michael R. "Pope, Chapman, and the Romantics." *Keats-Shelley Journal,* vol. 29, 1980, pp. 11–21.

Richter, David. "Reader-Response Criticism." *The Critical Tradition: Classic Texts and Contemporary Trends,* edited by David H. Richter, Bedford Books, 1998, pp. 917–33.

Riskin, Jessica. "The Defecating Duck, or the Ambiguous Origins of Artificial Life." *Critical Inquiry,* vol. 29, no. 4, Summer 2003, pp. 599–633.

Roberts, Adam. "Browning, the Dramatic Monologue, and the Resuscitation of the Dead." *The Victorian Supernatural,* edited by Nicola Bown, Carolyn Burdett, and Pamela Thurschwell, Cambridge UP, 2004, pp. 109–27.

Robinson, Charles E. "Mary Shelley and the Roger Dodsworth Hoax." *Keats-Shelley Journal,* vol. 24, 1975, pp. 20–28.

Rodwell, G. F. "On the Perception of the Invisible." *Macmillan's Magazine,* vol. 30, 1 May 1874, pp. 342–50.

Rossetti, Christina. *Time Flies: A Reading Diary.* Society for Promoting Christian Knowledge, 1885.

Rossetti, Dante Gabriel. "The Burden of Nineveh." *Victorian Poetry: An Annotated Anthology,* edited by Francis O'Gorman, Blackwell Publishing, 2004, pp. 350–56.

———. *The Letters of Dante Gabriel Rossetti to William Allingham, 1854–1870.* London: T. Fisher Unwin, 1897.

Rossetti, Michael William. *The Poetical Works of Percy Bysshe Shelley: including various additional pieces from ms. and other sources / The text carefully revised, with notes and a memoir, by William Michael Rossetti.* London: E. Moxon, Son, & Co., 1870.

Roth, Phyllis. "'The Jewel of Seven Stars'; Bram Stoker." *The Critical Response to Bram Stoker,* edited by Carol A. Senf, Greenwood Press, 1993, pp. 111–17.

Royle, Nicholas. "Our Mutual Friend." *Dickens Refigured: Bodies, Desires and Other Histories,* edited by John Schad, Manchester UP, 1996, pp. 39–54.

Rudy, Jason R. *Electric Meters: Victorian Physiological Poetics.* Ohio UP, 2009.

Ryan, Frederick. "Ireland and Egypt." *The Irish Nation,* 25 Sept. 1909; reprinted in pamphlet for the Irish Labour History Workshop, edited by Manus O'Riordan, Oct. 1984.

———. "The Spoil of Egypt—A Sordid Story of Modern Empire-Building" (a review of *Egypt's Ruin—A Financial and Administrative Record,* by Theodore Rothstein, with an Introduction by W. S. Blunt)," *The Irish Nation,* 10 Dec. 1910; reprinted in pamphlet for the Irish Labour History Workshop, edited by Manus O'Riordan, Oct. 1984.

Said, Edward. *Culture and Imperialism.* Vintage Books, 1993.

Saintsbury, George. *A History of English Prosody.* Macmillan, 1923.

Santayana, George. *Reason in Society,* vol. 1 of *The Life of Reason: The Phases of Human Progress.* Charles Scribner's Sons, 1905.

Schaffer, Talia. "Response to the V21 Manifesto." 2015. http://v21collective.org/responses-to-the-v21-manifesto/#response2.

Schmidt, Cannon. "Mother Dracula: Orientalism, Degeneration, and Anglo-Irish Subjectivity at the Fin-de-Siècle." *Bucknell Review,* vol. 38, no. 1, 1994, pp. 25–43.

Schor, Hilary M. *Curious Subjects: Women and the Trials of Realism.* Oxford UP, 2013.

Scott, Sir Walter. *The Antiquary.* Vol. 5 of The *Waverley* Novels, introductory essay and notes by Andrew Lang, London: John C. Nimmo, 1893.

——. "Dedicatory Epistle to the Rev. Doctor Dryasdust." *Ivanhoe.* Boston: Ticknor and Fields, 1866.

——. "Remarks on Frankenstein, or the Modern Prometheus; A Novel." *Blackwood's Edinburgh Magazine,* vol. 2, Mar. 1818, pp. 613–20.

Sedgwick, Eve Kosofsky. *Touching Feeling: Affect, Pedagogy, Performativity.* Duke UP, 2003.

Seeley, J. R. "History and Politics [I]." *Macmillan's Magazine,* vol. 40, no. 238, Aug. 1879, pp. 289–99.

Sexton, Thomas. "Ireland—Science and Art Museum, Dublin." *Hansard Commons (Hansard Online),* vol 275, col. 470, Dec. 1, 1882, https://hansard.parliament.uk/Commons/1882-12-01/debates/1bdd8a85-71b0-42ff-8bdf-c5928b75e839/ScienceAndArtDepartment—NewCentralMuseumDublin.

Sheehy-Skeffington, Francis. *Michael Davitt: Revolutionary, Agitator and Labour Leader.* D. Estes, 1909.

Shelley, Mary. *The Fortunes of Perkin Warbeck: A Romance.* London: G. Routledge and Co., 1857.

——. *Frankenstein.* Edited by D. L. Macdonald and Kathleen Scherf, Broadview Press, 2012.

——. "Introduction to Shelley's 1831 Edition." *Frankenstein,* edited by D. L. Macdonald and Kathleen Scherf, Broadview Press, 2012, pp. 347–52.

——. "Letter to Leigh Hunt, 9 September (11 September) 1823." *The Mary Shelley Reader,* edited by Betty T. Bennett and Charles E. Robinson, Oxford UP, 1990, pp. 404–5.

——. "Letter to [John Murray III], 8 September 1830." *The Mary Shelley Reader,* edited by Betty T. Bennett and Charles E. Robinson, Oxford UP, 1990, p. 409.

——. "Modern Italy (1829)." *The Mary Shelley Reader,* edited by Betty T. Bennett and Charles E. Robinson, Oxford UP, 1990, pp. 358–64.

——. "Note on Prometheus Unbound." *The Poetical Works of Percy Bysshe Shelley,* 3 vols., edited by Mary Wollstonecraft Shelley, London: Edward Moxon, 1847, pp. 1:367–76.

——. "On Ghosts." *The Mary Shelley Reader,* edited by Betty T. Bennett and Charles E. Robinson, Oxford UP, 1990, pp. 334–40.

——. "Preface." *The Poetical Works of Percy Bysshe Shelley,* 3 vols., edited by Mary Wollstonecraft Shelley, London: Edward Moxon, 1847, pp. 1:vii–xiv.

——. "Roger Dodsworth: The Reanimated Englishman." *Mary Shelley: Collected Tales and Stories,* edited by Charles E. Robinson, Johns Hopkins UP, 1976, pp. 43–50.

——. "Valerius: The Reanimated Roman." *Mary Shelley: Collected Tales and Stories,* edited by Charles E. Robinson, Johns Hopkins UP, 1976, pp. 332–44.

Shelley, Percy Bysshe. "A Defence of Poetry." *The Major Works*, edited by Zachary Leader and Michael O'Neill, Oxford UP, 2003, pp. 674–701.

———. *The Poetical Works of Percy Bysshe Shelley*, 3 vols. Edited by Mary Wollstonecraft Shelley, London: Edward Moxon, 1847.

———. "The Triumph of Life." *The Major Works*, edited by Zachary Leader and Michael O'Neill, Oxford UP, 2003, pp. 604–21.

Siegel, Jonah. *The Haunted Museum: Longing, Travel, and the Art-Romance Tradition.* Princeton UP, 2005.

Silyn Roberts, Siân. *Gothic Subjects: The Transformation of Individualism in American Literature, 1790–1861.* U of Pennsylvania P, 2014.

Simon, Leslie. "*Bleak House, Our Mutual Friend,* and the Aesthetics of Dust." *Dickens Studies Annual,* vol. 42, 2011, pp. 217–36.

Smajic, Srdjan. *Ghost-seers, Detectives, and Spiritualists: Theories of Vision in Victorian Literature and Science.* Cambridge UP, 2010.

Smith, Adam. *The Theory of Moral Sentiments.* Edited by Knud Haakonssen, Cambridge UP, 2002.

Smith, Alan Lloyd. "'This Thing of Darkness': Racial Discourse in Mary Shelley's Frankenstein." *Gothic Studies,* vol. 6, no. 2, Nov. 2004, pp. 208–22.

Smyth, Gerry. "Irish Literary Criticism During the Irish Revival." *1880–1940,* vol. 4 of *Irish Literature in Transition,* edited by Marjorie Howes, Cambridge UP, 2020, pp. 339–55.

Soares, Rebecca. "Morbid Curiosity and Monstrous (Re)Visions: Zombies, Sea Monsters, and Readers (Re)Writing Jane Austen." *Women's Writing,* vol. 25, no. 4, 2018, pp. 449–42.

Stead, W. T. "Looking Forward: A Romance of the Electric Age." *Science as Romance,* edited by Ralph O'Connor, vol. 7 of *Victorian Science and Literature,* Pickering & Chatto, 2012, pp. 331–60.

Stewart, Garrett. *Dickens and the Trials of the Imagination.* Harvard UP, 1974.

Stewart, Susan. *On Longing: Narratives of the Miniature, the Gigantic, the Souvenir, the Collection.* Duke UP, 1993.

Stiles, Anne. *Popular Fiction and Brain Science in the Late Nineteenth Century.* Cambridge UP, 2012.

Stoker, Bram. "The Burial of the Rats." *Dracula's Guest and Other Weird Tales,* edited by Kate Hebblethwaite, Penguin Books, 2007, pp. 93–117.

———. *Dracula.* Edited by Andrew Elfenbein, Longman Books, 2011.

———. *The Dublin Years: The Lost Journal of Bram Stoker.* Edited by Elizabeth Miller and Dacre Stoker, Robson Press, 2012.

———. *The Jewel of Seven Stars.* Alan Sutton Publishing, 1996.

———. "The Necessity of Political Honesty." Address delivered at Trinity College, 12 Nov. 1872; reprinted in Bram Stoker, *A Glimpse of America and Other Lectures, Interviews, and Essays,* edited by Richard Dalby, Desert Island Books, 2002, pp. 31–49.

———. "The Question of a National Theatre." *Nineteenth Century and After,* May 1908; reprinted in Bram Stoker, *A Glimpse of America and Other Lectures, Interviews, and Essays,* edited by Richard Dalby, Desert Island Books, 2002, pp. 75–83.

Stott, George. "Charles Dickens." *Contemporary Review,* vol. 10, Jan. 1869, pp. 203–25.

Stryker, Susan. "My Words to Victor Frankenstein above the Village of Chamounix: Performing Transgender Rage." *The Transgender Studies Reader,* edited by Susan Stryker and Stephen White, Routledge, 2006, pp. 244–56.

Sutherland, John. "How Does Victor Make His Monsters?" *Is Heathcliff a Murderer? Puzzles in Nineteenth-century Fiction.* Oxford UP, 1996, pp. 24–34.

Taylor, Jesse Oak. "Tennyson's Elegy for the Anthropocene: Genre, Form, and Species Being." *Victorian Studies,* vol. 58, no. 2, Winter 2016, pp. 224–33.

Tchernichova, Viktoria. "Browning's Regeneration of the Old Yellow Book." *RSV: Rivista di Studi Vittoriani,* vols. 15–16, nos. 30–31, July 2010–Jan. 2011, pp. 105–32.

Tennyson, Alfred (Lord). *Tennyson's Poetry: A Norton Critical Edition.* Edited by Robert W. Hill Jr., W. W. Norton, 1999.

Tracy, Robert. "Loving You All Ways: Vamps, Vampires, Necrophiles and Necrofilles in Nineteenth-century Fiction." *Sex and Death in Victorian Literature,* edited by Regina Barreca, Palgrave Macmillan, 1990, pp. 32–59.

Tromp, Marlene. *Altered States: Nation, Drugs, and Self-Transformation in Victorian Spiritualism.* State U of New York P, 2006.

Tucker, Herbert F. "The Dramatic Monologue and the Overhearing of Lyric." *Lyric Poetry Beyond New Criticism,* edited by Chavia Hosek, Patricia Parker, and Jonathan Arac, Cornell UP, 1985, pp. 226–43.

———. "Memorabilia: Mnemonic Imagination in Shelley and Browning." *Studies in Romanticism,* vol. 19, Fall 1980, pp. 285–325.

———. "Wanted Dead or Alive: Browning's Historicism." *Victorian Studies,* vol. 38, no. 1, Autumn 1994, pp. 25–39.

"The Universality of Electricity." *Punch, or the London Charivari,* vol. 35, Sat., 23 Oct. 1858, p. 165.

Ure, Andrew. "An Account of Some Experiments Made on the Body of a Criminal Immediately After Execution, with Physiological and Practical Observations." *The Journal of Science and the Arts,* vol. 4, no. 12, 1819, pp. 283–94.

Valente, Joseph. *Dracula's Crypt: Bram Stoker, Irishness, and the Question of Blood.* U of Illinois P, 2002.

———. *The Myth of Manliness in Irish National Culture, 1880–1922.* U of Illinois P, 2011.

Valéry, Paul. "The Problem of Museums." *Degas Manet Morisot,* translated by David Paul, introduction by Douglas Cooper, Princeton UP, 1989, pp. 202–6.

Valli, Eusebio. *Experiments on Animal Electricity, with their Application to Physiology, and some Pathological and Medical Observations.* J. Johnson, St. Paul's Churchyard, 1793.

Van Ghent, Dorothy. "The Dickens World: A View from Todgers's." *Sewanee Review,* vol. 58, 1950, pp. 419–38.

"Voting by Electricity." *Punch, or the London Charivari,* vol. 58, Sat., 12 Feb. 1870, p. 64.

Waits, Robert K. "Gustave Flaubert, Charles Dickens, and Isaac Pulvermacher's 'Magic Band.'" *Progress in Brain Research,* vol. 205, 2013, pp. 219–39.

Walpole, Horace. *The Castle of Otranto* and *The Man of Feeling* (by Henry Mackenzie). Edited by Laura Mandell, Longman, 2007.

Walton, Kendall L. *Mimesis as Make-Believe: On the Foundations of the Representational Arts.* Harvard UP, 1990.

Watson, George. "Yeats, Victorianism, and the 1890s." *The Cambridge Companion to W. B. Yeats,* edited by Marjorie Howes and John Kelly, Cambridge UP, 2006, pp. 36–58.

Whidden, James. *Egypt: British Colony, Imperial Capital.* Manchester UP, 2019.

White, Hayden. *Metahistory: The Historical Imagination in Nineteenth-century Europe.* The Johns Hopkins UP, 1973.

Wicke, Jennifer. "Vampiric Typewriting: *Dracula* and Its Media." *ELH*, vol. 59, no. 52, Summer 1992, pp. 467–93.

Wilde, Lady Jane (Speranza). *Poems*. Dublin: J. Duffy, 1864.

———. *Poems*. 2nd ed., London: Cameron and Ferguson, 1871.

Wilde, William. *The Beauties of the Boyne, and Its Tributary, the Blackwater*. London: James McGlashan, 1849.

———. *Narrative of a voyage to Madeira, Teneriffe and along the shores of the Mediterranean, including a visit to Algiers, Egypt, Palestine, Tyre, Rhodes, Telmessus, Cyprus and Greece. With observations on the present state and prospects of Egypt and Palestine, and on the climate, natural history, antiquities, etc, of the countries visited*. Dublin: W. Curry, Jun. and Company, 1840.

Winters, Ben H. "I Write with Dead People: How to Collaborate with a Corpse." *HuffPost*, 18 Mar. 2010, updated 25 May 2011, https://www.huffpost.com/entry/i-write-with-dead-people_b_347365.

Wolfreys, Julian. *Victorian Hauntings: Spectrality, Gothic, the Uncanny and Literature*. Palgrave, 2002.

"Wonderful and Horrible Effects of Galvanism." *The Odd Fellow*, no. 138, Sat., 21 Aug. 1841, p. 136.

"Wonders and Curiosities of the Electric Telegraph." *Australian Journal*, no. 103, Mon., 1 Dec. 1873, pp. 223–26.

Wood, Claire. *The Business of Death in Victorian Literature*. Cambridge UP, 2015.

Wood, Gillen D'Arcy. *The Shock of the Real: Romanticism and Visual Culture, 1760–1860*. Palgrave, 2001.

Woolford, John. "Browning Rethinks Romanticism." *Essays in Criticism*, vol. 43, no. 3, July 1993, p. 211–27.

———. "The Romantic Brownings." *Studies in Browning and His Circle*, vol. 24, June 2001, pp. 7–30.

Yeats, W. B. *Autobiographies*. Vol. 3 of *The Collected Works of W. B. Yeats*, edited by William H. O'Donnell and Douglas N. Archibald, Scribner, 1999.

———. *The Autobiography of William Butler Yeats, Consisting of Reveries Over Childhood and Youth, The Trembling of the Veil, and Dramatis Personae*. Collier Books, 1965.

———. "The Body of the Father Christian Rosencrux." *Ideas of Good and Evil*. A. H. Bullen, 1903, pp. 308–11.

———, editor. *A Book of Irish Verse, selected from modern writers*. Introduction and notes by W. B. Yeats, London: Methuen and Co., 1895.

———. "The Celtic Element in Literature." 1897. *Early Essays*, vol. 4 of *The Complete Works of W. B. Yeats*, edited by Richard J. Finneran and George Bornstein, Simon and Schuster, 2007, pp. 128–38.

———. *The Celtic Twilight*. Introduction by Kathleen Raine, illustrated by Jean Townsend, Colin Smythe, 1981.

———. *The Collected Poems of W. B. Yeats*. Edited by Richard J. Finneran, Simon and Schuster, 1996.

———. "Edmund Spenser." 1902. *Early Essays*, vol. 4 of *The Collected Works of W. B. Yeats*, edited by Richard J. Finneran and George Bornstein, Simon and Schuster, 1989, pp. 257–76.

———, editor. *Fairy and Folk Tales of Ireland*. Foreword by Benedict Kiely, Simon and Schuster, 1998.

———. "Introduction" to Lady Augusta Gregory, *Cuchulain of Muirthemne: The Story of the Men of the Red Branch of Ulster.* J. Murray, 1911.

———, editor. *Irish Fairy Tales.* Illustrated by Jack B. Yeats, London: T. Fisher Unwin, 1892.

———. *The Letters of W. B. Yeats.* Edited by Allan Wade, Macmillan, 1955.

———. "The Philosophy of Shelley's Poetry." *Early Essays,* vol. 4. of *The Collected Works of W. B. Yeats,* edited by Richard J. Finneran and George Bornstein, Simon and Schuster, 2007, pp. 51–72.

———. *Representative Irish Tales.* Compiled and with an introduction and notes by W. B. Yeats and a forward by Mary Helen Thuente, Humanities Press, 1979.

———. *Samhain,* Oct. 1902; reprinted in *Samhain: October 1901–November 1908,* Routledge (Routledge Revivals), 1970.

———. *A Speech and Two Poems.* Sign of the Three Candles, Dec. 1937.

———. *Uncollected Prose by W. B. Yeats,* vol. 1. Edited by John B. Frayne, Columbia UP, 1970.

———. "The Wanderings of Oisin." *The Poems: Second Edition,* edited by Richard J. Finneran, Scribner, 1997, pp. 361–91.

Young, Elizabeth. *Black Frankenstein: The Making of an American Metaphor.* New York UP, 2008.

Youngkin, Molly. *British Women Writers and the Reception of Ancient Egypt, 1840–1910.* Palgrave, 2016.

Zakharieva, Bouriana. "Frankenstein of the Nineties: The Composite Body." *Canadian Review of Comparative Literature,* vol. 23, no. 3, Sept. 1996, pp. 739–52.

Zigarovich, Jolene. "Epitaphic Representation in Dickens's *Our Mutual Friend.*" *Dickens Studies Annual,* vol. 43, 2012, pp. 141–67.

Zimmerman, Virginia. *Excavating Victorians.* State U of New York P, 2008.

INDEX

À la recherche du temps perdu (Proust), 142–43

Adorno, Theodor, 142–43

A.E., 234n2

Aldini, Giovanni, 24–27

Ali, Mohammed, 196

Allingham, William, 112, 232n2

amanuensis, 115

animism, 87–88, 230n13

Another Piece of Presumption (Peake), 69–72

Antiquary, The (Scott), 65

"Appeal to Ireland, An" (J. Wilde), 225n7

Arabi, Ahmed, 196

Arata, Stephen, 183

Arnold, Edwin, 152

Arnold, Matthew, 139

Aurora Leigh (Barrett Browning), 117–19

Austen, Jane, 41

Auyoung, Elaine, 81

Babylon Electrified (Bleunard), 232n27

Baldick, Chris, 90, 231n16

Barrett Browning, Elizabeth, 114–19, 233nn13–14, 233n16, 234n36

Barthes, Roland, 14, 136

Battle of Magh-Rath, The (O'Donovan), 235n30

Bazin, Germain, 161

Beauties of the Boyne, The (W. Wilde), 159–60, 238n31

Belford, Barbara, 198

Bellamy, Edward, 232n27

Benjamin, Walter, 32

Best, Stephen, 217, 221

Betensky, Carolyn, 229n32

Binyon, Laurence, 152–53, 236n34

Biographia Literaria (Coleridge), 45

Black, Barbara, 145, 235n13, 235n18

Black Africans, 229n32

Blagden, Isa, 115, 233n14, 233n21

Bleak House (Dickens), 82–83

Bleunard, Albert, 232n27

Blunt, Wilfred Scawen, 197

bodies. *See* corpse(s)

Bornstein, George, 163–64

262 • INDEX

Boswell, John Whitley, 195

Boucicault, Dion, 7

Boyd, Ernest, 226n27

Branagh, Kenneth, 77

Brinkema, Eugenie, 228n3

British Museum, 138–40, 146, 148–49, 152–53, 155

Bronfen, Elisabeth, 6, 9

Brooks, Mel, 38–39

Brooks, Peter, 230n1

Brough, Barnabas, 72–76

Brough, Richard, 72–76

Brown, Wendy, 4

Browning, Robert, 101–2, 232nn1–2, 233n21. *See also* "Essay on Shelley" (Browning); "Memorabilia" (Browning); *Men and Women* (Browning); "My Last Duchess" (Browning); "Porphyria's Lover" (Browning); *Ring and the Book, The* (Browning); "To a Skylark" (P. Shelley)

Budge, E. A. Wallis, 198

Bullock, William, 193

"Burden of Nineveh, The" (Rossetti), 143–48, 202

"Burial of the Rats, The" (Stoker), 199

Burke, Edmund, 21, 52, 68–69

Burton, Richard Francis, 198

Byron, Lord, 7, 44, 48

camp, 10–11, 213

Campbell, Matthew, 119

Carleton, William, 154

Carlyle, Thomas, 18, 31–33, 112, 114, 226n30, 232nn2–3

Castle, Gregory, 22, 154, 180

Castle of Otranto, The (Walpole), 65–66

Cathleen ni Houlihan (Yeats), 191, 213

"Cenci, The" (P. Shelley), 233n19

Chemers, Michael, 67

Christ, Carol, 6

"Christmas in the Elgin Room" (Hardy), 151–53

Citton, Yves, 219

Clark, Samuel, 194

Clay, Henry, 229n27

Cleopatra (Haggard), 237n12

Cleopatra's Needle, 198

Clifford, James, 202

Cohn, Elisha, 109, 232n30

Coleridge, Samuel Taylor, 44–45, 228n8

colonialism, 180, 183, 194, 201, 215. *See also* imperialism

Coming Race, The (Lytton), 232n27

Comyn, Michael, 166

Conan Doyle, Arthur, 7, 218, 237n12, 238n37

Cook, James W., Jr., 229n29

Cooke, T. P., 67

corpse(s): in Browning, 123–24, 128–29; in Dickens, 79–81, 85–87, 96–101; electricity and, 3; in Hardy, 151; Ireland as, 3; in M. Shelley, 40–42, 49, 52, 63–78; poetry and, 113–14; readability and, 4; in Rossetti, 144, 148–49; stories and, as interchangeable, 4

Crabbe, George, 217

Craft, Christopher, 188

Crimmins, Jonathan, 13

Crooke, Elizabeth, 158

Cuculain, 18, 20, 163

cultural appropriation, 23, 147, 149, 164, 180, 183, 199, 213

Daly, Nicholas, 202, 205

Darwin, Erasmus, 45

David Copperfield (Dickens), 231n26

Davitt, Michael, 196

Day, Jasmine, 201

dead bodies. *See* corpse(s)

Dead Women Talking (Norman), 8

Deane, Seamus, 156, 172, 212

"Death and the Antiquaries" (Rowlandson), 14

Delbruck, Hans, 38

Dickens, Charles, 28–29, 81–84, 97–98, 230n9. See also *Bleak House* (Dickens); *David Copperfield* (Dickens); *Great Expectations* (Dickens); *Hard Times* (Dickens); *Household Words* (Dickens); *Oliver Twist* (Dickens); *Our Mutual Friend* (Dickens); *Sketches by Boz* (Dickens)

Dillon, John, 207

Diothas, The (Macnie), 232n27

Dodsworth, Roger, 57. *See also* "Roger Dodsworth, the Reanimated Englishman" (M. Shelley)

Dracula (Stoker), 177, 182–91, 200–201

Duncan, Ian, 13, 52, 97, 231n24

Dying Modern (Fuss), 109

Egypt, 193–97, 210–11, 237n25. *See also Jewel of Seven Stars, The* (Stoker)

Egyptian in Ireland, An (Mitchell), 210–11

electricity: animal, 24–27; Burke and, 68–69; in Carlyle, 31–33; as cure-all, 232n27; in Dickens, 99–110, 231n26; in Doyle, 238n37; in "Essay on Shelley," 119–20; in *Frankenstein,* 2, 46–47, 67–68; galvanism and, 24–33, 99–110, 227n60, 228n64, 231n26; as instrument vs. energy, 30–32; in J. Wilde, 2–4; medicine and, 28–30; poetry and, 3; reanimation and, 3, 24–26; resuscitation and, 3, 31–32; in *The Ring and the Book,* 46, 128–29; as supernatural, 31

Elgin Marbles, 149, 151. *See also* Parthenon Marbles

epitaphic realism, 34, 81–82, 86–87, 93, 95

"Essay on Shelley" (Browning), 113, 119–27, 136

Fairy and Folk Tales of the Irish Peasantry (Yeats), 140, 161, 165–67, 172

"Fairy Doctor, The" (Yeats), 160–61

"Famine Year, The" (J. Wilde), 2

Felski, Rita, 11, 215–17, 219

femininity, 109–10, 185–86, 192, 203–6

Fielding, Henry, 85

Flower, William Henry, 236n39

Fortunes of Perkin Warbeck, The (M. Shelley), 59–61, 226n37

Frankenstein (M. Shelley), 5, 7; adaptations of, 20, 38–39, 67–78; creature in, 43–44, 66–68, 228n6, 228n10; Dickens and, 90–92, 95–96; electricity in, 2, 46–47, 67–68; Freeman on, 41–42; ghosts and, 42–43; historical imagination and, 63–64; historicism in, 13; history and, 21, 38–78; introduction to, 47–48; Ireland and, 19; Prometheus and, 19–20; reanimation in, 39–40, 43–45, 48–49, 63–78, 228n9; resuscitation in, 134; Scott and, 64–66

Frankenstein; or, the Model Man (Brough and Brough), 72–76, 229n27, 229n32

Fraser, Hillary, 134

Freccero, Carla, 9

Freedgood, Elaine, 23, 80, 83, 101

Freeman, Elizabeth, 41–42, 226n36, 228n2

Freud, Sigmund, 228n10

Fried, Debra, 93

Froude, J. A., 33

Fuss, Diana, 109, 113, 234n25

Gallagher, Catherine, 96–97, 105–6, 109, 231n20

Galvani, Luigi, 24, 45, 99

galvanism, 24–33, 99–110, 119–20, 227n60, 228n64, 231n26, 233n19. *See also* electricity

gender, 5–6, 109–10, 185–87, 203. *See also* femininity; masculinity

ghosts, 8–9, 11–12, 42–43, 230n14

Gibbon, Edward, 103–5

Gibbons, Luke, 191

Gigante, Denise, 44–46

Gladstone, William, 237n19

Godwin, William, 21, 57–60, 67, 184

Goode, George Brown, 236n39

Goode, Mike, 6, 50, 52, 56

gothic, 9–11, 41–42, 66, 77, 81, 90, 139, 148–51, 181–83, 191–92, 213, 220

Grahame-Smith, Seth, 221

graveyard, 79–81, 85–88, 94–95

Great Expectations (Dickens), 79–82, 85–96, 106, 230nn13–14, 231n17

Greenblatt, Stephen, 161

Gregory, Lady, 180, 191, 196, 211

Greiner, Rae, 54, 85, 230n11

Griffiths, Devin, 13

grotesque, 81, 84–85, 112, 116

"guilt thesis," 10

Haggard, H. Rider, 7, 237n12

Halberstam, Jack, 10, 229nn24–25

Hard Times (Dickens), 231n26

Hardy, Thomas, 123, 138, 141, 151–53

Harwood, Philip, 134

264 • INDEX

haunting, 9, 11–12, 41–42, 86–87, 138, 230n14

Heffernan, James A. W., 46, 230n33

Henley, W. E., 194

historical imagination: Godwin and, 60; M. Shelley and, 49, 56, 62–64; queer, 60; reanimation and, 2; Stoker and, 182–83, 186–87, 190, 199–200; sympathetic, 56–57; as term, 12; Yeats and, 166, 175, 179

historicism, 13–14, 19–20, 22, 40, 50, 56, 135, 140, 188

historiography, 6, 14, 17, 32–34, 39–42, 49, 52–55, 62–66, 134–35

History of Ireland (O'Grady), 16–17, 22–23, 140, 164

History of the Decline and Fall of the Roman Empire (Gibbon), 103–5

History of the Nineteenth Century (Michelet), 14–15

Hogg, James, 52

Household Words (Dickens), 231n17

Howes, Marjorie, 236n48

Huc, Abbé Everiste, 198

imperialism, 2, 23, 177, 182, 189, 193, 199, 207, 209, 237n18, 239n47. *See also* colonialism

In Search of Lost Time (Proust), 142–43

"In the British Museum" (Binyon), 153

Ireland: as corpse, 3; *Dracula* and, 182–83, 192; Egypt and, 195–97, 210–11, 237n25; *Frankenstein* and, 19; "heroic past" of, 210–11; in J. Wilde, 1–3; *The Jewel of Seven Stars* and, 191–99, 209–10; vampires and, 182–91; Yeats and, 157, 160

Irish Literary Revival, 3, 7, 18, 22–23, 180–81, 190–91, 193, 210, 212, 215

Irish National Museum, 139, 157–62

Iser, Wolfgang, 216–17

Ivanhoe (Scott), 21, 55

James, Henry, 110–11

Jewel of Seven Stars, The (Stoker), 4, 11, 178, 219–20; ending of, 237n1, 239n46; historicism in, 13; imagination in, 177; Irish nationalism and, 191–99, 209–10; reading and, 215–16; reanimation in, 179–81, 205, 213–14; researching of, 197–98; resurrection in, 178, 205, 213; resuscitation in, 178, 190; women and, 199–208, 238n38

Jordan, John O., 230n14

Joyce, James, 7, 180–81

Kasmer, Lisa, 59

Keats, John, 44, 138, 149–50, 235n18

Kennedy, Patrick, 167

Kiberd, Declan, 155–56, 211

Kingsley, Charles, 14, 54–55

Knoepflmacher, U. C., 120

Kornbluh, Anna, 13

Kristeva, Julia, 228n10

Lang, Andrew, 65

"Lay of Oisin on the Land of Youth" (Comyn), 166

Le Fanu, J. Sheridan, 7

Leach, Harvey, 73–74, 229n29

Lee, Vernon, 8–9

Levine, Caroline, 8

Levine, George, 80

Lewes, George Henry, 97–101, 231n21, 231n24

lifelikeness, 99–102, 105, 109, 112, 216

Limits of Critique, The (Felski), 219

Lire, interpréter, actualiser (Citon), 219

Lloyd, David, 83, 239n49

Looking Backward 2000–1887 (Bellamy), 232n27

"Los Amigos Fiasco, The" (Doyle), 238n37

"Lotos-Eaters, The" (Tennyson), 173–75, 236n47

Loudon, Jane Webb, 181, 193

Lowell, James Russell, 73

Lutz, Deborah, 91, 93–94, 217, 230n14

Lytton, Edward Bulwer, 102, 232n27

Macnie, John, 232n27

Mangham, Andrew, 84, 239n2

Mansfield Park (Austen), 222–24, 239n6

Mansfield Park and Mummies (Nazarian), 222–24

Marcus, Sharon, 217, 221

Markovits, Stefanie, 233n16

Martin, Amy, 23

Mary Shelley's Frankenstein (film), 77–78, 230n33

masculinity, 5–6, 60, 109, 129–31, 185–87, 203, 206–9, 212, 221

mash-ups, 7, 216, 221–22, 224

materialism, 41, 62, 68–69, 164

Maturin, Charles, 7

McCarthy, Anne, 232n30

medicine, electricity and, 28–30

Melmoth the Wanderer (Maturin), 7

"Memorabilia" (Browning), 122–23, 126–27

Men and Women (Browning), 115

Metahistory (White), 12–13

Michelet, Jules, 4, 14–16, 114, 134, 136, 184, 234n36

Miller, J. Hillis, 85, 87–88, 230n9

Milner, H. M., 228n8

Mitchell, Susan, 197, 210

Moers, Ellen, 228n10

Mole, Tom, 120–21

Moore, Thomas, 57, 235n30

Moran, D. P., 180

Morgan, Benjamin, 13

Morris, William, 163

Morus, Iwan Rhys, 69

Mullen, Mary, 23, 83

mummies, 7, 36–37, 44, 144, 148, 202–6, 215–16, 220–24, 235n13. *See also Jewel of Seven Stars, The* (Stoker)

Mummy, The (Budge), 198

Mummy!, The (Loudon), 181, 193

"Municipal Gallery Re-Visited, The" (Yeats), 141–42, 176, 179–80, 235nn10–11, 235n13

museums: in Adorno, 142–43; British Museum, 138–40, 146, 148–49, 152–53, 155; in Hardy, 151–52; haunted, 138; Irish National Museum, 139, 157–62; in *The Jewel of Seven Stars,* 202; in Keats, 149–50; "museum poems," 143–53, 162; in Rossetti, 143–46; South Kensington Museum, 140; in Valéry, 142; Yeats and, 156, 179–80

Museum Age, The (Bazin), 161

"My Last Duchess" (Browning), 113, 122–26, 133, 233n24

Myrone, Martin, 239n3

nationalism, 17, 35–36, 159, 165, 179–81, 191–99, 208–14, 226n30, 236n41, 238n29, 239n47, 239n49

Narrative of a Voyage (W. Wilde), 198, 238n31

Nazarian, Vera, 222–23

"Necessity of Political Honesty, The" (Stoker), 197

nonbinary, 60

Norman, Brian, 8

Northanger Abbey (Austen), 41

Novak, Daniel, 83–84, 230n5

objectivity, 35, 41, 60, 112, 121–24, 135

O'Brien, William, 158

O'Donovan, John, 235n30

"Of History and Romance" (Godwin), 21, 59–61

O'Grady, Standish, 14, 16–23, 140, 163–64, 211, 234n2

Oliver Twist (Dickens), 84–85, 231n26

O'Malley, Patrick, 23, 187–88

"On Seeing the Elgin Marbles" (Keats), 149–50

Our Mutual Friend (Dickens), 4, 81–82, 86, 96–111, 231n26, 232n32

"Ozymandias" (P. Shelley), 235n14

Parry, H. G., 218–19

Parthenon Marbles, 138, 149, 151, 162. *See also* Elgin Marbles

Past and Present (Carlyle), 31–32

Pater, Walter, 143

Peake, Richard Brinsley, 67–72, 229n23

Pearse, Susan, 160

Peltz, Lucy, 239n3

Peter, Walter, 139

Petrie, George, 159

Phillips, Wilson, 26

Pitt Rivers Museum, 235n24

Planché, J. R., 7

Plutarch, 65

Poems (J. Wilde), 1, 3

poetry, 1–3, 12, 35, 113–14, 121–23, 132–33, 135, 138–39, 143–53, 166–76. *See also* museums: "museum poems"; *Ring and the*

266 · INDEX

Book, The (Browning); "Wanderings of Oisin, The" (Yeats)

Polidori, John, 7

"Porphyria's Lover" (Browning), 113, 122–25, 133, 233n24

Poulet, Georges, 217

presentism, 2, 12–13, 22, 40, 226n21

Presumption; or, The Fate of Frankenstein (Peake), 67–69, 229n23

Pride and Prejudice and Zombies (Grahame-Smith), 221

"Problem with Museums, The" (Valéry), 142

Prometheus, 15–16, 18–20, 67–68

"Prometheus Unbound" (P. Shelley), 16, 18–19, 163–64

Proust, Marcel, 142–43

Pulvermacher's Chain, 28–30

queer, 11, 17, 41, 60, 111, 226n27

Radcliffe, Anne, 41

Ramazani, Jahan, 235nn10–11

realism, 34, 80–87, 93, 95–101, 109

Realistic Imagination, The (Levine), 80

reanimation: in *Dracula,* 187–88; electricity and, 3, 24–26; in *Frankenstein,* 39–40, 43–45, 48–49, 63–78, 228n9; gender and, 5–6; ghosts vs., 12; historical feeling and, 49–56; historical imagination and, 2; in J. Wilde, 2; in *The Jewel of Seven Stars,* 179–81, 205, 207–8, 213–14; in Literary Revival, 3; in M. Shelley, 39–40, 63–78; readability and, 4; Renaissance and, 133–37; in *The Ring and the Book,* 114–19, 127–34; in "Roger Dodsworth, the Reanimated Englishman," 56–63; in "Valerius, the Reanimated Roman," 49–56. *See also* resurrection; resuscitation

Renaissance, 133–38, 211

resurrection: in "The Burden of Nineveh," 148; in *Dracula,* 184; in *Frankenstein,* 39–40; in *Great Expectations,* 92–93, 95; history as, 134–35; in J. Wilde, 1, 3; in *The Jewel of Seven Stars,* 177–78, 205, 213; in Michelet, 15–16; in museum poetry, 151–52; in "Porphyria's Lover," 124; in *The Ring and the Book,* 131–32, 135–36; in "Roger Dodsworth, the Reanimated Englishman," 59; in *Sketches by Boz,* 87;

in "Valerius, the Reanimated Roman," 52, 54. *See also* reanimation; resuscitation

resuscitation, 6–12; in Dickens, 94; in *Dracula,* 185, 190; electricity and, 3, 31–32; in *Frankenstein,* 134; gender and, 6; in J. Wilde, 2, 5; in *The Jewel of Seven Stars,* 178, 190; Literary Revival and, 3; monologues and, 113; readability and, 4; reading and, 11; in *The Ring and the Book,* 5, 46. *See also* reanimation; resurrection

Ring and the Book, The (Browning), 4, 6, 46; electricity in, 46; poetry in, 12, 121–22, 132–33, 135; reanimation in, 114–19, 127–34; spiritualism and, 114–15; strangeness of, 112–13

Roberts, Adam, 114–15

"Roger Dodsworth, the Reanimated Englishman" (M. Shelley), 10–11, 39–40, 49, 56–64

Rossetti, Christina, 148–49

Rossetti, Dante Gabriel, 138, 141, 143–47, 155, 232n3

Rossetti, William, 233n21

Roth, Phyllis, 200

Rowlandson, Thomas, 14

Rymer, James Malcolm, 7

Said, Edward, 239n6

Santayana, George, 62

Schor, Hilary, 86–87, 110

Scott, Sir Walter, 8, 17, 32, 52, 55, 62, 64–66

Sedgwick, Eve Kosofsky, 10

Seeley, J. R., 12, 14, 22

Sense and Sensibility and Sea Monsters (Winters), 221

Shakespeare, William, 66

She (Haggard), 237n12

Shelley, Mary, 5, 119–27, 233n21. See also *Fortunes of Perkin Warbeck, The* (M. Shelley); *Frankenstein* (M. Shelley); "Roger Dodsworth, the Reanimated Englishman" (M. Shelley); "Valerius, the Reanimated Roman" (M. Shelley); *Valperga, or the Life and Adventures of Castruccio, Prince of Lucca* (M. Shelley)

Shelley, Percy, 3, 16, 20, 44–47, 65, 163, 235n14. *See also* "Cenci, The" (P. Shelley); "Prometheus Unbound" (P. Shelley)

Siegel, Jonah, 138

Silyn Roberts, Siân, 10
Sketches by Boz (Dickens), 87–89, 94, 230n13, 231n26
Smith, Adam, 21, 52, 229n15
"Smith and the Pharaohs" (Haggard), 237n12
South Kensington Museum, 140
spectrality, 8–9
Speranza. *See* Wilde, Jane
spiritualism, 8, 113–15
Stead, W. T., 227n62, 232n27
Stewart, Susan, 175–76
Stiles, Anne, 228n9
Stoker, Bram, 7, 13, 190, 197–98, 238n28. *See also* "Burial of the Rats, The" (Stoker); *Dracula* (Stoker); *Jewel of Seven Stars, The* (Stoker); "Necessity of Political Honesty, The" (Stoker)
Stryker, Susan, 228n10
subjectivity, 76, 84, 113, 122–24, 132, 207
Synge, J. M., 7, 154, 211

Tchernichova, Viktoria, 113
telegraph, 227n61
Tennyson, Alfred, Lord, 113, 173–75, 236n47
Thelwall, John, 68
Theory of Moral Sentiments, The (Smith), 229n15
Time Flies (Rossetti), 148–49
Tír na nÓg, 165–66, 168
"To a Skylark" (P. Shelley), 123
"To Ireland" (J. Wilde), 1–6
"To the Statute of Eumousia in the British Museum" (Arnold), 152
tombstones, 79–81, 85–86, 88, 94–95
Tucker, Herbert F., 234n29
Tynan, Katherine, 140, 154, 160, 235n8

Ulysses (Joyce), 181
Unlikely Escape of Uriah Heep, The (Parry), 218
Ure, Andrew, 26–27

V21 Collective, 13

Valente, Joseph, 10, 182, 190–91, 193, 236n48
"Valerius, the Reanimated Roman" (M. Shelley), 39–40, 49–56
Valéry, Paul, 142–43
"Valéry Proust Museum" (Adorno), 142
Valperga, or the Life and Adventures of Castruccio, Prince of Lucca (M. Shelley), 59
vampires, 7, 182–91
Vaucanson, Jacques, 24
Virgil, 59
vitalism, 29, 44–46, 67–68, 228n8

Walpole, Horace, 10, 41, 65–66, 85
"Wanderings of Oisin, The" (Yeats), 139–41, 156–57, 163–76, 236n41, 236n45
Wedgwood, Julia, 115–16, 122, 137
"Where My Books Go" (Yeats), 154–55
White, Hayden, 12–13
Wilde, Jane, 1–6, 167, 225n7
Wilde, Oscar, 1
Wilde, William, 159–60, 198–99, 201, 235n29, 235n30, 238n31
Winters, Ben H., 221–22
Wolfreys, Julian, 9, 46
women, 186–87, 199–208. *See also* femininity; gender
Wood, Claire, 96
Wood, Gillen D'Arcy, 149–50
Wordsworth, William, 230n10

Yeats, W. B., 3, 7, 16, 18, 139–40, 147–48, 153–57, 160–63, 167–68, 179–80, 211, 234n2, 235n8, 235n33, 236n34, 236n50. See also *Cathleen ni Houlihan* (Yeats); *Fairy and Folk Tales of the Irish Peasantry* (Yeats); "Municipal Gallery Re-Visited, The" (Yeats); "Wanderings of Oisin, The" (Yeats)
Young, Elizabeth, 228n9
Young Frankenstein (film), 38–39

Zigarovich, Jolene, 86, 230n10
zombies, 81, 96–101